PERIODS IN HIGHLAND HISTORY

*Alasdair Mór Grant, the Champion or **Ceann-tighe***

painted by Richard Waitt in 1714, showing the belted plaid as worn by a clansman and the
full arming of sword, targe, pistol, dirk and long gun

Periods in Highland History

I. F. Grant MBE LLD
Hugh Cheape

SHEPHEARD-WALWYN

First published in 1987 by
Shepheard-Walwyn (Publishers) Limited
26 Charing Cross Road (Suite 34)
London WC2H 0DH

British Library Cataloguing in Publication Data

Grant, I.F.
  Periods in Highland History;
  1. Highlands (Scotland)—History
  I. Title II. Cheape, Hugh
  941.1'5   DA880.H6

ISBN 0-85683-057-7

The publisher acknowledges subsidy from
the Scottish Arts Council towards the publication
of this volume

Typeset by St. George Typesetting,
Redruth, Cornwall
Printed in Great Britain by
St Edmundsbury Press, Bury St Edmunds,
Suffolk

Contents

Acknowledgements

Many of the illustrations for this book are drawn from the archives of the National Museums of Scotland and their copyright is vested in the Trustees of the National Museums of Scotland. They include plates from the following printed sources and collections (The bold numerals refer to the illustration number — see opposite):

J Romilly Allen, *The Early Christian Monuments of Scotland* Edinburgh 1903, **6**

Joseph Anderson, *Scotland in Early Christian Times* Edinburgh 1881, **10**

William Daniell, *A Voyage round Great Britain* London 1814, **42**

James Drummond, *Sculptured Monuments in Iona and the West Highlands* Edinburgh 1881, **18, 19, 23**

Alasdair Alpin MacGregor Collection, **3, 9, 17**

Montraive Collection, **44**

Scotland Illustrated Edinburgh 1850, **41**

Capt T P White, *Archaeological Sketches in Scotland* Edinburgh 1875-1878, **20, 22, 24, 27**

Grateful thanks and acknowledgements are due to the following for permission to reproduce the illustrations not included above:

National Galleries of Scotland, **40**
National Library of Scotland, **47**
National Museum, Dublin, **16**
Marquess of Bute, **30**
Earl of Seafield, **1, 32**
Michael Carmichael, **48**
George Dixon, **11**
William Drummond Moray, **29**
John Telfer Dunbar, **31**

List of Illustrations and Maps

Preface

This book has been long in maturing and we remember with gratitude time and help given in the past by Maj H F McClintock, Col Iain Grant of Rothiemurchus, Dr R B K Stevenson CBE of the National Museum of Antiquities of Scotland and Mr John Telfer Dunbar. We are also much indebted for the help generously given to us by Mr Eric Cregeen of the School of Scottish Studies, Mr D J MacCuish of the Crofters' Commission, Air Vice Marshal Calum MacDonald, Mr Donald Macdonald, Mr George Dixon, Miss Catherine Dickson, Mr C P Finlayson, Mr James Scarlett, Mrs Maclean of Dochgarroch, Miss Alma Grant, Miss Chrissie MacLeod, and colleagues of the National Museums of Scotland.

We make grateful acknowledgement for permission to reproduce copyright material in the illustrations to the Marquis of Bute, the Earl of Seafield, W S H Drummond-Moray Esq of Abercairny, the National Museums of Scotland, The National Galleries of Scotland, the National Monuments Record of Scotland, the Department of the Environment, Edinburgh University Library and the School of Scottish Studies, Edinburgh University.

Special thanks are due to Mrs Anne Grant, Mrs M Holt and Miss I G Boley who typed our work with such wisdom and care and Miss Helen Jackson who prepared the maps.

Introduction

It is convenient for the English nation that so many of the families of their kings provide useful names — Norman, Tudor, Jacobean and Georgian — that are the widely understood and generally accepted labels for the culture of successive historical periods. There may be no useful portmanteau words for the changes in style that went on during the times of the Plantagenets or the Wars of the Roses, but all through these times one has the feeling of correlated and organic development.

For Scotland before the Union of the Crowns, we have no similar terms and, apart from the reigns of Malcolm Canmore and his direct descendants, distinct periods in the social culture of the nation are not readily distinguishable. And so long as we have no convenient labels recording the periods of the general history of Scotland, it is not surprising that a sense of the sequence in events and social conditions in the history of the Highlands should also appear to be lacking.

In general views of the past in the Highlands, the names of only two men, both of them outsiders, at once come to mind. One is that of St Columba who came to evangelise the Highlands in the sixth century and whose name is so closely identified with the Island of Iona, the other that of 'Bonnie Prince Charlie' who led the Jacobite Rising of 1745. At the time of St Columba's coming, the Highlands were just emerging into written history and most people are vague about how things changed and developed during succeeding centuries. There is, for instance, a tendency to equate the organisation of the clans as we know them with the supposed organisation of an early tribal system of land tenure. In this book we shall trace the formation and development of the clans against the background of the social and political history of Scotland. In alluding to the Jacobite Risings, we hope to contradict the myth that they were a contest between Highlanders and the English or Lowlanders. Highlanders were in fact divided in their support for the Stewart and Hanoverian claims.

On the other hand, while it is a historical fact that there was a great deal of fighting in the Highlands, the idea that from ancient times the Highlanders charged downhill brandishing weapons that are usually termed 'claymores' is a popular misconception. The medieval Highlander used a cross-hilted sword and the Gaelic term *claidheamh-mór* (big sword), anglicised as 'claymore', referred to a double-handed variant of this type of sword. It was not until the seventeenth century that the basket-hilted sword, still worn with the full-dress uniform of Highland Regiments and popularly called the 'claymore', came into general use. The accounts of older battles describe how opponents tried to occupy and hold a strong point or the high ground. The downhill charge as a favourite battle tactic, like the basket-hilted sword, came in the seventeenth century. The origins of the wearing of the kilt instead of the more ancient belted plaid and of the use of regular recognised clan tartans are also debatable and controversial subjects.

Our ancestral music is often assumed to have been played on the bagpipe, complete with its three drones as we know it today. In fact a simpler form of bagpipe was being played in medieval Scotland as elsewhere in Europe. In the Highlands it only superseded the *clarsach* or harp as the esteemed musical instrument in the later sixteenth century, and a third drone only came into general use on the pipes more than two centuries later. Marches and reels are thought to have formed the repertoire of the pipes; as a matter of fact, it was considered derogatory to use the pipes for playing anything except *piobaireachd*.

The traumatic effects of the repressive measures taken by the government after the Jacobite defeat at Culloden in 1746 are obvious. As a consequence of entirely changed social and economic conditions that resulted, some chiefs and landlords abandoned earlier concepts of their duty and cleared their lands of their tenantry, sometimes with a gross lack of humanity, in order to form sheep farms. This has been widely publicised. Little is known and written about the chiefs and landlords who introduced contemporary measures of agricultural reforms and improvement. We point out the differences in appearance of wasteland that went out of cultivation before the agricultural reforms and may well have been cleared, and that which had subsequently been cultivated by the improved methods and had then become unprofitable.

Looking at the history of Highland Scotland from a generalised point of view in this book, we have defined seven periods of Highland history and described and correlated the distinguishing features within them:

1.   Before the eleventh century. A remote past, traces of which have survived in varying degrees in the Highlands.
2.   c.1050-c.1300. Feudal influences on the Highlands from the south. The beginnings of differentiation between Highlands and Lowlands.
3.   c.1300-c.1500. The Lordship of the Isles and patronage of the arts.
4.   Sixteenth and early seventeenth centuries. *Linn nan creach*, the 'Age of Forays'. Failure of government and the emergence of Highland characteristics out of political chaos.

5.   Seventeenth and early eighteenth centuries. Political antagonism of the Lowlands and concentration of cultural influences in the south. Development of a military role for the Highlands and the flowering of Gaelic poetry.

6.   After 1745. The breakdown of the old order and economic change.

7.   Later nineteenth and twentieth centuries. Survival within integration.

Period I

Before the eleventh century.
Survivals from a remote past and an early civilisation

In writing or speaking about the past it is very convenient to use portmanteau types of words that convey an overall idea of the general ways of life, the style of clothes and buildings, or the trends of thought current at the time. We talk of the Roman empire, or nearer our own time we speak of the Renaissance. On a smaller and more precise scale we have a series of well defined periods in English history, Norman and so forth. On the whole, the history of Scotland does not lend itself so readily to the making of such definitions. In dealing with Highland history it is easier to try to do this although the various stages show less of development than of adaptation to outside factors and of decline.

All through Highland history, one has to take into account the persistence of the influence of the remote past, and in tracing later developments, one has to keep this in mind. We begin the first period therefore in the times of pre-history. Down to recent times, Highlanders held such prehistoric remains as standing stones and grave slabs in such regard that there are large numbers of tales of misfortune attending anyone who put them to secular uses. One of the writers has personally been told of such. For instance a man removed one of these stones and used it as a lintel for his byre, and the cattle refused to stay quietly in the byre until the stone was taken away. A touching illustration of the old reverence for memorials of more ancient times is that the wall surrounding the cashel at Kilpatrick in Arran, the settlement of Columban monks, was built with a diversion in order not to disturb a Bronze Age burial.[1] Holes were deliberately made through some of the large stones. There is a tradition about some of them that bargains were clinched by clasping hands through the hole. One of the writers was often told that this was so in the case of the stone in the lonely Kirkyard at Dalarossie in the parish of Moy. The holed stones in the churchyard of Kilchousland in Kintyre were traditionally associated with marriage customs. A good example of the persistence of a more ancient belief is that of the knoll on the Island of Iona where St Columba used to meet with angels. In his *Life of St Columba*, St Adamnan called it *Colliculus Angelorum*, but it is now locally known as the *Sìthean* or 'fairy hill' and is probably an ancient burial ground. In the eighteenth century, the

1

people upon this island of particularly holy associations still poured an offering of porridge into the sea in the hope that an ample supply of sea-ware would be washed up to fertilise their land.[2]

The continuing veneration for some of the Columban Saints is itself an interesting survival. It is even more interesting to find the traces of yet more ancient beliefs embedded in traditions about them. For instance, the Presbytery of Dingwall in 1656 was taking steps to prohibit the people of Loch Maree from sacrificing a bull on the feast day of St Maelrubha who was the evangelist of the North West.[3] An eye-witness account of the healing rituals associated with St Fillan is retailed by so respectable a witness as a former Keeper of the National Museum of Antiquities of Scotland. The Saint's pool is in Glendochart in Perthshire. Crowds came to bathe in it in order to be healed. Each worshipper picked nine stones from the pool, took three turns round each of three cairns close by, left the stones in the pool and bits of their clothing on the cairn. Lunatics were thrown into the pool and had to spend the night fastened to a stone in the Saint's Chapel.[4]

Of course, the belief in the powers of witches, with a progression from respect for individuals with an exceptional skill in such things as the properties of plants or the vagaries of the weather to the imputation of evil powers, is widespread. It was common in the Highlands and instances recurred till well within the writers' memory. The burial of animals alive as a cure has been recorded so far apart as Kintyre and Moray.[5] The bones of animals were also sometimes buried under the foundation of a building. One of the writers was told by the former owner, Mackintosh of Raigmore, that bones of cattle were found under the foundations of the farmhouse of Cradle Hall, and workmen told her that they had come across chicken bones in the foundations when restoring the farm of Dalraddy in Badenoch. Cradle Hall was built in the eighteenth century and Dalraddy is unlikely to have been as old.

In noting the survival of such ancient beliefs, it is important to remember that they must have come down to us through a succession of domination by different cultures and races. An original patriarch has not been followed by the uninterrupted occupation of the whole land by his descendants. In referring to the clans in much later times the term 'tribal system' is often used, but although the term is applied to a primitive form of organisation, tribal laws can be very highly developed, as is evinced in the early Irish laws, and the semblance of such a form of society can develop in a very few generations as indeed happened in the case of Highland clans.

Sir James Frazer in his monumental work *The Golden Bough* has shown how pagan beliefs survived in agricultural custom all over Europe. In the Highlands there were many examples. Growing corn was protected by processions with lighted torches. Malign influences were propitiated by special festivals. For instance, at Beltane, the festival at the beginning of May, the herdsmen gathered together and prepared a fire. Each took a piece of oatmeal bread dressed with a mixture of eggs, butter and milk and, turning to the fire, threw a piece over his left shoulder as an offering to storms, birds of prey, and all other causes of damage to livestock. In his *History of the Province of Moray*, written in 1775, Rev Lachlan Shaw described how he had seen in Rothiemurchus, as a young man at the turn of the eighteenth century, herds at the May feasts with staves decorated with herbs, crops circled with blazing torches, the cutting of woodbine or honeysuckle and twisting it into circles when the March moon increased for the purpose of passing through them ailing children and cattle.[6] There has been a widespread belief both in the Highlands and in the Lowlands that the last sheaf cut in the harvest possessed magic properties. It might be hung on the wall in the house or it might be given to horses and cattle on Christmas or New Year's Day, or to the horses on the first day of ploughing. Considerable care was taken in forming this *Maighdean Bhuana* or Harvest Maiden so that it served a decorative purpose. In direct contrast were the *Gobhar Bhacach* (Lame Goat) and the *Cailleach* (Old Wife), the sheaves which were inflicted on those who were lazy or late with their harvest. This was a taunting and humiliating practice, which was more common in the Outer Islands, and was considered to bring ill-luck in its train. In Islay the last sheaf was kept in the house as a protection against the fairies.[7]

In the Highlands it was considered politic to refer to the fairies as the Good Folk, the Good People, or the Men of Peace, in Gaelic, *Daoine Sìth*, for often they were believed to be malevolent towards the human race. The Rev John MacDonald, minister of Alvie, Inverness-shire, wrote in 1845 that 'the venerable Principal Baird, whose labours of love will be long remembered with heartfelt gratitude in the Highlands of Scotland, has contributed, by his benevolent exertions, in an eminent degree to the expulsion of fairies from the Highland hills'.[8] The reason for the minister's gratitude was the scheme of 1824 for the education of the poor in the Highlands and Islands devised by Dr Baird, principal of the University of Edinburgh. But his concern was for the local belief in fairies and the identification by older folk of whirlwinds as processions of fairies, 'the host of the air', referred to in Gaelic as *sluagh*. The Good People were sometimes believed to be fallen spirits, but there is often a close connection between fairy lore and prehistoric remains; they shot 'elfbolts', which in reality were flint arrowheads, and many other Highland charms were really prehistoric artefacts such as bronze axeheads or spindle-whorls. The *sìthean* or fairy dwellings are often burial mounds or other prehistoric sites. In Ireland, the *Tuatha Dé*

Flint arrowhead, 'elfbolt', mounted in silver as a charm and preserved in Appin

Danaan, literally the 'Folk of the Goddess Danu' or more simply the fairy folk, are traditionally said to be derived from the early gods, and the fairy stories of the Highlands are full of remote and ancient influences. John Francis Campbell of Islay in his *Popular Tales of the West Highlands* (1860-62) has shown that many of them are distorted folk-history. Tales of small people and of giants, being traditions of small and tall ancient races, and the *gruagach,* the *glaistig*, the *bocan* and the *bruinidh* or brownie in some stories sound like the survivors of conquered races, surviving in remote places or attaching themselves to families of their conquerors.[9] It has been suggested that the fairy traditions associated with the MacLeods of MacLeod have their origin in the tolerance of the founder of the family for the earlier occupiers of the lands, notably the MacCrimmons.

There is good reason to think that respect for individuals with certain gifts goes back to the times of Nature Worship and that it survived in a clandestine way for a long time in the Highlands. The veneration for the Brahan Seer is an example. The association of witches with evil must also be of remote antiquity. An abundance of tales about local witches indicates its long survival. A contemporary of one of the writers, Mrs Otto Swire, had vivid memories of the complications in her aunt's house in Glen Urquhart because the housemaid was the niece of a local witch. The other servants did all the dirty work for her and took the blame for any breakages or mistakes. In her admirable *The Highlands and Their Legends* (1963), she gives a summary of this domestic dilemma.

The magic properties of a 'sword of light', the *claidheamh geal soluis* of the stories, and of a comb, which are often mentioned in Highland folk tales, may find their origin in the introduction of a new weapon, perhaps the fine sword of the Bronze Age folk, or to the much later sword of iron, and to the weaver's comb and the introduction of weaving. The widespread tradition that iron was the most effective protection against the fairies is even more suggestive of a historical origin, and it is a sign of the great persistence in the stories, made to meet altered conditions, that there are tales where the protective metal was the barrel of a gun.[10] One of the writers was told that a careless act that was said to allow fairies to enter a house, was the leaving of the band on a spinning wheel when one stops spinning, as the thread is then apt to break and become unthreaded. This was obviously a new cautionary tale, for spinning wheels did not come into common use in the Highlands until the second half of the eighteenth century.

The significance that was attached to rounded pebbles is an example of these intriguing submerged beliefs. Such pebbles are often found in association with prehistoric burials. For instance, when the Cairn of Achnacree in Benderloch was opened, the quartz pebbles deposited there shone in the lights of the excavators.[11] Quartz seems to have been preferred by the builders of chambered tombs, and in some instances, such pebbles have been found in burials which are far from deposits of quartz. One is surprised to find how large a part these pebbles played in the myths of the Gael, and in the Middle Ages pebbles in hollow stones were used in magical rites. On Iona, the *Clach Bradh* still survives at the entrance to St Oran's chapel, although the three crystal globes that were turned sunwise in its hollow were long ago thrown away as relics of superstition. The 'Black Stones' of Iona, so-called because of the utter damnation that was said to be incurred by the violation of an oath sworn on them, have disappeared but they played their part in the traditional history of the MacDonalds.[12] There are hollows on several of the West Highland grave slabs that look as if they were worn by the rubbing of a stone, and similar hollows are worn in the cloisters of Oronsay Priory. The medieval Highland crosses had flat bases with hollows worn in several of them, for instance, those at Oronsay, Kilberry and Kilmory in Knapdale. At Kilchoman in Islay, pebbles are still in the hollows and are said to have been thrown out several times but always replaced. It was said that women who wished for a son still turned these pebbles. When the cross at Kildalton was recently straightened, pebbles were found

Set of large cult stones placed on the grave of a Shaw of Clan Chattan in Rothiemurchus churchyard

under it; and a man who was employed on the restoration of Iona Cathedral described to one of the writers how the remains of many bodies were found in the crypt in wickerwork coffins and with pebbles placed beside them. Some of these pebbles have been embedded in the cement of the paving of the restored nave. In Rothiemurchus churchyard in Badenoch, there are four larger stones placed at the corners of the grave slab of Shaw, who traditionally led Clan Chattan at the fight on the North Inch at Perth in 1396. When the grave slab was renewed the pebbles were replaced A curse, it is said, will rest on anyone who removes them.

This cult for pebbles may have some connection with the veneration for crystal charm stones in the possession of some Highland families. The *Clach na Brataich* has been in the possession of *Clann Donnchaidh*, the Robertsons of Struan, since the eve of Bannockburn. It was always taken to battle and was carried at Sheriffmuir. Another characteristic of these crystal charms was the property of healing. Water into which the charms were dipped would cure diseases of men and murrains of cattle. The *Clach Dhearg* belonging to the Stewarts of Ardvorlich was still used last century to provide healing water. The ball of rock crystal of the Stewarts of Ardsheal, Appin, was finely mounted in engraved silver bands with a chain for dipping it into water. The Keppoch charm was dipped in water to the accompaniment of a prayer which has been preserved; this invokes St Bride, the Virgin Mary, the Trinity, Apostles and Angels and concludes with the words:

. . . .
A blessing on the gem and a blessing on the water,
A healing of bodily ailments to each suffering creature.[13]

Left: *Rock crystal charm of the family of Stewart of Ardsheal*

Right: *The Glenorchy charm consisting of a ridged reliquary stone in a sixteenth century silver setting*

Some crystal charms are oval in shape and ridged or 'hog-backed' on one side. These may be derived from reliquaries, and saints' relics and reliquaries themselves were used as charms. The Glenorchy stone which was owned by the Campbells of Breadalbane is almost certainly a reliquary stone which has been mounted, probably in the sixteenth century, in a silver setting with pieces of coral. One or two sixteenth century Highland brooches that have survived are set with crystals of reliquary type.

The most famous Highland charm stone is, of course, that of *Coinneach Odhar Fiosaiche,* the Brahan Seer. The following was told to one of the writers by a native of Uig in Lewis: it happened on a day of days that a young woman was herding cattle near a green mound that was an ancient burial place. It was a beautiful summer morning towards dawn, and the girl was sitting spinning wool with a *cuigeal* or distaff that was iron, not of wood. Iron has great power over those of the other world, and it was commonly believed in Lewis that human beings who had been lured into the *toman* of the Little Folk could only make sure of a way of escape if they stuck a steel pin or a dirk into the turf at the place where they were taken into the *toman.* Just before cockcrow the spirits of those who long ago had been changed were returning to their resting places. One of them, a richly dressed lady, spoke to the girl; 'Will you lift your *cuigeal* from where it is lying and let me come in to my place?' 'Who are you' was the reply, 'and why are you so late in coming back? What will you give me if I let you pass?' 'I was a Princess from Norway, and I had further to go than these others, and therefore I am later than they. And if you will let me pass I will give you a white stone. Give this to your first child, and as long as he has it he will have wonderful powers'. So the girl lifted her *cuigeal* and took the stone and the princess passed to her place. The girl kept the stone and she gave it to the son she bore and he became the famous Brahan Seer.

Well-worship was so general and widespread and there are many recorded examples. The change from veneration to 'folksiness' and from that to oblivion is vividly demonstrated for example in the popular attitude to the Mary Well, St Mary's Well, also known as the 'Clootie Well', in Culloden Woods near Inverness. About a hundred years ago, it was visited on the first Sunday in May as a solemn rite. Water from it was drunk just as the sun rose, and pieces of cloth, 'clooties', were dipped into this spring and rubbed on any sore or aching joint, and left hanging on a nearby tree. The people who actually remembered these practices, could not remember the dedication of the well. Later, the well became the object of an excursion on the appropriate day. A coin was dropped in, the water drunk and a wish formulated. The writers frequently heard of this custom but today, if one enquires about the well, people have forgotten about it and the customs associated with it.

There are many other instances of survivals of ancient beliefs and customs. One of the early Irish sagas, Bricriu's Feast, has as its theme the right of the Gaelic champion to a special portion of food at the communal feast — the *Curad-mir*, the Hero's Portion. The claims did not, of course, always pass unchallenged and from boasting, the warriors resorted to combat. This ancient theme of heroic society can be traced back to the Celtic peoples of the Continent. Classical writers describe the heroic feast and the Hero's Portion as a familiar custom of the Gauls. It survived in the perquisites of a chief's armour-bearer in the seventeenth century. Martin Martin described how this man had a double portion of meat assigned to him at every meal, and the measure of meat given to him was called the *Beatha Fir* or Champion's portion.

Our very appearance bears out that we are a mixed race. Nor is this diversity a modern development. The late Sheriff J R N MacPhail showed one of the writers a 'descriptive roll' of the recruits enlisted by MacLean of Lochbuie in 1794. Of the twenty-four men who came from Argyll, twelve were described as dark, three had dark hair and ruddy colouring, two had reddish hair and seven were fair. Other districts also varied, although the number of fair men was slightly higher in the east. Archaeological evidence suggests a certain amount of amalgamation between different races. Early Irish writings allude to subject races and non-free inhabitants of tribal territories, and Professor Eoin MacNeill considered that 'territories bore the name of the nobility owning them. They were not inhabited by a population all bearing that name or of the same name.' He also quoted a passage by Duald MacFirbis, the seventeenth century Irish genealogist, which is supposed to have been taken from an earlier manuscript in which the fair-haired Gaels were endowed with all the virtues and the more swarthy races with most of the vices.[14]

Although it is a moot point how far north the Romans actually ruled in Scotland, their influence was pervasive and disruptive of earlier customs. For instance it affected the form of the quern, that essential implement for food production, and encouraged the use of the fibula type of brooch. This was much developed and the finest Scots specimens of these date from between the eighth and twelfth centuries, and the taste for such adornments can be traced in the Highland flat ring brooches of later times. The effect of the Roman social ideas and of the displacement of hostile elements from within the borders of the Empire can only be assumed. A O Anderson in his *Early Sources of Scottish History* translates and arranges the written sources of the sixth to thirteenth centuries from which we learn about the people of the Highlands in this period of their development. To the South and the East were the advancing Angles and on the West, the vanishing Britons. Over a large part of the Highlands were the Picts. The failure of archaeologists and historians to make any authoritative statement about these people is most regrettable. One may venture the assumption that they were of mixed and not well integrated origin. The earliest recorded settlement of the Gael from Ireland was by Fergus Mór mac Erc about the year 500, but both in tradition and with obvious probability earlier landings must have taken place. Of the early Gael fortunately a great deal has been preserved, and we have plentiful evidence of their codes of law, their traditional history, their splendid epics, elaborate verse forms, and their beautiful craft work leading up to their most outstanding artistic achievement, their manuscript illuminations.

During this period Christianity was brought to the Picts by the followers of St Ninian and to the Gaels by St Columba. These peoples were at constant war with each other and with the Angles and Britons, on the whole the Picts being the most successful; but in 843, a date marking a definite period in Highland history, Kenneth mac Alpin, King of Scots, possibly by right of succession through his matriarchal descent (the Picts' right of succession being through the mother and not the father), and not conquest, succeeded to the Pictish throne. One of the enigmas of history is that apparently without armed conquest or disturbance, the less

numerous Gael were able to impose their language upon the Picts and
entirely to submerge their way of life. Almost the only tangible legacy
that the Picts have left is that of their carvings in stone, of which some
hundreds   survive   and   most   of   which   are   reproduced   in
J Romilly Allen's *The Early Christian Monuments of Scotland* (1903).
The meaning of the symbols that appear upon them — the crescent, the
broken rod, etc — has been lost but it definitely indicates a well defined
and uniform system of status and rights. When one looks at the carvings,
massive and intricate designs carried out with great precision, one has a
feeling of surprise that the people of whom they were characteristic
should so easily have lost their identity.

*Sculptured stone at St Madoes, Perthshire, in the form of a standing cross-slab of typical
Pictish Christian design with spirals and interlace*

The Gaels of Alba were closely associated with those of Erin, and it is important to bear in mind that at that period from about the fifth century onwards and in that corner of the Western world, Erin held an exceptionally high position. Although her locally more limited pre-eminence coincided with the spread of classical learning over a wider area where Latin was the accepted *lingua franca* of the Christianised academic world, yet just as in our materialistic times Americanised English is the most universal spoken language, so in Erin's immediate neighbourhood the speaking of Gaelic superseded Pictish and, a couple of centuries later, it was actually to replace Norse as the language of that mixed race, the descendants of the Norse conquerors of the greater part of the Western Isles and a considerable portion of the Mainland. Christianity was brought to the Angles from the north west. The church in Northumbria had been linked with the Columban church by the appointment of Aidan from Iona as abbot-bishop of Lindisfarne. But the Celtic rule of the church was then changed through the influence of St Wilfred to that of the Latin church which had been brought to England by St Augustine. The great classic civilisation with its strong literary traditions, what has been termed 'Latinity', prevailed and was gradually to push the Gaelic language and way of life to within the limits of what eventually became known as the 'Highland Line'.

In order to appreciate the relative power of Irish influence at this time, one must remember that Erin at this period, so far from being the 'distressful country', was in an enviable position. She reached a state of political consolidation at a comparatively early date. Although the concept of High King or *Ard Rì* did not become a reality until the twelfth century, the government had tended to become centralised from the fifth century onwards. Niall of the Nine Hostages, living in the early fifth century, had established his dynasty at Tara and the lay-out of the remains, although the structures are simple, indicates the existence of a well developed and centralised society. Erin's social life had not been disrupted by the invading Romans. Her mild climate with its abundance of winter feeding was particularly suitable for a simple stage of predominantly pastoral agriculture. Donatus, an Irish Bishop of Fiesole in Italy in the ninth century, wrote touchingly about the land of his childhood and described Erin in these terms: 'Far in the west they tell of a matchless land, which goes in ancient books by the name of Scotia (i.e. Ireland); rich in resources this land, having silver, precious stones, vestures and gold, well suited to earth-born creatures as regards its climate, its sun and its arable soil; that Scotia of lovely fields that flow with milk and honey, hath skill in husbandry and raiments and arms and arts and fruits'.[15] The rich collections in Irish museums of golden objects of beautiful craftsmanship, the finest in the western Europe of their day, testify that by finds of alluvial gold or by exchanges which a prosperous land could make in the ninth century, Ireland may have had more of the precious metal than any other country of western Europe. Certainly her craftsmanship was unrivalled.

Most important of all, her literature was in its finest flowering. The Ulster Cycle of heroic tales of the warriors of North East Ireland had been composed in the era of the long war between the provinces of Connacht and Ulster. This group of sagas concerns the legendary heroes and their king, *Conchobar Mac Neasa* or Conor, whose stronghold was at *Emain Macha*, the capital which was destroyed probably in the fifth century. The stories were, therefore, current in a pre-Christian age and maintained their popularity after the *Ui Néill* or 'descendants of Niall' had established their rule at Tara. With the introduction of writing at the time of the conversion of Erin to Christianity, a tremendous outburst of literary activity began. Christianity itself brought the Irish in touch with the mellowed civilisation of Rome and Byzantium, and it called forth the highest endeavours of the craftsmen in glorification of their new faith. It is no wonder that the people of Scotland should have treasured their connection with this fortunate isle. The tenacity with which the connection with Irish civilisation persisted in the Highlands was an essential feature in the history of their culture. The fourteenth century historian, John of Fordun, who evidently knew the Highlands well, noted in his great Chronicle the resemblance of the Highlanders to the Irish in language, manners and character, in spite of the Viking incursions and the eventual conquest of large parts of the Kingdom. Until the seventeenth century, this Gaelic civilisation was common to all people between the Butt of Lewis and Cape Clear.[16]

It is, however, important to remember that Irish civilisation was not taken over in its entirety when the kingdom of Alba was formed, and it is not safe to assume that any Irish institution, custom or law survived unchanged in the Highlands at a later time. It must be remembered also that the fortunes of Dalriada had been reduced to a low ebb before Alpin, father of Kenneth, succeeded to the throne, and when Kenneth mac Alpin himself was enjoying his great accession of territory, the terrible Norse incursion was beginning to threaten his Kingdom.

The invasions of the Norsemen which led to the loss of Shetland and Orkney, the Hebrides and of the most northerly part of the Scottish Mainland is thought to have begun with the peaceful occupation of the land by agriculturists, but this is unrecorded. The Viking raids, which devastated the civilisation of Ireland and Western Scotland, began in the late eighth century. The Irish annals mention a series of Viking incursions into the Hebrides in 793, and two years later, Iona was devastated and the treasures there had to be removed to Dunkeld. By this time, the raids had become a seasonal occupation for the Vikings and the raiders began to make permanent settlements. Finally, Thorfinn, Earl of Orkney (1014-1064), a vassal of the King of Norway, in addition to Orkney and Shetland, held the Western Isles and a considerable part of the Northern Mainland. In view of their position as conquerors of alien origin, it is most significant that from the mid-ninth century, the annalists should begin to write of the *Gall-Ghaidheal*, and that the grave goods found in local burials of the period should show a mingling of styles. Nevertheless, the Gaelic language with the Gaelic way of life retained its dominance over the Hebrides and the Western Mainland, although certain surviving words reveal a Norse influence. It is not surprising that such words should include some for weapons but other words are suggestive of a peaceful everyday life.

The Norse were developing their individual culture. Their very distinctive style of ornamentation like those of the Picts and the Gael employed elaborate interlacements. The original motifs were abstract in character and there is a slight feeling of menace in their beauty. Most events described in the later sagas were actually happening in our period. The terse prose and the matter of fact narration of deeds of reckless daring and insensate ferocity impart to this period of Norse vigour and activity a strangely elemental quality. The culture of the Gael, more sophisticated and with the potency of charm, prevailed over the robuster native culture of the Scandinavian conquerors.

The Norse were merchants, and the word *margadh* for market was borrowed by a people whose attitude to trade was manifestly different. Especially noticeable is the influence of Old Norse on vocabulary relating to the sea and fishing. Many of these words, such as *bàta*, boat, *sgioba*, crew, *acair*, anchor, and *stiùir*, rudder are still commonplace.[17] The Norse produced clinker-built galleys, of course, of great sea-worthiness and beauty. Their influence can be seen in the galleys of later times which were such an essential feature of life in the Western Highlands and which are portrayed on so many tombstones. Whereas the ancient Gaels were a sea-faring people, they seem only to have preferred currachs, boats or even ships formed of hides stretched on a wooden, wicker frame. The bay where St Columba landed on Iona was called *Port a'Churaich*. Martin Martin, writing at the turn of the eighteenth century, still repeated the traditional description of the Saint's coracle or currach. When St Brendan the Voyager set out to find the Earthly Paradise, he voyaged for seven years without success and on his return, St Ita told him that he would never reach the Blessed Land if he sailed 'in death-stained hides'. So he had a wooden boat built, and in it, at last reached the Earthly Paradise. Currachs are mentioned in songs and continued in use at least on inland waters presumably for such tasks as salmon fishing.

These were round or oval craft and not the sea-going type of St Brendan. Lachlan Shaw describes their use on the Spey as a rarity in his day although they continued in use here probably into the early nineteenth century for timber floating.[18]

In spite of what must have been a considerable infusion of foreign blood by the conqueror and settler, the number of clans that in their older genealogies claimed Norse descent, is not large. They include the MacLeods, the MacAskills, the MacAulays, the MacSweens and the Nicholsons. This is a significant indication of how deliberately the people discarded their Norse associations. Although Scandinavian influences are considerable, they have to be looked for. It was the privilege of one of the writers to hear Professor W J Watson, a recognised authority on the subject, point out that loan words from the Norse only form a small part of the total vocabulary, and, in general, one is left with a feeling of surprise at the homogeneity of the surviving culture of the Highlands between those districts where the Norse ruled for five hundred years and those where they never penetrated.

No doubt it was the menace of the Norsemen as well as the acquisition of much of the Pictish land that led to a shift in the area of government from the lands in western Argyll to the more central and fertile lands of the east. It is very significant that the very name and traditions of the site of Dunadd as the old *Dun Monaidh*, the capital of Dalriada, were forgotten. The Church also was affected. Although some monks remained at Iona, the annals record the transfer of the treasures and relics of Columba to Kells in Erin and to Dunkeld in the east. With the Saint's relics went the authority of his successors, so that the Church and ecclesiastical leadership were divided.

Although Erin and Alba differed in many respects, the social structure and its practical functioning were broadly similar in both countries. The basic element of society was the *Tuath*, the people or kindred. Within this, the smaller unit was not the individual but the *Fine* or family. This was the normal property-owning unit to which all its members were heirs in respect of landed and personal property. At the same time, all its members were responsible for the misdeeds of any of the others. More particularly, succession was determined by the narrowest of the kin groups, the *Derbfhine*, the certain or true kin, comprising the agnatic descendants of a common great-grandfather or, in other words, the ancestor and his descendants to the third generation. This principle can be seen working most clearly in the succession of the headship of a kindred of the kingship. But, to some extent, this hierarchical structure had broken down during and after the incursions of the Norse.

The succession to the kingship of Scots from Kenneth mac Alpin till it was challenged after the death of Malcolm III at the beginning of our next period can be seen to have switched between collateral lines, and several kings were killed by their successors. One institution recognised by the law tracts which could offset the disruption caused by succession struggles was Tanistry or the selection of a successor designate within a reigning king's lifetime. The *Tanaise Ríg*, 'second to a king', would probably be in practice the man who had most vassals to support him. Malcolm II, whose reign lasted the unusually long period of thirty years, chose his successor, possibly following the example of his father, Kenneth II, and his grandson, Duncan I, succeeded him in 1034 in the face of opposition from the men of Moray. They were led by Macbeth who also had a claim to the throne both as a grandson of Kenneth II and through his wife. The title of 'Tanist' occurred in later Highland records of the seventeenth century, although the principle of primogeniture was surprisingly accepted by the Highland clans, who generally made their choice of a chief in accordance with it.

Although the king of Alba as a whole approximated to the Irish provincial king, a system of local kingship probably also existed in Alba. The division of the country into seven districts or provinces, omitting Argyll but including Caithness, seems to coincide with the historical Pictland of before A.D.850. The rulers of these districts, as inferred from later records, bore the title of *Mormaer* which can be interpreted as 'Great Steward'. Mormaers therefore were in the highest ranks of the Gaelic nobility and were also administrators in an official capacity. They were to be found in the north east of Scotland but not in the west nor in Ireland. In the Irish annals, *Mormaer* and *Rí* were used synonymously, and in later feudal documents *comes* was used as the Latin equivalent, as it was also used for the Anglo-Saxon rank of earl. Later evidence suggests that the seven princes and the 'seven earls' survived the absorption of the Pictish kingdom in the ninth century.[19]

There are indications that the social structure and system of land administration were not seriously affected by the disappearance of the Pictish kingdom in the ninth century. The place-name, *Pett*, found in the modern form *Pit*, signified a unit of land or an 'estate'. It is common in the east of Scotland between the Firth of Forth and the Dornoch Firth. As well as forming locally descriptive names, it is also joined with proper names, such as Pitcormick in Strath Ardle, meaning 'Cormac's share', and Pitalpin in Angus, meaning 'Alpin's land'. This suggests that the Picts owned land individually and even that they continued to do so under the new Gaelic domination, but it must be remembered that all over the Highlands the Gaelic word *Baile* appearing in individual place-names may sometimes indicate appropriation.

The Gospel Book of the monastery of Deer in Buchan contains, as well as Vulgate texts, parts of the Gospels and also part of an Office for the

ISLANDS AND TRADITIONAL DISTRICTS

·········· Highland Line

Visitation of the Sick, in a ninth century hand; on the margins are a series of notes in Gaelic of grants of land made to the monastery. This includes *inter alia* the legend of the original grant to the monastery with a circumstantial story of St Columba and St Drostan. Since the *Notitiae* were written probably in the early twelfth century, much of the material, if it is authentic, must have been gleaned from tradition. There is other evidence of similar grants in Scotland and Ireland, and the *Notitiae* can be seen as one of the few scraps of evidence throwing light on social organisation and land-holding in Alba before the twelfth century. The second *Notitia* summarises grants of land to Deer such as 'Muiredach son of Morgann gave Pett Meic Garnait and the field of Toiche Teimne; and it is he who was Mormaer and was toisech', suggesting continuity from the Pictish kingdoms of east Scotland. *Toisech*, meaning leader, appears in both Irish and Scottish records as the head of a kindred, although the *Toisech* as an administrative official appears only in Scottish records such as the Book of Deer. He may have possessed the duties, tenure and privileges of the Scottish Thane with whom he was identified in later records, and it is more than coincidence that the Scottish Thanages are almost all within the former Pictland. The summary of grants also includes 'Malcolm, son of Kenneth, gave a king's share in Biffie and in Pett Meic Gobraig and two davochs of upper Ros Abard'. Here the King, Malcolm II (1005-34), assigns to the monks dues and services liable to be rendered by tenants of the estates named. The 'share' or 'cut' translates the Gaelic word *cuit* or *cuid*. These *Notitiae* show that a settled and organised system had actually existed and persisted with demarcated lands which paid fixed burdens.[20]

In these grants, the land measure of the davoch is used. This term derives from the Gaelic *dabhach,* meaning a large vat, but it was not similarly applied to land in Erin. The davoch in the old Pictland came to signify a definite area of land with fixed boundaries which would fill a cubic measure with its yield of grain. The land was assessed from the point of view of the amount of tribute or render that it would produce and, when it is possible to measure davochs, they vary in size in different areas. It was to disappear in documents of the earlier feudal period, but it must have continued in unofficial use, for it again became common in the Middle Ages, especially in the eastern half of Scotland north of the Forth.

It is characteristic of the fusion that went on during our period that (as we show in the next Period) in the early Middle Ages the Gaelic dues of *feachd* and *sluagh*, military expedition and hosting, *cain*, a payment in kind from land, and *conveth* or *coinmheadh*, maintenance or hospitality due to a superior, and also the Norse tax on land, *scat*, were all being levied on the Pictish davoch and on the 'ounceland' which dates from the

Norse occupation. The hybrid term, *tirunga*, i.e. *tir*, Gaelic for land, and *unga*, from the ounce of silver that was the Norse due, also appears as a land measurement. All are mentioned in feudal charters and in acts of parliament. Some indication of the long pedigree and the character of the old Gaelic system of tribute can be gained from the account of the Convention of Druim Cett held in 575. One of the issues concerned the standing of the Dal Riata of Erin with regard to the dues or taxes to be paid to the Uí Néill and to Aedan mac Gabrain of the Dal Riata of Alba. The judgement was given that: 'their *feachd* and *sluagh* should belong to the men of Ireland because *sluagh* always goes with the soil, but their *cain* and *cobach* (taxes) should belong to the men of Scotland'.[21]

The laws of Ireland specified very exactly the possessions that different grades of society were entitled to have. But the only document that describes the distribution of land in Alba is attributed to the mid seventh century; the *Senchus Fer nAlban* or 'History of the Men of Scotland' shows the variation in fortune that one would expect in human society. It describes the genealogies and the strength of the three kindreds which the sons of Erc had founded in Dalriada. The *Cenel Gabrain*, called after a grandson of Fergus Mór, possessed Kintyre, Knapdale, Arran and Bute; at a slightly later date a new kindred appeared in Cowal taking their name from Gabran's brother, Comgall, and giving their name to the district. The kindred mustered 560 houses and 300 fighting men. The *Cenel nOengusa* occupied Islay and had 430 houses and 500 fighting men. The *Cenel Loairn* territory stretched northwards from the Moss of Crinan and had been divided among the sons of Loarn. This kindred had 420 houses and 700 fighting men but the seventh hundred of this complement was composed of the men of the Airgialla. They were kindreds of vassal status, subordinate to the *Cenel Loairn* and also to the Uí Néill of Erin, paying tribute and providing fighting men for their armies. The name in fact signifies 'hostage-givers'.[22] This detailed account of the different grades of the inhabitants of an area is interesting to remember when we come to the development of the Highland clans of a later age.

As the *Senchus* shows, large numbers of folk lie behind the three kindreds or *cenela* and they cannot have been the direct descendants of Gabran, Loarn and Oengus. How the land was distributed among them we cannot be sure. In addition to military service, the men of these tribes owed sea-service levied at the rate of twice seven rowers for each twenty houses. The houses were grouped in villages generally consisting of thirty or multiples of that number, but in Lorn there had been much division to provide for numerous grandsons and great-grandsons, and these often held lesser numbers, sometimes as few as five. The details about the existence of these small groups is of especial interest when, at a later date, we come to the building up of the Highland clans. After the Norse penetration, their system of taxation was evidently applied to the old Gaelic organisation of the *baile* of twenty houses, for the land division of the ounceland or *tirunga* was divided into twenty pennylands. The ancient laws of Ireland were applied by the *brehon* or *brithem*, trained jurists who acted rather in the capacity of arbitrators, explaining the law to parties in a dispute and awarding the amount of compensation to be paid for injuries received.

In Scotland, archaeological excavation and laboratory dating methods have shown that some cereals, primitive barleys and emmer, a kind of wheat, have been cultivated from early Bronze Age times. Several finds from Scotland and Ireland of stone ploughshares show that simple *ard* ploughs were used but little else is recorded of cultivation methods. The Irish depended largely on pastoral agriculture supplemented by hunting, and their laws show that wealth and status were assessed in terms of the ownership of numbers of cattle. It must be significant that in the later stories of the *Fianna* they were still described as supporting themselves by hunting during the summer. In the feasts that the ancient tales so often describe, the food was meat and dairy produce. In the stories about the saints, tillage is rarely mentioned although monks certainly supported themselves by arable farming. Adamnan's *Life of St Columba* records incidents concerned with ploughing, sowing, reaping and grinding the grain (using the mill rather than a quern). The Gaelic people's attitude is in marked contrast to that of the Norse. Sagas such as the Orkneyinga Saga and Njal's Saga describe the active work on the land by Vikings in the summer and in between piratical expeditions. In the later Highland period, cattle-raising was very important for practical economic reasons but it also possessed considerable prestige compared with that of farming, tillage and the raising of crops.

The Gaels were accustomed to sending their cattle away for summer pasturing before the Norse conquests. The Norse also did so, but in districts once dominated by them the termination '-ary', in place-names, derived from the Gaelic *airidh,* sheiling, appears more often than the Scandinavian *shader* or *seadar*. The results of this transitional period can even be seen in farm implements. A single-stilted plough was used in the Hebrides as well as in Orkney and Shetland until the nineteenth century. Known in the Islands as the *crann nan gad*, it has been used in the Parish of Barvas, Lewis, within living memory. The Irish plough team of four horses yoked abreast remained the usual Highland plough team, and must have persisted until the turn of the nineteenth century. In the *Agricultural Report* for Perthshire of the 1790s, the writer described the 'short' yoke of four horses abreast as being the usual plough team in upland areas of the County; this was considered to save the harness or *graith.*[23] It had its effect on the arrangement of agricultural holdings in the Highlands, and it is perpetuated in the fairly common place-name Kerrow, derived from *ceathramh,* the Gaelic for a fourth. More important than such indications is the fact that in the succeeding periods down to the era of agricultural 'improvements' a very uniform system was general all over Scotland, both Lowland and Highland, and there are no indications that it was introduced from the south.

The real interest in tracing the survival of old institutions and the use of concrete things lies in the persistence of the ideas and ideals that lay behind them. In Erin, great importance was attached to lines of descent. By the seventh century, it became a cult to trace the royal pedigrees to mythical origins. In both the great story cycles, the genealogies of the heroes are carefully worked out. The Highlanders down the centuries were enthusiastic (and even, sometimes, imaginative) genealogists.

The wearing of the kilt is still considered the badge of the Highlanders. Clothes were always considered to be a matter of importance in Highland society. The Irish tales abound with descriptions of the beautiful clothes that were worn. In one of the great manuscript collections, Cormac mac Art who, according to the mythical history of Erin was a powerful king of the third century A.D., is described: 'Beautiful was the appearance of Cormac in that assembly at Tara, flowing and slightly curling was his golden hair. A red buckler with stars and animals of gold and fastenings of silver upon him. A crimson cloak in wide descending folds around him, fastened at his neck with precious stones. A torque of gold around his neck. A white shirt with a full collar and intertwined with gold thread upon him. Two wonderful shoes of gold with golden loops upon his feet. Two spears with golden sockets in his hands, with many rivets of red bronze.'[24]

H F McClintock in his *Old Irish and Highland Dress* has analysed the kind of clothes worn in the tales and on the figures carved on the monuments, and they show no approximation to the Highland belted plaid, the forerunner of the kilt, nor are checked fabrics mentioned. In the few pieces of early fabric that have been discovered, it seems that colour has been used sparingly and it is not until the seventeenth century that we find textiles made up with checks and stripes. The so-called 'Falkirk Tartan', dated to the mid-third century A.D., achieved a checked effect by using two shades of natural wool to produce a contrast in tone. The Highlander continued to weave extremely fine and beautiful worsted fabrics. This was especially noticeable in the sixteenth century.[25] The idea that the coarse carded woollen tweeds are particularly Highland emanated from the south in the nineteenth century.

The supreme beauty and craftsmanship of the ornaments of the Irish can be actually seen in the National Museum in Dublin as well as read

Silver brooch set with gold panels and gold filigree, eighth century, found at Hunterston in Ayrshire

about in their literature. The people of Scotland also made beautiful things and carried on the tradition into later times. Their supreme achievements were in the form of wonderful penannular brooches such as the Tara Brooch and the Hunterston Brooch. The Highlanders carried on this tradition down to the eighteenth century. In their early poetry their treasures were often recorded and in the Middle Ages were even carved upon their tombstones.[26]

Their love of dress and ornament allied to indifference to other amenities continued to be a marked characteristic. General David Stewart of Garth, writing of his youth in the late eighteenth century, said that the Highlanders willingly submitted to 'personal privations in regard to food and accommodation' in order to 'procure arms and habiliments which may set off to advantage a person unbent and unsubdued by conscious inferiority ...'. Lord Cockburn, in his *Circuit Journeys*, described the dress of a church congregation in Skye in 1841: 'They had all on red tartan cloaks or shawls and clean mutches of snowy whiteness, with borders of many plies'. He added: 'I can't comprehend how such purity can come out of such smoky hovels'.[27]

The Gaels have not handed down any great tradition in architecture.

But with their love of beauty, they embodied descriptions of wonderful dwellings in some of their tales. For instance, in the description of the house or mansion of his sweetheart, Cael of the Fianna sings in his *duan* or poem of praise of the gold and silver furniture set with crystals, the bed curtains like foxgloves, hung on slender copper rods and the roof with thatch of blue and yellow birds' wings.[28] Father Dieckhoff of the Benedictine Abbey at Fort Augustus and compiler of an important Gaelic dictionary used to describe how on his missions in the Western Highlands, he had seen examples of thatching made of different material evidently intentionally for ornament and giving the appearance of birds' feathers. In the 'Song of Cael', the walls of the dwellings were said to be white. The traditional dwellings in the Highlands are of drystone walling and never whitewashed, lime being too precious, and they are often referred to as 'black houses' yet, nowadays, when materials are available, the crofters' houses are generally lime-washed and stand out dazzlingly white against the dark hillsides.

The custom of fortifying hilltops and then of building strongholds was an ancient one in Alba; but, in spite of poetic fancies, it would be hard to imagine a dwelling more comfortless than was Dunadd, the capital of Dalriada. Excavations there, although they show signs of prolonged occupation, reveal only the remains of drystone walls and hut foundations upon the exposed summit. It is significant that among the few artefacts found, there were moulds for casting brooches and other ornaments. There is a fantastic tale of the competition of three brothers in rich possessions, extravagant hospitality and generosity for the loan of a magic cauldron said to kept there.[29] Cauldrons figure in several tales especially those involving feasts, and some examples actually survive. It is significant that the winner was chosen because of the greater numbers of his guests, in other words, the size of his following. If this was the case in ancient Erin and Alba, it would have been abundantly so in later times in the Highlands.

The Norse were better house-builders than the Gael, as excavations such as those at Jarlshof show, and they may have had some influence on the traditional type of house in the Outer Isles.[30] We know from Adamnan's *Life of St Columba* that the Saint and his monks used timber and wattle for their buildings on Iona; and even the very sites have disappeared. But in some of the early monasteries, small stone beehive huts or cells were built as in the Garvelloch Islands, and such settlements were surrounded by a cashel wall as at Kilpatrick or Kilbrendan in Arran and Loch Chaluim Chille in Sky. Such buildings and enclosures were also customary in Erin. Those humble buildings were the background to the fervent lives of the early evangelists. In them were visualised the tremendous visions of celestial glory described in St

Adamnan's *Life*. For instance, Virgno, a pious youth afterwards an abbot of Iona, 'burning with the love of God' entered the church one night to pray in the oratory. After about an hour, St Columba also came to the church 'and along with him a golden light descended from the highest heaven and filled all that part of the church. But the brightness of the same celestial light bursting through the inner door of the chamber, which was just a little ajar, filled the interior of that other small side house where Virgno was doing his best to hide himself — and not without a certain degree of intense fear'. In Erin a simple form of Romanesque did develop, but the surviving churches of the western Highlands are very simple; many are built without mortar and with undressed quoins.[31] In the later part of our period, in their need of protection for their churchmen and treasures from the raiding Vikings, the Irish evolved the round tower. In Scotland, the only surviving examples are in the Lowlands, at Brechin and Abernethy, to which Irish influence extended after the time of Kenneth mac Alpin.

As Francis C Eeles said, the period 'was one of very high artistic development in things of small size. It produced no great buildings; its churches, though numerous, were remarkably small; but in metal-work, in the writing and illumination of manuscripts, and also in certain forms of sculpture we may claim that it has never been surpassed'.[32] The prime flowering of these closely allied crafts reached its climax in Gaeldom

The Monymusk Reliquary or **Brec Bennoch** *of St Columba, late seventh or early eighth century*

about the ninth and tenth centuries. The complex stylised designs of interlace covering the entire space to be ornamented, are characteristically northern. In the finest period, zoomorphic abstractions were sometimes introduced into the designs, but never foliage. J Romilly Allen has pointed out in his *Early Christian Monuments* that the foundation of the patterns lies in the plait.

The skill of the Gael in working precious metals is shown in the wonderful collection of treasures in the National Museum in Dublin; but Scotland has an outstanding example in the Monymusk Reliquary, a lovely silver and enamel shrine in the National Museum of Antiquities, thought to be the *Brec Bennoch*, the Speckled Peaked One, of St Columba. The little shrine, which is no more than 4½ inches long and 2 inches wide, is carved out of solid wood and plated with silver and bronze and the plates engraved. Besides the typical Gaelic interlace patterning, it is enriched, like many other contemporary works of art, with designs based on the divergent spiral.

The supreme Gaelic art was that of illuminating. All the finest examples such as the Book of Kells and the Book of Durrow are in Ireland. The best surviving Scottish example of the period is known as 'the Book of Deer' and therefore presumably is of Scots origin and is rather an indifferent specimen of an illuminated manuscript. There is however a widely held belief that the Book of Kells was made upon Iona and transferred to Kells during the Viking raids. It is now kept in Trinity College, Dublin. It lies open but in a glass case and modern reproductions are arranged beside it to show some of the pages one cannot see, and it is most striking to notice how completely they fail to convey the over-powering effect of the combined complexity and beauty of the crowded and minute detail of the original. At Iona there was certainly the tradition of writing, for St Columba had set the example of copying the Scriptures; and there is a tradition that he gave a copy of the New Testament in his own handwriting to each of the churches which he founded. He had himself also penned the later sixth century Psalter known as the *Cathach* or 'warrior' and it is evident that a great deal of work continued to be done in the *Scriptorium* at Iona. Portions of annals written there formed the basis of later Irish annals such as the Annals of Tigernach. There is information of a few other Scots manuscripts. St Ternan, a leader in the mission to East Scotland from St Ninian's foundation at Candida Casa, is said to have had a copy of the Gospels in four volumes of which the Gospel of St Matthew was still preserved in a silver and golden casket at Banchory Ternan in Aberdeenshire down to the sixteenth century.[33] It has been claimed by some scholars that the art of illuminating originated with the Angles who had had the splendid Book of Lindisfarne. It may, however, be pointed out that the Irish had a long tradition of very fine design and craftsmanship in metal which the Angles lacked. Moreover, just as St Aidan brought them Christianity from Iona, skilled illuminators may also have come from there. Such a claim is based on the form of lettering. The Angles received through southern England the influence of the classical tradition in which the actual writing itself was far more important than it was in the Gaelic culture of a date later than when the Angles had come under the influence of churchmen from southern England and their Latinity and classical styles. Evidence in carvings on stones survives of this great Irish influence in contrast to the standing stones of the Picts and of the Angles. The oldest of the West Highland crosses such as St Martin's and St John's at Iona are entirely in the Irish tradition and were to inspire the West Highland carvings of the fifteenth century.

Perhaps the greatest legacy of the Gaels of Ireland to the later people in the Highlands was that of their literature, the oldest vernacular literature in western Europe. Here it is possible to give only the barest outlines of this great inheritance. The most important tales are grouped into two cycles, the Ulster or Red Branch Cycle, with a pre-Christian background, and the later, Fenian Cycle with its tales fixed in the third century A.D. There were also some contemporary stories from southern Ireland. However often these stories were repeated and elaborated, the

Cross of Kildalton, Islay, a free-standing high cross of the ninth or tenth century, with the prominent ring or nimbus linking the arms and shaft of the cross

characters in the different cycles were always kept entirely separate. This is stressed in the evidence before the Committee of the Highland Society appointed in 1805 to enquire into the nature and authenticity of the Poems of Ossian; and the confusion between the characters is one of the most suspicious points in James Macpherson's eighteenth century 'translations'.

In general outline some of the tales, such as the tragedy of Deirdre, have often been repeated and are fairly well known, but no summary can give an idea of their fascination — the mingling of a primitive ferocity and love of the marvellous with a strong strain of idealism and conduct, a dry sense of worldly wisdom, very subtle characterisation, great delicacy of perception, and a delight in beauty of colour and of form especially as found in the song and the flight of birds, the movement of the deer, the waves of the sea, the appearance of the land in changing seasons. From the wealth of beautiful passages the reader must choose what pleases him best. Unlike the gloom of Macpherson's productions, there was often a sense of fun and a dry humour, as in the many stories of the misadventures of Conan the Boaster. Perhaps the finest of the Red Branch stories is the *Tain Bo Cuailnge*, 'the cattle-raid of Cooley'. It is characteristic of the simple, pastoral economies of the Gael in that it deals with the rivalry of the men of Ulster and Connacht for the possession of a famous black bull.

The Gaels were fond of codes of advice as to proper behaviour, and there are several copies of 'Cormac's Maxims' preserved in later Highland manuscripts. The work is attributed to Cormac mac Art, the renowned third century A.D. Irish king, and it is written in the classical Gaelic common to Ireland and Scotland. After general good advice to his son Cairbre to be temperate and just, to encourage commerce and agriculture, and to defend his people, and practical hints on how to conduct his feasts, he advises discretion in behaviour. 'For if thou shouldest appear too knowing, thou wouldest be satirized and abused; if too simple thou wouldest be imposed upon; if too proud thou wouldest be shunned; if too humble thy dignity would suffer; if talkative thou wouldest not be deemed learned; if too severe thy character would be defamed; if too timid thy rights would be encroached upon'. Such high standards of behaviour were well in keeping with Highland sophisticated ideals of conduct. The distinguished manners of the people are mentioned by practically every early visitor to the Highlands. The earliest form in which these stories have come down to us is in prose with verse dialogue or short *rann* of poetry. They were evidently summaries for the benefit of the teller of the tales. Later versions were written out more fully.

The Ulster Cycle deals with the mythical kings of Ulster and their contemporaries before the rise of Connacht and Munster. In the earlier versions there are still traces of paganism. In several Gaelic tales an oath by the elements is almost exactly similar to that which the ambassadors from the Celts swore to Alexander the Great: 'If we do not fulfil our engagement may the sky falling upon us crush us, may the earth opening swallow us up, may the sea overflowing its borders drown us'. One of the episodes in the *Tain Bo Cuailnge* described how the god Lugh came to the rescue of his son Cu Chullain; perhaps it was so moving that the clerical revisers could not bring themselves to erase it. Cu Chullain is also credited with an earthly father.

Cu Chullain's chariot appears in West Highland tales written as late as the eighteenth century; and, as Mr Alistair Chisholm Mackenzie described, a Skye soldier in 1917 was heard singing a song written by a Lewisman in which the lines occurred:

Is chaidh ar giulan ann an carbad [chariot]
Null thar ghleanntan gorm an fhraoich

In the Fenian Cycle the sword was becoming of greater importance and the chariot had disappeared. Armour was not worn in the earlier versions of either cycle. In both there was some connection with Alba; for instance, Cu Chullain was trained in Skye, and his unwitting slaughter of Conlaoch, the son born to him there, was a tale much repeated in the Highlands and a gloomier and somewhat altered version appears in Macpherson's Ossianic 'translations'. The story of Deirdre and the sons of Usnach has a closer connection. Deirdre, with Naoise and his brothers, fled to Alba from her elderly betrothed, King Conchobar of Ulster, and many places are associated with them, such as Duntroon on Loch Crinan, Dunyardil or *Dun Dhearduil* on Loch Ness, and especially all about Loch Etive. It is told in the fifteenth century Glenmasan manuscript, and Alexander Carmichael heard the people of Barra still talking of the beauty of Deirdre of the white breast and her hair more yellow than the eastern sun in summer, and he took down the whole story there in March 1867 from a crofter, John MacNeill. A poem to a maiden on her marriage once widely known in the Islands, besides Christian attributes, spoke of the beauty of Emir, the tenderness of Deirdre, and the strength of Maeve, all characters of the Ulster Cycle.[34]

The Fenian Cycle is more popular in tone than the Ulster Cycle and not on the same heroic scale. The Fenians are generally believed to have been a sort of militia, a band of heroes whose fighting and hunting exploits formed the basis of countless stories. And the stories tell of the rivalry between Finn MacCoul (James Macpherson's Fingal), the leader of the Fianna of Munster, and Goll mac Morna, leader of those of Connacht, and of the growing enmity between Finn MacCoul and the

High King of Erin, and of the doings of these leaders and their kinsfolk. Finn is supposed to have lived A.D.200. There is evidence that in the seventh and eighth centuries tales about him were popular, and the oldest surviving texts, the *Leabhar na hUidhre*, Book of the Dun Cow, of the late eleventh century and the Book of Leinster of the twelfth century, were evidently taken from much more ancient sources. But as Dr Hyde says, the development of the Cycle was 'one of the most remarkable examples in the world of continuous literary evolution. I use the word evolution advisedly, for there is probably not a century from the seventh to the eighteenth in which new stories, poems and redactions of Sagas regarding Finn and the Fenians were not invented and put into circulation'. In J F Campbell's *Leabhar na Feinne*, the incidents of the Cycle as they were recorded in the sixteenth century *Book of the Dean of Lismore* and as orally repeated down to the nineteenth century were collated into a whole. He points out that the Cycle was current from c.900 till he was collecting in the 1850s and 1860s.

Many of the stories were bodily transferred to the Highlands. There are even several Ben Gulbens where Finn by guile slew Diarmaid in revenge for the taking away of his wife. There can be few districts where stories of the Fenians have not been localised. The Report of the 'Committee appointed to Enquire into the Nature and Authenticity of Ossian' stated in 1805 that they were also to some extent known in the Lowlands, for Blind Harry, Barbour, Boece, Gavin Douglas, David Lindsay of the Mount and Robert Kirk allude to them. They were the constant delight of the Gael, and Bishop John Carswell sourly remarked in the preface to his translation into Gaelic of *The Book of Common Order* in 1567, the so-called 'Knox's Liturgy', that Highland writers preferred 'the framing of vain, hurtful, lying earthly stories about the Tuatha De Danond and about the sons of Milesius, and about the heroes and Fionn Mac Cumhail with his giants, and about many others whom I shall not number or tell of here in detail'.[35] Or, as Stewart of Garth recalled from the days of his youth, when a visitor entered a hamlet, the first question after the introductory compliments was: '*Bheil dad agad air an Fhéinn?*' [Can you speak of the days of Fingal?]; and the whole community gathered to hear him. A considerable number of the stories survived as folk tales in the Islands well into the nineteenth century.

It is significant that in the long period of centuries when this loosely articulated mass of tales of greatly varying merit was current, the characters of the heroes are always clearly preserved — Finn wise and cunning, Goll fierce and surly, Conan the truculent boaster and butt, Diarmaid handsome, charming and beloved, Caoilte swift-footed and devoted to Finn, and Ossian the hero-poet who survived and mourned them all. In many later traditions, however, their stature is exaggerated to that of giants.

In Erin, the *Fìli* or poets held a very high position in society. They belonged to the *Oes Dàna*, the folk of gifts, the learned class whose rank and privileges equated with those of the nobles. The poet of the highest rank, the *ollamh*, was equal in rank and privileges with the king of a Tuath. The craft of the *File* may have originally been in the hands of the *Draoi*, the Druids, and the poet's universally recognised power of satire may have derived from a semi-supernatural function of an earlier, druidic era. Before the Church began to commit the laws, literature and saga cycles to writing from the seventh century, the *Oes Dàna* were the custodians of this rich oral tradition. In the rhythmic prose of the ancient law tracts, there are indications that some were composed in poetry, and metrical forms survive in the texts. The composing of eulogy and elegy was the main function of the *File* and the functions of the lower grades of poets and musicians were also defined. The *Oes Dàna* also included the *seanchaidh*, the historian, the *brithem*, the law-man, the *saer*, the wright or craftsman, and the *ligiche*, the man of medicine or leech.

The few surviving records of the Gaelic kingdom of Alba do not include mention of poets and poetic schools there, but we know that they were an established feature of society in the same way as the professional poets of Erin. There are references in Irish sources to the 'ollamh of Erin and Alba', showing how strongly the Gaelic culture of the two countries held them together, and a late eleventh century poem, the *Duan Albannach*, begins by addressing the men of learning of Alba:

O all ye learned ones of Alba,
Stately yellow-haired company.[36]

Our manuscript material survives from the period of the fourteenth to the seventeenth centuries showing how the bardic schools flourished and poets composed in the traditional metres so long as the Gaelic aristocracy held court. It has often been described how early Irish verse not only rhymed but used more elaborate metres than those found in any other language. A lengthy training was necessary to acquire the ready skill in a complicated but highly conventional system of metres. The organisation of the Church as it became established during this period was characteristic of the organisation of the Gaelic society of the times. Christianity had established itself in the Roman province of Britain by the late fourth century and there are traditions and indications of the visits of the early missionaries to the north east of Scotland, such as St Ternan, St Ninian, St Fergus and St Kentigern. But the most important period of evangelisation for Scotland and Ireland began in the sixth century, the period of St Columba's ministry. The conversion of Ireland was traditionally the work of St Patrick in the fifth century, and when the Church was securely established there, numbers of individual Churchmen went out to worship God in remoter solitude or to convert the heathen. Irish monasticism represented the adaptation of institutional Christianity to an existing society which has been described as 'familial, tribal and heroic'. The kin-based society with its men of learning and a highly developed oral tradition absorbed the monasteries. The administrative heads of the monasteries were abbots, often drawn from the kin of the founding families; and bishops, priests and deacons, though they had the same spiritual duties as in the Roman Church, were primarily monks and under the jurisdiction of the abbots. The office of abbot would be held by successive members of the kindred of the founding abbot, and in Iona the abbacy remained with the kindred of Columba, the Cenel Conaill of the Uí Néill, from his death in 597 until 704 when St Adamnan died, and his kindred continued to provide abbots at intervals long after that. This was characteristic of Gaelic civilisation where descent counted for so much. It is important to remember that the two Churches recognised each other.

Most of the great Irish monasteries had been founded in the sixth century. Their scholarship as well as their missionary zeal extended to Scotland, to England and then to Europe. The active monasteries sent out monks to found monasteries in other areas. St Columba was one of the most outstanding of these missionaries. It is our good fortune that through his biographer, St Adamnan, some idea of his personality has come down to us. He came to Alba in 563 with twelve companions, having already founded two monastic houses in Erin, and settled at Iona; and after its foundation, further missionaries went out from Iona. His coming was part of a great evangelistic movement, and at first there was independence and perhaps even rivalry between some of the missionaries. St Kenneth was closely associated with St Columba; St Brendan, St Maelrubha and St Blaan seem to have worked independently, although St Brendan was the friend of St Columba. Others, like St Comgall and St Moluag, were possibly his rivals. The monasteries founded by such missionaries were under the jurisdiction of the abbot and kin of the founding monastery. The monastic *paruchia* of *Calum Cille* thus embraced houses in Ireland, Scotland and northern England all of which looked to the Mother Church of Iona as their fount and head.

This early stage of development had a lasting effect on the Highlands, and all through the political and ecclesiastical changes that followed, the special local devotion to the evangelist particularly associated with the district continued — the cult of St Fillan about Loch Earn, of St Moluag in Lismore, St Kessog about Loch Lomond, St Maelrubha in Wester Ross, St Ternan in the valley of the Dee, St Finbar in Barra, and many

others. Like so much also, it passed into the great unrecorded folk
heritage of the people, to reveal its presence again and again in later
times. With the veneration for these Saints went veneration for their
relics, especially for their pastoral staffs, one of which, the Staff of St
Moluag, survives to the present day still in the custody of the descendants
of its original founder. One of the writers has had a personal account of
the long story of the survival of the *bachull* and of the family who are its
custodians by the present 'Baron of the Bachul', Mr Alexander
Livingstone. Their bells were simple four-sided hand-bells of bronze or
iron, such as the bell of Cladh Bhrennu in Glen Lyon. In our next period,
the organisation of the Columban Church was to be absorbed into that
of the great Western Catholic Church, but the old reverence persisted not
only for the evangelist who had first brought Christianity to a locality
but also to the bells and staffs associated with their ministry, the latter in
more cases where the name of the saint with whom it had originally been
associated had been forgotten. A very touching instance of the survival
of the old feeling of sanctity is given by Martin Martin writing at the end
of the seventeenth century of the deserted Flannan Islands. He describes
how the fowler coming there always felt that he came home because
'there was none ever yet landed in them but found himself more disposed
to devotion there than anywhere else'.[37] Sometimes it retained its vitality

*Hand-bell of iron and bronze from
Fortingall, Perthshire, associated with the
missionary journeys in the age of the Saints
of the sixth and seventh centuries*

into a later period not remote from our own as when, in the late nineteenth century, Alexander Carmichael heard the people of Barra invoking St Maelrubha, St Moluag, St Donnan, St Carnaig, St Modan and especially *Calum Cille* or St Columba to bless their lands and shielings.

At the time of St Columba, the Gaelic church had slight but friendly relations with that of Rome. Some accounts of his life tell of the sending of gifts to St Columba by Pope Gregory and that in return, St Columba sent the Pope his great Hymn the *Altus Prositur*. Controversy developed however on certain points of observance and over the method of computing Easter and the form of the tonsure. The Roman Church usages had been brought to England by St Augustine of Pope Gregory's mission in 597. They were accepted by the Church in southern Ireland in 633, by Northumbria at the Synod of Whitby in 664, and by the Pictish Church about 710. In spite of this, the other Church in Alba retained its own Celtic monastic organisation until it was replaced by a Roman episcopal Church organisation in the twelfth century.

It is significant of the impact of new southern influences and the coming differentiation of the Lowland culture that a cult for St Andrew should begin to arise. His relics were said to have been brought to Kinrimond or Kilrymont, later known as St Andrews, in the ninth century by Regulus who gave his name to St Rule's. Such was the popularity of this shrine that, in the eleventh century, Queen Margaret instituted the Queen's Ferry for easier passage between Lothian and St Andrews.

Both in Erin and in Alba, the second half of the eighth century saw a religious revival in the Church and an increase in the number of anchorites. They were called *Céli Dé*, meaning 'clients of God', and it is significant of the Church's close association with Gaelic civilisation that the secular term *céle* was used. A substantial body of nature poetry of eighth and ninth century date has survived, composed by solitary Culdees in communion with their surroundings. By the eleventh century, the Culdees were playing a prominent role in the Church. They had formed communities of regular clergy and these survived into the medieval period and were in full communion with the members of the organisation that succeeded them.

Other offices in both the Irish and the Scottish Churches were the *fer-leginn* and the *scoloc*. The rule of the Culdees laid special emphasis on learning. The *fer-leginn*, literally 'man of reading', was in charge of the school of a monastery and he was often an anchorite. Domangart, *fer-leginn* of Turriff, appears as a witness in the Book of Deer in one of the *Notitiae* dated to 1131. This office of the Celtic Church still existed in the thirteenth century. The term *scoloc* was used for the young cleric or scholar in the Church, receiving education in return for work, and also for the tenant of church lands, and the word survived in Gaelic as *sgalag*, meaning 'farm servant'.

Period II

c.1050-c.1300. Feudal Influences on the Highlands.
The Beginnings of Differentiation between
Highlands and Lowlands

This period saw the beginning of the cleavage between the Highlands and the Lowlands. Although Gaelic continued to be spoken in many districts from which it has now long since disappeared, Fordun in 1384 stated that 'the manners and customs of the Scots vary with the diversity of their speech. For two languages are spoken amongst them, the Scottish and the Teutonic; the latter of which is the language of those who occupy the seaboard and plains, while the race of Scottish speech inhabits the highlands and outlying islands. The people of the coast are of domestic and civilised habits, trusty, patient and urbane ...', and much more to the same effect. 'The highlanders and people of the islands, on the other hand, are a savage and untamed nation, rude and independent, given to rapine, ease-loving, of a docile and warm disposition, comely in person but unsightly in dress, hostile to the English people and language, and, owing to diversity of speech, even to their own nation, and exceedingly cruel. They are, however, faithful and obedient to their king and country and easily made to submit to law if properly governed'. It is the tragedy of the history of the Highlanders that they were so seldom governed with even a minimum of understanding, justice and efficiency.

The development of the differentiation between the Highlands and the Lowlands was of cardinal importance during the period. It was due mainly to economic causes. Over the greater part of western Europe, including to a lesser degree Scotland, there was a marked increase in commerce and industry, transport and communications, and the exploitation of natural resources, all of which resulted in a concentration of wealth and in improved amenities. The physical conditions of the area that we now call the Highlands hampered transport, commerce and industry. Natural resources were minimal, the proportion of land capable of cultivation was unusually low and of poor quality. The climate was severe and capricious, which was exceptionally bad for agriculture. These conditions should always be borne in mind.

The other great change which occurred in western Europe during the period was that of general social organisation, very markedly in the case of the Church, legal systems and arrangements made for civil administration — what today we call the 'feudal system'. This change spread to Scotland, first to the Lowlands and then to the Highlands as

34

the different areas came under the king's authority, and especially within the concept of feudalism, that of military and administrative service to a superior in return for occupation of land. The introduction of these as a formalised method of land-holding is the most important event in Highland history of the period. Adapted to conditions in Highland society during the next three and a half centuries, it was to persist there while it decayed in other parts of the country and was to accentuate the difference between the Highlands and the Lowlands.

In this period we see the gradual consolidation of the kingdom of Scotland in the south and south west, in the Western Isles and the parts of the Highlands that had been dominated by the Norse, and in other disaffected areas such as Moray. Although the most far-reaching social changes took place in the Lowlands, a new and foreign set of influences came to modify the traditional kin-based society and culture of the Highlands: it is in this period that we may detect the emergence of the nuclei of early clans. With so many great changes taking place in this period, a general idea of the nature of the reform of institutions and social organisation is as essential for Highland history as it is for Lowland or English history. We shall touch on the main aspects of these changes as they influenced Highland society.

Our second period opens with the reign of Malcolm III, Canmore (1058-1093). He consolidated his rule over eastern Scotland, which had been seized by Macbeth, and established a claim by his first marriage to the northern dominions of the Earl of Orkney, which his descendants then made good. His frontier with England continued to be a matter of bitter dispute throughout his reign and was the cause of his death at Alnwick in 1093. The sovereignty of the Hebrides, however, remained a matter of dispute between the Kings of Scotland and Norway until near the end of this period. One of the chief influences that was to bring about the great changes from a Celtic form of government and social organisation to a feudal one was that of Margaret, Malcolm Canmore's second wife. She was the grand-daughter of Ethelred, the last purely Saxon King of England. Thanks to the account of her life written by Turgot, a Benedictine monk and her confessor, her personality comes across to us unusually vividly. She was deeply concerned in Church affairs and was canonised in 1250. Her main concern was to eliminate outdated practices, although on occasion she gave help to the Celtic church communities of the Culdees. She was in full accord with the great revival that was enlivening the church in England, and when she founded a church at Dunfermline, she turned to Canterbury and Archbishop Lanfranc, who sent three monks from this centre of the new monastic movement. The foundation of the great religious houses was an important feature of European civilisation of the period; many of the

Scots nobles were to follow St Margaret's example and found houses of the Benedictine order, bringing in monks from England or elsewhere to do so. This was one of the many factors that brought the old Celtic Scotland into the main stream of Western European development. Her Church, which was dedicated to the Holy Trinity, grew into the wealthiest Benedictine abbey in Scotland and became the burial place of the kings of Scots, replacing their traditional burial place in Iona. In 1093, Malcolm and Margaret were both buried at Dunfermline.

Turgot refers to another influence from the south which may not have been inconsiderable in this period of European history when merchants and traders from Germany and northern Italy were travelling far afield. He described how Margaret encouraged foreign merchants to bring their wares to Scotland: 'and it was at her instigation that the natives of Scotland purchased from these traders clothing of various colours with ornaments to wear, so that from this period, through her suggestion, new costumes of different fashions were adopted, the elegance of which made the wearers appear like a new race of beings.'[1] The choice of Christian names gives some indication of the change in a family from a Gaelic to an Anglo-Norman way of life. It was to become a marked feature in the genealogies of the great Scots families as they became Anglo-Normanised. It is noticeable that Malcolm Canmore's eldest son by his first wife was called Duncan. Margaret's children were called Edward, Edgar, Edmund, Ethelred, Alexander, David, Matilda and Mary, all representing innovations from the south. The changes that were to transform the country began during Malcolm's reign and were carried on during those of his direct descendants. Their reigns form as complete a historical period in Scottish history as any that are called after a dynasty of kings in the history of England.

Malcolm's eight successors (except for his first-born, Duncan, who had no chance to prove himself) were all men of considerable organising ability. They succeeded each other in accordance with the principle of primogeniture which became embodied in the laws of the land. After Malcolm Canmore's death there was an attempt to revive the Gaelic custom of succession. His son Duncan was driven from the throne by Malcolm's brother Donald Bane, who claimed it under the complicated Gaelic custom of succession. He in turn was driven out with the help of William Rufus, King of England, and Duncan regained the throne for a very short time. But Donald Bane and his descendants were to make a good deal of trouble then and in later reigns.

There was another attempt to upset the system of primogeniture, leading to sporadic risings during the short reign of Malcolm IV (1153-65), who in consequence 'planted' the province of Moray with supporters of his regime, but there was no general pan-Gaelic support for the claimants. By the time of the death of Alexander III in 1286, the last direct descendant of Malcolm Canmore, when the rivalry among the claimants to the throne led to the disastrous invitation to Edward I of England to adjudicate, the old Gaelic custom of the selection of a Tanister, the chosen heir designate among the kindred, had become completely obsolete. The old system of succession perhaps may be detected faintly in the suggestion that the 'seven earls', the successors to the seven provincial rulers or mormaers, should be the adjudicators.

In considering the changes effected by these kings that directly affected the Highlands, one has to bear in mind that throughout their reigns their relationship with England varied from close friendship to armed conflict. The claims by the Kings of England to superiority over the Kings of Scotland was made and accepted, then at the end of our period extinguished by the first and second Wars of Independence. Within their realm of Scotland, this group of kings made great territorial changes. The Lothians and the south west were knitted more closely to the old kingdom of Alba, and the centre of control was gradually shifted southwards from Scone and Dunkeld. Meanwhile the seven provinces of Alba, which had enjoyed a formidable independence, were brought more closely under the control of the King of Scots. Moreover, the kings were able to regain from Norse rule first Caithness and Sutherland and then the mainland of Argyll. Finally, after King Hakon's expedition in 1263, Alexander III gained possession of the Western Isles. The latter extensions of territory were of course of cardinal importance in Highland history. During the period there had been a gradual extension of the authority of the Kings of Scots over the Western Isles. But all this is closely bound up with the history of Somerled, the ancestor of the two oldest Highland clans, and that of his successors and is best considered as part of the narrative of their rise to power. The Hebrides were finally ceded by Norway to the King of Scots in 1266.

Queen Margaret had exercised a strongly Saxonizing influence upon Scots affairs. Edgar, who succeeded Duncan and Donald Bane, although he owed a great deal to the help of the Norman King, William Rufus, had Anglo-Saxon affinities. The rest of the dynasty (Alexander I, David I, Malcolm IV, William, Alexander II and Alexander III) were more deeply under the influence of the Normans who were their close companions and held the important posts in church and state. In this, of course, the Scots kings were only moving with the times, for the Normans were exerting a permanent influence on the great reorganisation of social ideas and institutions and of the fabric of society that was going on all over western Europe. From a tenth century settlement of Vikings at the mouth of the Seine, the Normans had grown to be a major power in France. From here their influence extended to Italy, Sicily and the

Mediterranean, and the conquest of England laid the foundations of the twelfth century Angevin empire of Henry Plantagenet, one of the most important powers in Europe. Although the Normans came to Scotland by invitation and not as conquerors, great areas of land passed into their hands by royal gift or by fortunate marriages that were themselves, as feudal casualties, often in the royal gift. In fact, the arrival of the Normans has been dubbed by at least one historian as 'a Norman Conquest', and the influence of the changes that the country experienced in the twelfth century has been a dominating factor in the history of Scotland.[2]

Anglo-Norman families or those who had adopted southern Christian names and seem to have become feudalised in their ideas obtained a great deal of land in the most fertile districts of the Highlands. The Comyn family for example obtained the earldom of Buchan in the thirteenth century. They were justiciars, constables and later guardians of Scotland and they held the lordship of Badenoch and castles across the country from Lochaber to Strathspey. They also held Glen Urquhart which had previously belonged to the Durward. The latter was another Anglo-Norman, Thomas of Lundie, lord of Lundie in Angus, who as the king's doorward was an important officer in the royal household. He received a large part of the ancient earldom of Mar at the beginning of the thirteenth century when the succession to the earldom was in dispute. The Le Chiens, Fentons and Bissets held land in the Aird; the latter were also in Abertarf and they held land in Glenelg before the MacLeods received it by grant. The Manor of Rait, held by the Mackintoshes in the fifteenth century, was owned by a family of de Rait in the time of Alexander III and Edward I.[3] In the Black Isle, de Boscos, Mowats, Leslies and Grahams had land, and a Le Chien gained a footing at Farr in Sutherland. The large feudal estates of the Stewarts in the west originated with the grant of Renfrew to Walter fitz Alan, the Steward, whose family had come from Brittany. He had entered the service of David I in the 1130s and had been given a hereditary Stewardship.[4] A great family, *de Moravia*, of Flemish origin, were established in Moray in the 1130s, possibly as a consequence of the defeat of Angus, Mormaer of Moray (the great grandson of Macbeth, who was in alliance with Malcolm MacHeth who had claims to the throne) and the suppression of the old 'earldom' of Moray. The grant to Freskin the Fleming of Duffus with extensive northern territories by David I and the appearance in the records about 1136 of the name of the burgh of Elgin show how Moray, the old province of Macbeth, was being brought under royal control.[5] Many Flemings were among the incomers in Scotland of the twelfth and thirteenth centuries. With their medieval reputation as traders, they were important settlers in the new burghs; sporadic support for claimants to the crown in Morayshire, in eastern Inverness-shire, in the Black Isle and in Sutherland may have been partly inspired by dislike of the newcomers but on the whole, the intrusion of the Anglo-Normans themselves and of the fashion for Norman ways of life seems to have caused surprisingly little ill-feeling. Anglo-Normans, when they took service under the King of Scots or obtained land from him, became loyal Scotsmen and readily fought against the Anglo-Normans of England. As in all the other parts of Europe where their influence was felt, the coming of the Normans helped to bring about the adoption of a new social theory, that of feudalism, i.e., that the land of the whole country was the property of the King, who bestowed it upon subjects of his selection in return for specific services, military and administrative. The grants were embodied in charters and were heritable. By means of these feudal dues the country was defended, order was maintained and necessary outlays were met. At least, things would have been so had the system worked perfectly. It did not always do so, and one of the more fundamental topics of this book is to try to show how, in successive periods, its effects were different in the Highlands and the Lowlands.

It must be emphasised that the Anglo-Normans, influential and powerful as they became, were only enfiltered into the old system. What happened in the case of the earls is but an illustration. The ancient Scots Kingdom had been divided into seven provinces, each ruled over by a *mormaer*. This title was equated with that of 'earl', a Saxon term, which was also translated by the Latin term *comes* which was recognised as a high ranking title all over feudalised western Europe. Nevertheless some recollection of their original status survived until after our period, when in the disputed succession to the throne a proposal was made that the 'seven earls' should be called on to adjudicate. The succession to the earldoms with estates lying in the Highlands was by this time almost entirely by the normal practice of primogeniture. Buchan passed to the Comyn family by marriage with an heiress. In the case of the earldom of Atholl the old line of succession had died out. The title was then attended by ill-fortune and was temporarily held by a succession of families but eventually passed to a Stewart. In complete contrast, the earldom of Ross, which had largely passed under indirect Scandinavian control and had been regained by the Scots kings, was granted about 1230 to *Fearchar Mac an t-Sagairt*, who was probably the lay-abbot of Applecross, in reward for his services in helping to suppress a revolt led by the family of another claimant to the throne. It is an example of the lack of unity among the Gael to support the more ancient Celtic form of government. The earls of Ross did not remain distinctively Gaelic. Earldoms were to play a most important part in Highland history. The general pattern of the estates they held was to change and new earldoms were to be formed. In some cases, as in that of Menteith, Lennox and Angus, the growing changes between the Highlands and Lowlands were to cut across the old boundaries of the earldoms.

A type of organisation that was limited to the east coast (and the areas where Pictish occupation has left most evidence) was that of the thanages. About sixty-three thanages are known to have existed. They take their designations from names that were not Gaelic but probably Pictish and they belong to the same area as the mormaers. 'Thane' is an English title, of course, and first appears in Anglo-Saxon records of the seventh century; they were royal officers in charge of subdivisions of the shires of Northumbria, and from here seem to have been adopted by the kings of Scots. The system was grafted onto a pre-existing administration, that of the *toiseach* of whom we have record in the Book of Deer. The *toiseach* was both the lord of a kindred and a military leader. In the twelfth century, the Scottish thane was a royal officer in charge of royal demesne lands and responsible for the collection of *cain* and other dues. He was also responsible for the organisation of the common army service which was assessed in the earldoms on land divisions such as the davoch and the ploughgate.[6]

Eventually the administrative duties of the *toiseach* or thane came increasingly within the scope of those of the sheriff. This ancient form of social organisation has been fitted into the theory of the origin of one clan. According to the most acceptable of the genealogies of the Mackintoshes, the son of Shaw the founder was known as *Mac an Toisich*. Shaw had served in the force that Malcolm IV led in the subjugation of Moray, had been granted land and had been made Keeper of Inverness Castle. According to the genealogy, he was the younger son of the Earl of Fife and in later times the title of thane and earl had become mixed up.[7]

The sheriff and the sheriffdom, Anglo-Saxon in origin and Norman by adoption, was one of the most important institutions brought into Scotland in the twelfth century, and especially to the Highlands; it was to change with the passing periods. The sheriffs were not primarily judicial officers but administrative officers on the royal estates. Gradually their judicial functions developed to give them jurisdiction beyond the king's demesne. The office was granted by the crown for a period of years or during the king's pleasure and it is important to note that some of the early sheriffs, with names such as *Gille-Bride*, *Mac Beatha*, and *Gille-Muire*, were not Anglo-Norman incomers. The office later became heritable and families such as the earls of Lennox could receive a heritable grant of the Sheriffdom of Lennox. The number of heritable sheriffships steadily increased, suggesting that the office was a valuable one, and when the heritable jurisdictions were abolished in 1747, large sums had to be paid as compensation in every case. The growth of the sheriffs and sheriffdoms was one measure of the extension of royal government. By 1300, the whole of the Highlands came in theory if not in practice within the scope of the sheriffdoms. Their establishment can be dated approximately: Scone, 1128-1136; Stirling, c.1128; Perth, 1147-1153; Aberdeen and Banff, 1136-1137; The Mearns, 1165-1178; Moray, c.1172; Nairn, c.1204; Cromarty, 1264-1266; Skye, Lorn and Kintyre, 1293. William the Lion refers to his 'sheriff of Inverness' and his 'sheriffdom', although this was certainly not a closely defined unit and would have included Caithness, Ross and Argyll to the North and West. Alternatively, Inverness was the head court or *caput* of the Sheriffdom of Moray.[8]

In the absence of public buildings, the courts of the sheriffs were often held at some familiar landmark and such megalithic remains as 'Standing Stones' sometimes provided the meeting place for royal and baronial courts. These well-defined spots with their recognisable antiquity would enchance the dignity of the proceedings with ancient feelings of respect and awe. An outstanding instance of this occurred in 1380. Alexander Stewart, son of Robert II and Lord of Badenoch, known familiarly as the Wolf of Badenoch, cited holders of certain lands in Badenoch to appear at the *Standand Stanys* of the *Rathe of Kyngucy* to produce their title-deeds. The Bishop of Moray duly appeared, not to produce his deeds, but to protest against the Wolf's claim to lordship and jurisdiction. He stood outside the stone circle while the Wolf within ignored him. The Wolf, however, came to terms with the Bishop the next day.[9]

There is very little evidence of the legal system or of judicial office before the twelfth century but the proliferation of records in this period may give a false impression of origin. The key figure who emerges before 1300 is the justiciar who seems to exercise a jurisdiction on the basis of the sheriffdoms and, in the north, on the ancient provinces; he had jurisdiction both in criminal and in civil causes and many of the records show him supervising the old process of perambulation of marches. A threefold division in the Justiciarship gave the holders of the office responsibility for Lothian, Galloway and Scotland north of the Forth respectively. Although innovation appears to be the keynote of the reigns of the dynasty of Malcolm and Margaret, it would have been difficult to introduce concepts of sovereign kingship when a pre-existing system of customary and ancient laws survived. One of the old judicial officers, the *judex*, continued to function into the thirteenth century and the office, albeit in an attenuated form, survived into the seventeenth and eighteenth centuries in the Western Islands. *Judex* was used to translate *brithem* or *brieve*, as *comes* was used to translate *mormaer*. Matadin

Brithem witnessed one of the grants recorded in the Book of Deer. They were operating in the old provinces, and some were 'King's Brieves', and from record evidence we see that they had an important part to play in the administration of justice. The formal perambulation of marches to define territorial rights seems to have been his special function in the twelfth and thriteenth centuries, and his descendant of the seventeenth century in Lewis was also perambulating bounds and recording his judgements in verse, which is perhaps one reason for the extreme dearth of Gaelic legal manuscripts. The *judex* sank from a prominent position in the hierarchy to an insignificant one but remained with his more familiar title of the *dempster* who declared the doom or judgement in the later baron courts.[10] The *maer* or 'steward' who organised the collection of tribute was another official who survived from early Gaelic society. He acted like the *brithem* as a deputy of the *toiseach,* and, like the *brithem,* sank in status over time.

Behind the organisation of the thanages and sheriffdoms and medieval administrative units lay the earlier kin territories; the formal prose of Latin documents has tended to obscure the fact of their continuing significance. The inauguration of one of the kings of Scots gives a vivid illustration of the survival of ancient custom. The stronghold of the ancient Scots kings had been the rocky hill of Dunadd in Argyll and upon one of the rocks on its summit two footprints are carved where the kings were anciently inaugurated. But as late as the mid thirteenth century, almost at the end of our period, a most striking inauguration ceremony took place on the accession of a young heir, when the kingdom was unsettled and when no doubt every step to enhance a sense of continuity was taken.

The inauguration of the boy King, Alexander III, in 1249 was the occasion for the dramatic appearance of a 'highland Scot' who, as Fordun narrates, recited the Gaelic descent of the kings of Scots. When Alexander had been placed on the sacred stone on the Mote Hill of Scone, the *seanchaidh* came forward, fell on his knees before the King and hailed him in his mother tongue, saying these words in Scottish: 'Benach de Re Albanne Alexander, Mac Alexander, Mac Uleyham, Mac Henri, Mac David — and reciting it thus, he read off, even unto the end, the pedigree of the kings of Scots'.[11] This was not a coronation in the later sense with the anointing with the grace of the Holy Spirit through the offices of the church. The inauguration on a sacred stone in the open air was conducted, not by an abbot or bishop, but by the Earl of Fife, the premier nobleman of the land. In our next period, the idea persisted in the ceremonial installation of the Lord of the Isles and of course, down to the present day, the Sovereigns of Great Britain are crowned, sitting on a stone, the Stone of Destiny in a coronation chair. In the climate of that great age of European re-organisation, it is deeply significant to find that in spite of the mixed origins of the folk of Scotland in the thirteenth and fourteenth centuries, the growing sense of nationhood was associated with the Gaelic cultural background of the west and of Ireland, and with the royal line of Kenneth mac Alpin, Fergus Mór mac Erc and the mythical Fergus I, the original King of Scotia, descended from *Gaidheal Glas* and the eponymous Scota, daughter of Pharaoh.

The laws themselves were drawn up within this period mainly in accordance with the current ideology. Within them, fragments of more ancient laws survive. For instance in the *Assise Regis David* there was a law that anyone who should kill another's householhound should either 'wak upon that mannis myddin for a twelf moneth and a day' or be responsible for any *scaith* or damage done to his goods during that period.[12] Now, the story of how the Ulster hero Cu Chulainn acquired his nickname tells how in his childhood he killed a fierce hound that had attacked him; its owner Culann, the smith, complained to the king, and the child condemned himself to act as guard over Culann's possessions for a year and a day while the smith trained another hound, and he thus gained the name of *Cu* (dog) *Chulainn* (of Culann). The fostering of ancient ideas and customs must have been effective enough for Edward I to include among his ordinances for the government of Scotland in 1305 one to abolish the *Laws of the Brets and the Scots*. This treatise on status, applying to the British people of Strathclyde and to the Gaelic people of Alba, set out the *cré*, the blood-price, or compensation due to kindreds in cases of wounding or slaughter.[13] These *Leges inter Brettos et Scotos* were significant enough to be included in late thirteenth and fourteenth century manuscript compilations made after the devastations of the Wars of Independence and also in the late sixteenth century commentary on medieval Scots Law by Sir John Skene, the *Regiam Majestatem*.

Unfortunately although the principles of feudal organisation were clearly spreading, there are very few documents of this period that actually relate to the Highlands. The settlement of Moray with burghs, royal castles and accredited officials is clear. By the thirteenth century, Aberdeenshire had been feudally re-organised, with the country divided into baronies with the orderly placing of castles and parish churches. Argyll seems to have been similarly parcelled out in knight's fiefs following the campaigns of Alexander II and Alexander III. A series of writs of this period relating to Glassary and Cowal shows that the lands were then held of the king *in capite*; he referred to his tenants as 'knights and barons' and the new feudal status was swiftly Gaelicised in names such as *Mac a'Bharain*. In Caithness, which was not wholly within the Scottish realm until about 1200, the bishop, a member of the great de

Moravia family, distributed lands with which the king had endowed him to cadets of his own family on feudal tenures, besides organising the diocese into parishes.[14]

The penetration of feudal ideas and practices is interestingly shown by the changed wording of charters granted by the Lords of Islay, the progenitors of the Lords of the Isles. The text of a charter of the 1190s to Paisley Abbey has survived in the sixteenth century Paisley cartulary. Reginald, the son of Somerled, as Lord of Innse Gall, granted the Abbey eight oxen and two pence for one year from every house in his domain from which smoke issued, and thereafter one penny each year from every house from which smoke issued, and his heirs were to continue the gift or be cursed for failing to do so. His wife gave a tithe of her possessions to the monks and Reginald begged his friends and ordered all his people to help and aid the monks by sea and by land 'with the certain knowledge that by St Columba, whosoever of my heirs molests them shall have my curse'. The grant was repeated by his son Donald in similar terms, swearing by St Columba that evil-doers would suffer the pain of death. The witnesses included *Gille Caluim Mac Ghille Mhicheil* and 'many others of my own men'. Later charters by members of the family were worded in the conventional way of the Anglo-Norman writ and Norman and Normanised names appear among the witnesses, among them Robert de Bruce, Earl of Carrick, grandfather of the patriot king.[15]

The variety of land measures in use shows that there was continuity and fusion with the older organisation. The oxgate or bovate and the ploughgate or carucate were English terms almost invariably used in Scots charters of this period relating to the east side of Scotland from the Lothians to Moray. In the Highlands, where horses were used for ploughing, the term horsegang was generally used, signifying the fourth part of a ploughgate. The ancient davoch reappears in the thirteenth century in association with these measurements and often became the unit of feudal barony. It was subdivided into the half davoch or *leth-dabhach*, the quarter or *ceathramh*, and eighth or *ochdamh*. In the west, the davoch was equated with the Norse ounceland or *tirunga*. With the feudalisation of the country, another term came into use, the merkland. This was not an actual land measurement but was also, like the davoch, a valuation of the productiveness of the land and it was divided in turn into pennylands. Being an estimate of the extent of land required to pay a due of this amount, the area of land would of course vary according to its productivity. This assessment fell out of use in the eighteenth century, especially when estates were surveyed and measured in acres.

It is characteristic of this period, that the process of feudalisation was largely one of compromise and the crown relied heavily on the old forms of render such as military service and tribute. *Feachd* and *sluagh*, known in charters as *Scoticanum servitium* or Scots Service, was included in most grants of lands north of the Forth. That this term should have come into increasing use, replacing the more strictly feudal 'knight service', shows the continuity of social organisation that went back to the rule of the mormaers under the old line of kings. *Cain* or tribute was the form in which the crown collected foodstuffs. This continued as a payment in kind by tenants as part of their rent until the eighteenth century and later when it usually consisted of poultry, known as kain-hens. Associated with *cain* is *conveth* or *coinmheadh* signifying the obligation of maintenance or hospitality or a payment made in lieu of this. The duty of a clansman to give his chief *cuddich* or *cuid-oidhche*, a night's portion, the obligation to maintain a superior for a night, continued in the Highlands into the eighteenth century. Gradually these dues were commuted for money payments but even the efficient kings of this dynasty were not assured of receiving their revenues. When David granted 'the half part of my tithe from Argyll and Kintyre' to Dunfermline Abbey in 1150, he made the provision that it should only be in the years 'when I myself shall have received cain from there'. His grandson, when renewing the grant, renewed the provision.[16]

The Highlands were affected by the practice of giving the burghs monopoly trading rights over wide areas; this grew up in the twelfth century. The areas controlled by the burghs of Inverness, Perth, Aberdeen and Elgin were largely or entirely Highland. In return for bearing a share of the royal aids and taxation, they not only had a monopoly of foreign trade in the principal exports such as salmon, herring, wool, hides and skins, and the most valuable imports including wines and spices, which must have simplified the collection of any dues levied on these articles; they also had the monopoly of keeping taverns, and of making dyed and shorn cloth, and of holding markets within the districts allotted to them. For centuries Inverness was to claim the exercise of these rights all over the northern Highlands. Tain and Dingwall, Dornoch and Wick, and especially the first of these, disputed the rights of Inverness and gradually seem to have worn down the claims of this burgh. In the Highlands, as in the Lowlands, these privileges must have discouraged rural industries.

The growth of the burgh as a centre for trade and settlement is a European phenomenon of the twelfth and thirteenth centuries. The burghs were often strongpoints and *burgh* has the primary meaning of a fortified place. They were often garrison settlements around a castle and the strategic unit 'planted' in a hostile countryside. Such were Edward I's towns in Aquitaine and in Wales and his new town of Berwick in 1297. In the West at a rather later date, the burgh of Tarbert with its strong castle was to be strategically placed to serve in much the same way. Five

Castle Roy by Nethybridge with high curtain walls round a square enclosure

centuries later, James VI, in his policy of 'civilising' and deriving profit from the Western Highlands and Islands, carried out the same policy of establishing burghs. The burghs were the points where southern influences and, from them the English tongue, made their most significant inroads.

Visible signs of the penetration into the Highlands of feudal influences survive in the remains of the motte-and-bailey castles, which are fairly widely distributed in areas where Anglo-Norman influence was strong. A mound of earth with wooden buildings surrounded by a palisade on the top, like those portrayed on the Bayeux Tapestry, was the earliest form of a Norman castle and was introduced into England by William the Conqueror. When William the Lion subdued Ross in 1179 he constructed mottes, among others those of Edderdouer or Redcastle on the Black Isle and Dunskeath at Nigg which still survive. One of the most impressive examples of such a motte is the great Doune of Invernochty, Strathdon, on which the new regime in Mar was centred.

The royal castles of Inverness and Elgin, that did so much to hold down the North, were originally built in the next stage of development which began during our period, that of a strong stone wall surrounding wooden or comparatively slight buildings. Among many other examples are the oldest parts of Duffus Castle in Morayshire. The stark walls of Loch an Eilean Castle, of Lochindorb, and of Castle Roy in Abernethy are memorials of the power of their original builders, the Comyn rulers of Badenoch and Strathspey.[17] Most of the castles of this type in the eastern Highlands have been abandoned or rebuilt, but there was more continuity in the west. Many existing castles there were later given the addition of a strong tower and more strongly defended gateways, and they continued to be occupied, in the case of Dunvegan down to the present day.

Castles were in the Gaelic tradition. The Highlands are dotted over with defensive structures, hill-forts, brochs and similar buildings. Fordun, writing in the fourteenth century, mentions nine castles and two towers in the Western Isles, and down to the seventeenth century castles played an important part in the constant warfare. Whereas a social organisation centred upon the castle was a feudal innovation in Anglo-Saxon England, the Gael had always had something of the kind. In Ireland, the *rath* of the king or noble was the centre of the civil organisation of the people. In the Highlands there are many instances of continuity. Dun Evan on Colonsay, traditionally a stronghold of the MacPhees, is a primitive hill-fort, and the castles of Urquhart, Dunaverty, Dunollie, Dunstaffnage and Cairnburgmore are built on the sites of earlier strongholds. Probably the same is true of many others. Such buildings fitted into the new system in which the castle was not only the important element of a defensive strategy; it was also closely associated with patterns of administration. The timbered earthwork and the motte-and-bailey castle were the outward and visible symbols of a centralised monarchy and feudal lordship. The organisation of the country into sheriffdoms meant that the sheriff as the royal executive officer made his headquarters in the castle, the *caput comitatus*. He had to administer a large area and he had to be a man of rank and status to be effective. Previously the king had had few rights of interference in local affairs which had been the preserve of kindred, *mormaer* and *toiseach*. This may account for the way in which sheriffdoms were overlaying and absorbing thanages. Certainly the *caput comitatus* would appear as the awesome sign of a new order. The feudal lords also used their castles as administrative headquarters. Signs of the settled order of the age can be inferred from buildings such as the fine thirteenth century castle of Kildrummy; the curtain walls and four round towers enclose a chapel and hall in confidently opulent style by comparison with the starkly essential motte-and-bailey stronghold of a hundred years earlier.

Another sign of the changed times was the alteration in the battledress of the Gael. According to the most ancient versions of the Gaelic poems, the Gael did not wear protective body-armour; and Giraldus Cambrensis, writing in 1187, recorded that the Irish still did not do so. The same is specifically stated of the men of Galloway, and is implied for the Highlanders in contemporary accounts of the Battle of the Standard in 1138. These vividly describe the superiority of the men in armour. The English fought in close formation, 'shield was joined to shield, side pressed to side'. On the Scots side, the knights and 'English', that is , the Anglo-Norman or Normanised Scots, were grouped about the king on foot, while 'the rest of the barbarians extended round them on all sides roaring'. The 'barbarians' included the Galwegians (who, it is described, wore no armour), the Islanders and the men of Lorn. The men of Galloway claimed it as their right to form the front line, a contention in which they were supported by Malise, Earl of Strathearn who declared to King David: 'Why is it O King, that you rely on the will of the *Goill* since none of them with their arms to-day will advance before me, unarmed, in the battle'. The King accepted the claim, the second line was formed by the feudal host, the *Gall*, and others such as the men of Moray, and the third line was formed by the men of Lothian, the Islanders and the men of Lorn. The feudal host made up only a small proportion of the whole army, amounting to some two or three hundred armoured men; the *Gall*, though influential therefore, were numerically insignificant beside the *Gaidheal* whose battle-cry 'Albannich, Albannich!' was recorded by the chronicler Henry of Huntingdon as the battle-cry of the army of the Scots.[18]

The men of Galloway attacked and drove back the first rank of spearmen, 'but they were driven off again by the strength of the knights, and the spearmen recovered their courage and strength against the foe. And when the frailty of the Scottish lances was mocked by the denseness of iron and wood, they drew their swords and attempted to contend at close quarters. But the Southern flies swarmed forth from the caves of their quivers and flew like closest rain;' and after a gallant struggle the 'truly unarmed men' were routed. The speeches attributed to the leaders of the army show the contempt that was felt by the men in armour for those without it and, as Ailred of Rievaulx seems to suggest, the bad feeling between the Anglo-Normans and the Gael in the Scottish army caused their defeat. The superiority of the mounted knights is brought out in many contemporary accounts, such as that of the defeat of a Highland insurrection in the metrical chronicle of Andrew de Wyntoun and Sir Thomas Gray of Heaton's narrative of his own experience in the Wars of Independence.[19]

The Gael however learned by experience. The simpler and less costly forms of protective clothing, the habergeon or mail shirt or the aketon, a padded or quilted coat, were prescribed by the earliest known Scots arming act passed by the Scone parliament of 1318, to be worn by all above a certain rank.[20] In Ireland by the fourteenth century, the wearing of these garments or sometimes of the *leine-chroich*, the yellow shirt, a garment of thickly pleated linen dyed with saffron, had become usual. Apart from the *leine-chroich*, which does not appear upon the stone carvings, we know from the effigies on tombstones that the conical iron cap, the mail shoulder protection or *camail*, a mail shirt or sometimes the aketon and mail leggings were the universal fighting dress of men of position.

This was exactly like that of the Normans in the Bayeux Tapestry of the eleventh century. But some of the effigies also had splints fastened to their legs. This was an introductory phase to the wearing of plate armour. A most interesting illustration of how feudal institutions were penetrating the Highlands is the fact that the leading men in the Highlands adopted the practice of heraldry little, if at all, later than the Lowlanders. Evidence of this occurs very early in the next period.

There was no generally expressed resistance to the feudalising process, although the records are naturally somewhat one-sided. There may well have been suspicion and resentment over the changes of the period, dislike of the incomers and surprise at the presumption of the crown. On the death of Malcolm III in 1093, his brother Donald Bane, claiming his right of succession according to the Gaelic custom which would prefer brothers before sons, seized power, reversed the policy of Malcolm and dismissed his Anglo-Saxon favourites. Although this might seem to have been a national movement, he cannot have received the backing of the whole kingdom. He was twice driven out with English help before Edgar was placed on the throne. This was by far the most important rising, although all through the Canmore dynasty different sections of the Highland people rebelled; there were sixteen risings during the period, some of them lasting for years. But with the possible exception of Somerled's support for Malcolm MacHeth between 1153 and 1156, there is no evidence of a pan-Gaelic movement. Rather, on several occasions Gaels such as *Fearchar Mac an t-Sagairt,* afterwards Earl of Ross, were among the Crown's most active supporters against rebels. And when the royal authority was at its lowest ebb during the minority of Alexander III, the *Gaidheal*, far from forming a separate party, were to be found among the supporters of each of the chief rivals, the Durward and the Comyns.

Two of Scotland's great treasures show the continuity of old traditions of craftsmanship, the St Fillan's Crozier and the Guthrie Bell Shrine. The Crozier of St Fillan is enclosed in a silver-gilt case covered with the finest filigree ornamentation of ninth or tenth century workmanship. Known familiarly in Gaelic as the *Coigreach*, literally 'stranger' or 'one that comes from a neighbouring province', the pastoral staff thus personified became the symbol of office of the *Comh-arba* of St Fillan, that is, the heirs and successors of the founding Saint. The *Comh-arba* or

Left: *The Coigreach or pastoral staff of St Fillan, of copper ornamented with bands of niello*

Right: *Case or shrine of St Fillan's Crozier, silver-gilt casing ornamented with filigree work and set with a rock crystal, fourteenth century*

'coarbs' of St Fillan were the family of MacNab, in Gaelic *Mac an aba* or 'son of the abbot', who were hereditary Abbots of Glendochart and also held the Lordship of Glendochart. The Guthrie Bell Shrine may date from the twelfth century and was also worked on in later times although the iron bell is much older. The relics enshrined within these caskets, the bell and the staff or *bachull*, are those typical of the early Gaelic saints. Other survivals are the Kilmichael Glassary Bell Shrine of the twelfth century and a fragment of another crozier shrine. The *bachull* of St Moluag of Lismore, the sixth century missionary, has been preserved in the island for centuries. The Livingstone family who are its custodians hold the title of *Baran a' Bhachuill*. In 1544, Archibald Campbell, son of the Earl of Argyll, granted a croft known as *Peighinn na Bachla* on Lismore to the keeper of the *Bachull Mór*, and this same family still hold their sacred charge. Other croziers of which we have record do not survive; the *Bachull* of St Donnan of Eigg, for example, survived until the Reformation in the church of Auchterless of which he was the patron.[21]

The hereditary keeper of sacred relics as an office of Gaelic society was generally known as the *Deòradh* or Dewar; in one instance he survived long after this period and his office became woven into the feudal organisation of the country. There are later references to the Dewar's

Bell-shrine of bronze from Kilmichael Glassary, twelfth century, for covering a quadrangular iron saint's bell

Croft, as in the case of the hereditary keepers of St Ternan's Bell in the late fifteenth century, and the rights pertaining were not only heritable but could be assigned. Among the records of the provision made for the relics of early saints that of St Fillan is specially full.

An inquest held in April 1428 gives full details of the rights and duties of the Dewar of St Fillan's *bachull* and included renders of meal from each proprietor and tenant in the parish of Glendochart. The inquest also mentions that the Dewars received their office from the 'coarb' or ecclesiastical successor of St Fillan. A charter of James III confirmed the office of Dewar on Malise Doire or *Maol-Iosa an Deòradh* in 1487, recalling that his family had hereditarily possessed the *Coigreach* of St Fillan since the time of King Robert the Bruce and before and declaring that no one should impede the Dewar in passing through the country with the relics. The custody of the 'Brecbennoch' of St Columba entailed obligation to take it with the army on campaigns, and this duty was remunerated by a grant of the lands of Forglen in Banffshire. After Bannockburn, the keeper, who was the Abbot of Arbroath, resigned the lands and the duty of carrying the 'Brecbennoch' to Malcolm of Monymusk.[22] Evidence for the continuing veneration for Celtic Saints also survives in several service books that have fortunately been preserved and notably in that of Bishop Elphinstone's sixteenth century service book known as 'the Aberdeen Breviary.'

Among the treasures preserved in the National Museum of Antiquities are two small carved whalebone caskets fitted with locks and clasps. The larger and best preserved of the two, known as the Eglinton Casket, is about 10 inches long and is constructed of plates of bone bound with straps of bronze. The beautiful and precise interlace design carved on the panels formed by the metal straps is in the ancient tradition although neither of the caskets dates back as early as the ninth century. The decoration of each panel on the Eglinton Casket is self-contained and differs in the different panels.[23] Such caskets were evidently typical Highland possessions and a number are figured on West Highland carvings, for example, at Iona, Craignish, Kilbrandon, Tobermory, Kilninian, and Keills and Kilmory in Knapdale. These are the grave slabs of both men and women of the fifteenth and sixteenth centuries, so the caskets must have been family heirlooms, presumably of some antiquity.

We know that great care and skill went into the making and decorating of book shrines. St Columba's Psalter was preserved in a silver shrine or *cumdach,* and shrines made for copies of the Gospels attributed to early Saints or founders of churches have survived in Ireland. None have survived in Scotland as far as is known, but at least two were still in existence in the later Middle Ages when they were still venerated as objects of beauty and sanctity, and the word *cumdach* survives in modern Gaelic rendered as *còmhdach* for 'covering' or 'clothing'. The *Naomh-chiste na h-easbuig Fothad,* the holy shrine of the Gospels of

Casket of whalebone, its panels carved with interlace and bound with bronze straps, similar to such objects carved on West Highland grave slabs

*Book-shrine surviving in Ireland of the **Soiscel Molaise**, St Molaise's Gospel, ornamented with interlace panels of bronze-relief, eleventh century*

Bishop Fothad, one of the head bishops of the Columban Church, was still kept on the high altar of the Cathedral of St Andrews in the mid fourteenth century. What must have been an older *cumdach* was kept at Banchory-Ternan until the Reformation; it was the shrine of the Gospel of St Matthew, 'a metal case covered with silver and gold' bearing the name of the founding saint, the fifth century St Ternan.[24]

In the history of the church in Scotland during our period the mingling of old and new ideas and institutions is very marked. As we have seen, the organisation of the church in Alba seems to have been simple, although it had its distinctive religious order, the Culdees, and church dignitaries such as the *fir-leginn*. Individual *fir-leginn* are mentioned in twelfth and thirteenth century documents. In the Book of Deer for example, Domangart, *fer-leginn* of Turriff, witnessed a grant to the monastery of Deer in David I's reign. The Culdees had enjoyed royal favour in the late eleventh and early twelfth centuries, although we see David I offering the Culdees the alternatives of becoming Augustinian Canons Regular or of being expelled from their community. No doubt the Culdees were being superseded by regular cathedral chapters and monks and canons of the monastic orders from England and the Continent, but north of the Forth we have evidence of Culdee communities at Abernethy, Brechin, Dunkeld, Inchaffray, Iona, Loch

Leven, Monifieth, Monymusk, Muthill and St Andrews during the twelfth century. A few communities may have survived into the thirteenth century as colleges of secular clergy who would be attending to the spiritual needs of large areas like parishes. Culdees may have survived into the thirteenth century as colleges of secular clergy who would be attending to the spiritual needs of large areas like parishes. Culdees may have formed separate communities within monasteries as they did in one or two of the monastic houses of Ireland in this period. In 1164, the Annals of Ulster recorded the dignitaries of the community of Iona when an invitation was sent at the request of Somerled to *Flaithbeartach Ua Brolchain,* Abbot of Derry and head of the Columban monasteries in the north of Ireland, to be Abbot of Iona. They were Augustin, *mór sagairt*, Dub-shide, *fer-leginn*, Mac Gilleduib, *diseartach*, and Mac Forchellaig, head of the *Celi Dé*. This is an instance of the monastic community together with a Culdee community which may have been typical of the ecclesiastical organisation of the period.

It may be misleading to stress the differences between the Celtic Church and the Continental Church rather than the similarities. Without discussing the subject of liturgical differences, it is significant that the surviving liturgical books are in Latin, although of varying quality. An exception to this is a single rubric in the order of service included in the Book of Deer. 'Here give the Sacrifice to him' is written in Gaelic, signifying the Real Presence in the Eucharist rather than a service of memorial and showing that, fundamentally, the Columban Church was not a separate entity but a part of the universal church.[25]

According to Turgot, Queen Margaret concerned herself with liturgical matters and took part in many Church councils; at the principal council five topics were discussed: the duration of Lent; the refusal of the people to take communion at Easter on the grounds that they were unworthy; the celebration of Mass in some districts according to what was considered a 'barbarous rite', contrary to the practice of the Church; working on Sunday and the neglect of the Lord's Day; and secular marriage within forbidden degrees of kinship. These do not denote any fundamental difference of dogma with the Roman Church. It is difficult to discover how effective Margaret's attempts at reform were and she does not seem to have tried to change other more serious matters such as the secularisation of Church property and lay interference. Although she had a special regard and devotion for the newly introduced Order of St Benedict, she and her husband apparently gave their patronage to the Culdees. A twelfth century account of her restoration of the monastic buildings on Iona and the endowment of monks there is not altogether trustworthy, although it would not seem improbable for Malcolm and his wife to make some gift to this community. Turgot also describes Margaret's efforts to improve ecclesiastical ornaments and vestments.

The spread of new ideas is writ large on the church architecture of Alba in this period. The Gaels were not noteworthy as architects and the Highlanders of this period willingly accepted the great new architectural styles that were springing up in Europe. Traces of Norman and Early English influences are to be seen in surviving Highland churches. At Iona, the inserted doorway in St Oran's chapel and the oldest part of the Abbey church, part of the southern transept, founded by Reginald, son of Somerled, are Norman. So is the early part of the church of Fearn, Ross-shire. Nothing seems to be known about the date or history of the beautiful church of Killean in Kintyre with its strong Norman influence. The fine Early Pointed Gothic work of the ruined chapel at Dunstaffnage, with the lesser fragments that remain of the priory at Ardchattan, cannot have been built later than the end of the thirteenth century, for their builders, the House of Lorn, fell upon evil times shortly afterwards. The Nunnery at Iona was founded in late Norman or traditional style, and is thoroughly European and Romanesque in character.[26] This unity with the contemporary architectural styles of western Europe is in marked contrast to the styles of later buildings such as the irregular mixture of features in the later parts of Iona Cathedral and in the Church of Keills in Morvern.

In the course of the twelfth and thirteenth centuries, the ecclesiastical organisation of diocese and parish was taking the familiar shape of later times. Alexander I and David I have been repeatedly credited with the foundation of most of the bishops' sees but this is a simplification which is misleading. Although, from the eighth century onwards, there are occasional references to bishops, they evidently did not preside over definite sees.

The appointment of bishops and the development of dioceses was a slow and gradual process and it was not until the thirteenth century that a full diocesan system emerged with cathedral churches and chapters of canons and the diocesan administration of archdeacons and rural deans. The papal bull *Cum universi* of c.1192 to the Scottish king concerning the Church refers to nine Scottish bishoprics including Moray, Ross and Caithness but excluding Argyll; the see of the Isles or Sodor did not become a Scottish bishopric until later. The Pope had placed the dioceses of Orkney and Sodor, which included the islands of Arran, Bute and Man, under the metropolitan authority of the Norwegian archbishop of Nidaros or Trondheim in 1158. It was not until after 1378 and the beginnings of the Great Schism that Man and the Isles were separated, and not until the end of the fifteenth century that the abbacy of Iona and the bishopric were united and held by the same ecclesiastic. The diocese of Argyll was probably already in existence in the 1180s and had formerly been a part of the diocese of Dunkeld. From the beginning of its independent existence, its cathedral church was on Lismore; the choir still remains of the thirteenth century building. In 1240, Ewen of Lorn gave the Bishop of Argyll and his successors fourteen pennylands on the island. Until the end of the fourteenth century, the bishoprics of Argyll and the Isles, and also the bishopric of Ross seem rather shadowy and they certainly suffered from periods of interregnum. They were also poor. In the thirteenth century, when St Andrews diocese had an annual revenue of £8,000 and Moray of £14,000, Ross had only £350 and Argyll £280.[27]

The twelfth century also saw extensive building of parish churches which were served by priests and maintained by teinds or tithes. The abundance of evidence in this period obscures the fact that local churches, in some way fulfilling the same function as the later parish churches, had existed for some centuries. The monasteries had probably maintained the services of churches, and communities of Culdees had done the same. Place names with the element *eccles* suggests that an early church organisation had existed.[28] Parish churches often originated in the building and the endowment of local churches by landowners, but by the twelfth century the boundaries of parishes became defined and teinds for the maintenance of the churches were allocated. In Aberdeenshire, during the Anglo-Norman advance of the twelfth and thirteenth centuries, churches and castles were often built close together as part of an orderly social plan. But in the Highlands on the whole, parishes were formed where churches existed, and there was no organised and planned division of the country into parishes. Yet it is an impressive fact, documented in the monumental *Origines Parochiales Scotiae* for Ross and Caithness, that in that early and not untroubled age so many parishes were established with their churches and often additional chapels. For Argyll and the Isles the records are not so full but the vestiges of ancient buildings and dedications show that a network of churches existed that compares very favourably with provisions made after the Reformation. In fact, in many parts of the Western Highlands the parishes were so numerous that it was not possible to provide their incumbents with an adequate living.[29] A quatrain of a Gaelic poem in a later manuscript describes with feeling what might have been the material situation of many priests' lives:

> *Eglus fuar*
> *Agus cleirech tana, truagh;*
> ...
> A cold Church,
> A thin wretched cleric;

The body in subjection shedding tears:

Great their reward in the eyes of the King of Heaven.[30]

The eleventh and twelfth centuries were marked by a great spiritual revival throughout western Europe, stimulated by the newly formed religious orders. The Gaels were affected by this movement. Reginald Lord of Islay and his descendants, Duncan of Lorn, the Earl of Ross, the Bissets, the Lamonts and a number of the rising Campbell family all established houses of the religious orders of Benedictines, Cluniacs, Cistercians, Premonstratensians, Augustinians and Valliscaulians. It is perhaps significant that all the British houses of this latter Order, by its rule the most contemplative of all, should have been placed in or near the Highlands, at Ardchattan, Beauly and Pluscarden. The process of introducing religious orders continued in the thirteenth century. The newly-formed orders of friars began to arrive in Scotland about 1230 and by about 1250 the Black Friars or Dominicans had founded houses in Aberdeen, Elgin, Inverness, Stirling and Perth, all burghs bordering on the Highlands. These early foundations were all endowed by Alexander II.[31]

The re-organisation of the church had both material and spiritual disadvantages for the Highlands. A majority of the parishes were granted to abbeys, cathedrals or other religious houses and the revenues and teinds were thus diverted to their own use. Many churches were appropriated in this way immediately on being built and endowed. The crown took the lead in this process, especially David I, Malcolm IV and William, and lords and nobles followed suit. Holyrood Abbey is an outstanding example of how a religious house attracted such endowments in the few decades after its foundation. Highland parishes were presented to religious houses elsewhere. The Abbey of Inchaffray had churches in Argyll, for example, and a parish church in Perthshire was granted to an English foundation.[32] High Scots ecclesiastics periodically attended church councils abroad. Another serious evil was the costly appeals to Rome that drained away the resources of the church and were especially frequent in the poverty-stricken Highlands where the episcopal authority was weakest. The pitiful complaint of one of the suppliants survives, who after the dangers and labour of his journey to Rome was kept waiting there till all his support money was exhausted.[33]

One of the most important changes in the life of the Highlands about that time was the adoption of the Norse style of building wooden clinker-built ships, the beautiful and formidable galleys. The peoples of Scandinavia, with their abundance of iron, had wrought the axes and nails with which they learned to build their remarkable ships. Surviving examples like the Gokstad Ship have been found in Norse burials and are carefully preserved. The Gokstad Ship is a clinker-built boat, 76½ ft long with a 7½ ft beam, on a keel made from a single plank of oak, mounting a single mast amidships and using 16 pairs of oars. From its high, sharply raked stem its lovely lines are the very embodiment of the idea of speed.

The Gael in ancient times seem to have preferred skin-covered ships. The clinker-built *birlinn* of the medieval Highlander, as we see it portrayed on the tombstones and crosses, with its single masts and square sails, was the result of Norse influence. These carvings themselves lack the beautiful, raking lines of the Norse galleys and have more upright stems and sterns. One may perhaps assume that this was surely a device to fit them into the closely compressed designs, for the marked rake of the prow and stern persisted in the local type of fishing boat in Shetland and in the Western Isles *sgoth*. There was however one modification; by the fourteenth century the Highland galley was fitted with a rudder instead of a steering oar. Prized and loved they continued to be. They were constantly carved on the West Highland tombstones and cross shafts, and in Gaelic tales many a verse or *rann* tells of the 'speckled, towering sails', the 'tough, arrowy mast', and the shapely buoyant hulls. Highland poetry, songs and stories continued to glorify them. Alexander MacDonald, *Alasdair MacMhaighstir Alasdair*, composed a richly descriptive poem of 566 lines in the eighteenth century, taking as its theme a voyage from South Uist to Ireland. His 'Clan Ranald's Galley', *Birlinn Chlann Raghnaill*, is a masterpiece of Gaelic poetry and arguably the finest sea-poem of a sea-going people. Bishop John Carswell's liturgy, *The Book of Common Order*, follows the Geneva Book of 1556 closely, but introduces a beautiful prayer for the blessing of a ship putting out to sea, the *beannachadh luinge*, and Martin Martin also refers to such a custom; it was led by the steersman and the crew made the responses. Alexander MacDonald begins his 'Clan Ranald's Galley' with a ship blessing in metrical form.[34]

These galleys played an important part in the history of our period, in Somerled's career and in King Hakon's expedition for example. In the first War of Independence they proved themselves to be so formidable that King Robert the Bruce in his dying advice warned against their potential danger. Down to the end of the seventeenth century we hear of them continually. The more powerful chiefs could command a large number of galleys. John, first Lord of the Isles (1326-80) had a fleet of 60 ships, and in Donald Dubh's rising of 1545 he was followed by 17 chiefs with 180 galleys and 4,000 men. The provision of a galley or some form of sea-service was a frequent due on grants of land. For instance, in about 1343 MacLeod of Dunvegan, then styled as MacLeod of Harris, was granted eight davochs of land in Glenelg on condition that he had at all times a galley of 36 oars ready for the king's service. According to English documents of the sixteenth century, in calm weather their galleys could outrow the English boats. For war, for expeditions and raiding and, in peace, for commerce and travelling, the galleys of the Highlanders played a prominent part in the life of the people of the Western Highlands and Islands. When the Highlands were roadless, the waters of the western seas must have been in constant use. MacLeod was always crossing the Minch between his lands in Skye and Harris. Cattle were regularly ferried from the Islands to the mainland. Tales of raids by sea abound, such as the circumstantial account of the tricks played by Clan Ranald on the Macleans on a raiding expedition possibly of the fifteenth century. These accounts show that the sea was not a barrier to communications but a highway. The structure of the *iorram* or rowing song which glorified travel and the sea is probably very ancient.[35] As we shall try to show, the use of galleys had considerable influence on the social organisation of the people who were so dependent upon them.

Our period was one of adaptation, survival and change. In the Highlands it saw the beginning of a new form of social organisation that was to be of fundamental importance during the centuries that were to follow. In Erin, as in Alba, the word *clann*, meaning 'children' had acquired the wider meaning of 'kindred'. But by the twelfth century, the nuclei were forming in the Highlands of a wider type of organisation that was to develop gradually into what we now recognise as the Highland clans.

The subject of the clans and their origins abounds with acute controversy, and the people of the clans and their leaders vary so much in character that generalisation is impossible. Most of them have pedigrees which trace their origin to a remote past, often to origins difficult to verify; one of the MacLeod pedigrees goes back to a Scandinavian god and one of the Campbells' to a hero of the mythical Fianna. Many of them have more than one pedigree or revised versions of it, and in a later period, in the sixteenth century, the reason for this pedigree-making becomes evident. However, in nearly all these theories of origin, there comes a point about this time or during the succeeding two centuries, when the ancestor, a man of some position who can often be identified, was able to found a family which had the power to survive. As the family grew over time, the degree of kinship to succeeding chiefs lessened and ties of adherence or dependence tended to take its place. While there was still a need for close association for the purpose of mutual help and defence, this broadening of the base of clanship and the concept of *clann* was a natural development; it was not necessarily reflected in the surnames peopling a particular clan territory because patronymics were the customary form of naming in earlier times. The need for mutual defence had always existed, but its need and customs were to survive longest in the Highlands and Islands and within that area bounded by the 'Highland Line'. The imposition of systems of law and order as later understood depended upon accessibility, and it was not until improvements in communications and transport in a future age that this social and military system in the Highlands was dismantled. It may be impossible to find the fundamental reason why the clan-making impulse first appeared in this particular period. The establishment of the feudal system helped in the founding of some clans and hindered the development of others. The principle of recognised military service in return for land or protection, an important part of feudal organisation, was accepted as an important element in clan organisation and lasted as an essential duty in the Highlands long after it had died out elsewhere.

The rise of Somerled in the twelfth century — the progenitor of the MacDougalls and the MacDonalds — is an outstanding example of one way in which a clan was formed, and in a less formidable way, it happened over and over again as clans came into being. Somerled's name is Norse and means 'summer voyager' or 'summer warrior', so evidently he belonged to the *Gall-Ghaidheal*, the mixed population of the Hebrides. He had two pedigrees. In one, which has been proved to be substantially correct, he is traced back for nine generations to a Godfrey, son of Fergus, a historical character who was the same Godfrey son of Fergus, chief of a tribe in Northern Ireland who came to Scotland to reinforce Kenneth mac Alpin in his settlement in Scotland. This Godfrey was the leader of a powerful kindred, the *Uí Macc Uais*. Yet further back, the MacDonald tradition of Somerled's descent brings him through fourteen generations from Colla Uais, one of the traditional founders of the Kingdoms of Ireland. Colla himself was descended from the semi-mythical 'Conn of the Hundred Battles', and MacMhuirich the family poet celebrated this Clan Donald descent in his famous incitement to battle before Harlaw beginning:

O children of Conn, remember
Hardihood in time of battle:
Be watchful, daring,
Be dextrous, winning renown,
Be vigorous, pre-eminent,
Be strong, nursing your wrath,
Be stout, brave,
Be valiant, triumphant,
Be resolute and fierce,
Be forceful and stand your ground ....[36]

History is unclear as to exactly how many children Somerled had. Tradition suggests that, not surprisingly, he fathered children out of wedlock or that he had had one or more children by an earlier marriage. These were presumably provided for from some of his mainland possessions such as Morvern. The arrangements made for three of his sons by his second wife, a daughter of the King of Man, are of great importance in Highland history. Dougal, possibly his eldest son by this politically significant marriage, received Lorn, which then covered a large part of western Argyll, and the islands of Mull, Jura, Tiree and Coll. He is the progenitor of Clan Dougal. His second son, Reginald, received Islay and Kintyre. Angus, the third son, had part of Arran and possibly Bute. After warfare between Reginald and Angus and the latter's death about 1210, Reginald seems to have taken most of his possessions. Reginald himself had two sons, the eldest of whom received Islay and Kintyre and is the eponym of Clan Donald; Ruairidh, the next son, whose descendants were known as the MacRuairidhs or in later days as Clan Ranald, came off less well. His father Reginald's claims to the possessions of Angus had already been questioned by a yet more powerful feudal family, the Anglo-Norman Stewarts who had claimed Angus' possessions through marriage with his daughter and by arrangements that are unrecorded, he was able to obtain from the King a grant of Arran and Bute while Ruairidh received the rather inadequate compensation of a grant of Garmoran (the district between Ardnamurchan and Glenelg) and North and South Uist. This transaction is one instance of a persistent royal policy to keep the passage of the Clyde closed to Islesmen and their galleys and in the possession of the Stewart family.[37]

The Western Isles were not definitely ceded to Scotland by Norway until 1266 and both Dougal and Donald and their successors were in the difficult position of owing conflicting allegiances to the Kings of Scotland and of Norway. This gave them some degree of independence. The title of *Rí* or King was sometimes given to them. The remembrance of this was certainly present with Donald's later descendants, the Lords of the Isles. But although they had a semblance of semi-independence they did not fit into the aristocratic framework of feudal Scotland. They were constantly referred to by the rather indefinite title of 'Lord'. In the troublesome times of the first Wars of Independence, Alexander, Dougal's direct descendant, was known as Sir Alexander of Argyll and his son as John, Lord of Lorn. Donald's descendant was referred to as the Lord of Islay. Unlike such nobles on the mainland as members of the Stewart family and rather later the head of the Campbells, and of the family of Gordon which was given the feudal title of earl (and much land with it) and who owed their further advancement to using and abusing their feudal powers, the descendants of Donald, the Lords of the Isles, owed far less to royal patronage and were never the tools of the feudal system.

The end of our period came four generations after Somerled and only one after Leod. Their direct descendants could have only formed a family group within the large areas that they had inherited. They had not had time to evolve into the social entity that the Highland clans assumed. For then, as the royal authority spread and they came to hold their lands by charter from the King, the custom of primogeniture as laid down in their charters and according to the law of the land became obligatory. Provisions for younger sons were made as subordinates to the eldest son and heir. This became the almost universal custom among the clans, broken only in exceptional circumstances of extreme need.

In these families (as in many others) the strong clan-making tendency that became very marked in our next period began with the help of a grant of heritable possession of land and encouraged the adherence of the original inhabitants that this included. This was not so in the case of the Mackintoshes. It is incidental that Shaw, the founder, was a younger son of the Earl of Fife. He had been in the army sent to subdue Moray and Nairn and had been appointed to the office of Captain of Inverness Castle with some forest land in the hill country and a not inconsiderable holding of good land in the Laigh of Moray upon a very indefinite title as a reward for his services. His son became known as *Mac an Toisich*, son of the Chief, and the family developed into a clan. Not only so; Bean or *Beathann* and his family and Gillivray with his offered their allegiance to Mackintosh, and a pact for mutual protection was entered into and loyally carried out. The descendants of both Bean and Gillivray formed clans of their own but continued to be closely associated with the Mackintoshes. Shaw's family was associated in yet more clan-making. His great-great-grandson Ferquhard married the heiress of the chief man of the Clan Chattan, who occupied land in Lochaber, and is described by the scholarly historian of Clan Mackintosh as 'consisting of various families and septs bearing diverse names who had banded themselves together for the purpose of defence'. Ferquhard's son succeeded as Chief of Clan Chattan. This arrangement was displeasing to some members of Clan Chattan, and the descendants of the male heir, who was a churchman at Kingussie, formed a new clan, the Macphersons.[38]

The lands in Lochaber which had probably been held in an informal tenure were lost to Mackintosh and to Clan Chattan. It is important to remember that these clans, the Mackintoshes, the MacBeans, the MacGillivrays and the Macphersons, did not hold the main part of their land from the king but from subject superiors. The interactions of the feudal and clan systems were to play a very important role in Highland history during our next three periods.

Period III

The Lordship of the Isles, c.1300-c.1500

The period covered by reign of Malcolm III's successors with their Anglo-Norman feudalising policies proved to have been infinitely more beneficial for Scotland than the preceding one under the rule of the Scots kings. But with the death of Alexander III, the strong central control which seemed to be essential for the good functioning of the feudal system of government came to an end. In strict accordance with the laws of succession by primogeniture the Crown passed to a Princess in a foreign land. The possibility of the establishment of some interim form of government was lost by the dispute over the succession to the Crown. In accordance with feudal practice, the Superior, Edward I, Scotland's deadly enemy, undertook to adjudicate; the parallel of the wolf coming into the fold to select the next bell-wether suggests itself. All this is, of course, part of the general history of Scotland, but for Highlanders it is an illustration of the disastrous failure of a system of feudalised government where strong central control is lacking. Owing to various factors, feudal administration was to persist longer in the Highlands than the Lowlands, and during the next four hundred years the Highlands were to suffer from the frequent and prolonged periods when the governing authority in Scotland failed to fulfil its major function and to promote good rule and government.

An itemised account of the events in the first and second Wars of Independence does not fall within the scope of this book. It was hoped that the first War had definitely won independence for Scotland, just as in our own times the First World War was regarded as 'the War to end all Wars'. Unfortunately the Scots' triumph was soon followed by a long period of humiliating defeats, misrule and internal divisions that were not overcome until King James I returned from imprisonment in England in 1424.

Viewed from our particular aim of distinguishing periods of interest in Highland affairs, two points about the first War of Independence emerge. One is the attitude of the ancestors of the two early clans that we have noted — the MacDonalds and MacDougalls. Alexander, the head of the MacDougall family, was decrepit and his son, John, Lord of Lorn, took part with some distinction on the patriotic side until Bruce sacrilegiously murdered the Red Comyn, who was the MacDougall's friend, cousin and clan ally. John of Lorn then became Bruce's inveterate and very formidable enemy. His cousin, Alan, however had supported Wallace and continued to fight on the Scots side. In the case of the ancestors of the MacDonalds, the Lord of Islay was connected by marriage with the family of the Balliols. He was opposed to the claims of Bruce but was not so active as was John of Lorn. His younger brother, Angus Og, played an essential part in the support of Bruce in his darkest hour. Both families therefore had members upon each side, which was to be a characteristic pattern of Highland conduct, thereby safe-guarding the estate from possible forfeiture.[1]

It is noticeable that in the first War of Independence, the Highland clans were not sufficiently developed to be separately named. Angus Og, John of Lorn, the Campbells and other Highlanders are referred to as individuals rather than as heads of kin. But in his book *The Scottish War of Independence*, E M Barron stressed the importance of the part played by the men of the north in that struggle; and writers nearer the time tell of the part played by the Highlanders, especially at the battle of the Pass of Brander, at Bannockburn and in the assault at Byland. But many of their leaders were not of native Highland stock. William Wiseman, the Sheriff of Elgin, Sir Alexander Fraser, whose family had not yet become acclimatised in the north, and Sir Andrew Gray were the leaders of the force that climbed Ben Cruachan at the battle of the Pass of Brander in 1308, and at Bannockburn the men of Moray were led by Randolph, whom the King had created Earl of Moray in 1312, thus reviving the old earldom which had been in the possession of the Crown since 1130 following the death of the last of the *de Moravia* family. There can be no doubt that many of the clans fought, as their traditions assert, at Bannockburn; but almost without exception their organisations were not sufficiently powerful for the chroniclers to mention them. John Barbour, Archdeacon of Aberdeen, celebrated King Robert in his long patriotic poem called *The Brus*, completed about 1375. He described the King's personal *battalle* or division at Bannockburn, including the forces from the Highlands and Islands:

> And of Argile and of Kentyre,
> And of the Ilis, quharoff wes syre
> Angus of Ile, and But, all tha.[2]

Sir Neil Campbell, Angus Og and Donald of Islay were the only patriot Highlander leaders sufficiently important to be mentioned in the chronicles of the time, and similarly on the opposite side, we only hear of Alexander of Islay and John MacDougall of Lorn. In Barron's exhaustive lists of the men who supported Bruce or attended his first Parliament at St Andrews in 1309 there are few names from the West Highlands. In the list of those attending the Parliament and signing

Bruce's letter to the King of France, 'the barons of the whole of Argyll and Innse Gall' are lumped together. This omission, compared to the prominence accorded to the chiefs and their clans both in the civil wars of the seventeenth century and in the Risings of the '15 and '45, is very significant.

At the end of the first War of Independence, Bruce made grants and confiscations that materially changed the pattern of land-holding in the Highlands. During the interlude between the Wars, the creation of the Lordship of the Isles became possible. The evolution of the Lordship, its effect upon Highland culture, and its fall is the central theme of this period and one of the most important events in the whole of our book.

As a preliminary, however, it is desirable to set the scene and to consider the surroundings and the circumstances in which the Lordship emerged and which eventually made its survival impossible. Although the kings of Scots during our period were indifferent in ability, and David II, Robert II and Robert III are the most notable in this context, the Highlands at this time were not subjected to the disastrous practice indulged in by most ineffective rulers; it was not unknown for kings of Scots to delegate power to great nobles by employing them to rule the Highlands and thus to do their work for them. To some extent, this work was done for the Crown in this period by the Earl of Mar, who led the royal forces against those of the Lord of the Isles at the Battle of Harlaw and the second Battle of Inverlochy. The Earls of Mar, however, never established themselves as a dynasty; this was largely because the Earldom was regranted five times during our period, in three instances to relatives of the reigning sovereign. Although titles were regranted during the period, as for instance when Robert I created the Earldom of Moray for his nephew Randolph, and individuals rose to great power as in the case of Robert, Duke of Albany, who was also Earl of Fife and Menteith, the descendants of these men did not survive in a family succession. The great House of Douglas, which was so prominent in Scottish history in the fourteenth and fifteenth centuries and survived periods of disgrace and disfavour to maintain the power of its dynasty, barely concerned itself with Highland affairs or territories.

Events in this period particularly favoured the process of the development of clans. An obvious example is the way in which the fall of the great Comyn family, that had dominated the Laigh of Moray, Badenoch and Lochaber, allowed a group of clans to develop.[3] These clans, such as the Mackintoshes and Clan Chattan mentioned earlier, had already grown up in those areas of the Highlands and came to fill the vacuum created by the disappearance of the Comyn's lordship. Modern 'clan' maps are produced which show the whole of the Highlands parcelled out among the clans; though not within such clearly defined territorial boundaries, by the end of the sixteenth century the Highlands were more or less covered by the spheres of interest of the respective clans. In the fourteenth century it was not so. Bower's description of the northern Highlands in 1428 when James I came to Inverness to hold a 'parliament', after mentioning the Lord of the Isles' claim to the Earldom of Ross, goes on to state that the King had also summoned forty or fifty of the leading men 'who, low born as they were, held in utter subjection some seventy or eighty thousand others, and in their own particular tracts, they were regarded as princes and had all at their own arbitrary will, evincing not the slightest regard for the dictates of reason'.[4] Five of these men were named and were said each to command 2,000 men. Two of them, Angus Duff and Kenneth Mor, have been tentatively identified as the respective chiefs of the Mackays and the MacKenzies, and the general picture of the state of the Highlands that is conjured up is of unorganised units combining in time of need under the leadership of some outstanding individual.

The sparse population evidently consisted largely of unattached family groups. The guardianship of holy relics enabled some of their keepers to survive — the Livingstones for example, the Barons of the *Bachull* or Staff of St Moluag, have already been mentioned.

The widely dispersed name of Gillies, in Gaelic *Gill'Iosa*, the 'Servant of Jesus', must clearly have a religious origin. As is often the case, there are various versions as to the origin of Clan Chattan, but the fact that their leader was named *Gille Chatain Mhóir* supports the generally accepted assumption that they originated from a follower of St Cattan. One of the most striking instances of the tenacious survival of a clan is that of the MacDougalls. Dougal, son of Somerled, Lord of Argyll and of most of the Hebrides, and Ewan his son belong to a previous period. In the Wars of Independence, as already noted, John Lord of Lorn, son and heir to Sir Alexander of Argyll, took a leading part in opposing Bruce. His father had wished to make peace with Bruce, but it is interesting that he did not have universal support. Alexander complained to Edward I that 'barons of Argyll give me no aid', and eventually he surrendered to Bruce. John Lord of Lorn continued his resistance but was defeated and taken prisoner. Lorn was restored to his son but he unfortunately had only two daughters. By special arrangement, Lorn passed to the husband of one of them, a Stewart. There were sons as well as a daughter by this marriage but the daughter was married to her fourth cousin, Alan MacDougall, the male heir, being the descendant of Alan the brother of John, Lord of Lorn. His family had been living at Dunollie and it is possible that he had a good following of kinsfolk and family retainers, and also that it was sound policy by Stewart to give his daughter a considerable share of the family estate and the Island of Kerrera.

As already noted, Bower's account of James I's parliament at Inverness in 1428 named two leaders who were probably chiefs of surviving clans; Kenneth Mor, who is thought to have been chief of the MacKenzies, a clan whose period of predominance was to come nearly two centuries later, and Angus Dubh, the chief of the Mackays. As is so often the case, there are conflicting theories about the Mackays' origins. One theory derives them from the Picts; according to this, the Mackays are descended from Clan Morgan mentioned in the Book of Deer in the early twelfth century.[5] Other versions of their origin place them in the West Highlands. Reaching firmer ground, a probable ancestor was *Fearchar Lighiche*, the king's physician or 'Leech', who had a grant of land in Farr on the northern coast of Sutherland in 1379. (It is worth remembering that part of the country there had previously been held by a member of the *de Moravia* family). By the middle of the fourteenth century, the clan was firmly settled in their lands. In 1415, Donald of the Isles gave lands in Strathnaver in Sutherland to *Aonghas Aoidh*, who had married his sister. The surname Mackay is derived from this name *Aodh* which became the patronymic, and also gave its name to the country of the Mackays, in Gaelic *Duthaich Mhic Aoidh*. He is almost certainly the leader of four thousand men in Bower's account of James I's parliament at Inverness, and a Mackay is said to have been the leader of a joint force of Mackays, Rosses, Munros and Sutherlands that had opposed the Lord of the Isles rather earlier, in 1411. He was therefore obviously a popular and a powerful leader.

What is significant in considering our period is the large force of men outside a regular clan that would take the field. The Mackays continued to expand, yet by 1745 their entire strength was estimated at only 800 men.

So strong was the wish to organise into family groups — the clan-making tendency of the period — that Anglo-Norman or Lowland families who were planted in the Highlands, such as the Chisholms, the Frasers, the Grants and certain branches of the Stewarts, took on the organisation of a Highland clan. The ancestors of Fraser of Lovat only obtained lands in the Highlands in 1247 by marriage with an heiress of the Bissets, an Anglo-Norman family already in possession there, and the family seems to have taken some time to settle down in the Highlands. The Wardlaw Manuscript supplies a wonderful record of the evolution of this clan. By 1576, when the tutor or guardian of the heir trysted 'the whole numerous name of Fraser' at Tomnahurich to convey home the body of the deceased chief from Mar to Beauly, between eight and nine hundred men assembled.[6]

The families of Grants and Chisholms are of Norman-French origin; in both cases there are conflicting theories of an earlier Norse origin. In both cases, names of individuals are noted in the North some time before they are recorded as established land-holders there. The ancestor of the Chisholms obtained lands in the Aird through marriage, in which tradition and historical fact differ over the bride's identity. John le Grant acquired his first lands in Strathspey in 1434. His successors enlarged their possessions, acquiring much of their land in the fifteenth and sixteenth centuries, and in 1538, in a written document, the Grants were first alluded to as a *clan*.[7] Incidents in the general history of Scotland illustrate the growth of clan organisation. One of the sons of the Wolf of Badenoch led a raid into Angus in 1392 of 'three hundred and more' men and routed the forces that the sheriff was able to bring against him. This raid, called the 'dulefule dawerke' of Gasklune in Stormont, is described at length in contemporary chronicles, notably Wyntoun, and may have arisen over the succession to land in Strathnairn.

Its small size compared with later musters of Highland forces is significant. The leaders of the aggressors are recorded in a writ issued by Robert III directing them to be put to the horn for their part in the raid and particularly for the death of the sheriff of Angus and others. They can be seen to fall into six groups, drawn from six widely scattered districts where the Wolf held land. In these groups were the Duncansons and Robert de Athale, presumably the leaders of Clann Donnchaidh, and 'Slurach and his brothers, with the whole Clanqwhevil'. The identity of this clan has been the subject of endless discussion, but it may be Clan Chattan, under the leadership of Shaw of Rothiemurchus, 'Bucktoothed' Shaw, who led the clan in the battle on the North Inch of Perth. The link which united the force was therefore feudal service on a territorial basis, but there are indications of the existence of clans as a developing cohesive force socially as well as militarily. The Combat of the North Inch of Perth in the presence of King Robert III in September 1396 is an extraordinary event which caught the attention of fifteenth century chroniclers, whose accounts differ sufficiently in detail to obscure key facts such as the exact identity of the participants, although that the contest actually took place is vouched for by an entry in the Exchequer Rolls. The popularity of the story has been increased since Scott introduced it into *The Fair Maid of Perth*. According to the accepted account, two of the parties to a Highland feud each chose thirty men who fought each other to the death within a fenced enclosure, and this was viewed as a spectacle by the King, the Queen and their Court until only a handful remained. That such a spectacle could take place illustrates the callous attitude of the Lowland authorities.

It is of the greatest importance to realise that all up the eastern side of the Highlands, clans were building up who were unaffected by the culture of the Lordship of the Isles. For instance, one never finds the particular type of carving that is associated with its culture in the east or beyond a certain point northwards. With the exception of the Mackintoshes who claimed some land in Lochaber from the Lord of the Isles (which they were never able to occupy) and therefore occasionally had to help him, these clans offered him strong opposition. The Lordship never approached being a purely Gaelic organisation or a focus for Gaelic consolidation. The influence of the Lordship was not only confined within a limited area by indifference or even hostility from the number of clans growing up round it, but also two clans were gradually rising to power that were to be the main instruments of its destruction: first the Campbells and then, rather later, the MacKenzies.

The Campbells had reached a position of some standing before the Wars of Independence; Colin Campbell was baillie of the Crown lands of Lochawe and Ardskeodnish in 1296. This Colin was known as *Cailean Mór* and he probably gave the style *Mac Cailein Mór* to his descendants. His son Neil was the close companion of Bruce and married his sister Mary. His support for Bruce, especially in the vital years 1306 and 1307, ensured the later rewards to his family, especially of lands forfeited by the MacDougalls of Lorn. The family seem to have been well established in Lochawe when David II granted a charter to Gillespic Campbell of the lands there in 1369. Colin, Lord Campbell, created Earl of Argyll in 1457 or 1458, was an extensive landowner and close associate of the Crown and was the obvious agent to be employed in the destruction of the Lordship, from which he profitted greatly. The Campbells came to overshadow the development of other families in Argyll: the MacEwens, the Lamonts, the MacGillivrays, the MacGregors and the MacNaughtons. In the fifteenth century, offshoot branches had been planted at Glendaruel, Otter, Ormidale and Craignish.

The MacKenzies were another clan whose advancement deeply affected the history of the Highlands, but in their case this became significant only towards the end of this period. They were almost certainly of the same stock as the old Earls of Ross and held land in Kintail. When the Lords of the Isles succeeded to the Earldom of Ross, the MacKenzies had become their vassals but they supported the royal authority in two rebellions by the Lords of the Isles and their loyalty was well rewarded by the Crown. Their lands and influences were greatly extended by the part that they played in further insurrections by members of the Lords of the Isles' family and by the forfeiture first of the Earldom of Ross and then of the Lordship itself.[8]

A third clan was also later to come to prominence. Two years earlier than the creation of the Earldom of Argyll, in 1455, the King had created the Earldom of Huntly. The Gordon family owned valuable lands in the North East and had succeeded Randolph Earl of Moray as lords of Badenoch with superiorities over the powerful clans that were developing there. The Gordons, of Anglo-Norman origin, were to play a role in the Highlands similar to that of the Campbells and the MacKenzies.

Of the clans of mixed Gaelic and Norse origin, the rise to power of the most important, the MacDougalls and the MacDonalds, the descendants of Somerled, had already taken place during a previous period, but it is worth noting that the MacDonalds had established several branches that took on much of the individuality of clans, and during the period before the Lordship of the Isles, the MacAlisters, the MacIans and the MacDonalds of Glencoe had been established. During the time of the Lordship, Clan Ranald, who were the descendants of the heiress of the MacRuairidhs and of John, first Lord of the Isles, Clan Donald South, the MacDonalds of Keppoch, the MacDonalds of Lochalsh, and the MacDonalds North or of Sleat were all established.[9] After the fall of the Lordship those branches played their separate parts in the story of the Highlands.

In considering how the Lordship of the Isles came about it is worthwhile remembering the ancestry of the Lords of Islay. Not only had they the blood of reigning sovereigns in their veins through their remote descent from Conn of the Hundred Battles and more recently from the King of Man, but also Donald and his son had enjoyed a degree of semi-independence when the Kings of Scotland and Norway had both claimed their allegiance and when in the Norse chronicles they had been termed Kings. They were also related to the family of Balliol.

Angus Og received from King Robert the family possessions previously held by Alexander Lord of Islay, his elder brother, with the important exception of Kintyre. He was also rewarded by the grant of most of the island possessions of his cousin, the descendant of Dougal. He thus received Mull, Coll, Jura, Tiree and some lesser islands. In addition, he was granted Lochaber which had been forfeited by the Comyns. King Robert had definite reason for depriving Angus of what had been his particular share of the family estates where, in his castle of Dunaverty in Kintyre, he had actually sheltered the King in his hour of extreme need. The King was continuing the policy of his predecessors in keeping the control of the estuary of the Clyde under his own control. It was the menace of Highland galleys that King Robert wished to guard against. Like his predecessors, he entrusted much of the land to the favoured family of Stewarts. He also entrusted other members of it with the office of Sheriff for Kintyre and the adjacent lands. To demonstrate his sovereignty over this strategically important area in more spectacular fashion, he had himself drawn across the isthmus connecting Kintyre and

Knapdale in a galley as Magnus Barelegs, King of Norway, had done nearly three hundred years before him.

In addition he built a strong castle there. Angus Og's son John probably felt that he had some justification for the somewhat dubious steps that he took to regain the lands of his family. He supported Ewen of Lorn and the other disinherited lords, and he was for a time in alliance with the King of England, who bestowed upon him the futile grant of lands securely held by loyal Scots. Eventually his claim to Kintyre was recognised by the kings of Scots. Donald Gregory, in his *History of the Western Highlands and the Isles of Scotland*, unravels these very complicated manoeuvres. John also took a leading part in opposing the heavy taxation that was imposed upon the country to pay the ransom of David II and to finance his extravagance. In this he was supported by Campbell of Lochawe.

A very able man, he also made two highly advantageous marriages. The first was to Amie MacRuairidh, heiress to the old MacRuairidh lands, and thus he greatly consolidated his position. In spite of his previous disloyalty and conflict with members of the House of Stewart, after divorcing Amie, his second marriage was to Princess Margaret, who was the daughter of Robert II, himself the son of the High Steward and married to the daughter of Robert the Bruce. John's possessions included Kintyre, the main part of the Western Isles lying north of it, with a considerable extent of the west coast mainland in Lochaber, and north of Loch Ness. In 1354, he himself assumed the title of Lord of the Isles, *Dominus Insularum*. It is significant that he himself assumed it and it was long afterwards that his great-grandson received it formally as a grant from the King, although like John the first Lord, his three successors were at frequent variance with the Crown. John made special arrangements for the succession and did not follow the custom of primogeniture. He made Donald, his son by Princess Margaret, his heir for all his estates including the mainland property, passing over the rights of John, not only his eldest son but the son of Amie the heiress to these territories. It is infinitely to his credit that this son acted as regent for his younger brother and handed the estates over to him when he came of age. Younger members of the MacRuairidh family, by now generally known as Clan Ranald, did not accept this alienation of their mother's property and there was a certain amount of trouble. Throughout its history there was often to be dissension within the Lordship. John's activities may be said to have led to a climax when he assumed the title of Lord of the Isles. One of the symptoms of this troublous period of the Wars of Independence was the great change in the holding of lands, and one of the agents of this was John, whose very adroit manoeuvres culminated in his assumption of the title. This forms a prelude to our third period which is mainly concerned with the Lordship of the Isles.

There were four Lords of the Isles, whose rule spanned 150 years: John, the first Lord, Donald, Alexander, and John son of Alexander. Their possessions included all the islands to the north and west of the peninsula of Kintyre, excepting Skye and Lewis which they later obtained as part of the Earldom of Ross. Their mainland possessions included Kintyre and Knapdale, Morvern Ardnamurchan, Lochaber, Garmoran and other lands to the north of Loch Ness and, later on, the whole Earldom of Ross. They also acquired by marriage lands in the Glens of Antrim in Ulster which became the patrimony of *Clann Iain Mhóir*, 'Clan Donald South'. Their lands thus straddled the strategically important North Channel.

The title of *Dominus Insularum* was not bestowed on John of Islay by the Crown, and all four Lords, when circumstances were in their favour, adopted the position of semi-independent rulers. They were all in fact in frequent collision with central authority and seldom, if ever, on cordial terms with it. They established contacts with England and in acting in this way were obviously well aware that they came of royal stock. Within the Lordship itself, there were rivalries between the great branches founded by members of the family and such favoured supporters as the MacLeans. This more generalised account of the period concentrates upon the great cultural and social effects that the Lordship had upon the subsequent development of the Highlands, but it should always be borne in mind that the Lordship all through its lifetime was menaced by difficulties and hostile elements inside it as well as outside and was never the idyllic state that the imagination is prone to call up.

Almost from the start of his rule, Donald, the successor to John, became involved in a dispute with the Crown for recognition of his rightful claim to the Earldom of Ross. The dispute continued during his rule and most of that of Alexander, his successor. It involved the battle of Harlaw, probably the single episode in the history of the Lordship that is most widely known, and eventually it put the Lord of the Isles in a position of power in which a nobleman claiming some degree of independent sovereignty was obviously regarded as a threat to the state.

In itself, the Earldom of Ross was a rich prize, containing as it did some of the most fertile land in the Highlands, and it was especially desirable to the Lords of the Isles because it not only gave them the superiority of Skye and Lewis and completed their control of the whole chain of the Western Islands, but also provided them with new land wherewith to provide for younger relations and favoured supporters — a problem that became acute during the later times of the Lordship. At a period when the rule of the Crown was particularly ineffective and authority was exercised by the sinister figure of Robert, Duke of Albany, Regent and later Governor, the succession to the Earldom of Ross had been far from smooth or happy. In 1402 the heiress was a crippled girl, Euphemia, and Albany, then holding the office of Chamberlain to the feeble Robert III, encouraged or persuaded the girl to take the veil. He then arranged that the Earldom should be bestowed upon his own son, the Earl of Buchan. He thereby ignored the claims of Margaret, Euphemia's aunt and heiress. Margaret was married to Donald, Lord of the Isles, who prepared to enforce her rightful claim. In 1411 he mustered the manpower of the Lordship. From an initial gathering of 10,000 men he is said to have chosen an army of 6,000

The contemporary accounts of what followed are both contradictory and confusing.[10] The main interest is focused upon the final phase when Donald's army reached the Lowlands and it was expected and feared that he would attack Aberdeen. Lord Cromartie, drawing upon local tradition and with first-hand knowledge of the country, suggests that Donald made an attempt to capture Dingwall Castle, which would have been a prime objective in occupying the Earldom of Ross, using only part of his army and abandoning the project when he met with stiff resistance by several of the vassals of the Earldom, the Munros, the Mackays and the MacKenzies.' With his men, he rejoined the main force on its march eastwards. His avowed intention was to occupy some outlying land belonging to the Earldom within the sheriffdoms of Banff and Aberdeen. This seems to be rather a minor objective for a major expedition. The route he chose is equally surprising for, instead of following the line taken upon so many expeditions — that of crossing Lochaber and then following the course of the Spey till he reached the low country — he took a circuitous and strongly defended line. He captured the strong Castle of Inverness and made his way through the low country and the many defended parts of the Laigh of Moray, arousing the apprehension of the powerful men of the east coast and that of the citizens of Aberdeen. Donald's strategy is difficult to understand. Did he act in sheer bravado or did he plan to have the decisive fight for recognition of his wife's claim to Ross upon his enemies' land and not within the more difficult terrain of the Earldom that he claimed?

The Earl of Mar gathered an army of the local feudal notables and also three other Earls, a Sheriff and the Provost of Aberdeen with their followers. The open rolling country of eastern Aberdeenshire was well suited to the pitched battle that took place at Harlaw. It was considered to be of great importance. John Major, writing generations later, said that the schoolboys of Aberdeen were still wont to play at the Battle of Harlaw. The battle lasted all day.

'Red Harlaw' is commemorated in a rousing Lowland ballad:—

As I cam' on by Garrioch land
And down by Nether Ha',
There was fifty thousand Highlan' men
A marching tae Harlaw

.....

Romantic hyperbole has no doubt multiplied the numbers of those engaged in the battle, but while the chronicles of each side give circumstantial accounts of a victory for their own people, they also admitted to heavy losses. A later version of the same ballad echoed the sense of tragedy:

The noise and dulesome harmonie,
That ever that dreary day did daw
Cryin' the coronach on hie,
Alas, alas, for the Harlaw!

During the night following the battle, Donald and his men withdrew. There is no mention of any pursuit or rear-guard action. Unfortunately historical sources do not exist to explain for us the reasons for Donald's actions, and no further fighting by either side is recorded. Though the battle was remembered in Lowland balladry, it was also the occasion for the celebrated *Brosnachadh* or 'Incitement to Battle' by MacMhuirich which opens with the words: 'Sons of Conn, remember hardihood in time of battle ...'. That MacMhuirich should have chosen to present his subject in this context is noteworthy. Conn of the Hundred Battles in folklore is also given the title of 'High King of Ireland' and is not a local folk hero. In mythology, tradition and history, Ireland and Scotland were regarded as separate, and in the traditions about him, Conn is said to have raided Scotland, and so we may presume that he fought some of his hundred battles there. Somerled had traced his descent from Conn, and he was therefore the reputed ancestor of the immediate family of Donald himself and of the families of the other known descendants of Somerled.

Clan Ranald of Garmoran, MacIain of Ardnamurchan, and MacIain of Glen Coe were but a mere fraction of Donalds's army, which was put at the lowest estimate at 6,000 men and included his vassals, the MacLeods and the Mackintoshes. The *Brosnachadh* can be regarded as an example of the identification of his following with the royal descent claimed by a chief. This is the antithesis of the continental division of the population into Noblesse and Peasantry. It became a cardinal feature of the Highland way of life.

The actual family genealogy, which for obvious reasons was not alluded to, gives an interesting illustration of the complexity of contemporary social relations. Donald and Mar were first cousins, for

Donald's mother and Mar's father, Alexander Stewart (better known as the Wolf of Badenoch) were brother and sister, being the children of Robert II. Furthermore the Wolf of Badenoch was the second husband of Euphemia Leslie, Countess of Ross, and the divorced step-grandfather of Margaret, Euphemia's daughter and Donald's wife. There were two heiresses to Ross named Euphemia: the first who was descended from *Fearchar Mac an t-Sagairt*, 'Earl of Ross', and the second was her grand-daughter, the cripple.

Donald's defiance aroused the threat of retaliation and he was forced to sign a submission at Loch Gilp. But the struggle to obtain occupation of the Earldom of Ross continued during the rule of Alexander, the third Lord who, as Hugh MacDonald the clan historian reveals, had been 'proclaimed Earl of Ross and Lord of the Isles after the accustomed manner,' (no doubt upon the traditional Inauguration Stone in Islay), and involved in the two pitched battles of Inverlochy, one a defeat for the Lordship, one for the forces of the Crown, the capture of Inverness, the imprisonment of the Lord of the Isles and his mother and his abject surrender. This led to an act of bad faith and the total denial of justice on the part of the law-loving King James I and, at the end, the occupation of the Earldom of Ross during the rest of the lifetime of Alexander, Lord of the Isles.

The second John, last Lord of the Isles, vacillated between rebellions and submissions. He was involved in the struggle between the Douglas family and the King of Scots; in 1461, with the advice of his principal vassals and kinsmen assembled in council at his castle of Ardtornish, John granted a commission in the style of an independent prince to his representatives to confer with the deputies of the King of England, Edward IV. They met the English commissioners at Westminster and concluded a treaty known to history as the Treaty of Westminster-Ardtornish, the basis of which was the conquest of Scotland by the Lord of the Isles with the assistance of English forces and of Douglas, who had been banished by James II in 1455. The Lord of the Isles with his cousin Donald Balloch, Lord of Dunivaig, were to receive payments in time of war of £200 sterling per annum to the Lord of the Isles and £40 to Donald Balloch; and they undertook to become the vassals of the King of England and to help him in his wars in Ireland. After Scotland was conquered, those parts north of the Forth were to be divided between the Lord of the Isles and the Earl of Douglas. When this treaty was discovered, strong measures were taken, including John's forfeiture, and in 1476 John submitted. After the forfeiture of the Earldom of Ross, a new grant was made of the Lordship itself on feudal terms, including the island of Skye but excluding Kintyre and Knapdale and the Earldom of Ross. Fresh trouble, however, broke out and the feeble John could not control the more militant members of his family who tried to regain possession of Ross by force. In 1493 the Lordship of the Isles itself was forfeited for the second time and annexed to the Crown.

During the duration of the Lordship, its forces swept across the Highlands seven times to seize Inverness. On several occasions the town was occupied for years, and the royal dues were appropriated. The Castle of Inverness and the royal Castle of Urquhart were held for periods in both the fourteenth and fifteenth centuries.[12] But the Lordship was never able to face up to the united forces of the Crown. In spite of victories over locally raised forces at Inverlochy in 1431 and *Lagabrad* in Ross in 1483, and the indecisive battle of Harlaw, the Lords of the Isles never outpaced the threat of a united attack by the rest of Scotland, and Alexander and the second John were both obliged to make abject submissions to the Crown. Nor was the Lordship's leadership universally accepted within the Highlands. Among its most bitter opponents were the Mackays, the Frasers, the Munros and above all and increasingly the MacKenzies and the Campbells. The vassals in the eastern part of Ross were generally unfriendly to the rule of the Lords of the Isles, while those of Wester Ross showed greater devotion. In the Eastern Highlands the clans were definitely not friendly.

The Lordship of the Isles is of importance politically in Highland history because it provided at least the possibility of a separate Gaelic kingdom within Scotland, and in the dark days to come it was a focus for the traditional recollections of the old Gaelic civilisation. Even as late as the eighteenth century, a bitterly Whig visitor, the author of an anonymous tract 'The Highlands of Scotland in 1750', described the devotion of the Highlanders of the west to its traditions. He adds: 'the poorest and most despicable Creature of the name of McDonald looks upon himself as a Gentleman of far superior Quality and Dignity than a man in England of £1,000 a year'.[13] It is its glory that the people spoke of the Lord of the Isles as *Buachaill nan Eilean*, the Herdsman of the Islands. Many of the West Highland chiefs rose again and again to aid the representatives of the forfeited Lordship with the same consistent loyalty that they later showed to the cause of the Stewarts.

With one exception, the surviving charters of the Lords of the Isles are in conventional feudal form; they show that the ruler of *Innse Gall* maintained a semi-royal state. The signatures of the witnesses show that he had a council and a court of officers of state. Examples of most charters that grant and confirm land have survived in the Register of the Great Seal. By a charter dated 1466 and confirmed by the Crown in 1494, for example, John Earl of Ross and Lord of the Isles granted Duncan Mackintosh the Bailliary of Lochaber and confirmed him in lands already granted to his family together with the entirely conventional dues

POWER IN THE HIGHLANDS IN THE
MID-FIFTEENTH CENTURY

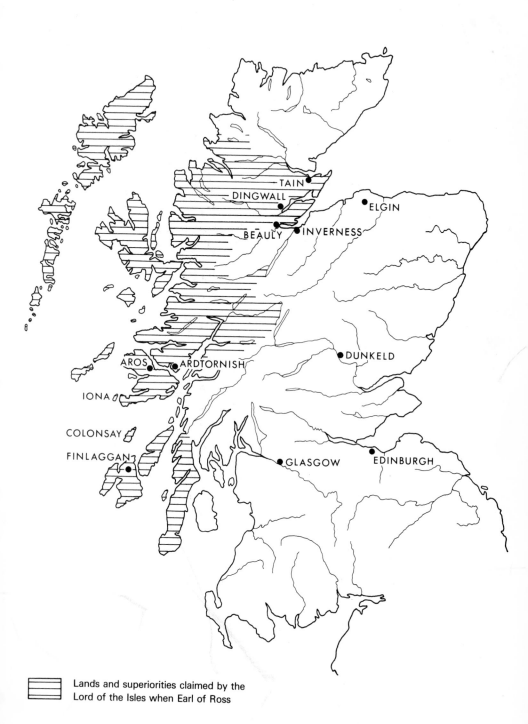

Lands and superiorities claimed by the
Lord of the Isles when Earl of Ross

and casualties. After the Lordship had passed to the Crown, James IV confirmed a charter in 1495 in the original phraseology couched in the style of a sovereign prince[14] granted by John, the last Lord, to his brother Hugh. These impressive Latin documents are important to bear in mind when analysing the Gaelic society of *Innse Gall*. One very different charter has been preserved. In May 1408, Donald, the second Lord, issued a charter in Gaelic, probably to a Mackay of the Rinns who fought under Donald Balloch at Inverlochy. It begins: 'In the Name of God, Amen. I, MacDonald, am granting and giving eleven marks and a half of land from myself and from my heirs to Brian Vicar Mackay and to his heirs after him for ever for his service to myself and to my father before me ...' The payment of four cows for MacDonald's table or forty-two merks yearly for certain specified lands followed, and the charter was dated on the ninth day of the month of Beltane. The signature is *MacDomnaill*. The wording of verbal grants by the Lords of the Isles handed down traditionally in Knapdale and Kintyre is similar; one ran: 'I, MacDonald, sitting upon Dundonald, give you a right to your farm from this day till tomorrow and every day thereafter, so long as you have food for the great MacDonald of the Isles.' [15] In both instances, the grantor uses the style *MacDhomhnaill*, adopting the patronymic of the thirteenth century Angus Mór of Islay or *Aonghus MacDhomhnaill*, Angus son of Donald, son of Reginald, son of Somerled. *MacDhomhnaill* had thus become the style of his successors, and it has been customary till our own day to address and refer to a chief simply by his surname or style in this manner.

The method of succession was by the feudal custom of primogeniture, although for political reasons John, the first Lord, was succeeded by Donald, the eldest son by his second marriage to Margaret, daughter of the heir presumptive to the throne, later Robert II. It is interesting to find that in this case Donald's younger brother, John Mór, Lord of Dunivaig and of the Glens of Antrim, was sometimes denoted as the *tanaiste*, as the chief designate during the lifetime of a ruling chief in accordance with the old Gaelic custom of electing an heir among the kindred. The term may have been generally used in Gaelic writings when it was intended that the succession should not go to the legal heir. Generally, the word for heir, *oighre*, was used. It was of course a matter of great advantage for chiefs of clans to obtain feudal charters for their lands and the feudal custom of primogeniture tended to become general.

Hugh MacDonald, the Sleat *seanchaidh*, gives some details of surviving and possibly roseate traditions of the administration of the Lordship. He was, of course, writing with the partiality of a devoted clansman and of a far-off time of happy memory. He was imitating the theoretic precision of the ancient Irish laws: 'The constitution of

government of the Isles was thus: MacDonald had his council at Island
Finlaggan, in Isla, to the number of sixteen, namely four Thanes, four
Armins, that is to say Lords or sub-Thanes, four Bastards or Squires or
men of competent estate, who could not come up with Armins or
Thanes, that is, free holders or men that had their land in factory, as
Macgee of the Rinns of Isla, MacNicoll in Portree in Skye, and
MacEachern, MacKay and MacGillivray in Mull, MacGhillemhaoil or
MacMillan, etc. There was a table of stone where this council sat in the
Isle of Finlaggan ... Moreover, there was a judge in every Isle for the
discussion of all controversies, who had lands from MacDonald for their
trouble, and likewise the eleventh part of every action decided. But there
might be still an appeal to the Council of the Isles. MacFinnon was
obliged to see weights and measures adjusted; and MacDuffie, or
MacPhee of Colonsay, kept the records of the Isles'.[16] Thomas Pennant,
Martin Martin, Anderson and Buchanan corroborate the traditions of
the sitting of the Council of the Isles at Finlaggan. '*Cum mensura lapidis
McCoull*' is mentioned in the precept of a charter of 1587-8 as being in
use in Coll, Tiree, Jura and Mull. Martin Martin notes the use of a
special version of the *omer* in some of the islands.

How far the system worked it is impossible to tell, but frequent
complaints of lawlessness in the Highlands are recorded. Many of the
troubles within the Lordship were due to conflicting grants of land. This
was especially the case in Lochaber and Garmoran, where there were
conflicting claims between branches of the family as well as between
other vassals. A far more serious weakness was the impossibility of
obtaining new lands to provide for the younger sons of successive Lords
and for favoured adherents such as the MacLeans and the MacNeills.
Under John, the last and weakest Lord, this difficulty increased. It led to
civil war between his kinsmen and his favourites, culminating in the
bloody sea-fight in Tobermory Bay. The custom of granting
superiorities, which Eoin MacNeill cites as an Irish as well as a feudal
practice, exposed the original inhabitants to the danger of expropriation,
as happened to the loyal MacDuffies of Colonsay by MacLean of Duart.
This difficulty of providing for sons and adherents was to prove a
problem in nearly all the clans.

The traditional accounts of the ceremonial and customs of the old
Lordship are very revealing. Hugh MacDonald records 'the ceremony of
proclaiming the Lords of the Isles. At this, the Bishop of Argyll, the
Bishop of the Isles, and seven priests were sometimes present; but a
Bishop was always present, with the chieftains of all the principal
families and a *Ruler of the Isles*. There was a square stone seven or eight
feet long, and the tract of a man's foot cut thereon, upon which he
stood, denoting that he should walk in the footsteps and uprightness of

his predecessors, and that he was installed by right in his possessions. He was clothed in a white habit, to show his innocence and integrity of heart, that he would be a light to his people and maintain the true religion. The white apparel did afterwards belong to the poet by right. Then he was to receive a white rod in his hand, intimating that he had power to rule, not with tyranny and partiality, but with discretion and sincerity. Then he received his forefathers' sword, or some other sword, signifying that his duty was to protect and defend them from the incursions of their enemies in peace or war, as were the obligations and customs of his predecessors. The ceremony being over Mass, was said after the blessing of the bishop and seven priests, the people pouring out their prayer for the success and prosperity of their new created Lord. When they were dismissed, the Lord of the Isles feasted them for a week thereafter; gave liberally to the monks, poets, bards and musicians. You may judge that they spent liberally without any exception of persons.'[17] This form of ceremonial had its roots in a very distant past. There is the footprint cut in the living rock on the ancient hill fort at Dunadd, and various customs were remembered at the turn of the eighteenth century when Martin Martin wrote that at the customary inauguration of a Highland chief he was placed on a cairn, surrounded by his friends and followers, and that his father's sword and a white rod were handed to him and a 'panegyric' delivered by an orator on the pedigree and prowess of his family. The ceremony appeared to include a blend of the panoply of Christian coronation with Celtic custom as with the inauguration of the kings of Scots at Scone. The formal recitation by *file* and *seanchaidh* with all the persuasive techniques of poetic eulogy and learning was thoroughly Gaelic and one of the institutions which clearly flourished under the Lordship.

Formal feasts were held within the Lordship in the ancient Irish tradition. An actual account of a feast at Aros about 1431, which also shows the growing weakness of the Lordship, is related by Hugh MacDonald. One of the guests, John, uncle and tutor to the young Laird of Moidart, in speaking with MacLean of Duart, who was the Lord of the Isles' favourite and of whom the MacDonald kinsfolk were bitterly jealous, said that he knew that it was MacLean's office as marshal 'to set the MacDonalds in order tomorrow at dinner, and that he should see all the principal men there placed according to their rank and station; but if MacLean would give him a black hound that he had, he would supply his place the next day. MacLean consented to this and gave the hound. At dinner time next day John stood at the end of MacDonald's table, and desired the laird of Ardnamurchan to sit down .... . Then he desired MacFinnon and MacQuire to sit, for MacQuire was an ancient Thane. Then he desired Beaton, the principal physician, then MacMurrich, the poet, to take their seats. Now, said he, I am the oldest and best of your surnames here present and will sit down; as for these fellows who have raised up their heads of late and are upstarts, whose pedigree we know not, nor even they themselves, let them sit as they please. MacLean, MacLeod of Harris and MacNeil of Barra went out in a rage and very much discontented. MacLeod of Lewis remained within; the other three were determined, as soon as an opportunity offered, to be fully revenged of John MacDonald for the affront, as they thought, he had given.'[18]

A number of the names of the traditional office-bearers to the Lord of *Innse Gall* survive. MacDuffie or MacPhee kept the records, Mackinnon had been marshal until replaced by MacLean and was the judge. MacMhuirich was the hereditary poet whose family held office from generation to generation from the thirteenth to the eighteenth centuries. They traced their descent from *Muireadhach Albanach* of the O'Daly bardic family of Ireland who is reputed to have fled to Scotland about 1213 having killed O'Donnell's steward. About twenty poems have survived in manuscript collections ascribed to the thirteenth century *Muireadhach*, two of them addressed to the Lennox family, possibly his first patrons in Scotland. The family held land in Kintyre, Islay and Colonsay at least until the later sixteenth century, but after the fall of the Lordship they seemed to relinquish their hereditary lands in Kintyre and transfer their allegiance to Clan Ranald. They were given bardic privileges, including the lands of Staoligarry and Drimisdale in South Uist, which they held heritably into the eighteenth century. They preserved many of the practices of Irish classical learning, including the literary language and classical metres, and some of their manuscripts survive, such as the Books of Clanranald. The ties with Ireland were maintained by members of the family in successive generations going across for part of their training in the bardic schools. Lachlann MacMhuirich, who claimed that he was eighteenth in descent from *Muireadhach Albanach*, told a Committee of the Highland Society at Torlum in Benbecula in 1800: 'That there was a right given them over these lands as long as there should by any of the posterity of Muireach to preserve and continue the genealogy and history of Clan Donald, on condition that the bard was to educate his brother's son or representative, failing of male issue, in order to preserve their title to the land'.[19]

The Beatons were hereditary physicians whose family has a record of service almost as impressive as that of the MacMhuirich family. The precedence given to Beaton at MacDonald's table as shown in the seating arrangement at the feast at Aros demonstrates that he was traditionally one of the most senior members of the learned classes. The family held lands near one of the mansions of the Lord of the Isles at Kilchoman in the south west of Islay and another branch was settled in Mull at Pennyghael on Loch Scridain where their herb garden is said to be traceable. The respective branches of the family bore the honorific titles of *An t-Ollamh Ileach* and *An t-Ollamh Muileach*, the term *ollamh*, doctor or professor, being reserved only for a very few of the professional classes. The reputation and prestige of these men spread far beyond the bounds of their native localities. By the seventeenth and eighteenth centuries, they were in possession of comparatively large collections of Gaelic medical and scientific manuscripts which were attracting the attention of scholars of the day. Like many other Highland families, they had alternative theories about their origins, one placing them in Ireland and the other in Lowland Scotland. They shared with other families the claim that they belonged to *Tochradh Nighean a'Chathanaich*, the tocher of the daughter of O Cathain or O'Kane; this lady brought a large retinue of men from her kin lands in Ireland when she married Angus Og of Islay in the closing years of the fourteenth century.

The paucity of law tracts among the surviving Gaelic manuscripts is rather striking. Sir Robert Gordon of Gordonstoun's description circa 1630 in his *Genealogical History of the Earldom of Sutherland*, of the functions of the Breve of Lewis at the beginning of the seventeenth century closely resembles that of the ancient *Brithem* of Erin: 'The Brieve is a kynd of Judge among the Islanders, who hath ane absolute Judicatorie, and unto whose authorities and censure they willinglie submitt themselves when he determineth any debatable questions between partie and partie.'[20] Sir Robert's account was at least an informed one, as he was himself a lawyer.

There were other traditional offices. The confirmation of a charter exists under which John Davidson, son of Gibbon Davidson, hereditary armour-bearer to the Lord of the Isles, held land in Kintyre. Martin describes how each chief had an armour-bearer, the *Galloglach*, allowed the special portion of food. *Mac o Senog* or Shannon, the harper, had four merklands in South Kintyre in return for his service, and Ranald MacAlasdair, harper, was still possessed of two merklands also in South Kintyre in 1596, long after the disappearance of the Lordship. The MacEacherns were famous sword-makers to the Lords of the Isles and had land in Islay at Kilchoman. Gilleonan MacNeill was standard-bearer to Alexander, third Lord. MacArthur was said to have been a piper to the Lords of the Isles and to have had lands at Proaig in Islay. His line certainly served MacDonald of Sleat in later times and founded their school of piping in Kilmuir. Other names found within the bounds of the old Lordship and derived from hereditary offices are MacSporran, the purse-bearer, members of whose family are buried on

Iona, MacLaverty, said to be the orator, and MacInstocker or *Mac-an-Stocair*, the trumpeter. It was of course customary for such officers as the smith and the piper to hold a grant of land in virtue of their office. In Mull, when Argyll took possession of Duart's lands in the seventeenth century, the lands of two hereditary pipers are mentioned in the rentals that were drawn up, the holdings of *Iain MacIain MhicEoghainn MhicAilein* and *Padraig MacDhomhnaill*. A MacDonald of Murlaggan was hereditary standard-bearer to Mackintosh, as shown in a legal document of 1727 in which he states that the family had performed the office since the fifteenth century. Mackintosh's hereditary bard was a MacIntyre, whose ancestor had been brought from Rannoch by William Mackintosh at the beginning of the sixteenth century. MacDonald of Sleat had a standard-bearer and a quarter-master who still exercised his right to the hides of cows about 1700. The chief also had his *Gocaman* or sentinel and MacNeill still maintained such a sentinel in 1695.[21]

The Lordship was defended by a succession of castles held by the Lord of the Isles himself or by kinsmen or adherents. Their ruins, such as Ardtornish and Aros, are places of impressive strength, but his favourite residence was on an island in Loch Finlaggan in Islay. Fordun refers to it as a manor or mansion and not a castle and it is significant that, although its ruins cover a large area, there are no remains of massive fortifications, a striking illustration of the security in which he dwelt in an age when most powerful men were glad of the protection of a castle.

From early times the exercise of hospitality was a paramount obligation among the Gael. One example, not perhaps of how things were, but of how a Highland chief would have liked them to be, concerned MacLeod of Lewis. It occurs in the Applecross Manuscript, a seventeenth-century history of the MacKenzies. Murdo MacKenzie, said to have lived in the fifteenth century, had been dispossessed and fled to his uncle MacLeod of Lewis. 'The form of MacLeod's house at that time was so princely that all men that came to it would gett maintenance for a year and a day before he would be asked from whence he came.' Murdo remained there for some time without divulging his identity. He won two pipes of wine in a wager, and MacLeod's 'Master of the Household' told his master that the stranger had 'the pairts of a free-hearted gentleman', and that he was distributing the wine amongst the 'rangall and poor ones of the Toun'. MacLeod sent for him, and Murdo revealed himself as MacLeod's sister's son and was given men and boats to regain his heritage.[22] The tale bears an extraordinary likeness to an ancient Irish story about Dunadd.

As in a purely feudal tenure, the holding of land was an important link between the Lord of the Isles and his kinsmen and vassals, and in nearly

Castle Tioram in Moidart with an enclosing wall and tower on a tidal island, late thirteenth century, possibly erected by the MacRuairidhs

all clans one of the important functions of a chief was that of a land-holder and defender. There was, however, as time showed, very much more to the relationship of chief and clansman than material ties. For instance, among many examples, in 1394 in the course of the Lord of

Innse Gall's frequent military expeditions, some of his forces occupied
Glen Urquhart and Glen Moriston, and lands there were given to his
followers, MacDonalds and MacLeans, the latter of whom were given
the keeping of Urquhart Castle. The Lord of the Isles was eventually
forced to relinquish Glen Urquhart and Glen Moriston and, after an
interregnum, they were granted to the Laird of Grant early in the
sixteenth century; but in the civil wars of the seventeenth century the
MacDonalds took the side of their own chiefs and not that of their
landlord.

The importance of the Lordship, however, lies not only in its political
and social order but also in its cultural aspects. It provides that
patronage for the arts of the Gael that was so much lacking in later times
and its influence was pervasive. The later Dr A O Curle, the
distinguished archaeologist, once commented to one of the writers that
the art of the West Highland carvings was so localised and belonged so
definitely to one period that there must be some assignable historical
cause for their production. In trying to discover the reason and the
correlation of dates and the former ownership of the land, the enormous
importance of the Lordship becomes apparent. As one might expect,
there are some fine outliers outside the bounds of the old Lordship, such
as those at Kilmichael Glassary, Kilbrandon, Taynuilt, Dalmally,
Kilmartin and especially at Ardchattan. The Lerags Cross at Kilbride is
typical of the finest work, except that it has a coat of arms carved upon
it. The cross at Inveraray is an import. Most of the other outliers, like
those at Innishail and in the churchyards of Kilbride and Glassary, are
inferior specimens. Although the art persisted for about fifty years after
the forfeiture of the Lordship, later specimens are, with the notable
exception of the tombs in St Clement's Church, Rodel, Harris, of a
debased form, like the tombstone at Lismore traditionally belonging to
Donald nan Ord, with exaggerated quillons on the sword hilt, or the
effigy on Inch Kenneth wearing later medieval armour. The greater
number and the finest stones are in Kintyre, Iona, Morvern, Moidart,
Mull and the adjacent islands within the old Lordship. More than a
dozen are positively dated by inscription as coming within the period of
its existence or quite soon afterwards.[23]

The design is produced by cutting back the background, although in
the finest specimens, notably those at Iona, there is little carving in the
round. The earlier West Highland crosses and carvings of the ninth and
tenth centuries have evidently influenced the new style of carving, but
there are great differences. In shape, the separate ring or nimbus round
the intersection of the arms and shaft of the free-standing crosses has in
nearly every case been replaced by a solid head; and the base, instead of a
wedge-shaped socket, has become a flat slab. A great deal of foliage has

Left: *Effigy of an armoured warrior, commemorating Bricius MacKinnon and his sons, late fourteenth century, Iona. The figure is wearing the quilted surcoat or aketon*

Right: *Grave-slab, c.1500, with a galley and distinctive plant-scroll decoration under the inscription to Angus, son of Angus Lord of Islay, the latter to be identified with the Angus Og who was murdered in Inverness in 1490*

been introduced into the design, but the characteristic fondness for interlacing continues to be an outstanding feature, although the divergent spiral, so characteristic of early Celtic work, has disappeared. Most of the designs are less well balanced and are very much more individual than in the earlier period.

Although there is a great deal of variation, some of the favourite designs are: 1. Full-length effigies of warriors and ecclesiastics carved in relief; 2. Panels of small effigies of men and women in Lowland dress; this style is particularly favoured in Knapdale and Kintyre; 3. A sword or foliated cross down the middle or one side, associated with interlaced designs, foliage, monsters or hunting scenes, or with objects such as galleys, shears, combs, caskets or other domestic utensils; 4. An overall design of intertwined foliage with sometimes a galley at the top, a type most often found on Iona; galleys appear more often on the northern carvings than the southern.

Having visited a number of the carved stones, one is left with the general impression that although everywhere there are a few exceptionally fine examples, perhaps the imported work of an expert, districts show certain tendencies. The carvings in Kintyre are the most massive and least symmetrical. These characteristics are gradually modified as one goes northwards, and those of Iona and Morvern are the most graceful, and those of Iona the best executed and most symmetrical. There is great originality but less beauty in the work from Tiree. There are local preferences such as for a 'marigold' design at Oronsay, and at Iona for an all-over symmetrical design of foliage within a border that is sometimes decorated with 'nail-head' ornamentation.

Some of the subjects carved on the stones evidently illustrate their owners' possessions or occupation, such as a harp, a casket, a rod — apparently one of office — a pair of shears, and by far the most frequent of all, a cross-hilted, double-edged sword of the period. Noting minute differences, one wonders if they are not often portraits of the dead man's own sword. The swords carved upon the effigies of the warriors give one an idea of the size of their weapons. They are of much the same length as a single-handed sword. The crosspieces are shaped as 'quillons', which is a Scottish characteristic, and the pommels on many of them have pear-shaped tops which is thought to derive from the Vikings. A few of the swords are carved down the whole length of a grave slab, though still cross-hilted and two-handed but with longer blades. They are of a type of Continental origin and would obviously be weapons most suitable for display and ceremonial. They are not specifically alluded to in written accounts of the fifteenth and sixteenth century when they came into use, but unlike the later basket-hilted swords, they are cross-hilted and thought to have given rise to the term 'claymore' or 'big sword.'

West Highland grave-slab at Kilmory, Knapdale, commemorating members of families of hereditary craftsmen, in this case possibly gold or silversmiths of the fourteenth or fifteenth centuries

The significance of some of the things portrayed has been lost, as for instance that of the goat-headed figures carved at Kilmory, Knapdale and Nereabolls, Islay. But the sword would probably denote a man qualified for military service, and a galley one of sufficient standing to owe service with a *long fhada*, 'lymphad', *birlinn*, or galley. The service of a galley was often specified as the return on grants of land, and the duty of repair and upkeep of galleys was imposed on those who held lands of the crown in the Western Highlands, so that the king could mobilise a naval force at short notice for service. A statute of James I's parliament at Perth in 1429 ordered that:

> All baronnis and lordis hafand landis and lordschippis nere the see in the west and on the north partis and namely fornent the Isles that thai haf galayis that is to say of ilk four merkes worth of lande ane aire ...[24]

But of what were the hunting scenes which appear so often, including one on the stone of an ecclesiastic at Keills, Morvern, and another on the

Left: *West Highland swords of the fifteenth century. A two-handed* **'claymore'** *and the earlier, lighter type of sword with characteristic downward-sloping quillons, typical of the swords on grave monuments*

Right: *Grave-slab with a hunting scene, Saddell Abbey, Kintyre*

cross-shaft at Kilmory, symbolic? The carving of an otter accompanying a salmon on a tomb at Saddell and on other Kintyre stones could hardly have been pleasing to the keen fisherman. It has been suggested that the animals on the stones were inspired by the 'bestiaries' fashionable at the time; on the other hand, the hunting scenes may have been simply the representation of the deceased's favourite sport. This is the most likely explanation because in Gaelic society, hunting the deer was a favourite occupation and was considered to be an important trait of character. Praise of *sealgair sìthne air frìth nan àrd-bheann*, the hunter of deer in the mountains, was a common phrase used in song; prowess on the hill and at the chase was the acme of nobility.

The erection of free-standing crosses in Ireland and Britain, which had been in decline since the twelfth century, was revived in the Lordship and survived it. The very fine Campbeltown Cross, for example, dates from the late fourteenth century, and the Campbell of Lerags Cross is dated 1516. Many of the crosses bear representations of the Crucifixion, some of which were erased in the Reformation as, for instance, on the otherwise well preserved and very fine Campbeltown Cross. Many of these Crucifixion carvings resemble conventional representations of the central theme of Christianity. Some others are curiously distorted and seem to be powerfully symbolic expressions of the sufferings of Christ and the agony of the Atonement beyond human powers of description. Outstanding examples are the strangely moving Figure on the Cross at Kilberry, Knapdale, and the smaller and broken cross at Kilmartin. On both these crosses, the style of the rest of the carving is quite conventional.

It is a tragedy that so many of the stone monuments mentioned by earlier writers such as Thomas Pennant in the 1770s and Capt. T P White in the 1870s have disappeared or have deteriorated. The record which they made in their day has enabled us to restore inscriptions and details which have since been obliterated by the passage of time. The earliest set of drawings to survive was made by a Welshman, Edward Lhuyd, a Celtic Scholar and Keeper of the Ashmolean Museum, who went on a study tour of Argyll in 1699 and recorded twenty five monuments. The inscription on a late fifteenth century cross erected by MacMillan at Kilmory, for example, was recorded by Lhuyd but is now illegible.[25]

The stones throw light upon Highland ecclesiastical vestments and on an old skill in embroidery. Earlier chasubles were originally circular, and they were only gradually reduced to the narrow form in general use from the sixteenth century onwards. A few carvings of conventional chasubles are found on Highland stones, especially in Kintyre. But ecclesiastical effigies on the Guthrie Bell Shrine and carvings in Arran, on Iona and Islay, show or indicate a style of chasuble formed, apparently, by some kind of ornamental gathering of the fabric, and which resembles earlier Irish examples.[26] These effigies have a noticeably upstanding 'apparel' on the amice; The 'apparel' is a strip of ornamentation on the linen of the amice which stands up stiffly as if heavily embroidered. This Highland peculiarity is, as far we know, not referred to elsewhere and is a personal observation. It is rather remarkable that these characteristically Highland vestments were being made at a time when in other parts of Scotland vestments were being imported, as for instance, by the Abbot of Paisley in 1459 and by the Bishop of Dunkeld. Heavy embroidery is also shown upon the clothes of two of the lay effigies at Oronsay and on that of the 'bloody MacDonald' at Saddell.

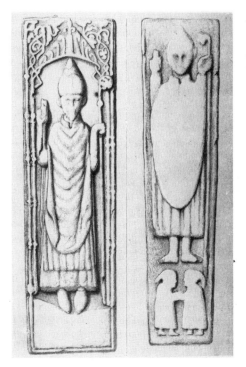

Mitred ecclesiastics, either abbots or bishops, with right hands raised in blessing and carrying staffs or croziers, the one on the left under a canopy, Iona, fourteenth century

It is convenient to pass to the implications of West Highlanders' battle dress as worn by effigies on tombs for written descriptions. Thus Robert Lindsay of Pitscottie, writing of 1460, says that the men of the Lord of the Isles were 'all armed in the Highland fashion with Halbershownes'. So customary had it become that in the later versions of tales of the Fianna they were equipped with mail shirts. Protective body armour had never been worn by these heroes in the earliest versions of the tales about them. The custom of wearing chain-mail was therefore grafted onto stories through time. For example, in a late version of a story about Fionn, every one of the Fianna, *an Fhian*, was said to be wearing 'a coat of mail of brightest hue'. The wearing of mail shirts also figures in clan tradition. A Campbell story, for instance, about the fourteenth century *Cailean Iongantach*, later Colin of Lochawe, tells how he was caught in a house set on fire by his enemies. He was wearing 'his coat of mail which after the antient forme was made lyke after a nett hanging down to their heels called in Irish a *luireach*'. His mail shirt became so hot that when he escaped he plunged into a pool which was afterwards always known as *Linne na Luirich*, the 'Mail Shirt Pool'.[27]

The adoption of the mail shirt from the Lowlands was well suited to contemporary methods of fighting which often seem to resemble the descriptions of battles in the ancient tales in which the fighting was mainly done by picked champions. In our period the importance of the exploits of outstanding warriors persisted. It comes out strongly in two accounts of the battle of *Blàr na Pairc*, one in the Applecross Manuscript, the other in a late seventeenth century Genealogy of the MacRaes. They include vivid descriptions of the combat between the standard bearers of MacKenzie and MacDonald, and the intervention of Big Duncan, the *sgalag mór*, in the duel between two of the leaders. In his *History of Greater Britain* of 1521, John Major describes a fight between two groups of 'caterans' in Strathnaver in the reign of James I, and says: 'the conflict was, as it were, by an equal number of duels and every man made an end of his antagonist, or contrariwise'.[28]

The provision of fighting equipment had its important social implications. A document giving the revenue of the eighteen score merklands of Islay, after stating their rentals in livestock, victual and money rent, added that besides this, 'ilk merkland man sustein daylie and yeirlie ane gentleman in meit and claith, quhilk dois na labour, but is haldin as ane of their maisters household men, and man be sustenit and furneisit in all necessaries be the tennent, and he man be reddie to his maisters service and advis'. The fighting strength of the West Highlands in time of insurrection or possibly at the time of the Tyrone rebellion in the sixteenth century was estimated at six thousand men, exclusive of the labourers of the ground who were not 'permittit to steir furth of the cuntrie quahatevir their maister have ado, except only gentlemen quhilk labouris not, that the labour belonging to the teiling of the ground and wynning of thair corns may not be left undone...'.[29] The cost of equipping a warrior in the current battle dress must have been considerable. The *daoine uasal*, the gentlemen of a clan, who could afford to arm themselves well, served a most important function as the fighters in the constant warfare waged by the more militant clans. There was also frequent employment to be had in military enterprises in Ireland. Clan Donald straddled the North Channel, as certain clansmen occupied land in Antrim during the fifteenth century. By the sixteenth century Highlanders were in Ireland in such numbers as to form an important element in the O'Neill and O'Donnell rebellions against Elizabethan rule. In his *Britannia*, the sixteenth century English historian William Camden described some of the inhabitants of Mayo in 1586 as:

> Scots transplanted from the Hebrides and the family of the Donnells from thence, called Clan Donnells, who are all galloglasses and as it were mercenary soldiers, armed with double-headed axes and coats of mail...

The classic medieval distinction between those who fought, those who prayed and those who worked still held good for the Highlands in this period, and fighting as a gentlemanly pursuit was therefore limited to comparatively few men. On the west coast of the Highlands there was special reason for the persistence of fighting with a small number of well-armed picked men, because their expeditions generally had to be made in galleys and therefore the number to be engaged was limited. Nevertheless, although specially well-equipped fighting men were a feature of the battle tactics and social organisation of the Highlands at this period, local folk, with the extraordinary mobility characteristic of Highland troops, also could and did fight, as contemporary accounts of the Wars of Independence abundantly show. This is important to bear in mind in describing the change in Highland dress and fighting methods in later times.

The carved stones suggest other points worth taking into consideration. In the first place, the manufacture of chain-mail and swords shows that a considerable number of skilled smiths lived in the Highlands. The tools of their trade — anvil, hammer and pincers — were carved on a few monuments and their names were also commemorated; in the Irish law tracts, the smiths as craftsmen were classed with poets and accorded a high position in society and so it is not surprising to find them erecting stone monuments in the same way as lay and clerical dignitaries. There are many traditions and stories about smiths in which they are sometimes accredited with supernatural and magical powers and, like poets and physicians, some families held office as smiths and armourers to the principal chiefs heritably for generations, such as the MacEacherns in Morvern and Islay and the MacNabs at Dalmally.

Another important point to note is ·that no effigy is depicted as wearing a kilt or belted plaid; they wear armour or some kind of battle dress, or ecclesiastical vestments. In the hunting scenes on monuments at Knapdale and Rodel, men are shown carrying conventional shields (not targes) and in a few, their armorial bearings are carved on them. A number of fourteenth century seals also bear heraldic devices.

We have but a pitiful fraction of the Highland manuscripts dating back to the period, though we know of the existence of many that have disappeared. The preservation of many of those that survive we largely owe to the controversy surrounding James Macpherson's *Ossian* in the late eighteenth century. The literature of old Gaeldom seems to bring us into closer touch with its people than anything else. They show that the Highlanders did not live in barbarous isolation and give interesting evidence of their links with contemporary European culture. In the manuscripts are versions of the wanderings of Ulysses and of the Aeneid and other classical epics. In most cases these Gaelic versions are greatly altered from the originals and are all arranged in the same form as original Gaelic stories; nevertheless it is remarkable that Gaelic should be the first language into which the classical stories were translated. For instance, the Book of Leinster, c.1147, has a version of the *Togail Troi* or Destruction of Troy, whereas elsewhere the earliest known translation is in French and was not written until about 1180. There are collections of pithy sayings, which have always been popular with the Gael and which were traditionally attributed to ancient kings and heroes such as Cu Chulainn. Some of the manuscripts contain history and genealogy; many of the pedigrees take the descent of families back to Biblical origins. There are many poems by contemporary Irish poets and also a number of tales, among them a version of the story of Charlemagne and Roland. The most interesting, however, and the most precious which the patronage of the Lord of the Isles tended to preserve were the great epics, the copies of stories from the Ulster and Fenian Cycles in the classical early form of prose sagas with speech-poems interspersed. The story of Cu Chulainn and Conlaoch and of the death of Cu Chulainn, that of the Children of Lir and, especially, the story of Deirdre and the sons of Uisneach, with many other tales from the Fenian Cycle, were favourites.

The rise to power of new political forces coincided with a new kind of prose narration and new forms of verse. The best known of these works is the one which scholars call the *Book of the Dean of Lismore*. This collection was made by James MacGregor, Dean of Lismore and Vicar of Fortingall, and by his brother Duncan between about 1512 and 1526. The manuscript contains over 11,000 lines of poetry in the standard literary Gaelic of the day but written phonetically, using the orthography of Lowland Scots. The great fascination of the *Book* lies in the fact that it represents the literary tastes and the kind of poetry that Highlanders of all stations of life were actually repeating so near to the close of our period. Many of the pieces have a strong local association with the Loch Tay and Fortingall area, and the whole collection shows a definite bias towards Perthshire and Argyll. We may presume that other districts of the Highlands and Islands had a similar wealth of Gaelic poetry. A part of the inspiration behind the collection may be inferred from one of the poems by Finlay MacNab of Bovain in Glendochart, in which he urges the MacGregor family to compile a book of poetry, or a *Duanaire* or song-book as he styles it. Finlay states that he already has material to hand from packmen and that more may be expected from the strolling bards. Heroic poems must have been a part of their stock-in-trade. The *Book of the Dean* includes about thirty pieces of this sort; four poems relate to the earlier Cu Chulainn or Ulster Cycle and twenty four to the later Ossianic or Fenian Cycle.[30] Some of these pieces are attributed to *Oisean* and *Caoilte*, the Fenian poets; those attributed to the former take the form of dialogues, bitter or pathetic, between St Patrick and *Oisean* as the last of the Fianna. The storytellers make the third century *Oisean*, son of Fionn, survive his contemporaries, sometimes in the otherworld or in the *sìthean*, to meet with the fifth century St Patrick. This satisfactorily explained the survival of the traditional lore and ballads and lent them authority. There are also a few narrative Ossianic poems, some attributed to *Caoilte Mac Ronain* and others to later poets. An early seventeenth century Irish manuscript, the *Duanaire Finn*, containing sixty-nine poems, is the other important source of Ossianic ballads. The form and text of all these poems show that they are much later than the days of *Oisean*; the ballad form of narrative poetry in Gaelic literature was part of a contemporary European movement beginning in the twelfth century, and this form of poetry in Scottish Gaelic appears for the first time in the Dean's Book. Although they were inspired by the same general European movement, these Gaelic ballads differed in theme and also in their form from the Lowland ballads that were appearing about this time. The Lowlands ballads were singable, the Highland ones more suitable for reciting. Besides these complete poems, almost all the pieces in the book, many of them highly topical, are shot through with allusions to the great Ulster and Fenian figures.

Almost all the poems in the *Book of the Dean* are written in the traditional classic Irish syllabic metres, loosely termed 'bardic verse'. Such a term is appropriate since much of the poetry only approximated to *dàn dìreach*, which was the strictest metre of the bardic schools. Some of the poetry in the *Book of the Dean* is in strict metre but some has been composed with some licence and contains lapses from this metre and from the literary language. *Dàn dìreach* is syllabic verse generally divided into quatrains or *rannan* which are four line verses with a fixed number of syllables. Each line consists of a certain number of syllables, being perhaps typically a heptasyllabic line though often consisting of more or less syllables, and each line ends on a stressed word of a certain syllabic length. This end-rhyme is complemented by internal rhyme between words in which the stressed vowels are identical. Rhyme or *comhardadh* depended therefore on the equality of stressed vowels in words of similar syllabic length, and the consonants subsequent to these vowels had to be of the same class and quality such as for example, the soft consonants P, T and C, or, in a different class, the hard consonants B, D and G. Aspirated consonants formed further classes of rhyme. The balance and flow of *dàn dìreach* is often maintained by rhyme between the last word in the first line of a couplet and a word in the second line of the same couplet; this is known as *aicill* or anticipation and is found in the verse in the *Book of the Dean*. *Comhardadh slàn* or perfect rhyme did not consititute an unwavering standard. Often, though vowels matched,

different consonant groups would be matched in which case the rhyme
was imperfect, *comhardadh briste* or broken rhyme; *uaithne* was another
correspondence in which the consonants were of the same class but the
vowels, although of the same length, need not be identical. Most of the
surviving Scottish bardic poetry, including what we have in the *Book of
the Dean*, does not exemplify the strict use of *dàn dìreach* but rather was
composed in the form known as *oglachas* with fewer and looser
rhymes.

Douglas Hyde has translated examples of Gaelic poetry such as *dàn
dìreach* in a way that demonstrates some of the methods of versification.
Maeve's Lament clearly shows characteristics such as *aicill*:

> Mac Mogachoirb Cheileas CLU
> Cun fearas CRU thar a ghaibh,
> Ail uas a Ligi — budh Liach —
> Baslaide CHLIATH thar Cliu Mail.

> Mocharb's son of Fiercest FAME
> Known his NAME for bloody toil,
> To his Gory Grave is GONE
> He who SHONE o'er Shouting Moyle.[31]

As already mentioned, in old Erin there were seven grades of *filidh* or
poet, the highest of whom bore the title of *Ollamh* or Doctor, whose
prestige was considerable and who was customarily assigned the status of
a *Rí Tuaithe* or petty king. For title *Ollamh* is given to several of the
contemporary poets in the *Book of the Dean of Lismore*. There is no
information whether a school of poetry existed in Scotland such as still
survived in Ireland. It is, however, interesting to find that in the late
seventeenth century Martin's description of how a poet composed lying
in the dark resembles the practice in the Irish poetic schools, where the
poets retired to 'a chamber deaf to noise and blind to light'. In earlier
times several orders of bard came below the *filidh*, but with the break-up
of the Gaelic polity they were now becoming merged both in Ireland and
Scotland. A Campbell genealogy written by Rev. Robert Duncansone in
the 1670s said that 'there were certain persons called Seanachies and
Bards who were antiquaries, and whose work it was from father to son
for many ages to keep ane account of the genealogies of great families,
and their actings, which ordinarily they did put in Irish ryme of a most
exquisit frame, of whose writings there is now little extant except some
fragments and traditions ....'[32]

From the *Book of the Dean* we know that in our period many poets
travelled about *air chuairt*, on circuit, entertained by munificent patrons,
though others belonged to and remained in the household of some chief.
Almost three hundred years later, Martin described the 'Orators' or

'Isdane', that is *Aos-dana*, the folk of songs, who kept the genealogies, made elegies and panegyrics, mingled socially with the chiefs and gentry and, becoming insolent and extortionate by the abuse of their power to satirise like the ancient *filidh* of Erin, lost their former profit and esteem and 'now are allowed but a small salary'.

Highly skilled the poets whose work is preserved in the *Book of the Dean of Lismore* certainly were; all but two pieces use the classical metres, and among the writers were people of position, including two Campbells, Duncan Campbell of Glen Orchy and Isabel, possibly a daughter of the Earl of Argyll. The art of the classical metres was not confined to the trained bards, and both in Ireland and in Scotland chiefs and nobels could turn their hand to composition, and one of the most famous composers was the fourteenth century Earl of Desmond, *Gearoid Iarla*. The House of Argyll was a patron of the ancient culture and probably skilled in the bardic arts in this period when it was beginning to inherit the pre-eminence of the Lords of the Isles; Finlay MacNab in his poem about the making of the *Duanaire* states that no poem lacking artistry should be taken to Mac Cailein to be read, suggesting that Argyll was a competent critic.

The great flowering of a less classical form of verse and an abundance of poets are suggested in the surviving sixteenth century manuscripts. But a more spontaneous and inspired verse, free of the rules of metrics which hedged in bardic literature, must have its roots deeper in the past than the documents of our period can show. The poems and love of lyrics of ordinary people must have a long history; from the later written tradition, we can infer a great fondness for prayers and chants and for the Ossianic literature of the Fenian Cycle, and the readiness by which the prose stories could be rendered in verse. We can also learn a little of it from traditions of the skill of extemporary versification possessed by everyday folk. There is an abundance of anecdotes of this power of ready versification. It is a well-known tradition that the Earl of Mar, wandering in the hills after the Battle of Inverlochy, met a woman herding cattle who gave him some meal and water which he mixed in the heel of his shoe. He then composed a couplet declaring that: *is math an cocair an t-acras* ..., hunger is a good cook and the barley crowdie in the heel of his shoe was the best food he had ever eaten. Mar then went on and hid in the house of a cottar who was later to claim recognition also in rhyme at the Castle of Kildrummy.[33] It will be remembered that this Earl of Mar was the natural son of Alexander Stewart, Wolf of Badenoch, which is an example of how Gaelic culture permeated all ranks of society, native and immigrant.

One of the few surviving anecdotes about the Lords of the Isles demonstrates the high regard for powers of extemporary versification.

MacDonald was walking, some say in Barra, some say in North Uist, when he saw a rough-looking black-haired lad sitting at the edge of a cornfield husking and eating the ears of grain as he basked in the sun and herded the cattle. Being a ready-witted poet, MacDonald said in verse; 'That raven there, you raven. Right well are you nibbling the ears of corn. It is my prayer to the King Above, that you will be without a claw and without a tooth.' To which the boy replied prompty, also in verse: 'If you are MacDonald, may the Lord recompense you. Where ever was heard a man of your kin satirising a boy over ears of corn.' The Lord of the Isles was delighted with the boy's ready wit; he took him under his care and the lad rose to high position. A later anecdote concerns Donald Gorm of Sleat; he was reputedly a resourceful poet and was an acknowledged expert on boat-building. He was invited to visit Barra to advise MacNeill about the building of a birlinn. For various reasons, he was dissatisfied with his reception and left, declining to discuss the design of the birlinn with his host. Just as he was about to embark, he gave MacNeill's boatbuilder a set of directions in verse: *Leagail bheag is togail bhog ...*, couched in deliberately ambiguous form and open to different interpretations. [34]

Although music and singing are often mentioned in the old stories, and this period was one of great musical development throughout Europe, there is little to tell us about actual Highland airs of this date. The elaborate metres of the period would be difficult to set to music that would appeal to the modern ear. Hugh MacDonald refers to the Lord of the Isles as patron of 'poets, bards and musicians', and this is probably an accurate reflection of the bardic hiearchy with the poet or *filidh* as the senior member, the bard acting as reciter to the *filidh* and the *luchd-theud*, the folk of strings, providing the accompaniment. The same heirarchy existed in Gaelic Ireland in this period; a Dublin apothecary, Thomas Smyth, in information submitted to the Privy Council in 1561, described the respective functions of the Rhymer or *Filidh*, the Reciter or *Racaire*, and the Harper:

> Now comes the Rymer that made the Ryme with his Rakry.
> The Rakry is he that shall utter the ryme; and the Rymer himself
> sitts by with the captain verie proudlie. He brings with him also
> his Harper, who playse all the while that the Raker sings the
> ryme.[35]

A Highland harp or clarsach is carved on a tombstone probably dating to the fifteenth century at Keills, Knapdale, and the resemblance between the detail on this and the surviving fifteenth or sixteenth century Queen Mary Harp in the National Museum of Antiquities of Scotland is particularly striking. It is said that the strings of the Highlanders' clarsachs were of brass wire and that they were played with the nails grown long or with a plectrum. The Highlanders were said to ornament their clarsachs with silver or precious stones or, if they could not afford this, with crystal. It was the favoured instrument of the Highlanders of the Middle Ages, and harps and harpers are constantly mentioned in stories, poems and contemporary documents. But Gerald of Wales, writing in the twelfth century, stated that the Highlander also played on two other instruments, the tympanum and the chorus. This last was probably a bagpipe in a simple form with chanter and blowstick only. The bagpipe was of course played all over Europe and there are many allusions to it in the Lowlands and in England. According to tradition, the Lord of the Isles had a piper, a member of a family of MacArthurs resident in Islay, but the references to the bagpipe and to pipers in the

Left: *Grave-slab in the ruined church of Keills, Knapdale, late fifteenth century, showing a* **clarsach** *remarkably similar to the Queen Mary Harp*

Right: *Highland harp or* **Clarsach**, *known as 'Queen Mary's Harp', decorated with designs of interlace, animals and geometric motifs, late fifteenth or early sixteenth century*

Highlands belong to later periods. It is significant that the period when the harp was flourishing was also the era of fighting by bodies of specially armed men, the kinsmen or associates of the founders of the emerging clans. It was to them that the *Brosnachadh* or Incitement to Battle was made by the *filidh*, probably accompanied by a harp. Neither the tones of the clarsach nor that of the human voice would carry impressively to large bodies of men in the open air, and with the development of the clans in the sixteenth and seventeenth centuries came the stimulus for a new type of music.

Among other surviving manuscripts there are medical works which belonged to the Beatons, the hereditary physicians to the Lords of the Isles, and the O'Conachers or MacConachers, a family of doctors in Lorn, who are mentioned in several documents. These works belong mostly to the fourteenth, fifteenth and sixteenth centuries and display great learning, quoting all the authorities well known to contemporary medical science such as Hippocrates, Euclid and Galen. In fact, Hippocrates the Greek physician is referred to as *iuchair gach uile eolais*, the key of all knowledge. Scientific works drew on other classical sources, especially Aristotle for example, and these were transmitted to the medieval west through the Jewish and Arabian thinkers of the tenth, eleventh and twelfth centuries such as Averroes and Avicenna. One of the foremost medical treatises was the *Lilium Medicinae* of Bernard Gordon, Professor of Physic at the University of Montpelier, the centre of medical studies in medieval Europe, a reputation it had won over from Salerno, the oldest of all universities and itself the meeting place of eastern and western Mediterranean civilisations. Published in 1305, the *Lilium Medicinae* was very soon afterwards translated into Gaelic and several copies of the translation exist. One of these, belonging to the Beaton medical family in Skye, was said to be worth sixty milch-cows, and so valuable that when the doctor crossed an arm of the sea the book was sent round by land. In the medical manuscripts, such matters as fevers, wounds, anatomy, heart disease and the properties of plants are discussed systematically. Charms are also frequently included and often sanctified by reference to saints or the Scriptures. But they also dealt with astronomy, astrology, philosophy and metaphysics; medicine and *materia medica* were not isolated disciplines but were intimately associated with the wider fields of reasoning, philosophy and the physical sciences. Until the fourteenth century, scholasticism reigned supreme, and those who sought to explain the universe and natural and human phenomena did so by reference to the main tenets of Christian faith. Thus, an early fifteenth century medical manuscript includes a Gaelic commentary on a Latin text of Isidore of Seville's glosses on the canons of Damascenus; though such a tract seems religious and theological, the manuscripts generally resort also to the practical, even recommending travel and continuous hard work as the most successful cure for infatuation.

Religious poetry and tracts and lives of the saints have been preserved in the manuscripts. The *Book of the Dean of Lismore* includes religious verse, and other manuscripts have poetry by different hands, often in the form of moral exhortation. The typical example might be the series of quatrains beginning:

A dhuine, cuimhnich am bas ...

'Man, be mindful of death ...

The lives of the early saints were favourite subjects for retelling and had of course been a well established aspect of Gaelic literature and religion since the eighth and ninth centuries. The manuscripts contain accounts of the lives of the Gaelic saints like St Patrick, St Colum Chille, St Ciarán, St Moling, and St Bride, and also of one or two of the saints of the early Christian Church of Egypt and Syria, the home of desert monasticism. They contain independent versions of familiar stories such as the one with an unexpected twist in the tail that it was Moses and not St Patrick who rid Ireland of snakes. Another favourite was the legend of St Philip the Apostle which was also given a particular slant not found in the standard canon of religious literature. In it, St Philip is sent to preach to the heathens of *Lochlann*, Scandinavia, the invaders of Ireland whose evangelisation followed centuries after that of the Gaelic peoples. The story also includes the motif of the 'Evernew Tongue'.[36]

Genealogy was treated as a serious subject in the Highlands. With the rise of the clans and with the decline of Norse power, there was a renewed closeness with Ireland, and a series of genealogies appeared in the fifteenth and sixteenth centuries, deriving nearly all the clans from early Irish sources. Although these genealogies cannot be reconciled into a general pattern, they do however seem to show a tendency towards a pan-Gaelic feeling, all too ineffective in practice, when so many clans, of course, notably the Mackays, Munros, MacKenzies and Campbells, bitterly opposed the Lordship, the bastion of Gaelic civilisation and the most likely focus of a pan-Gaelic movement. Genealogies, however, were put to some practical use in justifying an allegiance or making an alliance. For instance, there was the convenient tradition that the Irish wife of Angus Og brought in her train men of every surname among her father's followers, the *Tochradh nighean a'Chathanaich*. Among these were counted not only the ancestor of the Beatons but those of the Rosses, Munros, and Dingwalls, all three of whom had their own very different genealogies. This made a convenient pretext for claiming the loyalty of these families, who lived in the Earldom of Ross, which the Lords of the Isles subsequently acquired. In the case of consolidating the confederation of Clan Chattan, claims of a common ancestry were also stressed. In cementing friendship, the bond of a common ancestor was used. For instance, MacKinnons, MacNabs, MacQuarries and Grants all claimed kinship with the MacGregors, who themselves traced their descent from Alpin, father of Kenneth and the ancient kings of Scots, and they used the same badge, the *giuthas* or pine tree. All these clans had bonds of friendship or other associations with the MacGregors: after their proscription at the beginning of the seventeenth century, — among the punitive measures taken after the battle of Glen Fruin in 1603 — the Grants had to pay fines totalling 16,000 merks for sheltering MacGregors.

By the fifteenth century the ecclesiastical architecture of most European countries was developing national characteristics such as the Perpendicular style in England; but in Scotland no particular national style was evolved. Highland church building did not follow current styles as much as in the preceding period. A good example is the Abbey Church of Iona, where there has been so much reconstruction that the unity of the plan at the west end has been lost. Unlike the severely Norman features of the earlier parts of the building, the carvings of the capitals in the later parts, with their intertwined foliage and animals, are akin to that of the style of the West Highland tombstones and crosses. The few churches built within the period, such as Fortrose Cathedral and the Priory at Beauly, with their very long aisles, are individualistic in style. An extreme example is the Priory on Colonsay with slanting stone slabs instead of voussoirs over the windows. Castles built or occupied in the West Highlands continued to have the outer or curtain wall as the main defence, but with added emphasis upon an inner tower and a fortified gateway. But in the East Highlands a new style in castles was spreading, primarily built as large strong towers. A good example is the oldest section of Kilravock Castle near Nairn, built after 1460 under a licence granted by the Lord of the Isles during one of the expeditions to Inverness. In a few cases this style in castle building permeated to the west, as at Borve in Benbecula, attributed to Amie MacRuairidh, wife of John, Lord of the Isles, and Ardtornish in Morvern.

The small homes of the lesser folk of this period have not survived. But a fifteenth century poem in the *Book of the Dean of Lismore* gives a description, albeit a very rosy one, of the home of a lesser chief. It was written by Finlay the Red Bard in praise of the house of John MacGregor. The poet says that he has found the house of his choice, the house where the poets feasted. It was ablaze with wax candles and a banquet fit for kings was spread. The music of the harp and the ancient songs were to be heard there. The description of its construction is specially interesting. 'Thus did the masons leave aright the coupled house

Four-sided wooden mether or drinking cup of Irish and Highland medieval type

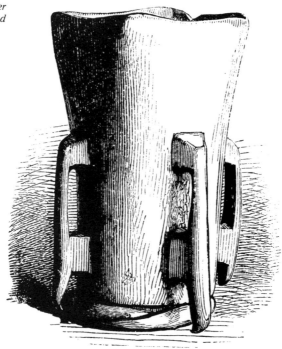

of MacGregor'. Down to times within living memory the traditional method of house-building in most parts of the Highlands was by setting the couples or pairs of wooden cabers upright in the foundations or lower courses of the walls and with their tops fastened together. This type of house was characteristic of the Central and Eastern Highlands and some were still being lived in at least as late as the 1930s.

Few valuables have survived from this period; the times that followed were too hard. The 'Dunvegan Cup', which bears the date 1493 and an inscription, is unique and is probably of Irish origin. It is richly ornamented with silver on wood and the square shape seems to have been typical. Examples of four-sided wooden cups survive, and in the old tales four-sided cups, *ceithir chearnaich,* are mentioned; Fionn is said to have had 'quadrangular cups', and such cups, beautifully made, were as magic vessels the objects of heroic quests.[37] Not only in story and tradition but also in sober fact we know that the Highlanders had valuables. In 1402, when Alasdair, younger brother of the Lord of the Isles, was absolved for burning and plundering Elgin, he presented a large gold torque to the Church and his leading men also made offerings of gold.[38] Silver gilt spoons of thirteenth century style and decoration were found hidden in the Nunnery on Iona, and gold finger rings and fillets ornamented with plates of gold such as were worn by women in the Middle Ages were found in the same place and also in Bute. Martin Martin's description of the older style of women's dress with finery and belts decorated with silver is strongly reminiscent of the few material remains. Such possessions certainly suggest prosperity.

Period IV

Sixteenth and early seventeenth centuries.
Linn nan Creach — the Age of Forays — and the emergence
of Highland characteristics out of political chaos

The history of Scotland during the sixteenth and early seventeenth centuries records momentous events, most notably the Reformation in the mid-sixteenth century and the Union of the Crowns in 1603. The Highlands were affected by these events as well as the Lowlands, although in some respects rather differently. The Union of the Crowns in 1603 put James VI into a stronger position from which to direct his policies for the Highlands that he had inaugurated after he had assumed power personally in 1587. For the Highlands, the main course of sixteenth century development continued until after the King's death.

It is difficult to summarise the tangled and often lurid history of the Highlands during this period, but three marked and constant features may be noted. Firstly, a fundamental change took place as the position of predominant power shifted from the Lord of the Isles to the House of Argyll. After its forfeiture Clan Donald still consisted of eight branches founded by the younger sons of successive heads of the family upon land held of them. There were ties of association with many vassals, including the MacLeods of Lewis. The significance of the elimination of these most important branches of Clan Donald and of the MacLeods of Lewis, and the acquisition of their land and much else beside by the Campbells and MacKenzies was far deeper than a change in the ownership of territories. The Lordship of the Isles had tended to be a separate Gaelic principality within Scotland, closely associated with Gaelic forces in Ireland. It had been a focus for Gaelic culture. Such patronage had encouraged the maintenance of a high standard in the distinctive arts of the Gael. On the other hand successive earls of Argyll now developed their expanding powers by a steady support of the *de facto* rulers of Scotland, especially during the recurrent eclipses of direct rule by the Crown. Comment is not necessary upon the methods by which the Campbells pursued their aims; what differentiated the period of their predominance from that of Clan Donald is the fact that, rich and powerful as Argyll and his kinsmen became after the end of the fifteenth century, they did less and less to support or encourage the arts of Gaeldom. The traditions of West Highland carving died out during this period and especially after the Reformation. Notable exceptions to the picture of decline are the MacLeod monuments in the early sixteenth century St Clement's Church

105

at Rodel, including especially the wall-tomb of Alasdair Crotach MacLeod, prepared for him in 1528. The family of MacMhuirich with its surviving tradition of literary service was supported by Clan Ranald, one of the branches of Clan Donald; and chiefs and leading men continued the old custom of giving hospitality to the poets and maintaining a family bard of their own. Poetry in Gaeldom, however, did not die: the innate genius of the people gave it a new force more spontaneous and more universal than was the work of the highly trained professional poets. *Piobaireachd*, that great development of the period in Highland music, was fostered by some of the leading families, most notably the MacLeods of Dunvegan.

The most important feature of our period was that the Highlands suffered even more than the Lowlands from the recurrent eclipses of the power of the Crown. Between the death of James IV at Flodden in 1513 and the assumption of full authority by James VI in 1587, there were thirty-three years when the sovereign was a minor, and three sovereigns (James V, Mary and James VI) succeeded as infants of a year old or less. There was always difficulty in re-establishing royal authority after these minorities, and all these reigns were troublous. After the forfeiture of the Lordship in 1493, James IV took great personal interest in his Highland subjects, making several expeditions to the Highlands and Islands in the

Survivals in a decadent style of West Highland grave-slab carvings in Appin and at Kilmichael, Kintyre

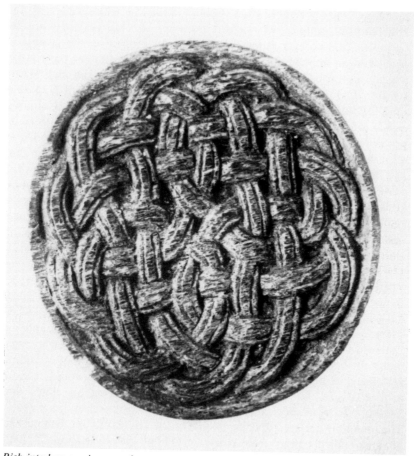

Rich interlace carving on a bone counter. Board games such as backgammon and chess were the popular diversions of the Gaelic warrior aristocracy and are frequently referred to in song and poetry

space of a few years; but his sudden revocation in March 1498 of the charters he had granted to the vassals of the forfeited Lord of the Isles, and his appointment of the Earl of Argyll as lieutenant over the old Lordship in 1500, with authority to let the lands, began the fatal policy of employing Argyll and also later Huntly as agents for the government. Although James V was a severe ruler, he, and later on, Mary of Guise, when she was Queen Regent, temporarily and partially checked the disastrous system.

A third outstanding feature of the period was that unfortunately, when James VI actually assumed personal rule at the age of twenty-one, a new element entered into the royal attitude. Desperately poor himself, the King was convinced that wealth could be extracted from the Highlands. Examples of wishful thinking at this juncture are an optimistic and roseate report by Sir Donald Monro on the Islands in 1549, and an anonymous account of the productiveness of the Islands which was probably drawn up for the King towards the end of the century. In 1597, when giving terms to Angus MacDonald of Dunyveg, the King stated that he wished to plant his lands in Islay, Jura, Colonsay and at Kilkerran (later Campbeltown), with 'burrow townis with civile people, religioun, and traffique of merchandice'. He constantly tried to raise the Crown rents of that considerable part of the old Lordship that had become Crown land. Argyll and his kinsmen Campbell of Cawdor were able to outbid the ancient proprietors in receiving grants of Kintyre after 1607 and Islay in 1614 in spite of last-minute counter-offers by Sir James MacDonald, at the time imprisoned in Edinburgh Castle. Perhaps basing his expectations on glowing reports prepared for him, the King granted commissions to gather the Crown rents referring to the Islands and their 'incredible fertilitie of cornis', as 'of auld, the maist constant and suire rent and patrimonie of the Croun'.[1] But Sir Alexander Hay of Newton, the Clerk Register, in a letter of 1614 'marvelled' at how much more highly the lands of the Western Isles were retoured or valued when compared with the payments by great men for lands in Fife and the Lothians.[2] The King exacted heavy compositions from chiefs who came under the ban of the law; and, with the deliberate intention of obtaining forfeitures of land in order to put it to what he imagined would be more profitable use, an act was passed in 1597 ordering all chiefs and landholders to produce their charters before the Lords of Exchequer. The preamble declared that the people of the Highlands and Islands had not only failed to pay their yearly rents, but that by reason of 'their barbarus inhumanitie' had made the fertile land and the rich fisheries unprofitable. But as the authorities knew, the Royal Burghs had a statutory right to a monopoly of the trade in herring, and this they guarded jealously in the face of constant evasion. It was in furtherance of these objectives of placing land at the disposal of the Crown and of protecting the fisheries that the terms of the 1597 act were framed. All chiefs and landholders who could not produce their charters and title-deeds and fulfil certain other conditions were to lose all claim to their lands. In those troubled times the difficulty of keeping charters was very great. For instance, in 1558, James MacDonald of Dunyveg obtained a new charter for his lands in Islay because all his 'ancient evidents, charters, precepts, instruments of sasine and other writs are burnt, destroyed and lost by war and other causes'. And we learn from family histories that Mackintosh, who had deposited his charters to the Lochaber lands with friends, 'suffered the penalty' until, through the good offices of the Clerk Register, the family was granted new titles. According to family traditions MacLean of Duart also lost some of his lands through failure to produce his charters. MacLeod of Dunvegan had great difficulty in saving most of his lands after forfeiture, although no direct action was taken against him. The most important action taken under the act was the forfeiture of the island of Lewis, owned by the *Sìol Torcuil* branch of the MacLeods. There followed the experiments of the 'Fife Adventurers', beginning in 1598. These are but examples and no return exists that might show the actual numbers of those who lost their lands or were seriously embarrassed by this legislation.

The Fife Adventurers were ten Lowland gentlemen of position including the Duke of Lennox, the King's young cousin and favourite. It was planned that they should develop the fisheries and other resources of the Island of Lewis and they were granted a lease of it for a term of years. They made a settlement at Stornoway in 1599, but the MacLeods, in spite of a family quarrel, captured it and the enterprise was given up.[4] A struggle for the possession of the Island developed between two families of the MacLeod *Sìol Torcuil* and the Adventurers. Kenneth MacKenzie of Kintail and later his brother Ruairidh, the Tutor of Kintail, intrigued with all three. Intervention by the State further provoked hostilities. In 1606, James VI induced two of the Fife Adventurers to resume their efforts to colonise the Island. Members of the MacLeod family succeeded in driving out successive Fife colonists, although neighbouring chiefs were prevented from assisting them in their resistance to invasion. One of the neighbouring chiefs, however — MacKenzie of Kintail — eventually gained possession of the Island by a mixture of force, intrigue, marriage and government support. Kenneth MacKenzie greatly improved his own position when he was made a permanent member of the Privy Council through which the King mainly conducted his dealings with the Highlands and Islands. At the same time, MacKenzie remained in close touch with one branch of the family of the MacLeods of Lewis. He then married the daughter and heiress of the last of the *Sìol Torcuil* claimants. Finally, after the ejection by force of the Adventurers, he received a Crown charter to Lewis in 1610 and exterminated the line of *Sìol Torcuil*. The whole episode abounds with deeds of violence and treachery from which neither the King and his agents, nor the MacKenzies, nor their victims the MacLeods of Lewis who were more sinned against than sinning, can be said to emerge with credit. MacKenzie received recognition for his work by being created Lord Kintail in 1609 and, having carried off the prize, his eldest son Colin was created Earl of Seaforth in 1623.

Another undertaking also inspired by the profit motive and mainly carried out by the Privy Council, spurred on by the King, was a concerted series of attempts to 'daunton' the island and west coast chiefs. In these attempts, for political reasons, there was a strong anti-Gaelic feeling. For instance, James VI, in his letter of 1608 to the Commissioners appointed for the improvement of the Isles, stated that he wished to remove the scandal of allowing part of Scotland to be possessed by 'suche wild savageis voide of Godis feare and our obedience'.[5] This tendency survived and even increased as the Gaelic language and culture became associated in the public mind with Jacobitism.

In August 1608 a powerful expedition was sent to the Islands and West Coast, and Andrew Stewart, Lord Ochiltree, and Andrew Knox, Bishop of the Isles, were given commissions to lead it. They had been supplied with terms to be offered to the local chiefs. These terms were not accepted at once, and the chiefs, who had been invited on board Ochiltree's ship in the Sound of Mull, were kidnapped. Under duress they promised submission, and they met with Bishop Knox as the King's Commissioner at Iona in 1609 and signed the 'Nine Statutes of Icolmkill' on the 23rd August. These statutes were reinforced by further agreements in 1616 and 1620. Some of the provisions such as the proscription of bards were not repeated and were inoperative. Others were amplified and enforced, and some were to have lasting effects. These included support for the reformed Church, attempts to reduce the landless population of the Highlands, such as the prohibition of 'sorning', that is the forcible exaction of hospitality, strict limitation of the import and consumption of wine and spirits, though home distilling of *aquavitae* was permitted, and the prohibition, subsequently modified, of the possession of firearms. The chiefs who subscribed to these agreements were subjected to a number of special enactments designed to reduce their position and individual way of life. The chiefs who subscribed the Statutes were Angus MacDonald of Dunyveg, Donald Gorm MacDonald of Sleat, Clan Ranald, the MacLean chiefs of Duart, Coll and Lochbuie, MacLeod, MacKinnon and MacQuarrie. By an order of the Privy Council, additional to the Statutes of Icolmkill, they were obliged to make a yearly appearance before the Privy Council. In a later agreement they were each obliged also to 'exhibit' a specified number of their leading men. The number of adherents in their households, their provision of wine and, in a later agreement, the number of their galleys were all specifically limited. They were to live in a 'comely dwelling' at a specified place and themselves cultivate a farm. Most important of all, under the Statues of Icolmkill, they were to send their eldest sons to be educated in the Lowlands, and this provision was extended to all their childen over nine years old. Other provisions bound them to assist the King's forces in action against rebels (who were of course often their allies or kinsmen). They were to charge a fixed rent for their land, and by a separate ordinance of 1617 the taking of *calps* was forbidden. This at least must have been a dead letter, as we know from documentary evidence, for calps were specified in Kintyre charters of 1670 and were being paid on Ulva at the time of Dr Johnson's and James Boswell's visit in 1773.[6] The chiefs were also forbidden to interfere with the Royal Burghs' monopoly of the herring industry. Terms constantly used such as 'gross ignorance', 'barbarous inhumanity' or 'incivilities' in these agreements which the chiefs had to sign were the stock-in-trade of the King and government and were most insulting.

The lesser people suffered severely. The marchings and counter-marchings in Islay and Kintyre for example in 1614-1615 and 1644-1647 caused considerable hardships, local destruction of crops, livestock and property, being exacerbated by disease and plague spread by armies on the move. The Earl of Argyll's own sinister comments after the Islay rebellion of 1615, 'I hoip now dayly to be busie in executionn....' and Sir Alexander Hay's allusion to the 'rebels of the Lewis' suggest that reprisals spared few.[7]

When Sir James MacDonald younger of Dunyveg was preparing to fly the country, his followers and the principal Islay tenants begged him to stay and die with them, for they had no hope of mercy from the Campbells. And there are traditions of the exposure of any of the inhabitants that were obnoxious to the Campbells on rocks covered by the sea at high tide, such as the story in the Manuscript History of Craignish of such treatment of Islay folk after the MacDonalds had been dispossessed. In 1625, through the oppression of his agent Donald Campbell, a natural son of Campbell of Cawdor, Argyll deliberately drove the MacIans to rebellion, exterminatedthe family of the chief, and secured Ardnamurchan for himself. After selling some of his other property in order to pay for the forcible occupation of Islay, Campbell of Cawdor sold that rich island to Campbell of Shawfield in 1726, as it had become unprofitable.[8] Andrew McKerral, in his *Kintyre in the Seventeenth Century*, has documented the plantation of the area, showing that it was a slower process and by no means as sweeping as earlier scholars had suggested. As the rolls of Kintyre tenantry of 1596 and 1605 showed, considered deterioration of land in the peninsula had taken place when Argyll received his charter to Kintyre and took possession. The failure of the burgh of Lochhead, later Campbeltown, founded about 1618, to develop rapidly and the ravages of war and pestilence in the years 1644-1647 must have greatly narrowed the horizons of Argyll's schemes. The Marquis brought lairds and scions of old families from Ayrshire and Renfrewshire after 1650 and also Campbells from other parts of Argyll and set lands to them, and a

Kintyre rental of 1678 shows that he had settled 139 Lowlanders and 103 Campbell tenants there, mainly in the parishes of Campbeltown and Southend, but 179 holdings were still left with old Kintyre stock.

Royal cupidity and that of the House of Argyll and the Campbell kinsmen were responsible for the persecution of the MacGregors. They were already in trouble in the fifteenth century, and after a series of outrages, repressive measures and reprisals were put in hand in which Argyll and his kinsman Campbell of Breadalbane benefited. The massacre of Glen Fruin in February 1603 put the MacGregors hopelessly in the wrong, and a series of acts of parliament forfeited their lands, proscribed their name, and inflicted other penalties. The most repellent failure was the strong profit motive shown in the proceedings of the King, Argyll, Breadalbane and their agents. Individuals were promised grants of lands for pursuing their MacGregor owners. Any help given to a member of the proscribed clan was made liable to a fine, and it was agreed that Argyll should pay the King £22.10s. out of every £100 of fines that he could collect for his offence. A vicious circle had become established, for the MacGregors, deprived of their land, had been forced to become predatory. Doubtless they also became scapegoats for other acts of violence, fire-raising and robbery but they were an obvious target for complainants before the Privy Council.[9] The MacIans of Ardnamurchan were also forced into piracy by the loss of their lands, after the conveyance of the superiority to the 4th Earl of Argyll by a MacIan heiress. The term 'broken men' became common currency in this period to describe those living by robbery and violence, and the records relating to the Highlands and also to the Borders abound with reference to 'notorious clans of robbers, broken men and sorners'. Specific and very oppressive legislation was introduced towards the end of the sixteenth century with the object of dealing with 'broken men'.

Already from the beginning of the period the disastrous system of entrusting supreme administrative and judicial powers to Argyll and Huntly as the most powerful magnates in the North deeply affected the social organisation of the Highlands. By means of their own feudal powers and constantly renewed commissions, of which Argyll himself received about twenty-five during the sixteenth century, still more flagrantly, the office of Justice General (the chief judge in criminal cases) was made hereditary in the Argyll family from 1514 to 1633. They acted as judges in cases in which their own interests and those of their adherents were involved; and they acted as executioners of sentences against their personal enemies and opponents and were the recipients of the forfeited lands and goods. In all too many cases they acted as *agents provocateurs*, and owing to some of the ups and downs of politics but occasionally to the success of their victims in exposing them, both Huntly and Argyll had their wings clipped from time to time. Alexander MacDonald of Dunyveg's letter to the Lords of Council in 1531 blamed the Earl of Argyll and his brothers for the troubles in the Islands. He described Argyll's 'verray proven malice and invy' and the government, becoming suspicious of the Campbells' activities and motives, revoked Argyll's commission and imprisoned him, though only for a short period. But they were almost always able to get their commissions renewed. They were useful agents for doing what the ineffective central authority could not do, and Argyll, in offering to collect the rents of Crown lands in the Western Isles, could claim that he and his friends 'hes als gret experience in the danting of the Ilis', when asking for another commission of lieutenancy. In 1607, having received Kintyre, he wrote to the King offering to hold Clan Donald and the Western Isles in check. Clan Donald, he said, was the strongest pillar of all the broken Highland men who never in any age were civil but had been the schoolmasters and fosterers of all barbarity, savageness and cruelty. In return for procuring their utter suppression, he asked for a charter for Islay, Jura, Colonsay and other islands.[10] In the early seventeenth century MacKenzie of Kintail, especially in connection with the Island of Lewis, was able to assume the same profitable office and a trio of magnates was thus formed.

There was, however, a considerable difference between the interests and rewards of these magnates. Huntly, with large estates in the east, obtained a great extension of his feudal superiority over the upper valley of the Spey and across to Lochaber in the mid sixteenth century. He disrupted the affairs of clans within his superiorities. His illegal execution of Mackintosh in 1550 is a well known example; but he did not expropriate. Argyll, on the other hand, continuously extended his own mainland and island possessions. When the heritable jurisdictions and ward-holding were abolished after the '45, Argyll's share of the compensation paid was £25,000 and Huntly's was £22,000, including compensation on his great Lowland fiefs, out of a total of £86,000 paid to the six feudatories in the North.

Information does not survive of the total of the sufferings inflicted on the country people by such grants, but a court held in Kintyre in November 1596 enrolled the names of all the tenants and rent-paying merklands in North and South Kintyre, including both occupied and unoccupied lands. Out of 344 merklands, 81½ were lying waste. Nine years later, in September 1605, a similiar court was held and its records show that the waste merklands in North and South Kintyre had increased to 113. These courts were convened respectively by Sir William Stewart of Houston, Commendator of Pittenweem, and David Murray, Lord Scone, the Comptroller, both with the King's commission and more impartial judges than Argyll and his kin. The obvious evils of the system are well put by Sir Alexander Hay, writing in December 1615, when he said: 'By many it is thought that if goode will did secunde the dewtye which they (Argyll and others with commissions in the Islands) are bounde to do, thir frequent Island imployments wold not occur so often.... for when thir imployments ar so profitable in present pay and a preparation for making suite at court for service done, how easie a matter it is to have some of these unhallowed people, with that unchristiane language, readye to furnish fresh work for the tinker, and the matter so carryed as that it is impossible to deprehend the plotte'.[11]

It was of course owing to the weakness of the government that such agents were employed to administer the Highlands. It was an abuse of the feudal system now grown decadent, by which Crown and government would find themselves ignoring or condoning illegal acts and outrages, or standing by while the great men and their followers feuded. In the North, the Earl of Sutherland was entrusted with the administration of law and order. It was in the feudal tradition that the main cause of unrest there was the rivalry between the noble houses of Sutherland and Caithness. Their struggles form the main theme of Sir Robert Gordon's *Genealogical History of the Earldom of Sutherland*. In his own words, 'sparks of rancour between Sutherland and Caithness constantly burst into flame'; and all the local clans were involved on one side or the other. Atholl and Moray were sometimes also employed as the royal agents in the Highlands, but owing to broken successions and other difficulties, neither of them achieved the same position as Argyll and Huntly. Especially during the second half of the period the MacKenzies of Kintail greatly increased their feudal position on the mainland of Ross, including the fertile lands of the East Coast and finally over the Island of Lewis. It must be remembered that it was largely by means of Highland followings that these agents for the Crown were able to exercise their powers. Huntly and Argyll especially did so by their feudal superiorities. This sometimes involved the lesser people in difficulties. A dramatic instance occurred when Queen Mary came to Inverness in 1562, during her campaign against George, 4th Earl of Huntly, and the Gordons. The Gordon vassals in Badenoch were called out to oppose her, but the young chief, Lachlan Mackintosh, who had joined the Queen in Inverness, hurried off and intercepted his Badenoch clansmen at a ford of the river Nairn and brought them to the Queen in spite of the 'raging' of Huntly's son.[12] Members of Clan Gunn lived on the lands of Moray, Sutherland and Caithness, but they refused to follow their respective superiors against each other, preferring to follow their own chief, who was a vassal of Sutherland, in war.

It takes some imagination to visualise a condition of society so completely at the mercy of the law of the jungle as were the Highlands in the sixteenth century. The laws of the land and their administration were ineffective. After the forfeiture of the Lordship, James IV reorganised the system of justice ayres, justices and sheriffs in 1504. Parliament at that time considered that 'thair hes bene greit abusioun of Justice in the north partis and west partis of the realme sic as the north Ilis and south Ilis. And therethrough, the pepill ar almaist gane wild'. The Hebrides to the north were to be served by a justice and sheriff at Inverness or Dingwall (a functionary far removed from the sources of disturbance) and the islands to the south by a justice and sheriff at Tarbert or Campbeltown; new sheriffs were also to be established in Ross and Caithness. But the gifts of lieutenancy and the legal rights of the great feudatories wrecked the legislative system. The term 'that the King's writ did not run' could be applied to many parts of the Highlands. Deeds of violence and unbridled wickedness by groups or individuals abounded, as the records of the Privy Council and clan tradition show. There are many examples; *Gilleasbuig Dubh* of Sleat, a notorious ruffian, murdered two of his brothers but was eventually recognised as Baillie of the extensive district of Trotternish in 1510. He himself was later killed by his brother's sons. The Glengarry MacDonalds burned the Church of Kilchrist in Easter Ross in 1603 with the congregation inside, an act which was celebrated in the clan piobaireachd, *Cill Chriosd* or Glengarry's March. A similar exploit was perpetrated by the MacDonalds who burnt Trumpan Church in the course of a feud with the MacLeods; the latter had already suffocated the population of Eigg in reprisal for yet earlier outrages, by building a fire in the mouth of a cave in which the islanders had taken refuge.

Punishment in such cases was usually inflicted by a grant of 'Letters of Fire and Sword' to the aggrieved party who was then entitled to execute the penalty, always provided that he was sufficiently powerful to do so. As an example of the circumstances and spirit of such a commission, the Earl of Moray had chosen a time when the chief of the Mackintoshes was a minor and had granted some lands which had long been occupied by Mackintoshes to an Ogilvie, and the Mackintoshes had savagely raided them. A proclamation was sent in the name of the Crown in 1528 to the sheriffdoms of the north east and to leading noble families, and all the freeholders, barons, captains of clans and gentlemen within their bounds, ordering them to proceed against Clan Chattan and, according to the usual formula in such cases, 'invaid thame to thair uter destructioun, be slauchtir, byrning, drowning and uther wayis', with the additional proviso to 'leif na creatur levand of that clann, except preistis, wemen and bairns'. The execution of the order was mainly entrusted to the Earl of Moray, the aggrieved party. Although he apprehended and executed a number of clansmen, the Mackintoshes eventually were able to resume occupation of the land.[14]

The Laird of Grant and his tenants were powerless to obtain redress for the ravaging of Urquhart and Glenmoriston in 1513 by Donald, son of Alexander MacDonald of Lochalsh, and in 1544-5 by Glengarry and Lochiel as allies of Clan Ranald. The latter were summoned by open proclamation at the cross of Inverness in August 1546 because it was understood by the Lords of the Council 'that thair is na sure passage to the dwelling-places nor personall presens of the saidis personis'. A fine of £10,770 Scots was imposed in their absence, which they made no effort to pay, and their lands were declared forfeit to Grant, who did not make the vain attempt of taking possession, and eventually, in 1600, he returned them to their *de facto* owners.[15]

It is a point of importance, in considering the organisation of the clans, to remember that they were generally able by force to retain possession of their lands; even the MacGregors managed to remain in occupation of some of their lands as lesser holders. Glengarry, MacLeod of Raasay, Lochiel, Keppoch and others continued to hold their lands by force of arms against the wishes of those with a formal title to them. In describing the islands of Raasay and Rona, Donald Monro in his report of 1549 commented that they were occupied by *Mac Ghille Chaluim,* MacLeod of Raasay, and held by the sword, but belonged to the Bishop of the Isles in heritage. The later report prepared for James VI made the same point. Lesser folks could also make the occupation of lands too dangerous and unprofitable for anyone else. In Sutherland about the year 1604, a certain *Aonghas MacCoinnich MhicAlasdair*, who had been dispossessed of the lands of Ardinch because he refused to pay an increase of rent, killed his cousin, his cousin's wife and their two sons to whom the lands had been given. When the owners tried to eject him, his rage 'went so far that he killed nyne persons, one after another, who interprysed to possess that land'. The owner then sold it to a more powerful neighbour, the Grays of Skibo, but a long feud followed before they gained possession of it. The said Aonghas killed the new tenant and took refuge in Strathnaver from where he harried the Grays and their property until he was himself killed by them.[16]

It was a cardinal weakness of the Highlanders that they never were fully united in a general Gaelic movement. Their martial activities were dissipated. Argyll, Huntly and Atholl owed much of their strength in manpower to their Highland superiorities. In Ireland, especially in the period of the Tudor reconquest in the sixteenth century, the Highlanders played an important part in the complicated politics of their neighbour across the water, with a considerable reputation as professional soldiers, the *gall-òglaigh*, anglicised as 'gallowglasses'. They were men of substance and traditionally heavily armed, and they could command a high price in war. They fought the English who were trying to impose direct rule on Ireland beyond 'the Pale'; they were recruited by Irish noble houses, such as the O'Neills and the O'Donnells, in their wars amongst themselves; they were also recruited by the English administration to resist the campaigns of the Irish; and they were recruited by their own folk, especially of Clan Donald, who had substantial interests to protect and foster in Antrim. In their turn, the Irish were recruited by the English to eject the Highlanders from Ireland as their numbers grew to disturbing proportion.

The tie with the old Lordship of the Isles persisted and its old vassals showed an enduring faithfulness to it. There were five or more serious attempts to restore the Lordship or to repossess the Earldom of Ross. During the lifetime of John, the last forfeited Lord, his son Angus Og led an expedition that won a resounding victory in Easter Ross and that occupied Inverness. He was assassinated about 1489 or 1490. John's grandson, Donald Dubh, made his first attempt — an abortive one — in 1501, having been liberated from prison in Argyll, as the chronicler described, 'by a Fenian exploit'. This was followed by an expedition into Ross in 1513 by Donald MacDonald of Lochalsh, a collateral who proclaimed himself Lord of the Isles, but he angered his followers and was killed in 1519, and the rising collapsed. In 1539 the head of another collateral branch, Donald Gorm of Sleat, made another attempt to seize Ross, but was killed while attacking Eilean Donan. About 1543, Donald Dubh, who had again been imprisoned, made his second attempt. The time was favourable, for Henry VIII was threatening Scotland and Donald Dubh acted in association with Matthew, Earl of Lennox, and the pro-English party in Scotland. Donald Dubh moved his supporters to Ireland, and assuming the style of Lord of the Isles and Earl of Ross, and with the support of the barons and Council of the Isles in July 1545 appointed a commission to treat with the King of England. The commission was signed by seventeen leading supporters. Donald Dubh's force was estimated at 4,000 picked men with 180 galleys, and in addition to this a force was left to protect the islands from attacks by Huntly and Argyll. But Donald Dubh fell ill and died in Ireland, his followers quarrelled over the allocation of the pensions and money which the King of England had granted them, and gradually all the leaders made their peace with the government. The direct line of the Lords of the Isles was now extinct. Nevertheless there was a last, less formidable rising in 1615.

All but the last of these risings were supported by almost all the branches of Clan Donald, with the notable exception of the MacIans of

Ardnamurchan. All the old vassals of the Lordship supported more than one of the risings, and the MacLeans and MacLeods of Lewis were consistently loyal. Otherwise Highlanders not only failed to coalesce but fought among themselves. Existing feuds, such as that between MacDonald of Sleat and MacLeod of Dunvegan, and between the Mackays and the Gunns, still flourished. Many became intensified or sprang up for the first time. The Campbells were at enmity with those of their neighbours who could show fight. MacKenzie of Kintail fought with the MacDonalds of Lochalsh, Glengarry and Clan Ranald. MacLean of Duart had a quarrel with the MacLeans of Coll and Lochbuie. He waged a war of extermination against MacDuffie of Colonsay. He had differences with MacDonald of Sleat, but his foremost feud was with MacDonald of Dunyveg, a feud which involved a number of other clans that supported these two powerful protagonists. MacIan of Ardnamurchan met with severe retribution for his murder of his distant kinsman, Alexander MacDonald of Lochalsh. Claims to Lochaber were the cause of a tangle of feuds; Mackintosh was vainly trying to enforce his parchment rights against Lochiel and Keppoch and two branches of MacLeans had conflicting claims there, while Huntly and Argyll struggled for the superiority. In the North, the Mackays, the Gunns, the Rosses and the Murrays had their own differences that were exacerbated in the intermittent struggle between the Earls of Sutherland and Caithness. These feuds were generally for the possession of land, but trifling incidents could make them flare up.

As a result of the state of almost constant warfare, the Highlands became covered by a network of offensive and defensive agreements. The great superiors bound their vassals to give them armed support when required by bonds of manrent. In return they granted bonds of maintenance, binding themselves to give them protection. The position was complicated by the fact that such bonds were often given to rival magnates, to Huntly and to his principal rival Moray or to Huntly and Argyll. At other levels, powerful chiefs and superiors also received bonds of manrent from small dependent septs and families: for instance, in 1590, the 'native men of Craignish', local families such as MacIosaig, MacMhuirich, MacCaluim and others, gave their bonds of manrent and *calps* to Ronald Campbell *MacIain MhicDhomhnuill*, Campbell of Craignish, who gave obligations of maintenance in return. A number of such agreements made in the course of the sixteenth century by Sir Duncan Campbell of Glenorchy were engrossed in a register showing how a chief could protect his interests by contracts of manrent and maintenance. As well as the obligation to serve in hosting and hunting and to ride and go in their lord's affairs, the lesser families undertook also to pay *calp of ceann-cinnidh*, that is the choice of animals claimed from tenants on decease by superiors.[17] This was roughly equivalent to the heriot of Lowland custom but had also come to be regarded as gifts due to chiefs or superiors from tenants in return for support and protection. Agreements were also entered into between different clans. Sometimes they emphasised a real relationship, such as that between the Mackintoshes and the Farquharsons, and sometimes a traditional one, as between the MacGregors and the MacQuarries. In this situation, any incident in the Highlands, however localised, was apt to set most of the north ablaze.

It is important to realise the chaotic condition of the country, because it explains how essential it was for a Highlander to belong to a strong organisation. A chief was essential to the maintenance of his clansmen. In the next century, the MacGregors were almost unique in managing to continue to exist without either a permanent chief or the possession of land. In such a society the clan was dependent upon its chief both as a leader and the holder of the title to land. Generally, when the family of the chief was exterminated, the clan broke up. This was so in the case of the MacLeods of Lewis, the MacIans of Ardnamurchan, the MacDuffies of Colonsay and the MacDonalds of Lochalsh and Islay. Bishop John Lesley, writing of Clan Mackintosh about the middle of the sixteenth century, said that their custom 'as of many others in the Irish country, has been at all times to acknowledge one principal for their chief captain, to whom they are obedient in time of war and peace, for he is mediator between them and the prince. He defends them against the invasions of their enemies, their neighbours, and he causes minister justice to them all in the manner of the country, so that none should be suffered to make spoil or go in sorning, as they call it, or as vagabonds in the country'. In the case of a powerful clan the prestige of the chief was immense. The historian John Major, describing Argyll about 1518, said that the people swore by the hand of *Cailean Mór*, just as in old times the Egyptians had sworn by the health of Pharaoh. The Wardlaw Manuscript gives unrivalled pictures of the work of successive chiefs of Fraser in training, protecting, organising and leading their clansmen.

In this turbulent period it was, however, as the fighting leader and as the landholder that the chief was most essential. In the case of some fortunate clans, such as the Grants and the Frasers, he did so by means of Crown charters. But, even so, his rights to occupation would not have been of much avail if he could not have made good his rights by force of arms if necessary. In the case of Mackintosh, the only part of his lands that he held by a Crown charter at this time was in Lochaber, and he was not able even to obtain compensation for the violation of his rights there until well on in the seventeenth century. In this period he held most of his lands by feu or other tenure from two rival magnates, the Earls of

Huntly and Moray, and during the earlier part of the century also from the bishop of Moray. The position of Mackintosh and of his neighbour Grant illustrates the difficulty in generalising about the clans.

Grant's lands in Strathspey were erected into a regality, the form of tenure in old Scots law that gave a subject the most complete control of his landed possessions and their occupiers. Although he gave some feus, most of his cadets received wadsets, that is, conveyance of land in reversion to a creditor. On the other hand, most Mackintosh cadets held land in feus or other tenures not from Mackintosh but from one of his superiors. Clan Mackintosh had a far more chequered career than Clan Grant, yet Bishop Leslie in a passage we have already quoted pointed out the Mackintosh as an example of a clan's devotion to their chief. There were clans who occupied their lands because they were too powerful to be turned out. The Earl of Sutherland owned lands occupied by the Gunns, especially in Strathullie, but was obliged 'to court their Favour and Friendship'. Fraser of Farralin in Stratherrick had no property of his own and was a tenant of *MacShimidh* (Fraser of Lovat), but 'as a considerable tribe owned this Man for their Chieftan, he was always much caressed by Lovat'.[18]

To hold his land, the chief was dependent on a powerful following. He provided for those who suffered in raids and for the widows of the fallen. Additional manpower was often welcomed, and 'broken men', unfortunates who had lost their holdings and were therefore condemned to a predatory life, were settled on the land. A Privy Council Minute of 1602 records that Glengarry had received some broken men on his lands 'with all glaidness of hairt'.[19] In their need for defence, the clans were becoming consolidated. As was pointed in Period II, their founders did not come to an empty land. In some cases the older inhabitants kept their identity as dependent groups within the clan. More generally they were absorbed. In the case of the MacLeods, the family history in their *Bannatyne Manuscript* gives examples of both, especially of families living on their lands in Harris and Bernera. The Highland custom of using the patronymic rather than the surname made the process of assimilation easier.

By the sixteenth century, the process of absorption by successful clans of lesser kin was far advanced. In Lochaber, the MacMartins of Letterfinlay, the MacSorlies of Glen Nevis and the MacGillonies of Strone, who had all formerly been associated with Clan Chattan, were forced by different means to take the name of Cameron, especially during the vigorous chieftanship of Allan Cameron of the Forays, *Ailean nan Creach*, in the reign of James III. The adoption of the land-holding chief's surname by old inhabitants was a common practice. The Lairds of Grant had extended their lands in Strathspey by canny but peaceful means during the sixteenth century, and it seems to have become usual for the local population to call themselves Grants or take the name of Grant. As an instance of this, a document of 1537 refers to a 'John McConquhy, in Garthrynbeg', and in a writ endorsed on the same document in 1581, this man's son describes himself as 'Duncane Grant in Gartinbeg, sone and air to umquhill John Makconachie Grant in Gartinbeg'. Here the name of Grant has been adopted as a surname in addition to the patronymic *MacDhonnchaidh*.[20] Fraser of Lovat had only established himself in the North at the end of the fourteenth century, yet two hundred years later the Frasers could be numbered at between eight and nine hundred men. Within Clan Chattan, many of the Davidsons or *Clan Daibhidh* whose fortunes were waning adopted the name of the more successful Macphersons. The condition of the Highlands and the extreme need to maintain as large a following as possible led, as can be shown, to great changes in the cultural life of the Highlands and affected the distribution of land.

It must be stressed that the Highlands developed a unique and characteristic institution out of a relationship that arose through bitter necessity. The bond between chief and clansmen could be one of a selfless devotion that shines through the darker episodes of the history of the Highlands. In telling of the way in which the hard-pressed followers of MacLeod of Lewis rallied again and again to Norman, the rightful chief, the writer of the early seventeenth century manuscript 'The Ewill Troubles of the Lewes' wrote: 'for all these Ilanders and lykewise the Hylanders ar by nature most bent and pron to adventur themselves, their lives and all they have for their masters and chiefes yea beyond any other people'. Even at the end of the seventeenth century it was customary for clansmen to pray for their chief when they said grace.

By the sixteenth century the extreme desirability of holding land by a legal title — charter, feu or lease — ensured that succession was by the legal heir. It is noteworthy that, although the welfare of the clan so largely depended upon the abilities of the chief, instances of his removal by the clan are extremely rare. One of the few examples was by the MacDonalds of Clan Ranald. It is worth telling as an illustration of the complications of Highland administration. The clansmen had disposed of an unpopular chief, Dougal, and had accepted as his successor Alexander or *Alasdair* who was his uncle, although Dougal's own two sons were his legal heirs but were then young. On Alexander's death about 1530, he was succeeded by his own illegitimate son, *Iain Mùideartach*, John of Moidart, who was able to obtain Crown confirmation for his lands. Unfortunately when, in 1540, James V made his ambitious voyage round Scotland and summoned the local chiefs to meet him, John of Moidart was, with several others, carried off to imprisonment. This was the opportunity for the legitimate claimants to the Clan Ranald inheritance to come forward. Apart from the two sons of the murdered chief Dougal, his grandfather had had a son by a second marriage late in life to a daughter of Fraser of Lovat. The Frasers who enjoyed the favour of the King began to intrigue on behalf of their kinsman Ranald *Gallda* or 'stranger', so-called because he had been brought up with his mother's people far away from Moidart. John of Moidart's title to the lands was revoked, and Lovat installed Ranald by a show of force. In a reversion of policy, the authorities released John of Moidart and other prisoners. The clan accepted him as leader, and Ranald was forced to flee. A prolonged struggle followed, in which Fraser of Lovat, with the valuable support of Huntly, who was responsible as Lieutenant of the North, and with the clans who were his feudatories, backed by the authorisation of the Queen Regent, tried to replace Ranald *Gallda*. But John of Moidart and the clan in their difficult, hilly country, resisted and were able to defeat the Frasers in July 1544 at the bloody battle of *Blàr na Lèine* at the head of Loch Lochy. John of Moidart finally received recognition of his right to the possession of his lands and transmitted them to his sons. His official designation was, however, changed from Chief to Captain of Clan Ranald, the customary designation in Lowland Scots for the leader of a clan who was not the legal heir in the direct line.[21]

When an heiress succeeded, the conflict between feudal law and the wishes and needs of the clansmen often became acute. The successful consolidation of Clan Donald under the Lords of the Isles in an earlier period was due to the failure in the male succession in the MacRuairidh family and the marriage in 1337 of the heiress with John, the head of the other branch of the family. So fortunate an arrangement was unusual. There was the risk that by the exercise of his feudal right a superior might endanger the clan in arranging the marriage of the heiress. Several cases of this occurred during the sixteenth century. A glaring example was the loss of Ardnamurchan by the MacIans to the Campbells. Another was the marriage of the Cawdor heiress to Argyll's younger son and the family of Campbell of Cawdor was thus founded. In the case of the MacLeods, the heiress became one of 'the Queen's Maries'. During her minority there was great discontent in the clan due to the claims of a cousin to the chieftainship. She was married to a Campbell but her uncle, the male heir, was able to compensate her husband and obtain recognition as chief and owner of the estates.[22] In the case of the succession of a minor, a male relative was chosen to act as 'captain' and generally, although not invariably, he loyally surrendered his trust when the heir had attained manhood.

The financial arrangement for maintaining the chief probably varied considerably. If he held land by charter or lease, he let or sub-let his lands and received rents in money and kind; but even in the seventeenth century some chiefs were receiving the old Gaelic due of the *calp*, the gift of the tenant's best beast at his death or when called upon to meet some special needs of the superior. For the payment of another old due, that of the 'cuddich' or *cuid oidhche*, there is much evidence still in the sixteenth century. This was, literally, a night-portion, or a night's lodging or entertainment due from the tenant to his superior, or the equivalent of this in value. The late sixteenth century description of the Islands prepared for James VI refers to the payment of cuddichs in most of the islands; among the dues paid by the people of Lewis was 'their Cuidichies, that is, feisting thair master quhen he pleases to cum in the cuntrie, ilk ane thair nicht or two nichtis about', which takes us right back to the heroic period of Gaelic Scotland and Ireland.[23]

Already in the previous period, the powerful Lords of the Isles had experienced the problem of finding land with which to provide for successive generations of younger sons and useful adherents. With the increased need for manpower in the sixteenth century, this was a difficulty that beset nearly all the Highland chiefs. The alternative solutions were to acquire new land, to reduce or, less often, to dispossess people living on their own land, or to denude themselves of their own patrimony. The need for more land was at the root of nearly all the enduring feuds. It was the good fortune of supporters of crown and government, such as, conspicuously, the Campbells and the MacKenzies, that they received a great many forfeitures and so were able to deal with this problem. The internal histories of most clans tend to be obscure, but that of the MacLeods of Dunvegan illustrates how, as the closeness of relationship with the reigning chief diminished, older collaterals lost their status, position and holdings. Sir William Fraser, in his *Chiefs of Grant* , shows how provision for his family varied according to the amount of land an individual Laird of Grant was able to acquire.

Three other developments may be noted. The increase in the holding of land by the tenure of the feu was coming into extended use and gave security of succession to many chiefs, and it became even more general in the seventeenth century.

Another very significant change was in the form of the clan traditions and genealogies, a matter of far greater importance to the clansman of those days than to the modern Highlander. The legislation requiring the production of charters affected the Highland consciousness very deeply. By the end of the seventeenth century a spate of new manuscript histories had appeared, among them those of the MacKenzies, Campbells, Camerons and Grants, in which descent was generally claimed from a distinguished Norman or other foreigner who is sometimes supposed to have married an heiress of the old Gaelic line, thus combining all possible advantages, and in all of which early and sometimes spurious charters are more or less circumstantially described. William Buchanan of Auchmar, writing in 1723, warned against 'the fondness of people's having the origin of their most famous men screwed up to as great a pitch of antiquity as possible, yea, sometimes above measure'. By this time some of the heat had gone out of the situation which had forced families to prove their claim to titles to land. But fashion in this continued to play a significant part. Earlier Gaelic manuscripts of genealogies which have survived traced the descent of the leading families from men of the Dalriadic past in Ireland and Scotland or from Fenian heroes. Diarmaid O'Duibne, one of the eponymous ancestors of the Campbells, for example, was a companion of Fionn, and the MacKenzies had traced their descent from an historical sixth century king of Dalriada. The move away from a Gaelic past bred some efficient propagandists such as John Pinkerton (1758-1826), who demonstrated a Norman ancestry for the Campbells and whose antipathy to the Gaels fired into activity William Forbes Skene, the first effective apologist of the modern era for the Gaelic and Pictish cause.

Most clans had their ups and downs during this troubled period and that which followed, but it is noticeable how much better those of the Central and Eastern Highlands fared than those of the West and the Islands. The MacDonalds of Lochalsh (1519) and of Kintyre and Islay (1614) were eliminated and so were the MacIans of Ardnamurchan (1629), the MacDuffies (1620) and the MacLeods of Lewis (1610). MacLean of Duart was one of the most powerful clans in the west during most of the seventeenth century, yet in the next century he was to lose the greater part of his land. Under great pressures the Camerons, the MacDonalds of Moidart, Glengarry and Keppoch, and the MacLeans of Ardgour, although they managed to continue to exist, suffered severely. But many of the clans of the east consolidated their position. The Laird of Grant secured possession of Glen Urquhart as well as consolidating his position in Strathspey.

Although Mackintosh endured times of danger in the seventeenth century, he was able to secure the lands of Dunachton in Badenoch and to force the Earl of Moray after 1624 to leave him in possession of Petty of which the Mackintoshes had long been in occupation. Further north, the Frasers were flourishing, and in the extreme north the Mackays and some other clans were also improving their position. The most notable change in the fortunes of a clan was in that of the MacKenzies. MacKenzie had held land in Kintail, but during the time of the Lordship he obtained a footing in central Ross. He took a leading part in supporting the government against the efforts of members of Clan

Donald to regain the Earldom of Ross, and received charters for forfeited lands in Wester Ross and for the more valuable lands in Easter Ross. After the Reformation the family acquired the former lands in the Black Isle and round the Cromarty Firth which had belonged to the Church. MacKenzie also obtained royal confirmation for lands he secured from MacDonald of Lochalsh and Glengarry. By 1544 he was sufficiently powerful to act independently and to refuse to obey a summons to serve under Huntly, acting as Lieutenant of the North. Later on, by doubtful means, he was able to buy Lewis and other lands from the Fife Adventurers in 1610, and to oust the descendants of MacLeod of Lewis finally from their lands, even though in the preceding years he had used them when possible to discomfit the Lowland incomers who represented a threat to own his schemes to obtain Lewis.[24] Eventually he secured a royal confirmation for his new possessions, having been created Lord MacKenzie of Kintail in 1609. His eldest son Colin was created Earl of Seaforth in 1623. The twenty-five or so clans mentioned by Duncan Forbes, Lord President of the Court of Session, in his estimate of Highland manpower before the 1745 Rising were all well established by the sixteenth century. It was a sign of the growing power of the chiefs, although a most inconvenient one for them, that the government was obliged more and more to use them in its efforts to enforce law and order. The earliest instance was an act of council of 1496, ordering that in the case of civil action against the islanders, of which many were pending at the time, the chief of every clan should be made responsible for the due execution of summonses and other writs against members of his own clan, under the penalty of being made liable himself to the party bringing the action. Ninety years later, in 1587, when the young James VI was beginning to assume personal power, an act of parliament was passed making it incumbent on all landlords to find sureties for the behaviour of their vassals, and a second act, applying to chiefs and captains of all clans, required them to find sureties for sums proportionate to their wealth and the number of their vassals and clansmen, for the peaceable and orderly behaviour of those under them, and making them liable for repairing any injuries committed by their followers and also making them liable to being fined for such offences.[25] The proceedings of the Privy Council show that the signing of an undertaking to observe the provisons of this act was continued far into the next century.

By the sixteenth century Europe had developed a considerable dress sense. In medieval times formal wear for clergy and laity had largely consisted of gowns or robes. By Tudor times a very masculine style had developed for men and an equally distinctive feminine style for women. People had obviously developed a dress sense. It is not surprising that about this time we begin to hear more about the clothes worn by the Highlanders. There had been portrayals of the dress of warriors and ecclesiastics upon the West Highland tombstones, but they portrayed the formal dress of the period. About the only hint about the dress of the people is that they went bare-legged; Magnus Barelegs of course was said to have acquired his nickname because he had adopted Hebridean dress. The Anglo-Norman knights at the Battle of the Standard scorned 'the worthless Scot with half-bare buttocks' of the twelfth century. John of Fordoun merely remarked that the Highlanders' peculiar dress much disfigured them. In the sixteenth century, they were becoming known as *Redshanks*, a term most commonly heard applied to the Highland mercenary forces in Ireland. In his letter to Henry VIII in 1543, John Elder, a Caithness man, boasts of it. He says that they were able to endure all the rigours of the weather, 'goynge alwaies bair leggide and bair footide' in both summer and winter, and that therefore 'the tendir delicatt gentillmen of Scotland call us Reddshankes.'[26]

With the bare legs went a cloak or a plaid. Blind Harry the Minstrel describes Sir William Wallace in one episode as wearing 'ane Ersche Mantill', and according to tradition, Bruce lost a plaid as well as a brooch to MacDougall's men in 1306. The fight on the North Inch of Perth in 1396 was evidently fought in the national undress; John Major said that the antagonists fought 'naked but for a plaid'. James III granted a charter to Argyll for certain lands in Lorn on payment of *unam clameden, nomine albe firme*, that is, the lands were being held in blench ferm or for the nominal annual render of a *chlamys*, the later Latin word for a cloak, or, in the Highland context, a plaid. A charter of 1596 is more explicit; Sir Duncan Campbell of Glenorchy granted one of his sons, John Campbell, some lands on payment of £10 Scots, a gallon of sufficient aquavitae 'et optimam clamidem coloratam vulgo ane fyne hewd brakane', here using the Gaelic word for plaid, *breacan*.[27] By the sixteenth century, the making of plaids in the Highlands was a considerable rural industry, for the burgesses of the Royal Burgh of Inverness were constantly trying to punish people for infringing their monopoly of dealing in them. In the sixteenth-century inventories of Inverness burgesses 'Highland hose', tartan plaids and Highland trews were often included. In an exchange of gifts between Hugh O'Neill, Earl of Tyrone, and Angus MacDonald of Islay in 1596, the Irish gifts were horses 'seven of the best horses in the country', the Highland gifts to the Earl, 'plaids and sculls', that is, iron skull-caps.

H F McClintock in his *Old Irish and Highland Dress* quotes nine contemporary descriptions of Highland dress in the sixteenth and seventeenth centuries. All but one of these descriptions mentioned the linen shirt; generally yellow is the colour specified, though its shape varied. Most of them also mentioned the plaid and generally described it as checked. More than half of the descriptions allude to the custom of going bare-legged. In two, a short jacket is mentioned, and two descriptions allude to trews. What seems to have happened is that with the decline of the methods of fighting of the Middle Ages, the customary clothes of the lesser people were becoming identified as the national dress. Already in the later sixteenth century, Thomas Randolph, the English ambassador, when going on a hunting trip in 1563, wrote to William Cecil, Queen Elizabeth's secretary of state: 'As many as are going to Argyll are preparing their Hyeland apparell' and continued that although he had clothed and accoutred himself as much as possible like everybody else, he would have taken more pleasure in returning home than from remaining in 'a safferon shyrte or a Hyelande pladde.' In 1618 John Taylor, the 'Water Poet', attended a hunting party held by the Earl of Mar in Braemar, and described the belted plaid as the general dress of all men including the nobility and gentry.[28]

Highland clothes were, moreover, becoming differentiated from Irish dress. Lughaidh O'Cleary, in describing a body of Hebrideans who came to the assistance of Red Hugh O'Donnell in 1594, noticed differences in clothing, 'for their exterior dress was mottled cloaks of many colours with a fringe to the calves of their legs; their belts were over their loins outside their cloaks'.[29] This could be an early description of a belted plaid. After the sixteenth century the *leine chroich* or saffron shirt is barely mentioned. Martin Martin in his *Description of the Western Islands*, published in 1703, says that the islanders had 'laid it aside' about a hundred years before.

The sixteenth century descriptions of Highland dress do not mention any articles of headgear, and some say that the men wore their hair long and went bare-headed. This was an old Irish custom, and medieval Highland poetry has many allusions to the long hair of the chiefs and heroes. It was not till the seventeenth-century descriptions that the flat bonnet appears as the typical Highland headdress.

By the end of the sixteenth century there were a number of castles in the Highlands. The 'tower-house' type of building had been added to or had taken the place of a simpler curtain wall. At Dunvegan there are two towers within the wall. The earlier one has been dated by Dr Douglas Simpson to the fourteenth century and he compares it with a tower definitely associated with Amie MacRuairidh, the first wife of John, first Lord of the Isles. One would venture to suggest that, even if some of the styles of the minor features in their construction are more ancient, these castles as a rule were not earlier than the families of the chiefs of the clans whose rise we have described. Owing to poverty and inaccessibility some time lag in the adoption of styles would not be surprising. There might of course be exceptions, as for instance in the case of Dunyveg in Islay, to which Norse features have been ascribed. The second tower at Dunvegan was built by Alasdair Crotach, c.1547, and is markedly more elegant and commodious.

Changes in battle tactics, due to the introduction of firearms, were going on all over Europe and led to a modification in the wearing of defensive armour. The arming acts in Scotland show that the Lowlands were in advance of the Highlands. There are many accounts that show that the old mode of fighting with mail-clad men still survived, especially in the West. The late sixteenth century anonymous report to James VI about the Islands said that a third of the six thousand men that could be raised in the islands 'aucht and sould be cled with attounes and haber-chounis, and knapshal bannetts, as thair lawis beir', signifying that they should have the quilted surcoats, mail coats and protective headgear. In 1545, during Donald Dubh's rising, the three thousand men who accompanied him to Ireland were described to the English king as 'very tall men' equipped with 'habergeons of mail, armed with long swords and long bows but with few guns'. Contemporary documents and tradition indeed show that even in the eastern Highlands the old accoutrements were still being worn. Some have been noted. One learns, for instance, that a MacKenzie was wearing a mail coat in a fight in 1583 with some Munros at Chanonry Point by Fortrose, and that about that time Mackintosh wore 'a yellow warcoat' when attacking Huntly's castle of Ruthven. Contemporary inventories at Inverness include a fine medley of arms — habergeons, bucklers or shields, steel bonnets, swords, dirks, bows and arrows and culverins. The tradition of mail-clad heroes lingered in folk poetry into the eighteenth and nineteenth centuries.

The Island clans, who were largely dependent on transport by galleys, would naturally prefer the use of smaller bodies of well-armed, picked men. But in the desperate feuds of the period it would be natural for hard-pressed clans to put every available man into the field. The increase was swelled by the reception of broken men, to whose numbers the troubles of the times were constantly adding. The authorities were of course concerned about this. The roll compiled in 1587, following the enactment of the General Band, of the names of landlords and baillies of lands in the Highlands and Islands where 'brokin men has duelt and presentlie duellis', contained 137 names. A list of broken clans and families made in 1594 for the Privy Council had 22 names of clans and 19 other kins' surnames.

More or less circumstantial accounts of four considerable battles fought during this period demonstrate the transition that was going on. If you walk over the ground of the battle of Gruinard, fought between

MacLean of Duart and MacDonald of Dunyveg in 1598, one can see where the fortunes of the day were decided by the taking and holding of a hill. In the battle of *Drum na Cupa* in 1431, the Mackays held a strong position on a ridge where the Sutherlands attacked them but were defeated by an ambush from the rear. Far more important was the fight between the forces of the forfeited and excommunicated Earl of Huntly and of the young Earl of Argyll with the king's commission, in the battle of Glenlivet in October 1594. Argyll's army was the more numerous, estimated at some six or seven thousand men, and almost entirely composed of men from the west. It was drawn up at the top of a rough slope 'arrayed in battell'. Huntly, whose forces were mainly mounted, made his way up the slope and attacked and defeated Argyll's men who had passively awaited him.

The battle of *Blàr na Lèine* of 1544 between Clan Ranald and the Frasers is well documented. A body of four hundred Frasers returning from the invasion of Clan Ranald's land along the south shore of Loch Lochy were intercepted by a larger force of the Clan Ranald. There was a head-on clash and the Frasers were defeated. The Frasers consisted of 'the flour of the gentry of the name', the gentlemen of the clan, and came from the fertile Aird and must have been far better equipped than the Clan Ranald, whose land is mountainous and who at the time were under great pressure. The battle is therefore an example of the advantage of manpower.

The downhill charge by lightly-clad men which was to become the characteristic and much dreaded Highland method of fighting required some weight of manpower. This was clearly evolving in the sixteenth century, and the increase in the number of clansmen used in fighting must have been a factor that brought about the change in the favoured musical instrument of the Highlanders. Although the tradition of the poet's incitement to battle, the *brosnachadh catha*, was still remembered in the eighteenth century, something much more resonant than the human voice with harp accompaniment was required to rally and stimulate large bodies of clansmen, and it is surely no chance accident that the bagpipe, that ancient and powerful musical instrument, should at this time have begun to come into prominence in the Highlands.

The bagpipe is a very ancient musical instrument and in varied forms has been widely distributed in different parts of the world, notably in Europe and Asia. With the proliferation of record evidence surviving from the Middle Ages, it can be seen that the pipes had become the universal musical instrument. They were of course the instrument of homely folk and used for entertainment and dancing at festivals, weddings and any social gatherings. They were also a favourite instrument at court, and James I was said to have been a piper of ability.

There is evidence of fees paid to families of musicians as early as the reign of Alexander III, and in the fourteenth century we learn of court pipers in the pay of David II. Among the royal payments to pipers, many were to English pipers. Until the sixteenth century, piping in England enjoyed considerable favour with the court and nobility especially in the reign of Henry VIII; there were salaried pipers at the English court, and there are references to English pipers being sent abroad for training in schools of minstrelsy on the Continent. In Scotland, the Treasurers' Accounts which survive from the later fifteenth century and especially for the reign of James IV give a clearer picture of crown patronage of pipers and minstrels, and in the same period, which was one of relative prosperity in burgh life, we begin to learn of official pipers in the Scots burghs. They generally had a toft or croft rent-free and were paid from the common good. Perth, a burgh on the fringes of the Highlands, maintained a burgh piper into the nineteenth century; he earned three shillings a week and a handsome sum by playing for well-to-do folk on Handsel Monday.

In the Highlands, the harp was the chosen instrument of the aristocracy and the literati. The bagpipe is not mentioned in the old tales of Ireland nor by any of the Highland poets whose work has been preserved in the *Book of the Dean of Lismore*. A solitary reference in the twelfth century by the monk Gerald of Wales to the Highlanders using the droneless bagpipe, the *chorus*, as well as the harp may have been subject to misinterpretation or at least is difficult to substantiate. It is evident, however, that by the sixteenth century the pipes were becoming the Highlanders' chosen instrument of war. George Buchanan writing in his Latin *History of Scotland* (1582) said that the Highlanders had substituted the bagpipe for the trumpet; and in his *L'Histoire de la guerre d'Ecosse* (Paris 1556) Jean de Beaugue, an officer serving with the French auxiliaries in Scotland, wrote of the occupation of Haddington by the English and the skirmishing in the Lothians in 1548 and 1549. He described the Earl of Argyll's contingent and commented that 'the wild Scots encouraged themselves to arms by the sound of their bagpipes'. A frequently quoted couplet from his long panegyric said to have been written in 1598 by Rev Alexander Hume, minister of Logie, includes the pipes with the instruments of war:

> Caus michtalie the weirlie nottis breike,
> on Hieland pipes, Scottes and Hybernicke.

Here is the suggestion also that the Highland bagpipe with its sonorous and strident tone had become differentiated from the Lowland and Irish pipes.[30]

It will be remembered that by the sixteenth century there was a change in the use of musical instruments in western Europe. From being merely an accompaniment to the human voice, instrumental music was attaining some importance for itself. The Highlanders were therefore abreast with a European movement in evolving a new style of composition for the great Highland pipe. In the late sixteenth and early seventeenth centuries, it seems to emerge suddenly as the fully developed art of the *piobaireachd*. We may be in error in trying to trace lines of development and points of influence, when a more characteristic progression of artistic expression is in the decline or falling away from the high point of a more or less spontaneous flowering. But several tunes by their titles antedate the sixteenth century, such as the Battle of the North Inch of Perth (1396), the End of the Great Bridge (1427), Black Donald's March (1431) and the Park Piobaireachd (1491) or the Battle of Blar na Pairce. It would be difficult to maintain categorically that these tunes are contemporary with the events which they commemorate. In the form in which we have them, they are probably later and fall within the classical period of *piobaireachd*. But there are excellent melodies in tunes such as Black Donald's March, and the likelihood is that they pre-existed as song airs and were taken up on the pipes and played in *piobaireachd* form by the masters of the art. The origin of the *piobaireachd* is a matter of debate. It is generally accepted that this form of musical composition appeared in the sixteenth century and has been adhered to ever since. There is, of course, no record of the actual notes of an air played at that date. It therefore seems best to trace how tradition and study of this form of music of our period has persisted.

The tradition is strong and universal that the supreme masters of *piobaireachd* were the MacCrimmons, the hereditary pipers of MacLeod of MacLeod, then generally known as MacLeod of Harris, and later as of Dunvegan. There are conflicting theories about their origin, but according to the MacLeod traditional poetry they came from Harris, and the fairy element in some of the local stories about them suggests an early origin. Traditionally their famous school of piping at Boreraig in Vaternish, Skye, was founded early in the sixteenth century; by the end of it, with fuller documentation, we begin to know more of this dynasty of great pipers, of Donald Mór MacCrimmon, born about 1570 and active in the time of Rory Mór MacLeod, and of Patrick Mór MacCrimmon in the next generation, born about 1595 and the composer of such great tunes as Lament for Mary MacLeod and the tragic Lament for the Children. It is a glorious achievement of the MacLeods that, engaged in constant feuds with their neighbours, supporting to extreme hazard the desperate attempts to restore the Lords of the Isles, in constant trouble with an oppressive government and its agents, and maintaining their families and people on the Atlantic shores of Skye and Harris, they should yet have given the support and protection needed for the flowering of this Gaelic art. And not only so, they also fostered the beginnings of the great revival in Gaelic poetry.

Ceòl mór, meaning great music, is the more precise term for what is generally called *piobaireachd*, a word unattractively anglicised as 'pibroch'. There are nearly three hundred tunes surviving today, consisting of marches and battle-tunes, gatherings, salutes and laments, most of them belonging to the period approximately 1600-1760. One of the earliest writers on Highland pipe music and the first to write it in staff notation was Joseph MacDonald, the son of Rev Murdoch MacDonald, minister of Durness; he was the author of *A Compleat Theory of the Scots Highland Bagpipe*, written on a voyage to India about 1761, where he was to take up a post with the East India Company. Unhappily for later generations of piping scholars, he died of fever shortly after his arrival aged only twenty three. His work survived in manuscript, to be published posthumously. But Joseph MacDonald was writing when the memory of days before the proscriptive legislation was still fresh, although in referring to pipe music as a relic of the past he was clearly pessimistic about its future. He wrote that the Highland pipes as a martial instrument would only be used for pieces of music specially written for them, for *piobaireachd* and jigs, and he divided pipe tunes into marches, including gatherings, and 'rural pieces'. This tradition among Highland pipers survived until relatively recently as the late Pipe Major John MacDonald, Inverness, suggested when he recalled his early tuition from *Calum Piobair*, one of the greatest exponents of the MacCrimmon tradition:

> I received most of my tuition from Calum Macpherson at Catlodge, Badenoch. Calum was easily the best player of *piobaireachd* I have ever known. He hardly ever played March, Strathspey and Reel, only *Piobaireachd* and jigs.[31]

Although individual tunes of *ceòl mór* are very different from one another and definitely of different degrees of merit, they conform to certain rules of composition and follow a definite plan. The tune begins with the 'ground' or *urlar*, or what Joseph MacDonald refers to as the *adagio*, being the tempo indication for slow time. The theme can usually be discerned within the *urlar*, which will include different variations of it. The length and variations of the musical phrases of the *urlar* tend to be laid out in a regular form and the piper can easily absorb the phrase-pattern of the tune. A characteristic variation of the *urlar* is 'thumb variation', that is the substitution of High A for a prominent note, such as E, or the 'doubling' by which a phrase is repeated at certain points to maintain an even flow in the melody. The *urlar* itself is followed by a succession of conventional variations, achieving a slightly quicker tempo in successive movements and involving increasingly elaborate grace-noting. The tune reaches its culmination in the *crunluath* and the additional, often optional, crowning movement, the *crunluath a mach*, by which the piper's skill can be judged. The conventions and achievements of *piobaireachd* place it firmly in the Gaelic learned tradition. The resemblance of the severe, intellectual music of *ceòl mór* to the old Gaelic style of ornament, complicated, stylised and covering the whole surface, and also to the elaborate metres of Gaelic poetry is very striking. The designs of the tartans, covering the whole surface of the fabric with the repetitive designs of the crossing threads, is surely a manifestation of the same spirit. And the old Highland way of singing the psalms has seemed to express the same artistic ability.

The dates of the introduction of the special features of the Highland pipes are matters of dispute. The authenticity of the few surviving old sets of pipes in their present form has been doubted, although different parts of sets of pipes are often original, such as the drones. The chanters, more subject to wear and tear and more frail by the nature of their construction, have been replaced on many sets of pipes. But the chanter is the ancient foundation of the bagpipe and the drones have been added to provide a steady harmonic. If the early chorus was a droneless bagpipe, pipes with drones begin to make their appearance in the thirteenth and fourteenth centuries. It is often suggested that the second tenor drone, tuned to the key-note of the chanter, was added in the sixteenth century and the bass drone which gives such a distinctive and powerful tone to the Highland pipes, not till about 1700. The thirst for definition obscures the fact that both two-drone and three-drone bagpipes were played, and it is only over the last hundred years that the pipes have adopted their fixed, fashionable and familiar form. According to Joseph MacDonald, the bass drone had long been in use but it had for a while been out of fashion with some Highland pipers in his day. The bass drone, tuning two octaves below the key-note of the chanter, is so characteristic of the Highland bagpipe that it is hard to believe that it did not make its appearance until after much of the good *ceòl mór* had been composed. A powerful bass was certainly later considered to be an essential feature of *piobaireachd* when, after 1821, two-drone pipes were debarred from the Highland Society annual competitions.

There is a very strong tradition that the old schools of piping used a syllabic notation to preserve their music and to pass it on to their pupils. Known as *canntaireachd*, it has survived in three forms, differing slightly from each other, MacCrimmon canntaireachd, MacArthur canntaireachd and Campbell or Nether Lorn canntaireachd. The last has survived in sufficient bulk in manuscript, for it was written out in the 1790s, to allow a reasonably complete system of notation to be recontructed and to be published through the work of the Piobaireachd Society in our own day. It would be wrong, however, to regard what we have of canntaireachd as a fixed formula to which master and player strictly adhered, although it has generally been used consistently by those acquainted with it. The principle of the vocal notation is the same for all sources. The notes of the melody are represented mainly by vowels, such that the vowel can have a specific pitch meaning, and the grace notes by consonants.

The teaching of piping could be done entirely by canntaireachd and has been within living memory according to the late Pipe Major John MacDonald, Inverness, and the late Pipe Major William MacLean, Killcreggan, who were both pupils of Malcolm Macpherson, *Calum Piobair*. Most pipers still use a loose form of canntaireachd to describe the notes of their music or to sing the tunes, and the tradition of singing with canntaireachd vocables survives in Gaelic, more especially with *ceòl beag* or light music.[32]

Another important development of this period was in poetry and song. As an era of troubled times, *Linn nan Creach*, the 'age of forays', it was also a period of transition, away from the strict bardic verse of the schools of poetry and learning towards folksong. It saw the development of singing in Europe as a whole, and song has been such a strong mark of the Highland character and such a vital feature of life and work. It saw the beginnings of popular verse in vernacular Gaelic, which was to come to the fore so markedly in the seventeenth century, and the decline in the use of the classical literary language. The Ossianic ballads, for example, were now passing into the vernacular Gaelic and folksong tradition, although they mostly kept to their syllabic metrical structure. They began to enjoy wide popularity and have only now disappeared from the song tradition. That the art of poetry was not necessarily the preserve of a professional elite must have been clear by the sixteenth century, although the gap between the literary language and the vernacular was perhaps not so great as has been made out. Compositions in the vernacular survive from the sixteenth century, as Professor W J Watson points out. A group of these is associated with the MacGregors, whose rapidly worsening circumstances destroyed the milieu in which bardic verse and the literary language could be cultivated. But their plight gave rise to some memorable poetry such as the song to MacGregor of Roro, Glen Lyon, which is rounded off by a warning to MacGregor to be ever alert to the dangers which surround him, finishing with the couplet:

> Though the hawk is noble
> He is often taken by treachery.

For much of the verse which survives from this period, though the language is vernacular, the style and metres were bardic. And the composers, when they are known to us, are generally lairds and chiefs. Men such as *An Cleireach Beag*, the Laird of Coll, *Fear na Pairce* or MacCulloch of Park, and *Gille Caluim Garbh* of Raasay would have been literate and in some cases obviously widely read. The mood and conventions of formal panegyric are carried over into folksong, with the eulogising and listing of heroic attributes and the rehearsing of the history and achievements of patrons and kin. An example of this from the early sixteenth century is a piece addressed to an Earl of Argyll by a Mull bard:

> I shall journey with my prepared song
> To the king of the Gael,
> The man who keeps his house crowded
> Happy and plentiful.

The poem closes with its first word repeated, *triallaidh*, providing that bardic gesture of a conventional *dùnadh* or ending. In this more or less conventional praise-poem, the bard offers his song in ready expectancy of the munificence of Argyll whose courage and virtues are described; *MacCailein* is seen as the great Gaelic chief and the very antithesis of the enemy of the Gael. Some songs, such as the very moving lament by his widow for Gregor MacGregor of Glenstrae, executed at Balloch (Taymouth Castle) in 1570, contain a human and emotive note much more characteristic of folksong than of classic formal verse. She addresses her grief to her fatherless child:

> If there twelve men of his name
> And my Gregor at their head,
> My eyes would not be shedding tears
> Nor my own child without friends.

> They put his head on a block of oak
> And they shed his blood on the ground,
> If I had there a cup,
> I would drink my fill.

The drinking of blood reminds us of the tragic Deirdre drinking the blood of her beloved Naoise, and this and the ancient symbolism of the apple later in the song makes it a bridge between worlds. The MacGregor songs provide a very moving counterpoise to the stark and bloody statements of the pursuit and extirpation of the clan in the Register of the Privy Council.

The classic poetry was syllabic but the new song poetry was stressed, that is, each line having a fixed number of stressed syllables gave a rhythm to the stanzas, each of which could be of varying length. There is evidence of a fundamental change in the stress pattern of language in this period, by which emphasis fell away from unstressed syllables and words, and this must also have helped to put the old syllabic metres out of fashion. It was in the sixteenth century that, as W J Watson describes, 'untrained or only partly trained poets who, when they used the structure of the syllabic metres, would disregard the refinements'.

Another influence in shaping new tastes in poetry was the tradition of the choral songs or songs of work, which were strongly stressed and already well established, being based on older metres. Some of these, though ostensibly the music of the folk, are aristocratic in their reference and resort to the conventions of classic panegyric. An early surviving example, possibly belonging to the later sixteenth century, is the lullaby or cradle-song to Donald Gorm MacDonald of Sleat, who died in 1617, *Taladh Dhomhnaill Ghuirm*, attributed to his foster-mother. This type of song with the split lines broken up by a chorus or refrain of vocables belongs also to an archaic tradition, the form of song lending itself both to the preservation of older songs or fragments and to extemporary versification. The composer visualises the child as a grown warrior (or she eulogises the grown man by the convention of the *taladh* or lullaby):

> *Ge bè àite*   *an tàmh thu an Alba*
> .....
> Whatever place in which you come to rest in Scotland
> There will be there, as is customary, music and storytelling
> Pipe and harp, merriment and dancing ....

As a climax to the song, she invokes a rune of protection on him:

> *Neart Chon Chulainn*   *fa làn eideadh*
> .....
> The strength of Cu Chulainn in full armour,
> The strength of the seven battalions of the army of the Fenians
> The strength of melodious Ossian and of Oscar renowned for his feats,
> To be between Donald Gorm and his shirt ....

One of the earliest surviving poems in stressed metre is attributed to the Laird of Coll; he praises a MacLean who was a notorious pirate in the song *Caismeachd Ailein nan Sop*, composed about 1537. But among the early songs in stressed metre the one which expresses the spirit and the disquiet of *Linn nan Creach* most dramatically is *Clann Ghriogair air fogradh*, 'Clan Gregor outlawed':

> I sit here alone by the level roadway,
> Trying to meet in with a fugitive
> Coming from Ben Cruachan of the Mist
> One who will give me news of Clan Gregor
> Or word of where they have gone.[33]

Period V

Seventeenth and eighteenth centuries.
Concentration of cultural influences in the south but
development of military importance of the Highlands.
The flowering of Gaelic poetry

PART I

The period between the death of James VI and the Rising of the '45 is of
special interest, because in it the Highlands occupied a position of unique
importance not only in Scots history but also in that of Great Britain.
During this time, the Highlands became not 'a home for lost causes' but
a springboard from which they might be revived. This is due to the
differences between the social organisation of the Highlands and that of
the Lowlands. As we have tried to show in an earlier period, the holding
of land was organised upon a feudal system and upon the obligation to
render military service and maintain law and order. But the organisation
was less effective beyond the Highland Line and the nucleus of the clans
developed in association with the feudal system. Largely owing to the
ineffectiveness of the central government, armed service and self-defence
continued to be an essential part of the social organisation. Of course, by
the seventeenth century there was a marked contrast to that of the
Lowlands, where these feudal obligations were becoming a dead letter.
Sir Walter Scott, in *Old Mortality*, in his racy account of a 'Wappen-
schawing' illustrates this. The period was, of course, one of acute
religious differences and of divided dynastic claims. It was a period of
civil wars, and the poverty-stricken Highland chiefs suddenly acquired a
temporary political importance compared to the far wealthier
landowners of the Lowlands. It is only necessary to recall the armed
campaigns in which the Highlanders took part — Montrose's campaign
in 1645, the army of the Engagement defeated in August 1648, Charles
II's campaign of 1651 which ended so disastrously at Worcester, the Earl
of Glencairn's royalist rising in the Highlands in 1653-54 against the
Cromwellian occupation, Lochiel's resistance to General George
Monck's forces after 1654 when Sir Ewen boasted that the Camerons
were the only free people within these kingdoms, the Earl of Argyll's
rising in May 1685, the revolt led by John Graham, Viscount Dundee,
against William of Orange and the Revolution Settlement in 1689, and
the Jacobite attempts of 1715, the brief episode of Glen Shiel in 1719 and
the '45. Religious as well as political differences were involved in many
of these campaigns, very notably those of Montrose.

James Fraser's remarks about the year 1644 in the Wardlaw
Manuscript, ... 'There is nothing heard now up and down the kingdom

137

but alarms and rumores, randevouzes of clans, every chiften mustering his men, called weaponshowes' might constantly have been said of the whole Highlands during these years.[1] In these risings it must however be remembered that there was never united Highland support for the cause at issue. The false idea that the 1715 and '45 Risings were fought between the English and the Highlanders, or the Lowlanders and the Highlanders, still persists. It is therefore important to note, for example, that General Wade himself estimated in 1724 that the fighting force of the Highlands amounted to 22,000 men, of whom 10,000 were the vassals of men well affected to the government.[2] The Jacobite army in the '45 has been variously estimated at about 6,000 or 8,000 men. The chiefs of some clans were not invariably on the same side as all the clansmen, and occasionally some clansmen were forced 'out' to join the forces in the field. Nevertheless, a devotion to a King they regarded as legitimate, as opposed to the *de facto* government, does now appear as a definite feeling among many Highlanders in this period. In a way it had superseded the idea of the Lordship of the Isles as a focus for the loyalty of a large area of the Western Highlands.

Of course, in Great Britain as a whole, the duties of armed service had been taken over from feudal levies by professional troops, and the use of gunpowder in small arms as well as artillery had transformed their tactics. With civil wars at home and participation in Continental wars abroad the effectiveness of the army was enormously increasing during this period. This is obvious. It is also important to bear in mind that at the same time the Highlanders also effected a dramatic improvement in their battle tactics. In propitious circumstances they more than equalled the fighting potential of the professionals. The possession of firearms was a luxury that only a limited number of Highlanders could afford even by the end of our period, and the Highlanders during the seventeenth century still largely depended upon bows and arrows. Bowmanship was much admired, of course, and there are many tales turning on feats of archery. The sixteenth century Lochaber poet, *Domhnall mac Fhionnlaigh nan Dàn*, complains when old age has deprived him of his strength to draw the bow, and as late as last century, an expert marksman in Lochaber was referred to as having as accurate aim as the poet, *cho cuimseach ri Domhnall mac Fhionnlaigh*. Although about 1589 the Tutor of Lovat had ordered in his regality court that the Fraser tenantry should have a gun beside their bows, subsequently we learn that the Tutor paid a visit to Glenelg, taking 100 bowmen with him. Master James Fraser remarks elsewhere in the Wardlaw Manuscript that in his own day 'that manly art is wearing away by degrees, and the gun takeing place'. However, so late as the middle of the seventeenth century, successive chiefs of the Frasers continued to exercise their men in archery.

When Lochiel was with the Earl of Glencairn in 1653, half his force had bows and arrows and he placed his archers in opposition to the enemy's horse 'which they galled exceedingly with their arrows, for they were excellent archers and seldom missed their aim'. Probably the last considerable force of bowmen to be seen in Scotland were Lochiel's 300 'quivered Numidians' in the force with which he opposed Mackintosh in 1665. This was only part of the Highlanders' out-of-date equipment. An eye-witness of the Highland Host wrote of the 'odde and antique forme' of the Highlanders' accoutrements with headpieces and steel bonnets 'raised like pyramids' and the like.[3]

More significant than the change from bows and arrows to guns was the change from the heavy cross-hilted sword to a basket-hilted lighter type of sword that came into use from the Continent. A detailed description of these weapons can be dealt with separately. It is the way that they were used and how this came about that is the primary consideration. The old battles among Highlanders seem to have depended upon contests by the leading champion upon either side or for one side to occupy a strong position and the other to have to dislodge them. This was the form of two important battles fought at the end of the sixteenth century — the Battle of Loch Gruinard between the MacDonalds and the MacLeans in 1598 and the Battle of Glenlivet between Huntly and Argyll in 1594. In both these battles the attacking force fought its way up and dislodged the defenders. It was the genius of Montrose who, in his victories at Tippermuir, Auldearn and Kilsyth, used to good account the mobility and aggressive qualities of the Highlanders in association with his Irish volunteers. Under the leadership of Dundee at Killiecrankie in 1689, the Highland charge carried all before it. The success of the Highland charge has had an important bearing upon military history and upon the estimation in which the Highlanders came to be held. There are eye-witness accounts of the Highlanders' new tactics and the new weapons they now had, muskets and pistols, targes and the lighter basket-hilted swords. Coming down the hill 'like a living flood', almost before the bayonets of the troops could be brought from the 'Present' to the 'Charge', the Highlanders were upon them; and the accounts of the battle of Killiecrankie in July 1689 make it clear that the plug bayonets which were being used by the government forces prevented the musket being loaded or fired in the onset.

Although they might have been far more affluent, they had not the power of raising a following. At Worcester, the royal army was confronted by Cromwell himself in command of veteran troops. The whole of the Rising of the '15 was doomed to failure by the ineptitude of Mar, and nowhere was this more evident than in his choice of Thomas

Forster, a general who allowed the expeditionary force to be surrounded at Preston. In 1745, in the retreat of the over-optimistic expedition that ended at Derby, the Highlanders fought a successful rear-guard action. At Culloden the Jacobite leaders had selected a battlefield that gave full advantage to the enemy's superiority in cavalry and artillery and none to the Highlanders' tactic of the downhill charge. Ill-fed and wearied by a futile night expedition, they were subjected to a prolonged bombardment, and their charge was unsupported by the rest of the Jacobite army. Yet they broke the enemy's front line with their charge and inflicted almost all the casualties that were suffered by Cumberland's army that day. The magnitude of the Highlanders' achievements as fighting men during this period is worthwhile stressing not only as a corrective to the long list of failures which circumstances have forced upon the Highlands but as the cause of the government's action in our next period. It is also only the prelude to the splendid fighting qualities that they were to show.

At home, there were gradual changes in administration. But 'justice' was still being done by the grant of special lieutenancies and of commissions of 'fire and sword' to the injured party, although the lieges did not make very enthusiastic response. Great northern nobles, especially Argyll, continued to use their heritable jurisdiction strengthened by their armed forces and interest with the Privy Council and at court. Argyll's expropriation of MacDonald of Islay and of the MacIans of Ardnamurchan by intrigue and deception has already been mentioned. In the 1670's, having successfully entangled MacLean of Duart in debt, he used his powers as heritable justiciary to seize the greater part of Mull for himself. His methods of increasing his feudal superiorities are vividly described by only one of the sufferers, MacLean of Ardgour, who had been forced into surrendering his lands to the king to be regranted to Argyll who in turn feued out the lands to their former owner. Argyll's superiorities could also put old loyalties to severe test. The MacLeods, long associated with the MacLeans in the tangled politics of the day, had earlier granted the superiority of their Glenelg lands to Argyll; they then found themselves cited in the Letters of Fire and Sword against the MacLeans, among those to whom the execution of the commission was to be entrusted. In fact, the MacLeods probably took no action in the matter.[4]

During James VI's personal rule a serious attempt had been made to clean up the cases of conflicting titles to land that had been the cause of many feuds. These were dealt with and a great many ambiguities were cleared up. Following the same trend all over the country, there was a decrease in the number of feuds and an increase in the settlement of disputes by actions in the courts and by enforced arbitration. It is

POWER IN THE HIGHLANDS IN THE
LATER SEVENTEENTH CENTURY

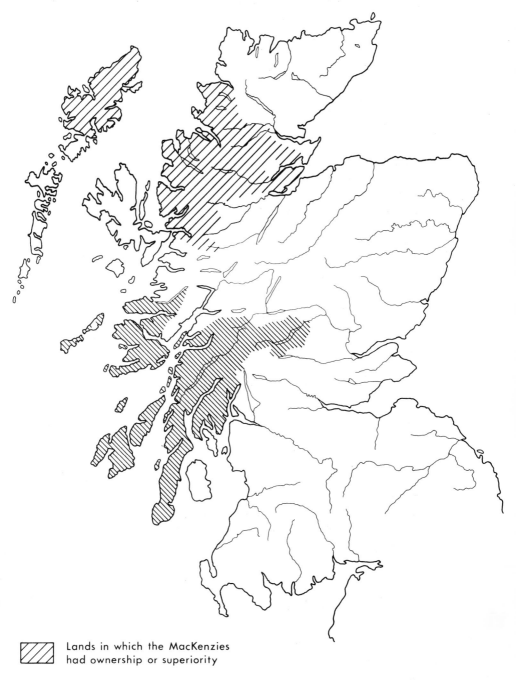

 Lands in which the MacKenzies
had ownership or superiority

Lands in Campbell ownership and over which Earls and Dukes
of Argyll and Earls of Breadalbane held superiorities

significant that the last clan battle was fought in 1688, at Mulroy in Glen
Spean, between the Mackintoshes and the MacDonalds of Keppoch over
a dispute about land.

The administration of the law, however, was not according to modern
practice. The Applecross Manuscript history of the MacKenzies (1667)
said that Colin of Kintail, *Cailean Cam*, who died in 1594, a 'tender
feeblie man', had many feuds with his neighbours 'against quhom he had
alwayis the lawes of the countrey, and his broyther Rorie Moire still
acted in the feilds and putt the law in execution'. Sir Robert Gordon was
constantly engaged in law business on behalf of Sutherland, and naively
described how the sides mustered 'all ther friends on either syd'.
Arbitration still had an element of *force majeure* in it. James Fraser, the
minister of Wardlaw, was present at the negotiations before the enforced
settlement between Mackintosh and Lochiel in 1664. He wrote:
'Mackintosh his men, about 500 in rank and file, lay on the east side of
the river at Haughs; Lochiel's men, 300, about Tomnifirich. Earth,
water, aire, rebounded at the sound of bagpipes Martiall misick. At the
sound of a trumpet the meeting sits at some distance, and my Lord
Bishop of Murray and the Laird Robert Cumming of Altyre, as
arbitrators and trenchmen passed betwixt them, and at last, the third day
being Thursday, matters were brought to an accommodation and
agreement, that it prevented litigation and cost in law. This was a noble
sight of gallant gentlemen and the clergy in decent grave garbs.' The
attempt at arbitration failed. The history of Clan Mackintosh gives a full
account of the failure of the Privy Council to ensure to Mackintosh the
lands on Loch Arkaig to which he had a legal right, of the complications
of clansmen owing military service to other branches of Clan Chattan,
of armed confrontation between Mackintosh and Lochiel, ended
by the intervention of an emissary of Argyll who by paying the compensation agreed to by Lochiel eventually secured the superiority of
Lochaber.[5]

The policy of the sixteenth century of obliging chiefs and proprietors
to sign the Band that made them responsible for the behaviour of their
tenants and clansmen was continued. For instance, in 1635 the Privy
Council ordered that all landlords and chiefs should make themselves
responsible for the behaviour of their followers; and Lochiel, Cameron
of Glen Nevis, MacGregor, MacDonald of Glencoe and Keppoch were
warded because no one would become surety for them. After the
Restoration this policy was again resorted to; sometimes its provisions
were carried to extreme lengths, and the order itself was renewed twice.
In 1678 the chiefs were made responsible for 'all of their name descended
of their house', and the more important were required to appear yearly in
Edinburgh, while the heads of lesser branches who 'by reason of their

mean condition' were not able to attend at Edinburgh were required to give in their names at Inverlochy'.[6]

During the period, repeated enactments were made to disarm the Highlanders, obviously with little effect. The enforcement of the order requiring the taking of an oath of allegiance led to the Massacre of Glencoe. This, one of the best known events in Highland history, is a shameful example of the maladministration of Highland affairs by the British Government. But a new and most important development was the succession of military measures taken in the Highlands by Cromwell, General Monck, and later William III and General Wade. They established permanent military posts at more than a dozen strategic points. One of the earliest was in the ancient fortified site of Castle Urquhart, which was garrisoned for about two years from 1690. When the troops abandoned it, they blew up the keep and entrance towers to prevent it ever being used again in the event of rebellion. Visitors to the holiday centre at Aviemore can see the impressive ruins of another military post across the Spey at Ruthven, built in 1719, on the site of an old castle. Similar barrack forts were constructed at Bernera Glenelg, Fort Augustus, then known as *Cill Chuimein*, and Inversnaid on Loch Lomondside. Gaelic speakers still call Fort William, *An Gearasdan*, the Garrison; there the military presence began with a turf and wattle fort thrown up by General Monck, and the position was consolidated after the Revolution with a stone fort. In 1725 General George Wade began to build his military roads. It should be noted that these were built to increase the mobility of the troops and did not in themselves create a marked effect on the economic or social development of the country. The Highlanders had always been extremely mobile, and for raiding, droving or pleasure they had moved very freely about the country. Of far greater significance was the policy of raising bodies of independent Highland companies wearing the dress, speaking the language and used to the methods of warfare of the people of the country. They were known as the 'Black Watch' or *Am Freiceadan Dubh*. They are said to have brought the Highlands into better order than had ever been known, but they had all been disbanded by 1717. General Wade formed six new independent companies of Highlanders in 1725, and in 1739 these were amalgamated and formed into a Regiment of the Line, which became known as the Black Watch and was enlisted for general service. In 1745, an additional Highland regiment, the Earl of Loudoun's, was raised, and then Duncan Forbes of Culloden, in his skilful containment of the Jacobite movement, raised a further eighteen Independent Companies.

It is a paradox that the effect produced by such repressive measures as the bodies of local levies and of the first Highland Regiment of the Line was to conserve Highland things. Although they were formed to repress the lawlessness and Jacobite proclivities of the Highlanders, the Independent Companies were raised through the organisation of those clans that supported the Hanoverian government. They were sometimes commanded by the chief, were officered by the cadets of the clan and the rank and file were their clansmen or tenants. The 1729 Companies were officered by Lovat, Campbell of Lochnell, Campbell of Fonab, Campbell of Carrick, Grant of Ballindalloch and Munro of Culcairn. It was found that the men would join only if the officers were members of the local gentry, even if mere children. How efficient was the clan organisation in raising these bodies can be seen in the extraordinary speed with which the 1745 Independent Companies were raised. Duncan Forbes of Culloden, who was entrusted with the task, only approached the chiefs in October; yet, in spite of abnormally bad weather, most of them had been raised and marched to Inverness by November 1745.[7] The raising of these bodies on a clan basis prolonged the value of a number of retainers which the pacification of the Highlands would naturally tend to reduce, and it played its part in the preservation of pipe music.

In addition to the efforts of the government, other forces were weakening the organisation of the clans during our period. Increasing contact with the outside world, English as well as Lowland, meant that new influences were at work. The chiefs and leading men, for example, were beginning to adopt Lowland and English ways of life, with more or less disastrous financial effect. The attempts to establish the government of the Reformed Church and the polemics of seventeenth century Presbyterianism helped to undermine the established ways of traditional society. In addition, the greater output of printed books and increased literacy meant that these issues could strike home in even the remotest communities. Nevertheless, because of the survival of older conditions in the Highlands and by adaptation to new ones, the clans continued to be important social organisations. No new clans were formed, and apart from acquisitions already noted, little land changed hands. But as has already been described, there was great variation in the structure of the individual clans. Clan maps, of course, cannot give any idea of the complexity of land tenure and occupation, or of the fact that in the Highlands feudal superiority was still an effective force. It is necessary to quote some examples to demonstrate that Highland society was complex and that this was no simple tribal system that had evolved.

The relations of the different inhabitants of a district varied very much. There were straths, especially in the Central Highlands, where there had never been a predominant clan, and such lands were under a great feudatory such as the Earl of Atholl. Even within the territories owned by a powerful chief there were very various degrees of relationship. To take one example of the infinite variation that occurred,

MacKenzie of Kintail, afterwards the Earl of Seaforth, that by the seventeenth century 'all the Highlands from Ardnamurchan to Strathnaver were either MacKenzie's property or under their vassalage, some few excepted, and all about him were tied to his family by very strict Bonds of Friendship and vassalage'. But dwelling in amity within MacKenzie's bounds were the Mathesons, the MacLennans, some Mackays and especially the MacRaes, and the late seventeenth century manuscript history of the latter clan by the Rev John MacRae of Dingwall shows how harmonious was the relationship between its men and the MacKenzies. The MacRaes were customarily constables of the key fortress of Eilean Donan and many MacKenzies were fostered with them. There were districts where the predominant clan was in a minority, as for instance in Lewis, acquired by MacKenzie in 1610. Although a rental of 1726 shows that the MacKenzies had been able to monopolise most of the large single tacks on Lewis, there were many joint-tenants who used patronymics such as John *MacMhurchaidh MhicIain* and Duncan *MacAonghais MhicIain MhicMhurchaidh* in Shawbost; this was of course the usual means of identifying individuals in Gaelic society. Down to the present day MacLeod, the name of the old possessors, is still the commonest surname.[8] Other occupiers such as MacIvers, MacAulays and Morrisons are still there in great numbers. In the '15, Seaforth's mainland tenants supported him with devotion and after the forfeiture of his estates and title continued to pay their rent to him. Those in Lewis showed far less readiness to do so. Assynt also had been captured from the MacLeods, and William Baillie of Ardmore reported to Lord President Forbes in 1745 that there were many MacLeods there who 'have been long keep'd in a sort of bondage in that Country, and have no turn for Arms'. A well-known example of clan loyalty is told by James Boswell in his Journal; he described how when they landed on Iona with Sir Allan MacLean of Duart, all the inhabitants 'who still consider themselves as the people of MacLean, though the Duke of Argyll has at present possession of the ancient estate, ran eagerly to him'.[9] There are examples of lesser clans on the lands of Campbell, MacDonald, Stewart, MacLeod and other chiefs. The Camerons were formed of a junction of branches of the clan such as the Camerons of Callart and the Camerons of Glendessary, and other clans such as the MacMartins and MacSorlies were added to them. In the case of the great confederation of Clan Chattan, a number of clansmen lived on land feued, rented or held in other ways by Mackintosh of the Earl of Moray, the Bishop of Moray and the Earl of Huntly. But MacGillivray, although a leading member of Clan Chattan, obtained a wadset of Dunmaglass from the Campbells of Cawdor in 1620 and this was converted into a feu in 1626. Another loyal supporter was Farquharson of Invercauld, although the family had long removed to Deeside and Braemar.[10]

In a *Memoriall anent of the True State of the Highlands* written about 1746, the author singled out the MacLeans, the Camerons, the MacLeods, the MacLachlans, the MacKinnons, the Stewarts of Appin and the MacDonalds of Sleat, Clan Ranald, Glengarry, Keppoch and Glencoe, as clans specially devoted to their 'Natural Chieftens .... whose followers are Generally all their Kinsmen Descended of their families and who have no manner of Regard either to Superiors or Landlord but where it chances to be their own Chieften .... Since they have an inherent attractive Virtue which makes their people follow as Iron claps to the Loadstone'. It will be noticed that several of these clans had been almost wholly dependent on their fighting adherents for their existence.

In such clans the powers of the chief were at their most patriarchal, but in all clans they were still considerable. For instance, General Wade, reporting on the state of the Highlands in 1724, said of the Highlanders: 'Their Notions of Virtue and Vice are very different from the more civilised part of Mankind. They think it a most Sublime Virtue to pay a Servile and Abject Obedience to the Commands of their Chieftans, altho' in opposition to their Sovereign and the Laws of the Kingdom, and to encourage this, their Fidelity, they are treated by their Chiefs with great Familiarity, they partake with them in their Diversions, and shake them by the Hand whenever they meet them'. He adds that the clans were divided into branches and sub-branches 'with Chieftans' who all showed descent from the original stock.[11] Edward Burt, on road survey duty with General Wade's forces in the Highlands, has a similar account written about 1725 of their 'blind Obedience' to and love of their chief and in a lesser degree to their particular sept, and also to those of the whole clan or name, 'whom they will assist, right or wrong, against those of any other Tribe with which they are at Variance, to whom their Enmity, like that of exasperated Brothers, is most outrageous.' Burt goes on to say: 'the Chief exercises an arbitrary Authority over his Vassals, determines all Differences and Disputes that happen among them, and levies Taxes upon extraordinary Occasions, such as the Marriage of a Daughter, building a House, or some Pretence for his Support and the Honour of the Name', and he goes on to describe how the clansmen would make a voluntary levy to support the estate and the person of the Chief in the event of forfeiture or other misfortune.

The income of a chief varied greatly from chief to chief and from place to place. It consisted, of course, of rents paid in money as well as in kind, and there was often the additional benefit of the *calp*, the gift that the chief customarily claimed, which we have already mentioned as continuing to flourish after its prohibition by the Statutes of Icolmkill. Occasionally, he received a voluntary 'aid' or contribution for such purposes as the education of the heir or the marriage of a daughter. A night's hospitality or entertainment was the often burdensome due which the chief more commonly exacted.

A very interesting and rare early rental from the Argyll Charter Chest for the Island of Tiree about 1662 gives an idea not only of the range of dues paid but also of the survival of an ancient land measure dating back to the days of the *Gall-Ghaidheal*. The rental must belong to the period when Argyll began to receive the rents of Tiree in reparation for the MacLean's indebtedness. It harks back to the days when the MacLeans were enjoying all the fruits of chieftaincy as well as feudal superiority. The island was valued in terms of the *tirunga* or ounceland, being the extent of land paying the old rent of an ounce of silver. Unusually, in describing the extent of Tiree as a tax paying unit, the equation is stated between the divisions and subdivisions of the island. Tiree extended to twenty ouncelands and each ounceland, which in practice represented a 'townland' with its dwellings and arable lands, was subdivided into six merklands or twenty pennylands or forty-eight *maills*. Each ounceland in Tiree paid £160 of money rent, stated quantities of grain and meal, cows, calves, sheep, cheese, butter, poultry and eggs. Other dues were seventy-five yards of coarse linen and a small 'sail and hair taikle to a galey'. Although a value was not put on it, the rental also included winter-quarters for MacLean and his retinue: 'And Tirie wes wont to quarter all the gentlemen men that waited on McLean all winter not under a 100.'[12]

It must be stressed that the functions of the chief had been and still were not merely a matter of sentiment but essential to the well-being of the clan. He had been and still was to a large extent the landholder on whom his people depended. He was their defender and military leader; and even when many of the feuds were ended in the sixteenth century, in the case of the more settled clans, his association with the Independent Companies and organisation of the Watch against cattle-thieves took the place of this earlier function. He represented their interests before the Privy Council and even at Court, and undertook the rather bellicose litigation of the period. Surviving muniments show how much work was done by chiefs in adjusting difficulties between their clansmen and those of other clans and in their law business. The voluminous Delvine Papers record the activities of an Edinburgh lawyer for his Highland clients.

In spite of the efforts of the government to discourage them, his duties as administrator of justice to his people were necessary in the remoter parts of the country. The economist Adam Smith in his *Inquiry into the Nature and Causes of the Wealth of Nation* (1776) stated: 'It is not thirty years since Mr Cameron of Lochiel, a gentleman of Lochaber in Scotland, without any legal warrant whatever, not being what was then called a Lord of Regality nor even a tenant in chief, but a vassal of the

Duke of Argyll, without being so much as a Justice of the Peace used, notwithstanding, to exercise the highest jurisdiction over his own people. He is said to have done so with great equity, though without any of the formalities of justice; and it is not improbable that the state of that part of the country at that time made it necessary for him to assume this authority in order to maintain the public peace'. So late as 1773, MacLean of Coll was still settling disputes and imprisoning malefactors. The chief was addressed by his patronymic, Argyll as *MacCailein Mór* and Fraser of Lovat as *MacShimidh*, or by a territorial designation such as *Lochiel*. We learn that in 1645 MacShimidh was 'so exact in genealogy that he could give an account of the meanest tenant's origin and parentage once hearing his name, whether stranger or native in all his Country'.

The Wardlaw Manuscript gives a detailed picture of the work of good chiefs in training their men, educating the children of the leading families by taking them into their households, and providing for the dependants of those who had rendered him service. After the Battle of Auldearn in 1645 in which the Frasers suffered heavy losses, 'there were 87 widdowes about the Lord Lovates eares'. But it is equally important to remember that the chief's very presence living among them was a focus for the social life of his people. His bard and piper enlivened them and perpetuated the strong traditions of poetry, song and music in Highland and Island communities. His countenance gave grace to their sports and festivities. The marriages and funerals of his family were their great occasions; the funerals of chiefs were generally most splendid spectacles. Most clans have traditions about specially magnificent ones. At the death of Lachlan Mackintosh of Mackintosh in 1731, the funeral feasting and entertainment lasted for a month, and on the day of the burial the funeral procession stretched from Dalcross to Petty. Master James Fraser, the author of the Wardlaw Manuscript, was a connoisseur; the funeral of Lovat in 1633 was 'sumptuous and splendid' and over 5,000 men from eight neighbouring clans attended.

A custom that did much to bind the chief and his leading clansmen together was that of fosterage, *comhdhaltas* in Gaelic, by which a child of the chief was placed in the care of a member of the clan to be brought up in his family. Many allusions and traditions show that the custom was an old one, but by the seventeenth century, formal bonds of fosterage were drawn up under which a given number of cattle was often given to the foster-father, an equal number becoming the property of the fosterling or he received other benefits when he came of age. Several contracts of fosterage survive from the seventeenth century, including a document in Gaelic for the fostering of Norman, son of Rory MacLeod, in 1614 prepared by the learned man and poet Turlough O Muirgheasain.

The honour of fostering the child of a chief was eagerly sought by the clansmen, and traditions abound of the loyalty and devotion shown by the foster-father and foster-brothers to their *dalta* or foster-child. Although the honour was great, the foster-parents' obligations could be burdensome. A contract of fosterage between George Campbell of Airds and *Domhnall Dubh MacEoghainn* and his wife dated 1665 illustrates the careful provisions specified from parent and foster-parent; he gives them in fosterage Isobel Campbell, 'his lawful dochter, for the space of seavin yeiris from Beltane nixt; ... gives to the said Isobel, as *Machellif* (fosterling's portion) tua new calfit kyne, with ane calf and ane stirk of ane yeir old, with ane tua yeir old quey, and that at Beltane next, with ane uther tua yeir old quey at Beltane 1667 yeiris ....' and the said Donald and his wife 'gives ..... tua farrow kyne' and further beasts at the terms, all cows and followers to be grazed by the foster-parents. The yield in milk of the cows was kept by the foster-father and the increase of stock was kept for the foster-child. In addition the foster-parents made over to the child 'ane bairn's part' of their goods and gear to be inherited by her. The primitive details of this surviving custom are worthwhile remembering when we come to consider how much the ways of life of the outside contemporary world were impinging upon these of the Highlanders. Fosterage created a depth of relationship which was proverbial in Highland society. *Comhdhaltas gu ciad 's cairdeas gu fichead*, fostership to a hundred degrees, blood-relationship to twenty, went the saying and there are stories that bear this out. The author of the Manuscript History of Craignish describes 'how sacredly the old Highlanders esteemed the relationship of Coaltship' in a fifteenth century instance in which one MacIosaig lamented the death of his foster-son more than the death of four of his own sons, all killed in a fight. The old man tried to kill his surviving son in his rage and bitterness, accusing him of cowardice for allowing his *dalt* to be killed in the fight. *Fear eil' airson Eachainn*, 'Another for Hector', commemorates the death of the eight foster-brothers of the chief of the MacLeans, Hector Roy of Duart, at the battle of Inverkeithing in 1651, when Hector Roy and hundreds of his clan all lost their lives. It is worthwhile quoting such incidents that illustrate the attitude of the people before indicating the forces that were to change it.[14]

All through the history of the clans the difficulty of providing land for the relatives, leading men and followers of a chief became acute when fresh land was not available. By the seventeenth century, broadly speaking, there were three classes of clansmen within a clan: the chiefs, the gentlemen who were close or distant relatives of the chief, and the ordinary clansmen. It was generally the policy of the chief to keep heritable possession of his lands or to provide for his sons and other relatives by long leases, up to a hundred years for example, or by a wadset. (The wadset was a form of mortgage in which the use of the land was granted in return for a capital sum and a low yearly payment. The land could be redeemed upon repayment of the original capital sum). Highland chiefs often provided for younger sons by giving them a wadset of a piece of land but retaining and exercising the right of resuming possession upon payment of an agreed sum. This was the policy of the Laird of Grant, and all up Strathspey there was a series of wadsets held by relatives of successive chiefs.

Such provision could become very burdensome on a chief. For instance, Simon the thirteenth Lord Lovat, who died in 1632, impoverished his estates by giving so many wadsets to his kindred: 'there was no earthly thing he put in ballance with his kindred, whom he would still keep by him within the country, nor would he suffer any of them to settle among neighbour clans.' Grants in Glen Urquhart had applauded the declared intention of Ludovic Grant, Younger of Grant, in the 1730s 'off planting Grants in this countrie, and turning out such as hade ther dependance on other chieffs and masters'. Because although Grant had acquired the barony of Urquhart in 1509 and the Grant lands on the north side of Loch Ness were part of the Regality created in 1694, it was felt that there were relatively few of the name of Grant in possession there. There was a quarrel in 1737 between the Grants and the Urquhart men over the marriage of a young heiress, and the Grants wrote to the chief that they wished that, 'one young pritty fellow of your name here turn out to be one of the most substantiall tennants in the countrie'. The successful suitor, a MacDonald, was later assaulted. The 'lugging' of the man, having both his ears cut off, protracted the quarrel.[15]

The lesser gentry, the wadsetters, tacksmen, or goodmen, as they were variously called, farmed part of their land and sub-let the rest to sub-tenants who generally paid rent in kind and services. For instance, in a report on Islay in 1776, the island was said to be occupied 'by two class of tenants, viz the great or gentlemen tenants and the small tenants'. The former possessed several quarterlands extending to three or four thousand acres. They sub-let to 'a sett of poor people' and 'the small tenants, four, five, six or eight of them, enjoys a quarterland promiscuously among them'. But as the mid-eighteenth century Gartmore Manuscript states: 'As the propinquity (to the chief) removes they become less considered till at last they degenerate to be of the common people, unless some accidental acquisition of wealth supports them above their station'. It is, however, rare to find an example of such a rise, and the trend was almost inevitably downwards. The manuscript history of the MacRaes gives a good account of the ups and downs experienced by a family of lesser gentry. There seems to be no record of resistance to the constant subdivision and re-allocation of land, but it must have contributed to the feeling of unsettlement and pressure and to the cattle-raiding that was an enduring cause of friction between the Highlanders and the Lowlanders.[16]

The gentlemen of the clan seem to have exercised considerable control over the chief, and it was they who chose a 'captain' and managed the affairs of the clan during the interregna following the fairly frequent successions of minors. Rev Lachlan Shaw, himself brought up in the Highlands, wrote in his *History of the Province of Moray* (1775): 'Anciently every chief of a Clan was by his dependents, considered as a little Prince, not absolute, but directed by the Gentlemen of his Clan. As the *Primores Regni*, and all who held off the King *in capite* were his Grand Council or parliament; so the Gentlemen and Heads of Families were to the Chief, by whose advice all things that regarded the Clan in common, or particular Families, were determined, differences were removed, injuries were punished or redressed, law suits prevented, declining Families supported and peace or war with other Clans agreed upon'.

The gentlemen played an important part in war. They were the best-armed fighters; the early habergeon or mail-coat and the later fire-lock or musket were expensive possessions. Sometimes the Gentlemen formed the entire fighting force. Sometimes they led the men of their branch when the main body of the clan was called out. In later times they were the officers of the companies and regiments formed in the Highlands. They helped to maintain order and to guard the more vulnerable districts from attack. The thirteenth Lord Lovat would 'flatly deny' any gentleman's son who wanted a lease of a farm 'in the incountry', telling him that 'gentlemen are appointed to watch and guard the country, and therefore ought to live upon marches, skirts and extremities thereof to keep off theeves and sorroners'.[17]

The growing number of the gentlemen and therefore the pressure upon them to find a means of livelihood during the seventeenth century are important factors that are obvious when it is remembered that the descendants of the owners of land had by course of nature increased through the centuries and that there had been almost no exit from the Highlands and no industrial development within it. The obvious means of providing for a landowner's children was by division of land, but under the system of primogeniture actual splitting up was impossible. What had happened was the creation of layers of ownership in rights of occupation. Generalized factual data for this obvious development are not available and, as every clan varied in its circumstances, would be impossible. Their own pedigree, the direct line of their own descent, was familiar not so long ago to many Highlanders. It requires considerably more genealogical skill to realize the inter-relation of families that wove Highland society into a complicated fabric. The voluminous texts upon MacDonald family groups or A M Mackintosh's scholarly summary of Clan Chattan Septs in his *Mackintoshes and Clan Chattan*, above all the actual tons of documents in the Seaforth Papers, are good examples of available material. The essential point is that society was not merely woven but felted together in different levels of prosperity. According to the degree of relationship with the holder of the land, material provision varied. Family fortunes differed. Yet a closely integrated society persisted. The seventeenth century must have seen this form of society at its most dense, for at the turn of the century, just as the pressure of accommodation upon land became intense, openings elsewhere became available. Especially after the Act of Union the availability of new openings in the South and overseas was most significant. Bailie John Steuart in his *Letter Book* and the first volume of the Culloden Papers show some younger sons became merchants or captains of ships. Many families like the MacLeods of Bernera were able to send a son to be 'bred to the law'. The Church supplied some openings because parish ministers were selected by the heritors of the parish. The greater number had obtained leases or tacks of varying size and farmed their land with the assistance of sub-tenants. By the early eighteenth century this system was coming under attack from the agricultural reformers. It was becoming out-moded, although under more primitive methods of farming it had surely had some good points. An analysis by one of the writers of an account book kept by a tacksman forebear, *Everyday Life on an Old Highland Farm*, fully bears this out.

The lesser country gentry rendered invaluable service to the preservation of the Highland traditions and poetry. As Lowland and English influences permeated Highland society from the top downwards, it was more and more the lesser gentry who supplied patronage and encouragement to poets and musicians and, themselves becoming increasingly literate as education opportunities increased, extended the sources of culture. There were poets among them. The seventeenth century Fernaig Manuscript, a collection of poems composed in the MacRae country and mainly written by a group of men of this class, contains many fine poems. Nor did their influence for the good of the Highlands end with their own departure. In the succeeding period much of the work of recording and preserving our Highland heritage was done by the Highland Societies that sprang up wherever adventurous Highlanders had made good in the world outside.

The lesser gentry were important agents in the development of the great cattle droving industry to England that became possible with the Union of the Crowns and which was the first indication that the growing industrial and commercial activity that in England was gradually boiling up towards the Industrial Revolution was penetrating the isolation and archaic social conditions of the Highlands. *Gille Chriosd* MacRae of Inverinate was reputedly the first man who drove cows from that country to the markets in the south in the seventeenth century, and annually bought beasts from neighbouring landholders for that purpose. It was said of him with regard to his generosity that 'if he was as frugul in keeping as he was industrious in acquiring, he had proven a very rich man in his own country'.[18]

The position of the chief and clansmen has been rather fully dealt with because the most outstanding point of this period is that the power of the clans and the feudal institutions of heritable jurisdictions and the due of armed service persisted as the viable social organisation of the Highlands down to the Rising of 1745. They were only put an end to by military occupation and the passing of legislation ending ward-holding and heritable jurisdiction in 1747. Nevertheless, working against the existing state of society, the seventeenth century saw the development of new institutions and ideas that were making radical changes inevitable. The question may well be asked: had the '45 never occurred, how would the changes have taken effect — by some equally sudden break or by peaceful penetration?

Although the difference between the Highlands and the Lowlands persisted in some ways — very notably in the survival of the duty of armed service in return for the occupation of land, a feudal concept beginning to die out elsewhere — yet the obvious signs of the penetration of Highland isolation increased during the seventeenth century. Unfortunately the direct result was the sudden raising of the standards of living regardless of any increase in the sterile over-crowded land to satisfy the new demand. The association with the Lowlands and England and the natural wish not to live in a way inferior to that of people of their own class was forced upon the chiefs in James VI's abortive attempts to exploit the resources of the Islands and Western Highlands. The Statutes of Icolmkill and subsequent orders of the Privy Council had forced the chiefs of some of the western clans to go yearly to Edinburgh and to have their children educated in the Lowlands. The MacLeod muniments show that this was no dead letter. In 1615 Rory Mor's sons were at school in Glasgow. Some of the chiefs from time to time visited London to see the king and obviously succumbed to the novel delights of the south. This drew stinging ripostes and satirical attacks from poets such as the Mull bard *Iain MacAilein* and the blind harper Roderick Morison, *An Clarsair Dall*. The latter composed his 'Song to MacLeod of Dunvegan' in which he attacks MacLeod for abandoning Dunvegan for foreign parts, *ann an daor chuirt nan Gall*, in the depraved court of the

Southerners, by contrast with his predecessor *Iain Breac* who had maintained a household in the old style, and for MacLeod's excesses and his extravagance by which the estate was burdened with debt. When the sons of other chiefs, such as Mackintosh, went south for their education, they became interested in affairs outside the Highlands. The custom of spending part of the year in Edinburgh was beginning, as was the interest in parliamentary elections and in the politics of the United Kingdom. This was notably the case with Argyll and with later Lairds of Grant. Although as a rule until the later part of the period it was still usual for chiefs' wives to be Highland or at least Scots, southern standards of living were spreading and also financial embarrassment; as the Blind Harper parodied the attitude of his chief: 'On the security of a townland or two, take the pen and sign a bond'.[19] The disastrous pressures that were to lead to the sale of so much land and the consequent erosion of ties between chief and clansmen were building up. This is a fundamental change in the period, less spectacular than many of the survivals or adaptations, but deep and permanent in its effect on the Highlands.

The serious weakness that began to appear in this period and was to become crucial later on, the acute financial embarassment of the chiefs, was exacerbated as they found that their resources were becoming increasingly inadequate for their style of living. Argyll himself, Chisholm, Lovat, MacLean, Grant, Mackintosh, Sutherland, MacLeod and many others became financially embarrassed. It is important to note that there is no evidence that this change in the way of life of the more important people encouraged any particular clan feeling. So far as their means allowed them, the lesser gentry also changed their way of life. There was no absolute social barrier in Highland society, although many of the lesser gentry entered the professions or commerce or, towards the end of our period, sought their fortunes overseas.

The belted plaid or its modification, the kilt, was worn by men of every rank; it was never a peasant dress. This is symbolic of the lack of social barriers, the familiarity between those of different rank and status, and the pride and feeling for dress in Highland society. Change, when it came, was more gradual and subtle. Brigadier Mackintosh, recalling in his old age some of his memories of the Highlands in his younger days, wrote of the change from clothes of home-grown, homespun materials to silks and broadcloth, of food garnished with English pickles and 'catch-up' sauce, and the change from the dram of good wholesome Scots spirits to the tea table and silver and china equipage.[20]

It is easier to trace the sale of large estates, but more difficult to trace the resumption of wadsets and the end of leases. The evidence for the departure of so large a number of the lesser gentry is also not obvious. The following is an unusually clear example of a general tendency. By great good fortune, the main part of the upper valley of the Findhorn, that is Strathdearn, was feued by the Earl of Moray during the seventeenth century with eight small estates. A M Mackintosh, the historian of Clan Chattan, has details on the pedigrees of the families who bought them. It is significant of the times that they were all members of the different branches of Clan Chattan, and also, though most of the purchases were ordinary commercial transactions, one feu was granted to Mackintosh in recompense for doing his work for him in catching a notorious freebooter. There is evidence that allows the conclusion to be drawn that they were all successfully engaged in the cattle trade, but as time went on, first sons and heads of families sought other occupations such as the army, the law, or commerce, and the revenue derived from their estates became inadequate for their support. By the end of the eighteenth century, all the estates had changed hands, some more than once.

For most of the lesser gentry during our period, the cattle-droving trade was a most important source of income. In early times, cattle had been sent from the Highlands to the Lowland markets. After the Union of the Crowns, the abolition of the barrier of the frontier allowed the trade to develop. Young stock, brought into good condition upon the shielings, were ferried from the islands, driven along the drove roads, changed hands in increasing numbers at 'trysts' all along the route and eventually were bought for wintering upon more clement English pastures.

This trade is an important landmark in seventeenth century Highland industry. It brought in much needed revenue, it brought the Highlanders into touch with England, it developed a commercial framework, albeit a shadowy one, of different men who raised cattle on a larger scale for this market, who made up small droves for their local tryst or who dealt directly with the English buyers. This was a significant change in a pastoral community that had been little affected by any commercial development of the Lowlands. The cattle trade was a part of great changes in the pattern of life in the Highlands. Scotland, an agricultural country, was poor. The Highlands with a lesser proportion of agricultural land, most of it of less good quality and with an even severer climate, was poorer than the Lowlands, although the disproportion in assets was not then so striking as in the present industrial age, for the Highlands contributed materially to the most valuable exports. A 1614 table of Scots exports recorded a total of £820,524 Scots of which nearly a third was for commodities that largely came from the Highlands, including £66,630 for hides of which £1,830 were for 'hart hyddis', £172,082 for skins, of which over £5,000 were from foxes, roe deer and rabbits, and £47,208 for salmon. The Highlands also produced a good deal of plaiding and helped to supply the lack of timber in the Lowlands, a trade which was to continue in the next period.[22]

Such trade, in contrast to the late eighteenth century, was unorganised. Thomas Tucker, an Englishman sent north to reorganise the customs during the Cromwellian occupation, reported in 1656 that all the people of Glasgow excepting the students of the College traded 'with theyr neighbours the Highlanders, who come hither from the Isles and Westerne parts; in summer by the Mull of Cantyre, and in the winter by the Torban to the head of loquh Fyn (which is a small neck of sandy land, over which they usually drawe theyr small boates into the Firth of Dunbarton,) and soe pass up the Cluyde with pladding, dry hides, goate, kid, and deer skyns, which they sell, and purchase with theyr price such comodityes and provisions as they stand in neede of from time to time.' In 1566 an order of the Privy Council declared that none should molest 'the Helandmen in bodiis or guidis' in coming to the Lowland markets, that 'guid nychtbourheid and abstinence fra all displesour and invasioun' should be observed between Highlands and Lowlands and that the surplus of the 'fruitis growand in the Laich and Hielandis' should be exchanged.[23] Three later orders were made concerning the non-interference with the payment of the Highlands' rent and dues.

The Highlands, however, were becoming increasingly unable to support their growing population. The old connection with Ireland and the employment of Highland soldiers there had ended, and was now being replaced by service abroad in the Swedish and other foreign armies, notably during the Thirty Years War. But economic pressure, especially among the less well provided clans, was at the root of the constant raids and feuds. Scott in *Rob Roy*, through the mouth of Bailie Nicol Jarvie, summarised the position. Having calculated that the total population of the Highlands was 230,000, of whom 57,500 were able-bodied men, he remarks colourfully: 'it's a sad and awfu' truth that there is neither work, nor the very fashion nor appearance of work, for the tae half of thae puir creatures; that is to say, that the agriculture, the pasturage, the fisheries, and every species of honest industry about the country, cannot employ the one moiety of the population, let them work as lazily as they like, and they do work as if a pleugh or spade burnt their fingers'; although about half of the others might make a little money by shearing the harvest, droving, or hay-making in the Lowlands, but that there remained 'mony hundreds and thousands o' lang-legged Hieland gillies that will neither work nor want' and 'mony hundreds o' them come down to the borders of the low country, where there's gear to grip, and live by stealing, reiving, lifting cows, and the like depredations! — a thing deplorable in any Christian country; the mair especially that they take pride in it, and reckon driving a spreagh (whilk is, in plain Scotch, stealing a herd of nowte) a gallant, manly action, and mair befitting of pretty men (as sic reivers will ca' themsells) than to win a day's wage by any honest thrift'.

The privileges of the Royal Burghs continued to interpose a formidable barrier to direct Highland trade. The merchants had a monopoly of the whole of foreign trade in the most important commodities. Inverness had her privileges over a wide area in the north confirmed by the 'golden charter' of 1591, and there are many recorded instances of the enforcement of the monopoly rights to trade in plaiding, hides and other materials, although so powerful a man as Lovat sold his salmon abroad and bought wine. The Royal Burghs also had a monopoly of the herring fishing. Inverness, however, by the seventeenth century had become largely a Highland community where Gaelic was freely spoken, and it served as a useful centre for the exchange of commodities produced and needed by the country people.[24]

It is important to remember that almost no wool was exported from the Highlands during this period, and that the small fine-wooled sheep supplied only the needs of the people. The export of plaiding, however, is often mentioned, sometimes checked plaiding and sometimes white or undyed. In 1592 certain tenants in the Isles paid their rents by sending to Glasgow 190 ells of plaiding, 22 hides and 11 otter skins. We know that the plaiding exported from Scotland was mainly coarse and cheap, and it is interesting to find that an account of Scotland of 1711 mentioned Highland plaids as 'a manufacture wherein they exceed all nations, both as to colour and fineness', and Martin Martin wrote that, 'the plaid ..... is made of fine wool, the thread as fine as can be made of that kind.'[25]

Before the Union of the Crowns, the people's cattle had from early times been their main source of sustenance and of the means wherewith to pay their rents. Other needs such as seed corn after a bad harvest, iron goods and small luxuries had to be imported into the Highlands. In 1502 Grant's grandson was selling marts to the king, and there are records of cattle being driven from Kintail and Trotternish in 1502 and in 1600, and John MacKenzie, captured at the battle of Pinkie in 1547, paid his ransom 'with cowes that was raised throw all his land'. The tocher of a bride was often paid in cattle, as for instance at Borlum and Dochgarroch in 1723.[26] Besides the trade in live cattle, enormous numbers must have been killed for their hides, but the growth of the trade in live cattle instead of their hides which took place after the Union of the Crowns must have adversely affected the people's dietary.

The stocks of cattle had sometimes been very large. In the raid into Glemoriston in 1545, Glengarry carried off about two thousand head, for which the Laird of Grant sought compensation. In the seventeenth century the export of cattle on the hoof to England increased and prices rose. The chiefs and tacksmen raised large herds of cattle and derived most of their income from them. In 1609 the chiefs of the Western Isles petitioned against a proclamation made in Argyll which forbade the inhabitants of the mainland from buying marts or cattle, horses and other goods from the Isles, because they could pay their rents only by the sale of cattle, horses and other goods in the mainland markets. The proclamation was at once withdrawn.[27]

The great cattle-droving trade, so important to the Highlanders, was developing. The manuscript history of the MacRaes gives us some racy anecdotes about *Gille Chriosd* or Christopher MacRae, who flourished in the early seventeenth century and was said to be the first man in Kintail to engage in the droving trade. He bought cattle from MacKenzie of Kintail, MacLeod of Dunvegan and MacDonald of Sleat, and drove them to the south where he sold them. He must have been in a flourishing position to indulge his convivial tastes. The following tale does not bear on economic matters but is characteristic of the times. Donald Gorm Mor of Sleat, who was married to a daughter of MacKenzie, had spent all the money which he had had with him while on a visit to Perth. So he left his wife there while he went home to get some more. Christopher, having sold his drove, found her in this predicament, lent her money, and conveyed her home, where he was entertained for some days. On leaving, and 'being still warm with drink', he called for a large cup of strong waters in which to pledge Donald Gorm. His host felt himself bound to return the compliment and exclaimed that he hoped Christopher did not intend to kill him with such large potations. Christopher incautiously remarked that it would be but natural, seeing that his father had killed MacDonald's father, his father being the redoubtable archer, Duncan *MacGhille Chriosd*, who had shot down Donald Gorm at Eilean Donan; MacDonald took the jest in good part, but his people drew their dirks and would have killed the boastful drover had his host not conveyed him personally to his boat.

The Highlands became covered by a network of drove roads which brought the cattle from the Highlands and Islands to the markets in East and Central Scotland. Each year from May to October, markets or trysts were held at places such as Muir of Ord, the fairs of Buchan and the Garioch and the Trinity Tryst by Brechin at which the cattle changed hands between drovers and dealers. In the last quarter of the seventeenth century Crieff in Strathearn on the edge of the Highlands became established as the main tryst, a position of prominence it was to hold until 1760s when rising prices and the growing interests of English dealers drew the tryst south to Falkirk. By the 1790s, 20-30,000 beasts were being sold here annually at the October tryst alone.[28]

Beside a legitimate cattle trade, the raiding of cattle, which had gone on from early times and was celebrated in song and prose, was intensified. This is so characteristic of this violently mixed period that it is worth describing in more detail. It was widespread: in fact, cattle spuilzie provides one of the most repetitive notes of the Register of the Privy Council in the seventeenth century. The clans whose pursuit it was were those whose increase in numbers had outstripped their lands' capacity to support them; among them were Glengarry, the MacDonalds of Glencoe and Keppoch, the Camerons, and also the MacFarlanes and the more needy cadets of other clans. The landless MacGregors were, of course, frequently cited as the perpetrators of such outrages.

It was the age of great caterans or *ceatharnaich*, and many accounts survive in fact and legend. In the Wardlaw Manuscript, for example, James Fraser describes *Iain Dubh Cearr*, Black John the Left-handed, who terrorised large areas of the north and exacted tributes from towns and villages, as 'a plague and scurge upon the country' who raided the Lowlands of Angus and Kincardineshire, Banff, Aberdeen and Moray from his refuge in the Cairn o Mounth. A more colourful figure is James Macpherson, born about 1675 and hanged at the Cross of Banff in November 1700 for his cattle reiving activities; he was a fiddler and composer, and 'Macpherson's Rant' is said to be the tune that he composed before his own execution. James Grant of Carron, *Seumas an Tuim*, began his career of outlawry in 1615 and continued until 1645 when, fighting in the battle of Auldearn, he earned a remission and pardon for his crimes, retired to his home and eventually died peacefully at an advanced age. His extraordinary career included evasion of the band of forty dispossessed Mackintosh tenants who were offered the restoration of their holdings by the Earl of Moray in return for the robber's capture, and later on, his escape from Edinburgh Castle aided by his wife. Such careers often had a strong element of tragedy as, for example, that of Donald Donn of Bohuntin in Glen Roy, one of the Keppoch MacDonalds. He was a notable poet, a very active reiver and a renowned lover whose amorous adventures were as famous as his thieving activities. He was in love with a daughter of a laird of Grant. Not surprisingly, the Laird used his influence, Donald Donn was captured and executed about 1691. When he was being beheaded, the severed head is said to have uttered the words *A Cheit, tog an ceann*, Kate, lift the head.[29]

Until well into the eighteenth century, there was little distinction between dealing and stealing and no shame was felt for 'driving a spraigh'. A song by a MacGregor to her love, *Bothan Airigh am Braigh Raithneach*, composed about 1680 illustrates contemporary attitudes. She describes how he would bring back clothes and attractive gifts for her from the fairs and then says:

> Why should we be without cattle
> When the Lowlanders have herds?
> We shall get cattle in the Mearns
> And sheep from Caithness.

The raiders specially victimised adjacent parts of the Lowlands and they also raided more peaceful clans. A letter from Lochiel to Grant in 1645 illustrates the prevalent morality of this. He promised compensation to Grant for the theft of cattle and damage done by his men, having mistaken the property of a kinsman for 'Morrayland, quhair all men taks their prey'. Banffshire and Aberdeenshire suffered severely, a particularly vicious raid being carried out in 1743 when the Black Watch had been withdrawn for foreign service, and Angus was fair game for the *ceatharnaich* who frequently crossed the country from Moidart and Lochaber. A particularly vicious raid occurred in 1602 when the MacDonalds of Glengarry drove off about 2,700 cattle from the grazings of Glen Isla, Glen Shee and Strathhardle. They were pursued by Angus men, who overtook them at the Cairnwell, and a battle ensued which was long talked about in the locality. Stirlingshire, Dunbartonshire and the Lennox were also open to attack, being on the fringes of the Highlands, and the harvest moon was locally termed there 'MacFarlane's lantern' because of his activities in the autumn, the favourite season for raiding.[30]

The raiders' favoured routes and the places where they concealed their cattle can still be pointed out. Some chiefs extracted a tax from reivers who passed through their lands; Rev William MacBean recalled the tradition in 1792 of the 'raiders' collop' which was levied on the caterans who passed on the ancient route through Moy and Dalarossie, collop being *calp* or *colpach*. Some of the victims paid 'black mail' as it was termed and thus bought off the raiders. A notorious example of extortion and intimidation was Coll MacDonald of Barrisdale in Knoydart, who was reputed to gain about £500 a year in black mail. The polite term for this was a payment 'to keep good neighbourhood'. The mighty Marquis of Argyll paid out about 3,000 merks after the raids on his lands of 1640 'because he was afraid of being continually molested by the Brae Lochaber men'. Others employed spies to trace the stolen cattle and to offer a reward to recover them. This was known as 'tascal-money' and much reviled by many as quite contrary to the spirit of the operations. The more usual remedy was to pay chiefs along the routes that the raiders took to maintain a 'watch' and to intercept them. Cluny Macpherson and Mackintosh of Kylachy organised such watches, and traditions of the exploits of one of their men, John Beag MacAndrew, who lived at Dalnahaitnich on the Dulnan, are still told in Strathdearn.

In fact, the exploits of the reivers seem to have lingered on in people's memory, in some areas more than almost anything else of the past, and are a valuable part of Highland folklore and tradition.[31]

By the early eighteenth century the domestic industries of spinning linen yarn, spinning woollen thread and knitting stockings, that were to help to carry Scotland through the hard times of the eighteenth century, had spread to the more accessible parts of the Highlands. They were important in Perthshire and in the burgh of Inverness.

It was an age of growing enterprise in the South, and undertakings such as attempts to discover and work metals, the all important materials in this age of booming activity, were made but met with little success. At this early stage, the landowners generally took the initiative in supplying the capital, the new technology and commercial organisation required. Among such enterprises was the shipping of iron ore to such places as Furnace on Loch Fyne to smelt it by means of the abundant scrub-wood and to ship back the pig-iron. Attempts were also made to discover and to mine mineral deposits in the Highlands, as for instance, lead in Islay and at Strontian, but with little success. Undeterred, such ventures continued to be made throughout the century. Even more minute were local attempts to smelt small deposits of iron ore, as for instance at Letterewe on Loch Maree, or even iron ore derived from peat bogs. The remains of some fifty of these little furnaces have been discovered scattered over the country.[32] The shortage of iron was acute during our period and for years afterwards. Because it had to be imported and the people could not afford to pay for it, the scarcity or absence of metal (apart from that used for weapons) conditioned the lives of the people until the great reform in agriculture which did not take place in the remoter and poorer districts until the very end of the eighteenth century or even later, and the plough, that essential agricultural implement was made of wood, except for an iron sock and coulter, in the most fertile and advanced districts such as Strathspey and the Laich of Moray only a few decades earlier.

In collecting implements and household plenishings for a Highland Folk Museum, it is possible to make a fairly accurate estimate of the fertility of the local soil from the presence or absence of iron. For instance, implements for toasting were specially useful for cooking when the hearth was on the ground in the middle of the floor or between two stones against the wall. From more fertile districts, one finds them in great variety; in the poorest, a stone or a support of charred wood had to suffice. It may be noted that in some districts timber also was scarce and had to be replaced by wattle, basket work and woven grass. When considerable activity was being stimulated from the south to find and use Highland resources, it is extraordinary that control of the fisheries which

James VI had made such efforts to develop had been allowed to slip into the hands of the Dutch with their well organised fleets of well equipped boats — the 'busses'.

A feature that distinguishes this period from the later eighteenth century is the absence of most kinds of craftsmen. In the Old Statistical Account of the 1790s, in parish after parish even in well developed districts, weavers and blacksmiths and, rather surprisingly, tailors are listed, but never masons, joiners or carpenters. Masons and wrights were brought in from outside to build castles and the houses of the most affluent. Even there, it can sometimes still be seen that the planks of the flooring were not sawn but were cut with the adze. If one examines the remains of really old ruined cottages, one sees that the surviving woodwork was shaped with the adze and pegged together with small pieces of wood in holes burnt out by a heated iron rod. There must have been a dearth of craftsmen, and convenient tools were rare possessions. Martin Martin, writing very late in the seventeenth century, recorded that St Kildans visiting Dunvegan were shocked to see that walls of masonry were covered by tapestry.

A significant indication of the absence of local craftsmen is in the number of tales of the dangers in fording Highland rivers because of the lack of bridges. The introduction of skilled craftsmen was an important development in the next period. The Highlanders during the sixteenth century must have had great difficulty in adjusting the exotic things that they imported to their more homely surroundings as well as paying for them from their very limited material means. This is only one symptom of a time of great contrast and changes.

The main imports consisted of grain and, for those who could afford them, a variety of miscellaneous articles. The accounts of a merchant in Campbeltown in 1672 show that he supplied saddlery, hardware, soap, spices, sugar, gloves, ribbon, saffron and the dyestuffs of indigo and cochineal, besides wine. Bailie Steuart of Inverness's *Letter Book* gives details of much the same selection of imports, and we know that Lovat imported wine and spices in exchange for his salmon. We have the record of a ship that came to the Western Isles with a miscellaneous cargo including cochineal, used for red dye, a most difficult colour to get from native dye plants.[33]

The amount of wine consumed in the Highlands must have been very great. In the repressive measures taken against six of the west coast chiefs in the early seventeenth century, their supply of wine was limited, but not one would think, to a niggardly extent although it might have been a serious limitation to the open handed hospitality expected of a Highland chief. MacLean of Duart and MacLeod were restricted to four tuns of wine each, Clan Ranald to three tuns and Coll, Lochbuie and

MacKinnon to one tun each and they were to ensure that none of their tenants bought or drank any wine at all. (The capacity of a tun varied, although a tun of wine was standardised at 60 gallons in 1644. The English tun generally contained 252 gallons). To curb more general drinking and drunkenness, an order of the Privy Council was added to the obligation of the chiefs in 1616 against excessive drinking and stated that 'the great and extraordinary excesse in drinking of wyne, commonlie usit among the commonis and tenantis of the Yllis, is not only ane occasioun of the beastlie and barbarous cruelties and inhumanities that fallis oute amangis thame, to the offens and displeasour of God, and contempt of law and justice; but with that it drawis nomberis of thame to miserable necessitie and povartie, sua that they are constraynit, quhen they want from their awne, to take from thair nightbours.'[34] Under the orders limiting the import of wine, householders were allowed to make as much *aqua vitae* as was needed for the use of their own families. The drinking of *aqua vitae* had become more common during the sixteenth century. There are references to it in Kintyre (where the farm of Crosshill at Lochhead in the seventeenth century paid six quarts of *aqua vitae* in rent), Ross-shire, Sutherland and Inverness, and although ale was still the commonest drink, the drinking of spirits was evidently spreading. By the seventeenth century, the word *usquebaugh*, from *uisge-beatha*, had come into general use, and as Martin Martin describes, the Lewis folk made a lethal liquor four times distilled called *uisge-baoghal*. In the satirical poem on the Highland Host by the Covenanting Commander, William Cleland, the Highlanders were said to carry a tup's horn filled with *usquebay*. By the eighteenth century the anglicised version 'whisky' seems to have come into use and we find Bailie John Steuart using the word in 1736. When Prince Charles Edward was in Skye, he could get nothing but 'whisky' in the inns; ale and beer were found only in gentlemen's houses.[35]

During this period there was a decline in the use of the Highland galleys and birlinns. The traditional histories of the Highlands such as the Applecross Manuscript and the history of the MacRaes abound with incidents in the early seventeenth century that show how constantly galleys were used. But in an inquisition made by the Privy Council into the numbers of galleys and birlinns owned by the West Coast chiefs, the number of boats is surprisingly small. Duart had two galleys and eight birlinns and his brother one galley. Argyll himself, Coll and MacLeod each had one galley, and Coll also had two birlinns. Clan Ranald, MacLean of Ardgour and MacPhee each had one birlinn. MacKinnon had only an eight-oared boat. It is possible that some of the chiefs were not willing to reveal more than they could help. The Privy Council order describes a 'galley' as a vessel with 16 to 24 oars, and a 'birlinn' as one with 12 to 16 oars. The very complete accounts preserved at Dunvegan show that the last birlinn built by MacLeod was in 1706.

The reason for this decline is nowhere given. The discouragement of galleys was part of the government's policy, but this, considering the state of the Highlands in the seventeenth century, is hardly an adequate explanation. For instance, in the expedition of 1608 to the Isles, Andrew Stewart, Lord Ochiltree, the King's lieutenant, wrote to the Privy Council that he would execute their commission to destroy 'lumfaddis, birlingis and Hieland galleyis'. And in the terms to be offered to the West Highland chiefs was one that all their boats except those needed to transport the royal rents were to be destroyed; and in the special terms imposed on the six chiefs in 1616 was one limiting each to one birlinn or one galley of 16 or 18 oars. The decline in the use of galleys and birlinns was evidently a rapid one. It is obvious that more modern sailing craft must have taken the place of the galleys with their banks of oars and square-rigged sails. This must have involved the building of boats with keels and new skills in seamanship to learn to tack. So far as we could discover, there is a lack of contemporary information about this. One gathers that the change was slow in coming. It is surprising that the coastal trade of the West and North should have been done by Inverness boats and that so many rowing songs should have survived and that there are eighteenth century allusions to singing at sea.

The period is unfortunately notable for some extremely bad harvests. No doubt, as the Highlands became more and more crowded, the people became more and more dependent upon the weather conditions. Also as they became more literary, comments upon it have survived. For instance, the chatty and discursive Wardlaw Manuscript has many comments upon it. The 'Seven Ill Years' of King William must have been abnormally bad, but the unreliability and harshness of the Highland climate, which to us is an inconvenience and a serious handicap to the tourist industry, was in the days of subsistence farming a serious threat to the people's well-being and sometimes even to the health or even the lives of the weaker members of the community.

In the seventeenth century new and formidable disruptive forces were operating against the cultural life of the Highlands. The four Scots universities of St Andrews, Glasgow, Aberdeen and Edinburgh were in existence by the end of the sixteenth century; Lowland Scots literature had been developed by the writings of Robert Henryson, William Dunbar, Gavin Douglas and other 'makers' of the golden age. The sixteenth century and the seventeenth century therefore saw the survival of a literary movement. But Lowland culture almost ignored that of the Gael. It is significant that James Philip in his very sympathetic *Grameid* should have derived the place-name Culnakyle from Old King Cole instead of from its obviously Gaelic origin, and has produced a myth entirely unrelated to Highland tradition for the people of Glen Roy. He is, however, almost unique in writing sympathetically of the Highlanders. With the seventeenth century there had developed a new bitter tone in writing of them, and the hostility expressed for the Highlanders by the Lowlanders in the seventeenth century had developed a note almost of hysteria. A few examples must suffice: King James VI's attitude is well known. The letters of Andrew Knox, Bishop of the Isles, entrusted with their administration as Steward of the Isles, teem with grossly insulting references, as when he warned the king that his own promises to 'that falss generatioun and bludie pipill' should not be honoured, or referred to the 'inordinaire levinge of that pipill' or urged that 'that pestiferous clan' Donald should be rooted out of Islay. When in 1609 Sir James MacDonald was brought to trial before the Privy Council, the indictment began: 'Forsamekill as, frome your verrie youthe, ye be tranit up in all maner of crewall barbaritie and wiketnes, and following the pernitious exampill of your godles parentis, kynsmen and cuntrie people'....'. Sir James in a dignified reply pointed out the impropriety of Argyll's testifying against him because of his territorial interests and his activities.[36] The tone of vituperation persisted into the era of the Enlightenment. A sermon preached before the S.P.C.K. in 1750 declared that the Highlanders like 'a dark torrent through a peaceful land spread fear and death on every side.'

The vigorously asserted allegations of the Highlanders' barbarity seem to have been considered a justification for the indulgence of similar behaviour by the Lowlanders, of which abundant examples occur. The massacre of Glencoe in February 1692 is only one instance; Bishop Knox and the chancellor, the Earl of Dunfermline, broke faith with the defenders of Dunyveg in 1615 and a massacre followed. In the reprisals by the Covenanting armies there were many examples of discrimination against the Highlanders, such as those by Argyll and General Leslie in Kintyre. Such perfidious and bloody acts were accompanied by a sanctimonious pretension to moral superiority for which actual evidence is conspicuously lacking. But the most naive surprise was sometimes expressed at the good conduct of the Highlanders. One comment on the Highland Host, for example, was, 'Never did 6,000 thieving ruffians with uncouth weapons make so harmless a march in a civilised country', and Daniel Defoe in his *Tour through the whole Island of Great Britain* reported that the Highland chiefs were 'as polite and as finished gentlemen as any from other countries, or even among our own, and if I should say, outdoing our own in many things ...'

The Highlands had not been without educational provision. In the sixteenth century and earlier there had been schools in the religious houses of Ardchattan, Rosemarkie, Fearn, Beauly, Kinloss and Kingussie, and there had been so many Highland students at Aberdeen Grammar School that Gaelic was allowed to be spoken. By the end of the sixteenth century there had come a change. From 1586 we find that the Masters of Lovat attended Lowland universities instead of being educated at Beauly Priory; and the sons of many other important chiefs, such as Mackintosh, the Earls of Sutherland, MacLeod of Harris and MacKenzie of Kintail were educated in the Lowlands. Sometimes such education was in deference to royal wishes. James VI wrote in 1608 to Wiliam Mackintosh of Raitts and Benchar, who was bringing up his nephew the young Laird of Mackintosh, ordering him to make provision for his dispatch 'to one of the Universities here', in other words, in England. Sometimes the clansmen desired it for their chief. About the middle of the century the gentlemen of the Earldom of Sutherland made a voluntary levy to pay for the education of the young Earl at a university.[37]

The seventeenth century saw another important educational development. Serious attempts were made to transmit the teachings of the Reformed Church in the 1560s, such as the educational provisions of the First Book of Discipline. The reformers had pronounced a wholly new ideal of a national system of education based on the parish, but the clearest statement of this had to wait until an act of the Privy Council of 1616 and successive acts of parliament of 1633, 1639 and 1646, all of which were concerned not only to establish schools and schoolmasters but also to make adequate financial provision for their maintenance. The 1616 act recommended that there should be a school in every parish so that, in the spirit of James VI's ambition, 'the youth be exercised and trayned up in civilitie, godlines, knowledge and learning, that the vulgar Inglishe toung be universallie plantit, and the Irishe language, whilk is one of the cheif and principall causis of the continewance of barbaritie and incivilitie amongis the inhabitantis of the Ilis and Heylandis, may be abolisheit and removit.' The new educational campaign was therefore also an attack on the Gaelic language and way of life. In later statutes, Gaelic was specifically forbidden in the Highland parish schools. The same policy had been pursued in the dealings of the Privy Council with the Western Highlands. We have already noted that in the Statutes of Icolmkill of 1609, the chiefs had to agree that 'the ignorance and incivilitie of the saidis Isles had daylie increasit be the negligence of guid educatioun and instructioun of the youth in the knowledge of God and good letters', and all gentlemen and yeomen were to send their heirs to be educated at schools in the Lowlands to speak, read and write English. In the 1616 obligation that six of the Western chiefs were obliged to sign was the provision that all their children over nine years of age should be sent to school in the Lowlands to learn reading, writing and speaking in English, and that none should receive recognition as heirs to their father or be received as a tenant on crown land who had not received this education. The order of the Privy Council accompanying this agreement contained the same provisions in the usual insulting terms, attributing the principal cause of the continuance of 'barbaritie, impietie and incivilitie within the Yllis of this kingdom' to keeping the children at home.[38]

After the Revolution, the king and parliament enacted that in future all vacant stipends in Argyll should be applied to educational purposes. The act of 1695 granted the rents of the bishopric of Argyll to the Synod of Argyll for 'Erecting of English Schools for rooting out of the Irish Language and other pious uses'. Since the folk of the area had been reluctant to pay, soldiers were to be quartered on them to enforce it. By 1698 the rents were financing twenty-five English schools, thirteen peripatetic English schools and five grammar schools. That the animus against Gaelic was largely political and that the need for being able to speak it was recognised by Argyll himself is clear from the careful provision made in the 1730s for the teaching of Gaelic to his own heir. His foster-father, Campbell of Glenorchy, undertook to have 'ane discreite man that is ane scollar, and that can speike both Inglis and Erise, quharof I think thair may be had in Argyll'; and his mother who was a Douglas, daughter of the Earl of Morton, wrote in 1637 ordering that the boy be held to speaking Gaelic.

The Highlanders were aware of the advantages of the Lowland's learning. The schoolmaster of Channory of Fortrose, in a petition to parliament for help in consequence of the damage done by the troops of General Leslie in 1646, stated that the school was attended by the children of the country, especially from the Highlands and Islands, as it was 'the next adjacent school to them'. The number of grammar schools in the north, especially on the east coast, was steadily growing. Sometimes gentlemen would join together to employ a tutor, usually a University student, or would send their sons to private schools run by the ministers. It is significant that in a bond of union signed by the leading men of Clan Chattan in 1609, out of twenty six signatures, half were made by 'hands led at the pen'. When a similar bond was made in 1664, only one out of twenty eight signatories could not sign his name. Literacy and learning were growing in the Highlands, but this was literacy in English and not in Gaelic.

The new parishes in the Highlands were very large; and even so, progress was very slow in setting up parochial schools in them. In the description of Lewis about 1680 by John Morison of Bragar he says that there was only one school in Lewis: it was in Stornoway, and maintained by the Earls of Seaforth; in it Latin and English were taught to 'heads of every family', that is only the sons and daughters of the tacksmen. Kirkhill and Kiltarlity had schools by 1671, but even most of the more accessible districts in the Highlands had to wait until the end of the seventeenth century or even later for a school. Rev Lachlan Shaw, writing in 1775, commented that there were hardly any schools in the province of Moray except in the royal burghs, till after the Revolution, and added 'I well remember when from Speymouth to Lorn, there was but one school, viz at Ruthven, in Badenoch'. The parish schools of course were specifically intended for teaching English. The initiative for the seventeenth century legislation on education came largely from the church. In 1646, the year of the important act for founding schools, the General Assembly passed a resolution demanding the implementation of the 1609 statute of Icolmkill regarding education in English, and the setting up of an English language school in every Highland parish. The Synod of Argyll was exceptionally enlightened in the matter of education and was the only Synod that made a provision, in 1650, that scholars who could read English were to be encouraged to translate the Bible to the others; the reason given was that 'because the knowledge of the English language is so necessary for the weall of the Gospell, the Scriptures not being translated in Irish'.[41]

It was largely to supplement the inadequacy of parochial schools in the Highlands that the Society in Scotland for Propagating Christian Knowledge was formed in Edinburgh through the efforts of some private individuals in 1709. Its patent of institution stated that it was formed for 'the further promoting of Christian Knowledge and the increase of piety and virtue within Scotland, especially in the Highlands, Islands and remote corners thereof, where error, idolatry, superstition and ignorance do mostly abound, by reason of the largeness of the parishes and scarity of schools'. It enjoyed the support of the General Assembly, it was strongly anti-popish and unfortunately it equated the progress of civilisation with the elimination of Gaelic and the spread of English. All the masters it employed were obliged to subscribe to a formula against Popery and to undertake to 'discharge their scholars to speak Earse'. As most of the children could speak only Gaelic, this condemned them to learning merely by rote. By 1715 the Society had set up twenty-five schools in the north, and by 1750 it had 150 schools. Its itinerant schools were scattered far and wide in remote glens and on distant islands where no parish schools existed, as for example, most spectacularly, on the island of St Kilda as early as 1711.[42]

The Church, however, ignored its most immediate duty. The provison of a Bible in the language of the people was central to the Protestant faith, and it was in unhappy disregard of this duty that the church authorities, episcopalian and presbyterian, did not supply a Gaelic translation of the Scriptures until the very end of the seventeenth century. By contrast, the people of Wales had three Welsh editions of the Bible by this date. The eventual production of a Gaelic Bible was due to the initiative and hard work of Rev Robert Kirk of Balquhidder and Aberfoyle (1644-1692) who had an edition of 3,000 of Bishop Bedel's Irish Bible and 1,000 of O'Donnell's New Testaments printed in London. The original text, in Irish type, was rendered in Roman type but was of course unfamiliar in vocabulary, idiom and orthography to all but the learned. Even when printed, the General Assembly was culpably indifferent to these Bibles, and it was a matter of years before they were brought north from London and distributed.

This dereliction of duty by the Church in Scotland had been noted in England. An ordinance of the Commonwealth Government of 1658 'for planting the Gospel in the Highlands' stated that although the Gospel was sufficiently preached in the Lowlands, 'yet little or noe care hath been taken for a very numerous people inhabiteing in the Highlandes,' who had been left in complete lack of religious teaching, and they ordered that £600 a year from the revenues of Scotland should be found to provide for this neglect. This provision did not survive the Commonwealth, but the authorities in Church and State were not entirely complacent over their neglect of the Highlands. For instance, in 1644 and 1690 Acts of Parliament were passed ordering that the stipends of vacant parishes should be devoted to the training for the ministry of youths who had the Irish tongue.[43] Efforts were also made to train and place Gaelic-speaking ministers in the Highlands, and because of their shortage, there was a ruling that no minister able to speak Gaelic should be settled in a Lowland parish. An example of a devoted covenanting missionary is David Simson, a Lowlander who learned Gaelic in order to work in the Highlands and who was made minister of Killean in Kintyre in 1656. Various efforts also were made to replace the sweeping reduction in Highland parishes that had followed the Reformation. In medieval times there had been an abundance of churches and chapels. For so poor a land, the plan was evidently too ambitious and the parishes too small, but it showed evidence of good Christian intentions. Not only were there many small parishes, but also many chapels. About two dozen of the old parishes had more than one additional chapel within their bounds, and some had four or five, or even six. After the Reformation many of the parishes were amalgamated. For instance, the parish of Kirkhill consists of the old parishes of Wardlaw with the Church of St Mary or St Muireach and Farnua dedicated to St Curitan and also including the cell at Bunchrew and the priory church at Beauly. This is only an example of what was happening all over the Highlands. In the

Islands the situation was even worse. The parishes of Ness with six chapels and nine more on adjacent islands, together with Sleat and Strath on Skye were for a time all united into one parish.

Unfortunately, national politics and the abdication of James VII in 1689 and the controversies over Church goverment and the Oath of Allegiance led to further religious divisions, in some parts of the Highlands as well as the Lowlands. Apart from any religious connection, Gaelic and Jacobitism were becoming widely associated in the Lowland mind. The only printed books in Gaelic were Bishop John Carswell's service book (the translation of the *Book of Common Order* of 1567), a translation of John Calvin's Catechism in 1630 or 1631, and a Gaelic version of the Shorter Catechism printed in 1653 by the energetic Synod of Argyll.

Unfortunately, the earlier stages of the Reformation may have been instrumental in destroying much of the Highland heritage. Bishop Carswell, who was himself an accomplished Gaelic scholar, in his introduction to the Gaelic translation of the Book of Common Order, tells of Argyll's work in 'destroying the false faith and false worship and in burning images and idols and in casting down and smashing altars and places where false sacrifices were offered of old'. The Synod of Argyll has often been blamed for the destruction of the library at Iona, but the evidence for this vandalism and even for the existence of a library at Iona is slight. One account written in 1693 accuses the Synod of destroying 'the registers and records' of Iona and also the crosses, of which numbers are said to have been thrown into the sea. There are traditions that the road outside was littered with manuscripts until they were gathered together and burnt. Others are said to have gone as waste paper and some used for wrapping snuff in the shops at Inveraray.[44] The Lords of the Isles were said to have kept records and there were documents engrossed by their record keepers, the MacDuffies of Colonsay, and there is some evidence for the compilation of annals at Iona. Manuscripts are said to have been taken from Iona to Douai in northern France where there was a Scots college, and a Gaelic translation of St Augustine's *De civitate Dei* made at Iona was still (in the eighteenth century) in the possession of the MacLachlans of Kilbride, a family well known for its literary interests and manuscript collection.

The attitude of the reformed Church was largely due to the ready association of ideas of the Gaelic and Highland ways of life with the Roman Catholic Church and the Jacobite cause. During the seventeenth century, in the face of penal laws and periodic agressive proselytising by the established Church, some areas remained true to the Roman Catholic faith, notably Barra, South Uist and Benbecula, Eigg and Canna, Knoydart, Morar, Moidart and Glengarry, and areas of Aberdeenshire

and Banff such as Glenlivet and Strathavon. The number of priests in
these areas was often pathetically small, and the need for Gaelic speaking
priests and missionaries was difficult to satisfy. The Irish Franciscan
mission to Scotland beginning in 1619, notable for the persons of Fathers
Cornelius Ward and Patrick Hegarty, effected a considerable 'revival'
and caused leading men such as Clan Ranald to reaffirm their
Catholicism and Campbell of Cawdor to be converted. Father Ward,
himself of the notable Irish poetic dynasty of *Mac a'Bhaird* had gained
access to Cawdor in 1624 in the guise of a poet and won him over after
three days of argument. A Scottish Mission was established in 1653 and
the first Vicar Apostolic, Bishop Thomas Nicolson, made his tour of the
Highlands in 1700. Probably due also to the response of areas such as
Strathglass and Braemar, a minor seminary that had been established on
an island on Loch Morar in 1712 was replaced in 1715 by the college at
Scalan in Glenlivet, which became the centre of Roman Catholic
missionary activity for the rest of the eighteenth century. Especially after
Bishop Nicolson's tour and the Roman Catholic sympathies of James
VII, the progress of this counter Reformation greatly alarmed the
General Assembly, which reported to the Privy Council in 1714 that
priests were swarming 'like Locusts, running from house to house
gaining Multitudes to their Ante-Christian Idolatry'.[45]

The authorities were minatory in ordering the Highlanders to observe
the reformed religion. In the Statutes of Icolmkill the first article
narrated that one of the chief causes of 'the grite grouth of all kind of
vice proceiding partly fra the laik of pastouris plantit and partly of the
contempt of those quha ar alreadie plantit' and that all ministers should
be 'reverentlie obeyit', their stipends paid, the ruinous kirks repaired,
'the Sabothis solemplie kepit', and sinners, including those who had
contracted handfast marriages punished.[174]

The order to repair their parish churches was repeated in 1622. The
appointment of two political careerists, John Carswell and Andrew
Knox, to the Highland episcopacy was most unfortunate. Carswell, as
Superintendent of Argyll and Bishop of the Isles, enjoyed considerable
ecclesiastical revenues and he was also a considerable landowner in his
own right. In Argyll tradition, a Gaelic quatrain preserves his memory in
an unflattering light:

> *Carsalach mor Charn-asaraidh*
> *A tha coig cairt 'na chasan —*
> .....

> The great Caswell of Carnassary,
> Whose legs are five quarters long —
> His rump is like the back of a crane,
> and his empty crop greedy and capacious.

In pleasant contrast to so much else in the seventeenth century the attitude of the Highlanders to religion, or rather to polemics, was tolerant or passive. Unfortunately this has changed to the fervour, bitterness and dissension which developed in many parts of the Highlands in the nineteenth century. The Puritan movement of the sixteenth century had little effect on the Highlands, and on the whole they showed a preference for old ways of thought, although they were sometimes influenced by the religious views of their chief. The story of the chief who stood at the crossroads and knocked down with his stick any of his tenants who tried to take the way to the Roman Catholic chapel is told of Hector MacLean of Coll with the wholesale 'conversion' of the Isle of Rum in 1725, and also of MacDonald of Boisdale, and gave rise to the nickname, *creideamh a'bhata bhuidhe* or the 'creed of the yellow stick' for Presbyterianism. The revival of episcopacy at the Restoration was placidly accepted, and after the Revolution, the bitterness that was shown in the south was conspicuously lacking. Many of the non-juring clergy were allowed to remain in their parishes, accepted by their people and tolerated by the local presbyteries. At Glenorchy the congregation refused to allow the non-juring clergyman, Mr Dugald Lindsay, to be displaced and he remained undisturbed in his charge for more than thirty years. Strathnairn, Appin and Easter Ross were strongly episcopalian. The itineraries of Bishop Forbes show how great was the people's attachment to the episcopalian services. Unfortunately political fears embittered religious differences and statutes were made and enforced against the non-juring clergy, and the severer statutes against the Roman Catholics were also revived.

Some of the chiefs were very active and sincere in trying to bring the benefits of religion to their people. The first Earl of Seaforth was especially energetic and caused a kirk to be built in every parish in his estates, including the island of Lewis that he had so dubiously acquired. On the other side, regardless of discouragement and persecution, the MacDonalds of Glengarry never accepted Protestantism. In spite of the risk of heavy penalties, the sons of the family were educated at Douai or elsewhere abroad, and some of them returned to be missionary priests in Scotland.

The depressive effect of the concentration in the Lowlands of all centres of learning was accompanied by the decline of the old Gaelic professions. There had been famous families of Highland doctors, notably the Beatons. One or two of the family may have been official historians to the MacLeans of Duart, because a writer in 1716 mentioned 'Mr John Beaton, the last of the Shenachies a Man pretty well skilled in Irish Antiquities' who had had a 'catalogue' of genealogy of the MacLeans. In 1558 a member of the Beaton family was attending Lord Lovat, but this seems to have declined in the seventeenth century, and in 1622 a doctor from Perth was in attendance on the Lovat of that date — who died. In the West, the family were more firmly established. In 1609 Fergus MacBeth obtained a crown charter for lands in Islay formerly granted to him 'by the Lord of the Isles of our Kingdom of Scotland', having been 'legally entered in the office of principal physician within the said Island, and for the administration of the said office'. Twenty years later, however, the family disposed of their lands. But there was still a Doctor Beaton in Islay some years later. Another branch had lands in Mull and had become attached to the MacLeans. The tombstone of one of the family at Iona dated 1657 is inscribed 'Joannes Betonus MacLenorum familiae medicus'. MacLeod of MacLeod had Beatons as his physicians, and the family was settled at Husabost in Glendale for their services. At least one member of the family seems to have served the Sleat family as well as Dunvegan. Martin Martin, at the end of the seventeenth century, mentions a Fergus Beaton in South Uist who possessed Gaelic medical manuscripts. He also mentions wonderful cures worked in Skye by a Neil Beaton, an 'illiterate empiric' and 'without the advantage of education'. He said he had been taught by his father. In the 1870s, a descendant of the Skye Beatons still lived in Uist and showed great interest in botany and the properties of plants. When Doctor Garnet visited Mull in 1800, there was no doctor on the island and anyone desiring medical treatment had to go to Inveraray. With the decline of medical skill went an increase in the reputation of Highland charms and uncanny powers. Gaelic was used for the charms mentioned in the seventeenth century witch trials in Bute, although otherwise English was spoken. Down to the end of the nineteenth century numbers of such charms survived in the Western Isles, and many of them are very touchingly devotional. There also survived in the Highlands a considerable traditional knowledge of the properties of curative herbs.[46]

The Breves of Lewis are mentioned in the tangled family history of the *Siol Torcuil* or MacLeods of Lewis in the early part of the seventeenth century. Traces of Gaelic law treatises concerning different subjects down to about this period have survived, although nothing on the scale of the Irish legal manuscripts, treatises and commentaries. The Statutes of Icolmkill discouraged the exercise of jurisdiction by the chiefs. How far the hereditary jurisdictions in the Highlands and that of the chiefs were according to Gaelic law there is nothing to show. Sir John Skene's *Regiam Majestatem* was published in 1596 and for the first time gave a precise definition of the laws of Scotland, and no doubt the knowledge of this book spread in the Highlands as well as the Lowlands. It is also interesting to note that the *Regiam Majestatem* took account of some traditional Gaelic terminology.

PART 2

In this period of great divergence in the ways of life and the constant clash between old institutions and new conditions, the Gaels were stirred to greater poetic self-expression than perhaps in any other period in their history. It is, however, entirely within the spirit of the period that this form of expression should vary from the traditional and classical to the spontaneous and narrative and finally to a new power of typical self-expression.

During the seventeenth century the story of Gaelic poetry followed two divergent trends. The classical metres were still used, and their practitioners, the trained and learned men of the schools, continued to occupy an honoured place in society. But the basis of this society was being undermined in the changing circumstances of the seventeenth century Highlands, and untrained bards were coming to the fore. Their language was the vernacular Gaelic of the day, some more colloquial than others. The spirit and subject matter of the poetry that survives from this period still reflected the influence of the old bardic verse, and eulogy and elegy in the old classical language and metres were still being composed well into the eighteenth century. Sir Norman MacLeod of Berneray, for example, who died in 1705, had three elegies written for him, two in syllabic metre and one in stressed metre.[1]

Poetry at least could provide a stable element in an unstable world and could reflect the old heroic qualities which were so greatly admired, celebrated in verse and emulated in the field. And when the new metres emerge, they bear the signs not so much of innovation but of an established tradition. The contemporary stressed metre is characterised by the short-lined verse and stanzas of differing length, which is a more ancient form of verse, essentially Gaelic in origin, than the classical metres which were derived from Latin hymn metres of the early Church. The distinctions between *Filidh* or Poet, Bard and Musician, and Historian or Genealogist were being worn down during the seventeenth century, although the hierarchy was still recognised. Martin Martin commented of 'the orators' that 'until within these forty years, they sat always among the nobles and chiefs of families in the *sreath* or circle.' The word *sreath*, meaning circle or rank, denotes the customary seating arrangement in the chief's household. Although the practice of poetry in the upper echelons of society was therefore the preserve of a few — the successive generations of the bardic families who were chosen to undergo the rigorous training in metrics and poetic disciplines — it would be wrong to place too much emphasis on the gap between bardic and vernacular poetry. The same scope and subject matter were to be found in both; political poems, religious and moralistic verse, satire, love poems (Niall Mor MacMhuirich's poignant love poem, *Soraidh slàn don oidhche a-réir*, is a fine example in classical metres), are to be found as well as the conventional praise poems and the common rhetorical techniques. Traditional learning, its survival and transmission must have been an inspiration, not the mere recollection of the past.

The most renowned of the bardic families were the MacMhuirichs. They had been associated with the Lords of the Isles from the thirteenth century to the turn of the sixteenth, and Clan Ranald, as the chief of one of the branches of Clan Donald, maintained that support in the liberal fashion befitting professional poets into the eighteenth century. They held the four pennylands of Driomasdal in South Uist and also the farm of Staoligarry which they still held in the eighteenth century by virtue of their office. The prestige of their office, their standing in the community and some aspects of the mystical associations of their art can be gathered from Martin Martin's description of them in the 1690s. He recalled that the poets' township had been considered a sanctuary, and it is curious that the traditions of this great dynasty that survived into modern times tell of magical abilities and a certain cunning. In the seventeenth century the family were still composing in the classical metres and traditional vein, lauding their own chiefs and addressing other chieftains. paying respects to their houses, kin and mutual alliances. The MacMhuirichs wrote pieces not only for Clan Ranald but also for the MacLeods of Dunvegan and the MacKenzies of Gairloch. The family wrote down *seanchas*, that is history, chronicles and traditions as well as their poetry, and the *Leabhar Dearg*, the so-called Red Book of Clan Ranald, is their monument. They wrote of the past and they also recorded events of their own day, as for instance, Niall MacMhuirich's account of the Montrose campaigns.

If the MacMhuirichs preserved the old learning, they were certainly not unaware of the changes of their day. Niall MacMhuirich, for example, wrote poems in the literary language and in seventeenth century Scottish Gaelic; in his old age he wrote a bardic elegy for Allan of Clan Ranald, who died after the battle of Sheriffmuir in 1715, and he also wrote a song in stressed metre. His contemporary Cathal MacMhuirich was well aware of the changes that were taking place. On the death of four members of Clan Ranald, his patrons, in 1636, he wrote:

> The heroes of the Clan of Conn are dead,
> How bitter to our hearts is the grief for them.
> We shall not live long after them,
> It is perilous for us to be separated from the brotherhood.
> They did not stint their gifts of clothing to the poets,
> Their horses, nor their gold cups;
> Now that they have gone under the clay and are hidden,
> To be left after them is a lasting sorrow . . .

> Because those of Clan Ranald have gone from us,
> We poets cannot pursue our studies;
> It is time for the *ollamh* to go after them,
> Now that there will be no presents to the poets.[2]

At the end of the eighteenth century, Lachlan MacMhuirich, who could describe himself as eighteenth in descent from Muireach Albanach of the thirteenth century, gave a statement about the family to a committee of the Highland Society enquiring into the poems of Ossian. He was illiterate; his family had lost their lands and their learning. The last of the family to have been a professional bard in the fullest sense was his great uncle, Donald MacMhuirich, the tacksman of Staoligarry, who had also gone to Ireland for part of his training. The family manuscripts were dispersed in the time of Donald's son, Niall, when the Red Book itself was given to James Macpherson. Lachlan said that the family had had a large collection of manuscripts which had been scattered and he himself had seen two or three cut up by tailors to make measures or patterns. A South Uist crofter told Campbell of Islay in 1871: 'My father had a book printed in Irish Gaelic full of all the songs of Ireland. Clann Mhuirich gave him the book Fear O'n Gharbh-thir, a big book', and in describing the manuscripts, he said 'Clan Mhuirich had seven cart loads'.[3]

The chiefs and leading families in the Highlands and Islands still continued to support and encourage the poets in the seventeenth century, and naturally a typical feature of the poetry was praise of the household and its munificence. And throughout the period the bards moved easily between Scotland and Ireland and from house to house, lavishing praise where it was appropriate or deserved. Niall Mor MacMhuirich, the Clan Ranald poet, for example, was unstinting in his praise of MacLeod's hospitality in 1613 in his poem *Sé hoidhche dhamhsa san Dún*, 'Six nights had I been in Dunvegan'. This must have been a memorable occasion if we are to believe that:

> We were twenty times drunk every day,
> To which we had no more objection than he had …..[4]

Certain chiefs maintained the old style and establishment even when their own circumstances were desperate. An outstanding example of this is the MacLean household at Duart before its final downfall in 1679. Duart's heavy indebtedness through most of the seventeenth century did not deter him from having both *Filidh* and *Bard*. Rev John MacLean, writing to Robert Wodrow in 1701, makes reference to the last learned poet at Duart, *Maol Domhnaich MacEoin*, who had died about 40 years previously. He was a member of the family of *O Muirgheasain*, originally from Inishowen, and had been '34 years at the schools in Ireland'. Another *O Muirgheasain* was in the Dunvegan household. It is obvious from the tone of reference that it was rare for the chiefs to be maintaining a *Filidh*. The Bards, composing in stressed metre and not using the literary language, still employed all the conventions of clan panegyric. Tradition records that Duart had a salaried bard in the seventeenth century, *Eachann Bacach*. His lament for Sir Lachlan MacLean, who died in 1648, is well known. *Thriall bhur bunadh gu Pharao*, 'Your stock went back to Pharaoh', is a poem which begins as a traditional elegy and moves on to a religious and nature imagery with a freedom more redolent of later poetry and folk song.[5]

The rich and powerful house of Argyll had become better known for their political activities than for any concern for Gaelic culture, yet they too maintained a family of hereditary bards and genealogists into the seventeenth century. The MacEwans, who may well have served the MacDougalls in an earlier period, held lands on Loch Melfortside for their services. They may also have been the source of Bishop Carswell's knowledge of the old learning and have made the 1630 translation of Calvin's Catechism. Their praise of the house of Argyll is, as might be expected, fulsome and flattering in conventional terms. These poets represent a tenacious survival of old standards. More significant was the new poetry. The new poets came from every walk of life, but the first of whom we have much knowledge belonged to the families of the chiefs and their kin. The early seventeenth century poet, *An Ciaran Mabach*, 'The Dark Stammerer', was a brother of MacDonald of Sleat. The Keppoch family produced a remarkable series of poets, *Gilleasbuig na Ceapaich* and *Aonghus Odhar*, Gilleasbuig's daughter Julia, better known as *Sileas na Ceapaich*, *Iain Lom*, the great grandson of *Iain Alainn* of Keppoch, and his son, and *Domhnall Donn* of Bohuntin, also related to the chiefs of Keppoch. The Fernaig Manuscript was compiled by Duncan MacRae of Inverinate between 1688 and 1693 and it is notable for demonstrating not only the wealth of poetic talent in Highland society but also the interest and awareness of Highlanders in the widest issues of the day and their enthusiasm for poetry. It includes some verses dating to the early sixteenth century and other old pieces such as a bardic poem on the Seven Deadly Sins and some Ossianic dialogues.

Duncan MacRae composed songs and collected those of others, many of them relatives and mostly men of standing such as the MacKenzie lairds of Achilty. Most of the poems in the Fernaig Manuscript are political or religious in one sense or another; about half of the poems are Episcopalian and Jacobite, taking a stern line against Presbyterian churchmen and the government of the Revolution. They heartily dislike William of Orange and Mary, who, as a Stewart, they considered had betrayed her family. Their actions are compared with the revolt of

Absalom against David and they therefore deserved Absalom's doom. The author of one poem denounces the fickle loyalties of the traitors who took the Whig side in 1689:

> They will change as a stream changes
> James yesterday, the Prince to-day.[6]

The two names most commonly associated with the composition of stressed poetry in vernacular Gaelic are Mary MacLeod and John MacDonald. Mary MacLeod, also known familiarly as *Mairi Nighean Alasdair Ruaidh*, lived from about 1625 to 1707 and spent the greater part of her life in the household of MacLeod of Dunvegan. According to tradition, she was related to MacLeod, and her surviving poetry, which is conventional in theme, consists mainly of eulogies and laments for her chief and his kinsfolk.

John MacDonald, the famous *Iain Lom*, a slightly younger contemporary of Mary MacLeod (c. 1625-1710), was also closely related to his chief, MacDonald of Keppoch. He took a personal part in many of the famous events of his age, and his poetry thus provides us with a most illuminating insight into Highland history. About 3,000 lines of his verse have survived, and he concerns himself not only with the politics of clans but also with national politics, with the Revolution and the Act of Union for example. His invective and satire, the traditional and much feared weapon of the poet, was famous, hence the epithet *lom* which most probably signified a caustic temperament. He bestowed his satire freely where it was deserved, be it on kings or Campbells. He was with Montrose and his second-in-command, Alasdair mac Colla,at the battle of Inverlochy fought on 2nd February 1645. He celebrates this encounter primarily as the victory of Clan Donald over the Campbells. *Latha Inbhir Lochaidh* finishes on a ferocious and merciless note against the enemies of his people:

> Did you know the *Goirtean Odhar*?
> It was well manured,
> Not by the dung of sheep and goats
> But by the blood of Campbells after congealing.
>
> To Hell with you if I pity your plight,
> Listening to the distress of your children,
> Lamenting the company which was in the fray,
> The wailing of the women of Argyll.[7]

This intensity is also to be found in the long poem in which he calls for vengeance on the murderers of the young chief of Keppoch and his brother in 1663, the *Murt na Ceapaich* well known in Highland history. Towards the end of our period the Jacobite cause inspired another group of contemporary poets. One of the best known of them was John Roy

Stewart. His lament for the losses at Culloden and his adventures as a fugitive before he escaped to France are still remembered in Strathspey.

Every district of the Highlands and Islands had its poets. The learned poets and other professions such as the doctors belonged to the areas mostly within the bounds of the old Lordship. The new poets came from all parts and seem therefore to be independent of the influence of the classical poets of the Lordship and can be seen as the manifestation of indigenous Gaelic poetic talent. Many anecdotes survive which show that the old skill of improvisation in verse had not disappeared. In a tale of the desperate revenge by Neil, one of the last of the MacLeods of Lewis, upon the Morrisons, the family of the Brieves of Lewis, one of the Morrisons spontaneously composed a rowing song or *iorram* to inspire his brothers. According to tradition, when Neil MacLeod himself was executed, one of the officers said roughly, 'Hurry on the old bodach' to which he replied in verse that were he on the deck of a ship, keeping his feet among the rolling waves and fast sea, it would not be he who would be called an old fellow.[8]

Ephemeral verse such as this and many compositions of unlettered and anonymous men and women have tended to attract less attention than the well-fashioned quatrain. Some of it has been in circulation, however, for up to three hundred years in oral tradition. Most significant in this corpus of song and poetry are those that accompanied and gave rhythm to tasks of work. Those that accompanied the fulling of the cloth after weaving, the *òrain luaidh*, are best remembered because this work has gone on until comparatively recently in the Islands. Other work songs were the rowing songs, shearing songs for the harvest, and quern songs, although these tasks fell out of use some time ago. The lyrics themselves, of course, could be transferred between tasks. The tradition survived because of the functional role and also because of the social role; they were sung by bands of women, and many of the songs are the compositions of women. 'Chorus songs' would perhaps be a more appropriate title than 'waulking songs'. They generally have a single line or couplet structure, with a chorus or refrain of words or apparently meaningless vocables. In the same way as *canntaireachd*, however, the chorus or refrain of vocables recall the tune. This is a very old tradition known in medieval Europe and surviving in the Western Isles when it had disappeared elsewhere. When Alexander III travelled by the high road through Strathearn in the thirteenth century, it was the custom for a band of women to meet him and sing before him. This was the *bannal* or band which we meet with in the later sources. It was a flexible tradition, quite naturally if composition was by extemporisation at work; a few chorus songs were older songs or ballads, and some incorporated bits of older songs. The Arthurian ballad, *Am Bròn Binn*, The Sweet Sorrow, was adapted as a waulking song. The long and justly famous song of *Seathan mac Rìgh Éireann*, possibly dating back to the sixteenth century, is remarkable as a woman's song, but the authorship of this, like many others, is unknown. The chorus song tradition did not stand apart from the literary or sub-literary tradition, however, and poets such as Mary MacLeod, Iain Lom and Alexander MacDonald composed chorus songs.

The later bardic poetry of the MacMhuirichs and others abound with allusions to the great figures of the ancient cycles of Gaelic literature. Not only were the traditions preserved but literate men also took a pride in writing and transcribing manuscripts. The MacLachlans of Kilbride, for example, were building up their manuscript collection in the seventeenth century, and it is largely due to the small lairds' and tacksmen's families that we now have Scottish Gaelic manuscript collections preserved for posterity in our national institutions. A notable seventeenth century manuscript written by Ewan MacLean about 1691 contains a collection mainly of heroic tales such as the long and popular tale of the Travels of Conall Gulban which was very popular with the storytellers, and also a version of the Ulster cycle tale of Mac Da Tho's Pig. The *Lilium Medicinae* was still being copied and handed down, and one learned medical treatise, transcribed in 1679 or thereabouts, quoted many authorities, and referring to Avicenna of the early eleventh century and the doctors in accord with him, remarked:

> It does not become us to contradict
> the pronouncements of the Doctors but
> to bury them with honour.[9]

The MacMhuirich *seanchas* in the Red Book of Clan Ranald was the last great piece of Gaelic prose in the literary language of the learned orders. But within a hundred years, publishing in Gaelic, both of original work and of translations of English religious classics, had begun, and was to grow significantly in the first half of the nineteenth century. If the writing of Gaelic prose in the learned tradition died out in the eighteenth century and if only a fraction of the learned manuscripts survived, oral tradition and the enthusiastic memory of the country folk preserved much of the great literary heritage. How effectively they did this is shown by the collections of the nineteenth century scholars such as John Francis Campbell of Islay.

There were developments in Highland music. In the sixteenth century, as in other countries, the harp had been losing ground to another stringed instrument, the viol, a forerunner of the violin. In the seventeenth century, the fiddle was evidently making its way in the Highlands. Lachlan MacKinnon, *Lachainn Mac Thearlaich Oig*, a famous poet, was an excellent performer on both the violin and the harp, as well as being the best deer-stalker in his day. The story of James Macpherson and 'Macpherson's Rant' at the end of the century is well known, and Martin Martin thought that the Islanders had had a fiddle of their own, although he gives no details. In Strathspey, one of the districts pre-eminent for fiddle music, the earliest family of fiddlers of whom we know anything were the Browns of Kincardine, and there was also a family of Cummings of Freuchie. One of them, Alexander, was piper and violer to the Laird of Grant in 1653 with a salary of twenty merks yearly. Meanwhile, the harp was declining in favour but was still played. An anonymous description of Scotland in 1597 stated that the Highlanders 'delight in musicke, But chiefly in Harpes, and Clairschoes after their fashion.' Rev Robert Kirk stated in his *Secret Commonwealth* that the harp was still played in Atholl at the end of the seventeenth century, and there are some references to harpers in the service of chiefs. One harper had the 'kyndnes' of lands in Mull in 1674 in return for his services. Like the classical poets, the harpers studied and travelled in Ireland, and Irish harpers in return crossed to pay court to the Scottish nobility both Highland and Lowland. The most famous of the Highland harpers was Roderick Morison, *An Clarsair Dall*, who customarily played for the MacLeods of Dunvegan. He died about 1714. *Sileas na Ceapaich* preserves the memory of another harper who died in the 1720s, in her 'Lament for Lachlann MacKinnon' which describes very vividly the popularity and function of such musicians; as *Sileas* says: 'I would be sure to get news from you about everything'. Murdoch MacDonald, *Murchadh Clarsair*, was harper to MacLean of Coll, and retiring from office in 1734, he died in 1738. He was said to be the last of the harpers, but there is evidence of one in the MacLeod household as late as 1755.[10]

The Highland bagpipe had already emerged as an instrument of war, and in the troubles of the seventeenth century pipes and pipers attached to regiments had appeared early. For instance, as early as 1586, Captain Balfour in the Scots brigade in Holland had employed two drummers and a piper, and in 1626 Sir Donald Mackay's regiment in the Swedish army had thirty-six pipers. All the accounts of the constantly renewed civil wars abound with allusions to the pipers and their effectiveness on the spirit of the men. For instance, when James Reid, a Jacobite prisoner at Carlisle in 1746, pleaded that he had been a piper and not an active combatant, he was condemned because no Highland regiment ever marched without a piper, and therefore in the eyes of the law the bagpipe was an instrument of war. James Philip alludes to the 'screaming pipes' at the gathering of Glengarry's men in 1689. In the camp at Nairn before Culloden, Cumberland noticed the pipers of the Independent Companies

and the Argyll Militia carrying their pipes and asked 'What are these men
to do with such bundles of sticks?', and he said that he could give them
better weapons. An officer replied that his Royal Highness would be well
advised not to do so, for those were the pipes, the Highlanders' music in
peace and war, and that without them they would be of no service.

The seventeenth century was indeed the period when piping reached its
zenith. Patrick Mor MacCrimmon, by tradition one of the finest pipers
of all time, was born about 1595 and died in 1670, and a succession of
great MacCrimmon pipers followed him. With a unanimity rare in the
Highlands their superiority was invariably recognised. When Charles II
was inspecting his army in May 1651 before the march south that was to
end so disastrously at Worcester, he was told that all the pipers
acknowledged MacCrimmon as their 'patron in chiefe'. The King gave
MacCrimmon who, in terms of dates, must have been Patrick Mor, his
hand to kiss and the piper instantly composed the well-known tune 'I got
a kiss of the King's hand','' or *Thug mi pòg do làimh an Righ*. In the
'45, when Donald Ban, the leading MacCrimmon of the day, was
captured in a skirmish by Prince Charles Edward's men at Inverurie, all
the pipers in the Jacobite army refused to play until he was released.[11]

Of course, piping was not merely useful in wartime but a much
esteemed art which was listened to seriously with a well-informed
appreciation of the finer points. One gathers this from many incidents.
Almost nothing was played but *piobaireachd*. One of the most important
duties of the family piper, as we know from tradition, was to play at the
chiefs' funerals which were very important occasions.

Rev James Kirkwood described for Edward Lhuyd in the late
seventeenth century how 'Pipers are held in great Request so that they
are train'd up at the Expence of Grandees and have a portion of land
assign'd and are design'd such a man's piper'. MacLeod is said to have
had three pipers, one for each of the districts of his estates, and the
piping school of the MacCrimmons at Borreraig had been established in
the sixteenth century, traditionally in the time of Alasdair Crotach.
Meanwhile, the Lowland pipers were losing ground. For instance, in
1630 Aberdeen gave up its piper because piping was 'ane incivill forme to
be usit within sic a famous burghe and being often found fault with, als
weill by sundrie nightbouris of the toune as by strangers'. The bagpipe
was now regarded as the characteristic Highland musical instrument.
Thomas Kirk, a Yorkshireman, in his *Modern Account of Scotland* of
1679, wrote of Highland music: 'not the harmony of the sphears, but
loud terrene noises, like the bellowing of beasts; the loud bagpipe is their
chief delight .....', and more to the same effect. Of course, the pipes can
never appeal to every ear, and some Gaelic poets complained of them,
and their praise and dispraise were popular subjects with the poets. The

older generation may have felt that the pipes were an unbecoming instrusion by comparison with the gentle tones of the harp, although there were also poems satirising harpers. These criticisms are often cited but they mostly seem to suggest good-humoured banter rather than serious satire. Niall Mor MacMhuirich composed a poem in vernacular Gaelic on the history of the bagpipe from its beginning, *Seanchus na Pìob bho thùs*. He finishes by suggesting that the music of the pipes and the funeral lamentations of women are the most devilish types of music in existence.[12]

In modern times the best known symbol (sometimes a very controversial one) of a clan is its tartan. It is, however, most difficult to prove when actual distinct setts of the tartans belonging to the different clans came into being, and even if it was before the end of the eighteenth century. Two points must be remembered. Firstly, one must bear in mind that there are very ancient records of other distinguishing marks of the different clans. In the first place, there were the banners. Their use was an early development and they appear in the traditional story cycles. An early ballad in the *Book of the Dean of Lismore* names the banners of the nine warriors of Fionn, and this is well known in Gaelic tradition. Banners are mentioned at the battle of *Blàr na Léine* in the sixteenth century. In Dundee's campaign, James Philip recorded that the MacLeans carried a blue banner, the Stewarts of Appin a blue one with yellow figures, and Cameron of Glendessary who led the MacGregors, a red one.[13] They were also carried at Culloden. As late as 1775, Rev Lachlan Shaw wrote that every clan had its war cry and its badge 'whereby they might be known, as they had no military habit or livery'. The war cry or slogan is also an ancient custom. In the Middle Ages the Scots burghs were said to have had their 'slughorns' or slogans. They are said to have played a part in more recent history, for when in February 1746, Loudon made a night march from Inverness with 1,500 men to surprise Prince Charles Edward at Moy, the blacksmith of Moy, Donald Fraser, with five men hid behind peat-stacks, fired their guns, and called out the slogans of the loyal clans as if the whole Jacobite army were there.

There are more allusions to the wearing of clan badges, and Sir Thomas Innes of Learney in *The Tartans of the Clans and Families of Scotland* summarises these. It was remarked that among the Highlanders who took part in the Highland Host, quartered on the disaffected districts of south west Scotland in 1678, 'the Glencoe men were very remarkable, who had for their ensigne a faire bush of heath, wel-spred and displayed on the head of a staff'. The *Grameid*, although fulsomely clothed in romantic poetry, is a lively and sympathetic eye-witness account of the beginning of Dundee's campaign; it describes the contingents of Glengarry, Glencoe, Clan Ranald, Keppoch and Sleat, and goes on: 'These all being chiefs sprung from the blood of Donald, they among themselves form 20 companies, and unite the clansmen in one battalion. They all bear similar arms, and carry into battle, as the emblem of their race, a bunch of wild heather hung from the point of a quivering spear'. The author also noticed that the Frasers wore a sprig of yew, still the badge of this clan. It is interesting to note that a certain number of the present clan badges follow the theories of the Highlanders' traditional origins. All branches of the MacDonalds and also the MacAlisters wear heather, while the Campbells and the MacArthurs, who were an early branch of the same stock, wear the bog-myrtle or gale. The Davidsons, Mackintoshes, MacBeans, Farquharsons, MacGillivrays and MacQueens, who are all branches of Clan Chattan, wore the very similar cranberry or blaeberry. The Grants, MacGregors, MacKinnons and MacQuarries, who claim a traditional descent from an early king, wear the pine. The MacLeans of Duart and the off-shoot branches of Coll and Ardgour wear the holly, but Lochbuie, who disputes the seniority with Duart, wears the blaeberry. The MacKenzies, who like the MacLeans claim descent from a Dalriadic king, also wear the holly. All the Stewart branches wear the oak and the thistle. The Camerons wear the oak and the crowberry, and the MacPhees, some of whom took refuge with the Camerons, wear their badge.

After the chiefs adopted the practice of matriculating their arms, members of their clan in some cases took to wearing their crest as a brooch or on some article of personal adornment: the Grant's burning mountain and the MacLeod bull's head are examples. But as they are part of heraldic insignia, they should be worn only if the device is encircled by a band or other symbol denoting that the wearer is an adherent of the chief.

In the struggle between the Hanoverians and the Jacobites, the wearing of cockades was the most important mark of identification, and the wearing of a black cockade with a red cross worn saltire-wise on it was explicitly ordered for the Independent Companies. In the trials of Jacobite prisoners after the '45, the wearing of the white cockade was accepted in the depositions as a proof of guilt, and as one witness said: 'We thought every man who wore it had joined the rebels.' James Ray of Whitehaven, a volunteer with the Duke of Cumberland, took part in the battle of Culloden and described the means by which a Highlander escaped from him in the pursuit after the battle. He came up with the wounded Highlander, who called out to him: 'Hold your hand, I'm a *Campbell*. On which I asked him where was his bonnet. He reply'd that somebody snatched it off his head. I only mention this to shew how we distinguished our loyal Clans from the Rebels, they being dress'd and equipped all in one Way, except the Bonnet, ours having a red or yellow Cross of Cloath or Ribbon, theirs a white Cockade'. At the first opportunity the man made off.[14]

It is rather strange that in other insignia which appear in our records, stories and traditions, tartans were not mentioned. For how long and to what extent distinguishing clan tartans were worn is very uncertain. The word is derived from a French term for a light kind of cloth of any colour, but an entry in the Treasurer's Accounts in 1538 for the purchase of three ells of 'heland Tertane to be hois to the Kingis grace' for James V suggests that in Scotland it had acquired the meaning we now attach to it. On the other hand, it may have denoted the fine fabrics or 'hards' in which the yarn was combed. The Gaelic word for tartan or the plaid is *breacan*, from the adjective *breac* meaning spotted, striped or checked. In his long poem 'The Birlinn of Clan Ranald', Alexander MacDonald described the sky at the beginning of the storm: *Chinn gach dath bhiodh ann am breacan air an iarmailt*, 'all the colours in a tartan plaid were gathered in the sky'.

Telfer Dunbar in his *History of Highland Dress* (1962) and McClintock in his *Old Irish and Highland Dress* (1950) have collected what early information we have about the wearing of tartan. In the sixteenth century, when we have descriptions of the distinctive Highland dress, a great many of them allude to striped or marlit (meaning chequered or patterned) plaids. For instance, George Buchanan, writing in 1582 said: 'They delight in marled clothes, especially that have long stripes of sundry colours; they love chiefly purple and blew. Their predecessors used short mantles or plaids of divers colours sundry waies devided; and amongst some, the same custom is observed to this day; but for the most part now they are browns, most nere to the colour of the hadder; to the effect, when they lie amongst the hadder, the bright colour of their plaids shall not betray them.'

The wearing of checked fabrics by the Highlanders is therefore of ancient origin. Besides the affinity cf such patterns with their other arts, there is a technical reason for this. Dyeing by the professional town dwellers was generally done to the completed web of woven fabric in a large vat. In the Highlands the wool is dyed before spinning, generally before carding. A vat large enough to dye a length of stuff or enough yarn to weave a uniform web would have taxed the resources of a rural people like the Highlanders, and the trade of dyeing was a jealously guarded burghal monopoly. To make really brilliant colours, especially red and blue, with native vegetable dyes is a difficult and tiresome process; and although dyestuffs were imported into the Highlands at least as early as the seventeenth century, they must have been both scarce and costly. They would go much further if used as overchecks. Among early pieces of tartan and plaids which have been preserved, some in fact have grounds of the natural colours of the wool, or of yellow which is a comparatively easy dye to get from native plants. On the other hand, there were always pressures towards uniformity. In the first place, there might be an element of fashion; but as James Scarlett with his skill as a weaver has pointed out to us, communities or districts would tend to approve the same general pattern, as might be suggested by the similarities between the Mackintosh, Grant and MacGillivray tartans. There was also the weavers' inclination to save time and trouble in setting up a warp by using the same proportion of coloured threads. Martin Martin's remark that the pattern of the cloth a man was wearing indicated where he came from — which is often cited as evidence of the weaving of tartan — might well apply to the weaving of district patterns.

During the time when the belted plaid was first noted by outside

James Moray of Abercairney, c.1739, showing the belted plaid worn by a laird and the details of its arrangement

observers as a distinctive dress, that is in the seventeenth and eighteenth centuries, there is no unequivocal contemporary account of clan tartans, although there are passages that can be made to imply their existence, just as there are others that convincingly suggest that they were not worn. A certain number of portraits survive of figures wearing tartans, and also pieces of the actual fabric. In the case of the portraits, it is striking that a number of different patterns of tartans are worn by various members of the same clan; Richard Waitt painted the portraits of members of clan Grant between 1714 and 1725, but the sett of the tartan in only two of them shows a very close resemblance, and those two are of the chief's retainers, his piper and champion. None of the subjects wears a tartan with the sett of the modern Grant tartan with its azure stripe. In some other portraits the figures wear more than one tartan. Some of our modern clan tartans are obviously copied from or founded on the examples worn in the portraits, but some of the old patterns are quite

John 3rd Earl of Bute and George III's Prime Minister, dressed in tartan trews, jacket and plaid

unlike anything worn at present, as for instance, that in the seventeenth century portrait by Michael Wright of an unidentified chief in the Scottish National Portrait Gallery. Surviving pre-1745 tartans are unlike modern tartans; many of them are asymmetrical, and some have grounds of natural colour or yellow. They do, however, show certain general distinct affinities in colour, pattern and weave. This bears out Martin Martin's description of the plaid; he said it was of 'divers colours; and there is a great deal of ingenuity required in sorting the colours so as to be agreeable to the nicest fancy. For this reason the women are at great pains, first to give an exact pattern of the plaid upon a piece of wood, having the number of every thread of the stripe upon it .... Every isle differs from each other in their fancy of making plaids as to the stripes in breadth and colours. This humour is as different through the mainland of the Highlands, in so far that they who have seen those places are able at first view of a man's plaid to guess the place of his residence.' Alexander Carmichael remarked that in the Islands the pattern of the tartan or other cloth to be woven is first designed on a small piece of wood. Whether this 'piece of wood' was indeed a sett-stick or some other kind of tally or *aide-memoire* has been a matter of debate.

The whole subject of tartans has aroused considerable controversy. Feelings may run high when we discuss what has become, for better or worse, a symbol of Scottish nationhood, both Highland and Lowland, whether tartans are 'genuine', especially with reference to their clan associations, the simplicity or complexity of the sett or pattern, and their antiquity. A debatable statement of their early origin is the *Vestiarium Scoticum* prepared by the Sobieski Stuart brothers and published in 1842. Of the seventy five tartans illustrated, very few can be proved to antedate the book itself, and the work has been discredited largely because the sixteenth century manuscript on which the designs were supposed to be based was either suppressed or never existed. Such was the interest and popularity of tartans at the time, however, that many of the tartans introduced by the *Vestiarium Scoticum* are worn to this day.[15]

As the late Lord Lyon, Sir Thomas Innes of Learney, pointed out, we do not recognise institutions while they are growing but only when they are an established fact, and 'we may be sure that neither clan or district tartan were originally invented as such'. In the seventeenth century when the belted plaid had become the recognised dress of the Highlanders and the clans had become much consolidated, there is evidence that the idea of a special dress for the chief's close followers was taking form. The wearing of a livery by the followers of a great man was, of course, neither new nor particularly Highland. The men of the fifteenth century Earl of Warwick, 'the king-maker', wearing red jackets embroidered with the ragged staff, is only one illustration. In the *Grameid*, James Philip describes a similarity in the clothing and equipment of the particular followers of some of the chiefs who rallied to Dundee. Raasay's men were described as wearing plaids and bull-hide tunics, while Stewart of Appin's two hundred men wore fur bonnets. Glengarry and his three hundred men all wore plaids 'woven with phrygian skill in triple stripe' of red, and his cousin Allan with one hundred men all wore a red stripe. The men of Glen Roy all seem to have worn yellow and blue. No distinguishing dress is described for the followers of Lochiel and Duart, who both had eleven hundred men, though Duart himself and his brother both wore a plaid with yellow stripes. One must, of course, make considerable allowance for the writer's poetic licence. A letter, dated 1618, has been quoted by Innes of Learney from Sir Robert Gordon, then Tutor of Sutherland, to Murray of Pulrossie 'requesting him to furl his pennon when the Earl of Sutherland's banner was displayed and to remove the red and white lines from the plaides of his men so as to bring their dress into harmony with that of the other septs'. Already in 1703 the desire for uniformity by the chief of clan Grant had been shown, for when he entertained some great men at a hunt, one of the guests related that he 'ordered 600 of his men in arms, in good order, with Tartane Coats all of one colour and fashion'. The order survives in the Court Book of the Regality of Grant and specified that his tenants were 'to have readie tartan short coates, trewes and short hose of red and grein set dyce all broad springed', and were to be armed with guns, swords, pistols and dirks.[16] The idea may be paralleled with the custom of some great proprietors in the nineteenth century who dressed their estate employees and gillies in a special pattern of tweed, a custom which is not unknown today. The wearing of similar tartans by the men of the Independent Companies and the Black Watch would naturally encourage such a tendency. The Independent Companies certainly wore a dark tartan. This would distinguish them from plaids with a brown or yellow ground, which would seem to have been the everyday wear of the lesser clansmen. It would be more expensive, but they were mainly the sons of relatives of the lesser gentry. General Wade in his instructions for the 1725 Companies directed that the tartans worn by the units should be as 'near as they can of the same Sort and colour'. After the Black Watch was embodied as a regiment, they wore the tartan that still bears their name, the distinctive black lines and blue on a dark green ground, but whether this was originally a clan tartan is uncertain.

When one divides Highland history into periods, it seems to be a strange thing that the main factors that contributed to the exact classification of clan tartan should all be mainly in a later period — that of the eighteenth century, especially during its second half. Definite

features of that time — the increase in the number of Highland
Regiments which encouraged standardisation, the organisation and
commercialisation of the handcraft textile industries and, above all, the
fashion for Highland things and Jacobite traditions — all these
contributed to a deliberate attempt to classify and standardize something
that had come to represent in the public mind a way of life and a state of
society that had vanished.

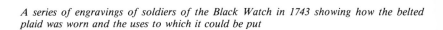

*A series of engravings of soldiers of the Black Watch in 1743 showing how the belted
plaid was worn and the uses to which it could be put*

It was during the period of the sixteenth and seventeenth centuries, and even the early part of the eighteenth century, that to belong to a clan and have the protection of a chief was essential for the individual's well-being, and the pride and self-sacrificing devotion to chief and clan grew up. Life was hard and dangerous but it had its moments of adventure and excitement and sometimes of triumph. It was not only for the Stewart cause that a man 'had to keep his head with his hands'. The elaborate checks and bright colours (so difficult to obtain) were only a part of the people's creative artistry and sensitiveness to beauty in poetry, epic tales and music and in response to the world about them that was the heritage the Gael brought from Erin and flowering in the seventeenth century. Traditions that are often hazy and sometimes greatly distorted but have genuine and ancient roots are embodied in the modern Highlander's love of his clan tartan. The outstanding fact about the Highland dress was that it was the general dress of the whole community and in no sense a peasant dress. Contemporary paintings exist of really splendid figures wearing both the belted plaid and the trews, for instance, Michael Wright's picture of an unknown gentleman thought to be the Earl of Breadalbane about 1660 in the Scottish National Portrait Gallery. The author of *The Present State of Scotland* (1711) commented that the plaid might seem 'uncouth, because not us'd elsewhere; yet it must be own'd, that as they are us'd by those of the better sort in the Highlands, they make a manly as well as a decent Habit.'[17] Charles Fraser-Mackintosh remarked that the dress of the richer folk differed only in the use of finer cloth, brighter colours and silver ornaments, the dress of all Highlanders being otherwise essentially the same. 'A Plain, general and authentic account of the Conduct and Proceedings of the Rebels, during their stay at Derby' gives this description of the Highlanders in what was one of their finest hours: 'A Crew of shabby, lousy, pitiful-look'd Fellows; mixed up with old Men and Boys; dressed in Dirty Plaids, and as dirty shoes, without Breeches; and wore their Stockings, made of Plaid, not much above half-way up their legs, some without Shoes, or next to none, and with their Plaids thrown over their Shoulders, (divested of their Arms) they appeared more like a Parcel of Chimney Sweepers than Soldiers'.[18]

Dress was as important to the Highlander as to his ancient Irish forebears. We have quoted Stewart of Garth's description of the Highlander's indifference to amenities in order that his clothing might be right. Tailors were employed to make his clothes when so much else about him was home-made. For instance, in the country parish of Alyth, out of a total population of 1060 there were four tailors; and the minister of Dunoon reported that his Highland parishioners were more given to dress and were less thrifty than the Lowland ones.[19] The dress of the

Highlanders, the belted plaid or *feileadh-mór* and the trews cut on the cross worn with a plaid, had become definitely recognised by the seventeenth century. A number of portraits show what they looked like. The wearing of trews cut on the cross and shaped to the leg has died out. Martin Martin described how they were made and stated that they were worn by the better-off people. Among the most interesting illustrations are a series of prints by Van der Gucht of 1743, showing how the belted plaid was put on and worn. Edward Burt in his *Letters* said it was 'set in folds and girt round the Waist, to make of it a short Petticoat that reaches half way down the Thigh, and the rest is brought over the Shoulders, and then fastened before, below the Neck', and in the case of the lesser folk 'sometimes with a Bodkin, or sharpened Piece of Stick, so that they make pretty nearly the Appearance of the poor Women in London when they bring their Gowns over their Heads to shelter them from the Rain'.

The rest of the Highlanders' dress was not markedly different from that worn in other countries, except that the jacket was noticeably shortened to allow for the belted plaid to be looped over it. The tradition of the short coat lingered long after the country people had given up wearing the Highland dress. Alexander Carmichael collected several poems alluding to it in the second half of last century. In early days, the sleeves were often slit at the cuff to allow for the wide shirt sleeves that were then still in vogue. The Highlanders, however, retained the fashion for slashed coats long after it had gone out elsewhere. Slashing appears in many of the contemporary portraits, and William Cleland alludes to 'a slasht coat'.

The sporran was of functional use when the belted plaid was worn, as it took the place of a pocket just as did the reticule with the flowing clothing of medieval Europe. There is considerable debate as to when the kilt as distinct from the belted plaid came into use. It is among the articles of Highland dress detailed in the Act proscribing the wearing of Highland dress passed after the '45, and there is a good deal of evidence that it was quite widely worn by then. The most popular version of a story about its invention is that a Mr Thomas Rawlinson, the manager of an English foundry company working in Glengarry about 1720, employed a tailor to make him a kilt as more convenient than the belted plaid and that Glengarry had a similar one made for himself. The question is whether a similar garment had not already been used in the Highlands. Stewart of Garth and the Sobieski Stuart brothers both thought so, but Sir John Sinclair did not.

It must be remembered that the Highland economy had been a pastoral one. For herding and droving and also raiding, the belted plaid was a most suitable sort of garb. By the seventeenth century there were increasing contacts with the South. There were several abortive attempts to develop mines or extract iron ore from peat. Other managers may have felt like Rawlinson. It is probably of more significance that in varying degrees the gentry were adopting southern ways of living in which the kilt would be a more convenient dress than the bulky belted plaid. That the kilt was adopted and continued to be worn rather than the substitution of entirely southern dress and the abandonment of the belted plaid is a tribute to the tenacity with which Higland ways of life were adapted to new conditions. A much less important or controversial change in the men's dress was the introduction of the blue bonnet. The dress of the women, as one would expect, changed more radically with the times.

Martin Martin has a description of the dress of the women. The ornaments are so elaborate that they could be worn only by very rich women. He calls the woman's plaid an 'arisad', saying that it was white, 'having a few small stripes of black, blue and red. It reached from the neck to the heels, and was tied before on the breast with a buckle of silver or brass, according to the quality of the person'. According to Martin's description, it could be a very fine dress, and the poets praised it and the wearers. John MacDonald of Aird, Benbecula, composed a rousing song at the time of the 1715 Rising in which he said:

The *Earasaid* is most becoming
On many a surpassingly beautiful maiden
Between Balavanich
And the Sound of Barra ...

The rest of Martin's description sounds fanciful, the brooch, for instance, was 'broad as any ordinary pewter plate'. The plaid and the headdress, the kertch or coif, do, however, appear in other descriptions; one written in Camden's 'Britannia' gives a description of the women in Breadalbane before the proscription of the Highland dress: 'The women's dress is the kirch, of white linen pinned round behind like a hood, and over the foreheads of married women, whereas maidens wear only a snood or ribbon round their heads; the *tanac* or plaid fastened over their shoulders, and drawn over their heads in bad weather; a plaited long stocking, called *ossan*, is their high dress.'[20] The 'tanac' or *tonnag* was a small square of checked or of any woollen material, used like a shawl over the shoulders. It was fastened before with a brooch of bone, bronze, copper or even silver or gold. The kertch was the symbol of the dignity of the married estate, and there is a tradition that the bride's mother bound it round her daughter's head on the morning after the wedding and presented her to the company assembled for the festivities. During the later part of the eighteenth century, however, the women entirely gave up wearing it and wore mutches instead.

The 'Hen Wife' at Castle Grant in 1706, by Richard Waitt. This is a rare illustration of the kertch or bréid as worn by countrywomen of the seventeenth and eighteenth centuries

For several reasons old Highland brooches are interesting. An old story shows that brooches were traditionally women's wear. The seventeenth century manuscript history of the MacDonalds includes a traditional tale of the fourteenth century. It concerned Duncan, one of the eponymous ancestors of the Robertsons of Struan. Duncan had become a great reiver and this was brought to the notice of the king, who was Robert II (1371-1390). 'Duncan put on a woman's habit, and a great brooch in his breast, alleging that he himself was Duncan's mother and

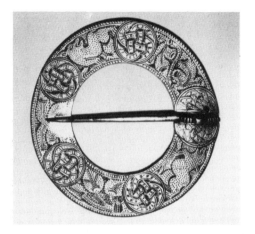

*Circular Highland brooches of brass of the seventeenth century, used by women to fasten on the plaid or **earasaid***

so went to Stirling to intercede for Duncan'. The fraud was taken in good part, and Duncan founded the fortunes of the Robertsons in Atholl. It will be remembered that in Burt's and Martin's accounts of Highland dress, the men were said to fasten their plaids with a bodkin or piece of wood. Another incident connected with a brooch brings one in touch with an aspect of the way of life of the period infinitely darker than the bloodshed of the fighting. In a confession in a trial for witchcraft in Bute in 1662, the woman who had been accused of curing 'Glaik', is said to have taken the child in her arms and went to gather 'a herbe called achluiuisge after this manner ...... eschewing meiting or speiking with anybody by the way and eschewing also all high wayes and when she comes to the place quhair the herbe is she takes a broch and layes it upon the herbe and plucks up the samin throw the broch in the childs name and then brings it home eschewing speiking or meiting with any by the way and seiths it upon the fire without suffering either a dog or catt or anything to pass betwixt hir and the fire till it be boiled quhair of she administers drink to the child three severall tymes and heales it.'[21] With the belief in witchcraft, some faint tradition that a brooch could be used as a talisman, as had sometimes been the case during the Middle Ages, may have survived. The earliest dated examples were of a typically Highland form of circular brooch and are seventeenth century. They were large and flat and were formed of an ingot bar of brass or occasionally of silver, hammered into a plate and bent into a circle with the ends joined and notched to form a hinge for the pin which was split at the end so that the narrowed part of the brooch could be slipped into the cleft. In the earlier brooches, the surface is divided into compartments by four or six circular panels which were filled in with traditional designs of interlaced ornament or grotesque animals. At the beginning of the eighteenth century a new design appeared; a chevron or triangle was introduced between the panels, giving the effect of a star, and not much later, a leaf design running round the brooch was used. From about 1710 to 1780 silver brooches with a niello inlay came into vogue. Although these brooches are Highland in character, the finest surviving examples of the later form of ornamentation actually come from the North East. Money was more plentiful there to pay the craftsmen or cairds who must have made them. In St Kilda, down to the time of the evacuation, the women wore plain round brooches.

The outstanding feature of this period was the fighting strength of the Highlanders. This was due to the new fighting tactic of the charge or rush of numbers of lightly but effectively armed men. For this charge to be effective, a new type of sword came into use. The massive cross-hilted sword that had been so often portrayed upon West Highland monuments of the fifteenth century, which had been effective in combats by champions in the defence of a fixed position, was, by the sixteenth century, being replaced by lighter swords with different kinds of hilts. The sword was still a weapon of prestige, but the change at this particular point of time was of essential importance in Highland history. The lighter broadsword with a basket hilt was not a Highland invention. It had been introduced into the Lowlands or had been evolved during the sixteenth century, and during the early part of the seventeenth century

*Basket-hilted sword with an imported blade marked **Andria Ferara**. The hilt by John Allan of Stirling and dated 1716 is richly decorated with chased work and inlaid with silver*

was the kind of sword in general use there. It was only by the end of the century that it had become especially associated with the Highlanders. It was only gradually that it had made its way there because of the prestige of the big, two-handed, cross-hilted sword which itself had been only a comparatively late introduction from the Continent. A story from the Wardlaw Manuscript describes a man being cut in half 'by one slash' of a two-handed sword 'which they mostly used'. This was the sword that was called the *claidheamh-dà-làimh*, the two-handed sword or the *claidheamh mór*, big sword, anglicised as 'claymore' and now erroneously applied to the lighter basket-hilted sword. The use of the claymore lingered on, perhaps because for many it remained a mark of status. So considerable a man as Campbell of Craignish carried one in the first half of the seventeenth century and also had an armour bearer. It was becoming merely a status symbol. The basket-hilted sword had spread to the Highlands and had become general long before the eighteenth century and was the cutting and slashing weapon associated *par excellence* with the Highland charge. When Argyll received the weapons from the MacLeans in Mull in 1679, there were 185 swords, 95 guns, 3 pistols, 5 Lochaber axes and 'ane two handed sword'.[22] Many broadsword blades were imported from Germany and Spain, the frequently spurious mark *Andrea Ferara* being taken as a sign of quality. Some specimens survive which are old claymores cut down. The bards of the clan period frequently refer to *lannan Spàinnteach*, meaning Spanish or Toledo blades, as though these were the most prized possessions, but swords were also made in the Highlands. Garnett describes the latter-day representatives of the hereditary armourers, the MacNabs of *Barr nan Caistealain* by Dalmally. The MacRurys were hereditary smiths and armourers to the MacDonalds of Sleat, and a branch of the family also worked in North Uist as smiths. Though blades were imported, there were many guard and hilt makers working in the Scottish towns. They developed a fine style during the seventeenth century and sometimes they signed their work. All these sword makers were Lowland. The particular type of basket-hilt had originated in the Lowlands, and there is no tradition of Highland craftsmen developing a style in its making. The high period of the craft was c.1700-1746, although demand for swords continued keen until the end of the eighteenth century from the various Highland regiments and cavalry.

As a result of the social conditions of the Highlands down to the passing of the Disarming Act of 1746, it was customary for the Highlanders to go about fully armed. General Wade, boasting in 1727 rather prematurely of the disarming of the Highlands under his ineffective attempt at disarmament, said that at his first coming to the Highlands, arms were 'Esteemed part of their Dress' and 'were Worn by the Meanest of the Inhabitants, even in their Churches, Fairs and Markets, which looked more like places of Parade for Soldiers, than Assemblies for Devotion or other meetings of Civil Societys'.[23] Burt, in his *Letters from the North of Scotland* wrote: 'When any one of them is armed at all Points, he is loaded with a Target, a Firelock, a heavy Broadsword, a Pistol, Stock and Lock of iron, a Dirk; and besides all these, some of them carry a sort of knife, which they call a Skeen-ochles (*sgian achlais*) from its being concealed in the Sleeve near the Armpit'.

It was, of course, an ancient custom, but it is highly characteristic of the times of the seventeenth century that the arms that the Highlanders carried underwent considerable changes. Two were of great importance. The change in the type of sword that was used has been indicated. The other was the introduction of firearms, which was to lead to the great changes of the next period. In the early seventeenth century the axe or

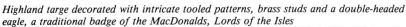

Highland targe decorated with intricate tooled patterns, brass studs and a double-headed eagle, a traditional badge of the MacDonalds, Lords of the Isles

tuagh was still sometimes carried. It had been the traditional weapon of the *Gall-òglaich*, the Highland mercenaries who had fought in Ireland in the sixteenth century. In the time of Montrose's Wars we have a good account of one individual Highlander's arms and of the fight he put up at the Battle of Auldearn. 'He turned his face to the enemy, his sword was at his breast, his shield on his left hand, and a hand-gun in his right hand.' From the account of the fight that followed, related by Niall MacMhuirich, we know that the 'shield' was evidently a targe and that he also carried a dirk. The targe came to be closely associated with the lighter basket-hilted sword in the Highland charge. It seems to have been of more recent introduction and, unlike that particular type of sword, it was of Highland origin and was made of bull's hide stretched upon two layers of oak board arranged with the plies running different ways. The leather was often ornamented with tooling in the traditional patterns as well as by studs and plates of metal which became more ornate by the end of the century. One early reference to them is in a fight between the MacDonalds and the MacKenzies at the end of the sixteenth century.[24] Philip, in the glamorous pages of the *Grameid*, several times alludes to the glitter of brazen knobs upon the Highlanders' targes. After the '45 targes went out of use.

The dirk also was an important part of Highland equipment. It was used in the final deadly encounter of the charge, and disarming acts were difficult to enforce against it. It was mentioned by Lindsay of Pitscottie in 1575. Burt in his *Letters* said it was 'above a foot long' and only sharpened on one side: 'They pretend they cannot do well without it, as being useful to them in cutting Wood, and upon many other Occasions; but it is a concealed Mischief, hid under the Plaid, ready for secret stabbing; and in a close Encounter there is no Defence against it'. It was a Highland development from the medieval dagger, and the ornamentation of its hilt and pommel developed during the seventeenth century. The bands of the traditional interlaced carving were extended until by the early eighteenth century, when the finest specimens were made, the whole hilt was covered and metal mounts, often of brass and sometimes of pewter or silver, had by then been introduced. Sometimes the blade was an old sword cut down and the wood of the pommel of heather or ivy roots was fashioned by local craftsmen. So far as the writers know, the *sgian dubh*, now an ornamental addition to Highland dress, is not mentioned in any old account nor does it appear in old pictures.

During the constant warfare that went on, not only in Britain but over much of Western Europe during the seventeenth century and in this period, firearms were coming more and more into use. In spite of the general poverty of the Highlands and the fact that the long and the cross-

*Group of dirks showing the
evolution from the long
knife of the seventeenth
century to the Army
officer's dress weapon of the
Victorian era*

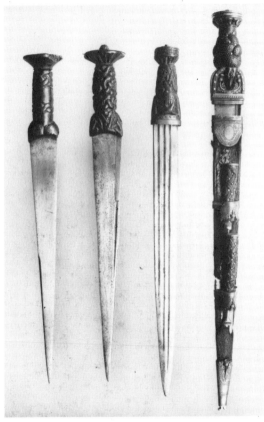

bows were still being used far into the seventeenth century, those who could afford them were obtaining guns from the Continent or the Lowlands. From their first introduction they were used for hunting. The Statutes of Icolmkill had prohibited the West Highland chiefs from using them, but then allowed them to use them for sport within a mile of their dwelling. The chiefs evidently were not deterred. In 1679 the followers of the MacLean chief, MacLean of Duart, were said to be armed with 'swords, pistolls, durks and other weapons invasive'. The poetess, Mary MacLeod, in her *Luinneag MhicLeoid* celebrated the possession of firearms as compared to that of bows and arrows, and Duncan Ban MacIntyre wrote a well-known poem to his fowling piece.[25] The Records of the Hammermen of Dundee show that guns were made there from the late sixteenth century, and a special style was developed with long barrels and much decoration. Spanish guns were imported — some in the 1719 Rising — and the gun used to shoot Colin Campbell of Glenure in 1752 was said to have belonged to Dugald MacColl and was 'a big long Spanish gun and his name for it was *an t-Slinneanach*, the broad shouldered one'.[26] The Lairds of Grant had an unusually large number of guns, which are now preserved in the National Museum of Antiquities of Scotland. They included guns from several Lowland towns but others were made in Strathspey. William Smith in Duthil, who had a tack from

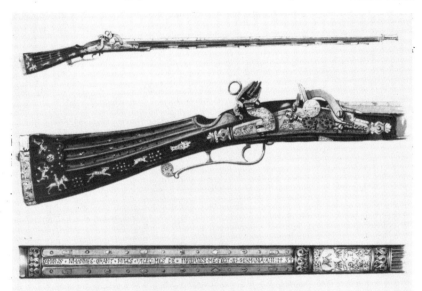

Long Highland sporting gun of the Lairds of Grant, with richly decorated and inlaid barrel and stock. The type of the lock and its decoration and the style of the stock with deeply carved fluting was characteristic of these Highland weapons

Flintlock all-steel pistol with scroll or 'ramshorn' butt, made by Thomas Caddell of Doune in the late seventeenth century or c.1700. There were several generations of gunmakers of this name in Doune, Perthshire, from c.1640 until c.1780

the Laird of Grant in 1675, was a gunmaker and examples of his work survive.

The Highlanders took to the use of pistols as well as guns. The earlier ones were imported or made in various Lowland towns. No doubt due to the great cattle fair that was held at Doune, Highlanders bought a great many of their pistols there, and a special type was developed, distinguished by the scrolls or 'ramshorns' decorating the end of the butt. The finest of these pistols were made about 1650 to 1750 and enjoyed a great reputation.

By the late eighteenth century their actual use had passed away and pistols, with dirks and powder horns, became ostentatiously made articles of costume not generally worn. Powder horns of flattened cow's horn and locally made are interesting because of the decoration incised upon them and are illustrative of the people's taste. There are traces of the survival of the traditional types of ornamentation. In the second quarter of the eighteenth century they went entirely out of use and were replaced by metal or leather pouches.

Powder horn of flattened cow's horn, dated 1678 with every surface filled with decorative carving including animal and bird symbols possibly of heraldic significance

Period VI

After 1745. The impact of change, without and within

PART I

The Rising of the 1745 marks the beginning of a new period more definitely than is usual in social history, even although many of the great changes that were intensified or initiated by the last Jacobite Rising and its suppression did not make themselves felt till about the 1780s.

The Rising was unmercifully suppressed by the government and the military, but this was in no sense a 'Scotch Rebellion' or an English-Scots confrontation. The arch-criminal both in fact and in tradition was William Augustus, the young Duke of Cumberland, commander-in-chief of the Hanoverian Army, a force whose savagery in victory far outstripped the pretended savagery of its Highland opponents. Cumberland earned his name of 'the Butcher' in the aftermath of Culloden when a long and dreary catalogue of atrocities was committed by his troops carrying out his indiscriminate orders to the letter. Those Englishmen like Cumberland and William, Earl of Albemarle, his successor as commander-in-chief, with little personal knowledge of Scotland, tended to see the whole Scottish nation as sympathetic to the Stuarts and, in their thoughts and actions, reflected the massive Hanoverian and Whig fear of Jacobitism. The House of Hanover, quite realistically, lived in dread of being unseated from the throne so recently acquired, and their lieutenants such as Robert Walpole fired that dread by furiously sniffing out Jacobites under the bed at home and all over Europe.

Irrespective of popular views, the '45 was more like a civil war in Scotland. Though contemporaries wrote about and referred to 'the Highlanders', a considerable part of the Jacobite strength was drawn from the episcopalian shires of Aberdeen and Banff, and areas of Angus and Perthshire which were by the eighteenth century more Lowland than Highland. There were many Scots and many Highlanders in Cumberland's army, and three Scottish regiments fought prominently at Culloden; three of his most notorious officers bore Lowland names, Major Lockhart of Cholmondley's Regiment, Captain Caroline Scott of Guise's Regiment and especially Captain John Fergussone R.N. of the Furnace. The Highland Independent Companies, recruited from the pro-government clans, have a far from untarnished record. For instance, the Companies under the command of Lord Loudon, MacDonald of Sleat and MacLeod of MacLeod visited Glenmoriston and after they had committed some unprovoked murders, 'went a rummaging up and down the Glen, destroying all the ploughs, harrows, etc., pots, pans and all household furniture, not excepting the stone querns, with which they grind their corn, breaking them to pieces and driving along with them such cattle as ... they found in the Glen'. The Rev Robert Forbes, Bishop of Ross and Caithness, had this account from a Glenmoriston man who had witnessed the devastations. Between 1747 and 1775, Bishop Forbes devotedly collected eye-witness accounts of the events and personalities of 1745-46 and recorded them in his book, *The Lyon in Mourning*. This has many signed statements by his informants of acts of brutality to the wounded after the battle of Culloden, in the prisons of Inverness, on the ships that took the wretched prisoners to London, and of widespread devastation with brutality in all districts suspected of Jacobite sympathies. The only excuse that can be offered for the calculated and systematic brutality is the fear the Highlanders had inspired, but cowardice is scarcely a creditable excuse.

Legislation was introduced to prevent the possibility of another rising. The acts to abolish heritable jurisdiction and wardholding of 1746 and 1747 brought to an end the feudal powers of the great tenants-in-chief, especially those in the Highlands such as Argyll, Atholl, Sutherland, Moray and Huntly. Their own obligations or money payments to the crown were diverted to church building, and the feudal dues of military service and casualties owed to them by their vassals were commuted to a money composition in the form of feus. Compensation was offered to the holders for the loss of their hereditary judicial powers. The great Highland feudatories Argyll, Huntly, Atholl, Seaforth and Breadalbane received £81,000 out of a total of £152,000. Altogether, 160 claims totalling £602,127 were made, but partly because owners of forfeited estates were not eligible, the claim of only one other Highland landowner, the Laird of Grant, was recognised. The appointment and payment of sheriffs depute by the government probably filled a useful need, as the unofficial judicial functions of the chiefs declined along with their other powers. The penal laws against the episcopalians were tightened up and the non-jurors driven underground.

There were no privileges that could be withdrawn from the chiefs in clan organisation, and the Highlanders in general were dealt with by the Disarming Act of 1746. This was much severer than the earlier attempts to disarm the Highlands, and effective provisions were made for its enforcement. The possession of arms and the wearing of Highland dress and of tartan were prohibited. The proscription of dress stated that after 1st August 1747, any person, man or boy, found wearing 'Highland clothes', plaid, *feileadh-beag*, trews, or shoulder belts, or wearing a

O THE ROAST BEEF OF OLD ENGLAND, &c.

Starving Jacobite at the Gate of Calais shown in a satirical print by William Hogarth of 1749

dress composed of tartan or parti-coloured cloth, should be imprisoned for six months for the first offence and if again found guilty, transported for seven years. The following oath was administered:-

> I, A B do swear, and as I shall answer to God at the great day of Judgment, I have not, nor shall have, in my possession any gun, sword, pistol, or other arm whatever, and never use tartan, plaid or any part of the Highland garb; and if I do so, may I be cursed in my undertakings, family and property — may I never see my wife and children, father, mother or relations — may I be killed in battle as a coward, and lie without Christian burial in a strange land, far from the graves of my forefathers and kindred; may all this come across me if I break my oath.[1]

Duncan Forbes of Culloden was strongly opposed to the passing of the prohibition of Highland dress, though he thought disarming should be strictly enforced.

The Act was not repealed till 1782. Its provision in regard to the possession of arms was evidently thoroughly enforced; and the carrying of them seems to have gone out. This sudden change is illustrated by the descriptions of one of the greatest social occasions in the old days in the Highlands — the funeral of a chief. Rev James Fraser's enthusiasm for these functions is obvious; his Wardlaw Manuscript abounds with descriptions of how neighbouring chiefs exhibited their own importance as well as respect for the departed by the size of their attendant following, all heavily armed. After the passing of the Act, the numbers in attendance might be as great and the liquor certainly as plentiful but it is specifically stated that the attendants were unarmed. James Boswell mentions in his *Journal* that there was hardly a targe to be found in the Highlands, and that after the Disarming Act they were used as covers for butter-milk barrels. The MacDougalls of MacDougall described to one of the authors how the targes at Dunollie had been used for covering meal kegs. But in the case of the prohibitions against the plaid and the tartan there was a good deal of variation. In the pro-Hanoverian districts a good deal of Highland dress was still being worn. Boswell was in Skye when the Act was still in force, yet many of the people he met were wearing the kilt; for instance, Allan MacDonald of Kingsburgh wore a tartan plaid, blue bonnet with a black cockade, a brown short coat, a tartan vest with gold buttons, 'a bluish filibeg' and tartan hose, a 'purple kilt', black waistcoat, a short brown cloth coat with gold cord and a large blue bonnet. As Boswell remarked: 'I never saw a figure that was more perfectly repesentative of a Highland gentleman'. The 'usual figure of a Skye boy' he described as 'with bare legs, a dirty kilt, ragged coat and waistcoat, a bare head and a stock in his hand'. In the Reay country also, where the Mackays were hostile to the Rising, the proscription was not enforced. It was otherwise in the predominantly Jacobite districts. The disturbed state of the country and dire economic necessity were leading to an intensification of raiding. The worst offenders were said to come from Rannoch, Glencoe, Lochaber, Glengarry, Knoydart, Glenmoriston and Laggan in Badenoch, which were singled out for thorough supervision and disarmament in 1747. Parties of soldiers were posted in the more disturbed districts and the straths the raiders generally passed through, and they were instructed to enforce the proscription of arms, dress and tartan. The local sheriffs and justices of the peace, however, were ready to accept every excuse for the release of the men arrested for wearing Highland dress, such as that the plaids had been dyed, that it was a woman's plaid, that the accused was wearing a girl's petticoat, or that a sewed-up kilt was a pair of trews. Nevertheless on the whole in these districts the Act was successfully enforced, at least in the years immediately after its passing. It was no doubt a useful excuse for 'pulling in' a suspected Jacobite, as John MacDonell of Scottos found to his cost, or for pressing a man for the Services, as happened to a

Highland merchant so late as 1778.[2] But by then in general it must have become a dead letter, because tartan was advertised for sale in Edinburgh, and at the Highland Society of London's first piping competition held at Falkirk in 1781 the competitors were required to wear Highland dress; and by all accounts, it was evidently the usual dress of the drovers.

Highland dress therefore came not only to be tolerated in the Highlands but, by an extreme and ironic reversal of attitudes, to be highly esteemed as the dress of the Highlanders and also as the national dress of Scotland by the beginning of the nineteenth century. In August 1822, when the ageing and corpulent George IV visited Edinburgh only 78 years after its wearing had been proscribed under severe penalties, he and Sir William Curtis, the Lord Mayor of London, donned the kilt as a pretty tribute to Scotland. Under the meticulous management of the 'Wizard of the North', Highlanders were especially in evidence in the capital for the occasion. It should be noted that the new attitude and enthusiasm were British and originated in the South and inspired some distaste among Scots. It is amusing to compare the correspondence of George IV's ancestor, James VI, with his Privy Council in referring to his Highland subjects, with this latter-day travesty of the wearing of the *feileadh-beag* as portrayed in contemporary illustrations.

One can trace a number of factors that produced the change, such as a revulsion from past brutalities, admiration for the devotion of those who had suffered in a romantic cause, the glamour of the House of Stuart as compared to the unglamorous House of Hanover. These feelings arose in very high circles. For instance, it was noted in the year 1748 of Lady Mackintosh, known as 'Colonel Anne' for her part in raising a regiment from her husband's clan to fight for the Prince and imprisoned for a short time: 'being at London was caressed by Ladys of Quality of the same way of thinking, was very intimate in the Prince of Wales' Family and so favourably received by the publick that she never met with any Insult on account of her principles. Allan Ramsay, the fam'd Scots painter, took a likeness of her, a thousand copies of which were bought in a short time'.[3] The purchase and furbishment in tartan of Balmoral Castle is a concrete example of the continued appreciation of things Highland by the Sovereign. The Highlands, in fact, in spite of all the disasters still in store for them, became fashionable, and this was eventually to prove to their definite financial advantage as deer forests and grouse moors became the most valuable kind of property in the Highlands. The subject has now gone out of fashion, but down to the mid-twentieth century the final phases of the Jacobite movement, the Risings of the '15 and the '45 and Prince Charles Edward's escape, gave to the Highland people a new subject of folklore. Stories were repeated, locations pointed out, any personal line of descent from Jacobite heroes was recorded, and more ancient folk tales were superseded. To older people, such as one of the writers, the modern change in attitude in the last forty years has been very noticeable.

The development of the fashion for Highland things is largely due to two authors, James Macpherson, the 'translator' of Ossian, whose main influence was not direct and whom therefore it will be more convenient to deal with later on, and Sir Walter Scott, the Wizard of the North. Scott himself has gone out of fashion and it is not easy to realise how great and pervasive was his influence upon his contemporaries. He was a leading figure in the great Romantic Movement which transformed European aesthetics and against the results of which we are still reacting. One result, an appreciation of the beauties of 'Caledonia stern and wild' which he wove into the poetry and novels that enthralled our forebears, is fortunately with us still, very much to the benefit of the tourist industry.

A more tangible factor in the change of attitude of the British people towards the Highlanders was owing to the pressures of a prolonged period of warfare and of national danger. Highland troops rendered a long and distinguished period of military service, reaching its culmination at the time of the Napoleonic Wars. We have said something about the earlier use of Highlanders as soldiers in the formation of the Independent Companies and of the Black Watch, the 42nd, in 1739. Highlanders had also enlisted in other regiments and had customarily fought abroad with 'Scots Brigades' in France and the Netherlands, and Duncan Forbes as early as 1738 had pointed out the possibilities of diverting the martial spirit of the Highlanders by enlisting them for service abroad. Walpole, however, would not risk it. When the situation in North America and on the Continent veered towards war in 1756, William Pitt the Elder reversed this policy. In his own words to the House of Commons, from the mountains of the north he drew 'into your service a hardy and intrepid race of men, who, when left by your jealousy, became a prey to the artifice of your enemies, and had gone nigh to have overturned the State .... These men were brought to combat on your side, have served with fidelity, have fought with valour and conquered for you in every part of the world'.

Between 1757 and 1761 nine regiments were raised, but were disbanded in 1763 at the end of the Seven Years War. The peace which led to their disbandment was a brief one, and in 1778 four Highland fencible regiments were raised. Once more they were disbanded at the peace of 1783, but when war broke out once again with France in 1793 and our unprepared country met with severe defeats, Alan Cameron of Erracht, by his persistence, obtained leave to raise the Cameron Highlanders, and other leading men in the Highlands followed suit. In 1793-4 eight Highland line regiments and a number of fencible regiments were raised, such as Lord Reay's Highlanders, and many more fencible and militia regiments were added during the Revolutionary and Napoleonic Wars.[4] In the zeal for national defence that spread over Scotland, the Highlands bore a most distinguished part out of all proportion to the size of their population. Rev Dr Webster estimated the population of the Highland counties at 337,000 in 1755, and at the time of the first official census in 1801, it had grown to 381,576, in spite of emigration.[5] The men in the Highland fencible regiments again and again volunteered to transfer to fill the gaps in the line regiments fighting overseas, and only the few instances when they refused are publicised. From the formation of the Black Watch till the end of the Napoleonic Wars, the total corps raised in the Highlands amounted to fifty battalions of the line, three of reserve, seven of militia, besides 26 battalions of fencibles, and 34,785 local militia and volunteers. Many Highlanders also served in the army raised by the East India Company and saw action against the French in India.

The organisation of these regiments was based on that of some of the great clans. MacKenzie of Kintail, Lord Seaforth, the Laird of Grant, and others offered to raise a regiment and had the gift of the commissions in it. The officers were mainly cadets of the chief's family and were responsible for recruiting most of the men. To a considerable extent the raising of these regiments helped to cushion the change from the tie of clanship to the cash nexus. Military service gave a career and an escape from overcrowded conditions at home. Regiments such as the MacLeods and Fraser Highlanders were disbanded in America and the men given grants of land there. Those who came home greatly enriched local society by their wider experience, as many contemporary writers, both visitors like James Boswell and residents like Elizabeth Grant of Rothiemurchus and Sir Aeneas Mackintosh of Mackintosh, testify. In puzzling out old records and accounts it is pleasant sometimes to come across the term 'Chelsea Man', meaning that the man was in receipt of a pension for military service. Colonel John MacInnes recorded the military careers of men of *An t-Eilean*, the Isle of Skye, up to the latter years of the last century, and it is an extraordinary catalogue of service to the British nation at home and abroad.[6] There can be no districts in the Highlands and Islands that could not produce a record of the same kind.

The services rendered by the Highlanders were of great importance besides the immediate one of helping to save Britain in her hour of peril, as well as the scope it gave to many Highlanders suffering from the economic pressures of the times. They restored to the Highlanders, defeated in two Risings, severely repressed and the victims of increasing economic frustrations, a reason for a well-founded pride in their race. They were also perhaps the most important factor in the preservation of the Highland dress and of piping and they laid the foundation of the industry of weaving and differentiating tartans.

The influence of Sir Walter Scott and of the military service rendered by Highland soldiers was immediate, obvious and direct. The influence of the second great writer, James Macpherson, was not so direct. He was in fact a potent force in creating the so-called Romantic Movement in late eighteenth century Europe; this denotes the change in ideas and attitudes in literture and art among the leading aesthetes in Europe. It turned out to be a favourable influence for the Highlands to which the cultured world looked for its primitive poetry. The spirit of European Romanticism was not of course in any way part of the Gaelic tradition, and the spiritual and imaginative inspiration which derived from it imbued terms such as 'Highland', 'Celtic' and 'Gael' with qualities foreign to them. Macpherson's European reputation and popularity led to a blazing controversy at home over the authenticity of his 'translation' of the poetry of Ossian, and also to a searching enquiry into Gaelic literature in which valuable oral and manuscript material was salvaged which would otherwise almost certainly have been lost. The desire to investigate the authenticity of Ossian also prompted the visit to the Highlands of several distinguished literati, including the redoubtable Dr Johnson. These travellers recorded an account of their travels and descriptions of Highland society at a time of fundamental change.

Macpherson was born in 1736 at Kingussie in Badenoch and for a time was schoolmaster nearby at Ruthven. It was while he was acting as tutor in the family of Graham of Balgowan at Moffat that he met the poet John Home, the author of *Douglas*, who asked him if it were true that ancient poems existed in the Highlands, a few having been translated and published in 1756 in the *Scots Magazine* by Jerome Stone, a Fife man teaching in Dunkeld. After some hesitation Macpherson showed him what he said was a translation he had made of a ballad on the death of Oscar, a character in the Fenian Cycle. John Home showed this exciting discovery to Dr Carlyle of Inveresk, Dr Hugh Blair, Professor Adam Fergusson and Principal William Robertson, all shining lights among the literati of Edinburgh. With their enthusiastic encouragement Macpherson in 1760 published *Fragments of Ancient Poetry collected in the Highlands of Scotland and translated from the Galic or Erse Language*, purporting to be compositions of epic poetry by the third century bard Ossian. Macpherson announced that he knew of more and longer Gaelic poems, and subscriptions were quickly raised to enable him to go on a tour to collect all he could. He was accompanied by the competent Gaelic scholars Lachlan Macpherson of Strathmashie and Ewan Macpherson and returned with a number of poems taken down orally and with some manuscripts. He spent some time translating this material, and in 1762 and 1763 he published *Fingal*, an epic in six books, and *Temora*.

The sales of his books were enormous. Before the end of the century, 'Ossian' had been translated into almost every language in Europe, and the next forty years saw translations in Czech (1827), Hungarian (1833) and Polish (1840). Macpherson himself did well out of his literary efforts. He made a good deal of money, obtained some lucrative 'places' and ended up as Member of Parliament for Camelford and a landed proprietor in his own strath, having bought the estate of Raitts from Mackintosh of Borlum.

Criticism of his work that made its own rather different mark on Highland history took a little time to develop, but under the massive leadership of Dr Johnson it had become very bitter by 1773, the year in which the entire collection was published in the new edition, *Ossian*. Confident and fresh from his visit to the Highlands, Johnson denounced Macpherson: 'I thought your book an imposture'. This scathing note was taken up by Malcolm Laing who described Ossian as 'a patchwork of plagiarism' and Macpherson as 'one of the first literary imposters of modern times'. He published a line-by-line analysis of the text to prove his point in 1805. The controversy spread beyond Britain, and the Italian and French editors in the first respective translations in 1763 and 1777 went to great pains to support the poems' authenticity. Dr Johnson's main points of criticism were that Gaelic was too barbarous a language to be a medium for such poetry, and that it was impossible that ancient Gaelic manuscripts should exist. Macpherson was defended by many fellow Gaels. In 1783, Highlanders in India subscribed £1,000 to enable Macpherson to publish the originals on which the poems were founded. The list of subscribers to a book written in his defence by John and Hugh MacCallum reads like a roll-call of the clans, and among his supporters were Ewen MacLachlan of Aberdeen University, a fine classical scholar, and also the sharp-tongued Rev Donald MacNicol. From learned discussions, the opponents descended to abuse; the MacCallums remarked that Dr Johnson was disappointed that he could find nothing more barbarous in the islands than himself.[7]

After Macpherson's death and burial in Westminster Abbey in 1796, a Gaelic version of his poems was published by the Highland Society of London in 1807, but it is merely a translation of his English poems, written in modern Gaelic in his own hand or that of an amanuensis. In 1805 the Highland and Agricultural Society of Edinburgh's Committee appointed to enquire into the nature and authenticity of Ossian, after an exhaustive investigation, announced that ancient poetry existed in the Highlands, and 'that it was common, general and in great abundance; that it was of a most impressive and striking sort, in a high degree eloquent, tender and sublime', and that Macpherson, although he used incidents and sometimes 'almost literal expressions', had altered, enlarged, elaborated, omitted and generally changed the compositons in accordance with his own ideas. This report is important not merely for assessing the merits of Macpherson but also as an indication of a new appreciation of the culture of the Gael.

The later and more scholarly study of Gaelic literature, the rise of which was largely due to the Ossianic controversy, has made clear that Macpherson mixed up details of the Ulster and the Fenian Cycles, which had never been done in the old prose versions and only in the latest and most debased versions of the ballads and popular tales, and that his accounts of manners and customs, mythology and history, were inconsistent with those of the genuine Gaelic literature. Although he was indeed a fabricator, his Gaelic sources are apparent in his work, if his treatment of them was generally arbitrary. Many of the sequences in his plot, especially in *Fingal*, closely follow the ballad originals as collected at the time in the MacLagan, Turner and MacNicol manuscripts. Macpherson's *Dar-Thula*, for instance, is based on the Deirdre story but he adapted it to fit his scheme; this was of course popular in oral tradition, and Alexander Carmichael collected a full version of it in Barra. His later *Temora* is less faithful to the originals, as though he was then more confident in his ability to produce an epic.[8] Macpherson does not use the old ballad forms of Gaelic poetry, the fixed number of syllables, alliteration and assonance. His amorphous and sententious style is the very antithesis of the old concise modes. The following extract gives a general idea of his style:

The spirit of Loda shrieked, as rolled into himself,
he rode on the wind. Inistore shook at the sound.
The waves heard it on the deep. They stopped in their
course with fear; the friends of Fingal started at once;
they rose in rage and all their arms resound.

Macpherson indeed is generally credited with being the originator of modern ideas of 'Celtic gloom'. As two of his enthusiastic admirers wrote in 1816: 'Ossian is perhaps the only poet who never relaxes, or lets himself down into the light or amusing strain ... He moves perpetually in the regions of the grand and the pathetic.' A more able exponent of this interest in ancient Gaelic poetry was the learned minister of Campbeltown, Dr John Smith (1747-1807). He was a stern Evangelical, but like many of his type in the Church he was not a man of narrow interests. Gaelic scholar, antiquary, agriculturalist, translator and active churchman, he also turned his hand to poetry. In 1780 he published his *Galic Antiquities*, which included fourteen ballads, and in his *Sean Dana* (1787) he published the Gaelic originals, having the advantage over Macpherson of being able to compose in the two languages.[9] As Campbell of Islay pointed out in *Leabhar na Féinne*, these translators believed that their work was an authentic reproduction, only 'their ideas on authenticity differed from modern ideas on the subject', and texts were treated as things to alter and enlarge 'to suit contemporary taste'. To assess the influence of Macpherson's writings upon world literature is outside the scope of the present work. We must remember with gratitude that the Ossianic controversy led to the collection and preservation of the precious remains of Gaelic manuscripts and to a new interest in Gaelic literature.

Macpherson may be seen also as the father of the Highland tourist industry. To prove him genuine or spurious brought pioneering travellers including Johnson and the attendant Boswell to the *terra incognita* of the Highlands. It was a glorified but extraordinarily uncomfortable form of treasure hunt. Gradually the Romantic Movement, to which Macpherson contributed so much, educated persons of taste into an appreciation of Highland scenery. Edward Burt, who had been in the Highlands in the 1720s, had described the Highland hills in his *Letters* as 'monstrous excrescences' and the views as 'most horrible'. But ideas were beginning to change by the beginning of the nineteenth century. John MacCulloch, of a Galloway family but born and brought up in the south of England, trained as a doctor and went on a series of tours through Scotland gathering data on geology and mineralogy. In his four volume *Highlands and Western Isles of Scotland* of 1824, he industriously catalogued and assessed the country and its scenery in the form of a series of letters to Sir Walter Scott. In his observations, he reserved most of his praise for the open valleys and straths. The road over the Spittal of Glenshee he dismissed as not worth description and the Cairngorms as 'a mass of rude uninteresting mountains'. The early visitors to the Highlands, both writers and artists, had very similar tastes. The Highlands had depressed the late-eighteenth century landscape-painter Joseph Farington, for example, who had drawn such inspiration from the English lakes, and Thomas Pennant, the English naturalist and antiquary, had described the Highlands in terms as impolite as Burt. It was Sir Walter Scott and artists such as Horatio McCulloch who first taught the visitor something of the stark grandeur of the high hills. In the early years of the nineteenth century, artists sought out the landscape of Ossian and Scott. The publication of *The Lady of the Lake* in 1810 drew them to Loch Katrine and the Trossachs, and *The Lord of the Isles* (1816) turned their attention to Skye and Loch Coruisk. McCulloch's paintings of 'Loch Katrine', 'Glencoe', 'Inverlochy Castle' and his imaginative amalgam 'My Heart's in the Highlands' vividly portray the highly charged sentiments of the day.[10]

In writing of influential contemporary descriptions of the Highlands, it is only fair to consider an antagonist. A very different attitude to the Highlanders was that of John Pinkerton (1758-1826). An industrious researcher but with strong prejudices, he published in 1787, *A Dissertation on the Origin and Progress of the Scythians or Goths*. According to the *Dictionary of National Biography*, 'its chief purpose was to expound a peculiar hypothesis as to the inveterate inferiority of the Celtic race'. The same conclusion coloured his monumental *History of Scotland from the Accession of the House of Stewart to that of Mary* (1797). It was news to the Highlanders that they were 'celtic' or that, as Pinkerton pointed out, they with Welsh, Bretons and Basques were the 'aborigines of Europe'. The MacCallums, the champions of Ossian, described Pinkerton's account of the Highlanders as 'a venomous bog of filthy slanders', although George Buchanan, more than two hundred years earlier, had noticed the kinship of the language of the Gael, the Welsh and the Bretons. Pinkerton's history was a valuable source book, especially for the reign of James V and before the publication of so many of the Scottish records, and his pungent style makes him very readable. He deeply influenced much subsequent thought with his theories of a Celtic 'race', though the term 'Celtic', generally loosely used, should be properly applied only to a group of languages and to a form of culture.

Although the Highlands were attracting the eye of sentiment, social changes were taking place which were to transform the very image which the outside world was seeking to discover. One of the most important changes is summed up in the old saying that before the '45, a man's standing depended on the number of men he could bring into the field, after it, by the number of cattle he could bring to market. The defeat of the Jacobite forces in the '45 Rising and the measures taken after it by the government to make the Highlands equally amenable to the enforcement of law and order as the rest of Britain are vitally important events in Highland history. The Jacobite defeat and the pacification of the Highlands, however, only gave a twist or emphasis to problems which had been building up since the preceding period.

It must be stressed that the gentry of the Highlands were entirely dependant upon agricultural earnings from their land, and of this only a small proportion was suitable for agriculture and even that was mainly of poor quality often inaccessible and subject to a severe and unpredictable climate. Under a primitive method of agriculture the extent to which cattle could be raised was the main source of income. Before the disarming of the Highlands, it was essential for the well-being, even survival, of the chief and clan that the manpower maintained by the land should be as large as possible. The surplus available for payment of rent from what was almost entirely subsistence farming was small even in the good years. To judge from such rentals as are available, it was frequently in arrears.

The Highland gentry's poverty and pride of birth were proverbial, and during the seventeenth century they were coming more and more into contact with Lowland Scots and Englishmen. It had become usual for the sons of the chiefs to go to school in the South and often on to a university and, in the case of the Roman Catholic families, to be sent abroad. In the early eighteenth century younger sons were finding their way to India or the New World. Marriages into families outside the Highlands also became more frequent. It was inevitable that the Highland gentry should have felt more and more acutely the difference between the simplicity of their life at home and the comparative opulence of that of the people with whom they came into contact, and that therefore in trying not to be conspicuous by their poverty, many families were becoming heavily involved in debt. What would have eventually happened had the old conditions of lawlessness continued can only be surmised.

On the whole the gentry of the Highlands adjusted their social life well to the changed conditions following the '45. As in the seventeenth century, they had lived mainly on their properties, taking their pleasure in sport and other local activities like the horse races held at Inverness. There were great gatherings at the marriages and especially at the funerals of their neighbours. They also tended to have their own houses in the nearest towns, such as Inverness or Elgin, where they would spend the winter.

The habit already beginning as early as the sixteenth century, of going to Edinburgh for the winter or even to London, was now quite general. Boswell's description in his *Journal* of Dr Hector MacLean's daughter who had been taught to do shellwork, and who received him and Dr Johnson in a beaver hat with a white feather when they arrived at supper-time, is one whimsical illustration showing the changing climate of the times. These changes had economic results and did much to depress the ancient culture of the Gael as its natural patrons moved away socially and intellectually from their roots. The eighteenth century saw the end of the hereditary offices maintained by the chiefs, the family seannachies of Clan Ranald, MacDonald of Sleat and MacLeod, the hereditary physicians, and also the colleges of piping.

Fortunately, the early visitors to the Highlands, especially Johnson and Boswell, have left us descriptions of eighteenth century Highland society. Coming from the class-conscious south, they noted the ease with which people of all ranks mixed while still treating the chief and his family with respect. It is difficult to remember, in reading visitors' accounts of an almost idyllic society, that it was under severe economic pressure and experiencing great social changes. We learn how in the home of MacLeod of Raasay the whole company joined in the singing. The clearest indication of the growing economic pressure was in the frequent references to emigration by the friends and connections of their hosts. But these were not regarded as occasions for gloom, and there was even a cheerful song and dance called 'Emigration'.

Some chiefs were able to weather the economic pressures, as for instance MacLeod of Raasay, so much quoted by Boswell. Sir Aeneas Mackintosh of Mackintosh in his *Notes Descriptive and Historical* of about 1780 furnishes a detailed description of how a chief could at once treasure old tradition, realise and fulfil his duties as chief, and adjust his way of life and his scale of expenditure to the conditions of the time. Others had inherited greater financial burdens. Boswell and Johnson described with admiration how young Norman MacLeod of MacLeod kept up the patriarchal traditions of his ancient family and entertained his clansmen in Dunvegan Castle. Norman MacLeod, however, eventually went overseas like so many of his race. He served with distinction in the Indian Army, rising to the rank of general, but he had to sell valuable land, and his successor still had to struggle to maintain the encumbered estate. Both Mackintosh and MacLeod remitted the payments of rents and arrears in bad years, and so did many others. The Parliamentary Committee which took evidence in 1783 about the distress and famine caused by the disastrous harvest of the preceding year and the severe winter following it noted the details of the many examples of cancelling rents and giving out meal and seed corn. The worst affected areas were in the northern and east central Highlands, where 'not a peck of bear can be had in the country for gold, love, or any money'. With a forceful comparison, a letter from Badenoch stated: 'The poor Highlanders .... of this country were never in such distress since the time of King William'.[11]

Some chiefs, however, could not adjust to the changing times. Alasdair MacDonell of Glengarry of the early nineteenth century, who with a fantastic arrogance tried to play the part of an ancient chief complete with a 'tail' of followers, was an anachronism. He ruined his estate in trying to keep up this style of living, but in the ancient tradition he supported the culture of his race, and it is to his credit that he helped to finance the studies of Ewen MacLachlan, the fine Gaelic scholar, and maintained *Ailean Dall*, Blind Allan MacDougall, as his bard. Only gradually did the burden of chief as distinct from land-holder become separated. There have been many worthy descendants of the old chiefs, and the tie of sentiment between chief and clansmen has not entirely died out. As we shall hope to show, a notable example in the mid-nineteenth century was to be the labours of some chiefs to relieve distress during the potato famines. Nevertheless, the organisation of the clan as a functioning institution had ended. In 1852, when there was a lawsuit as to whether the heir at law of MacGillivray of Dunmaglass, not being a member of Clan Chattan, could succeed to the chieftainship of the clan, the Court of Session declared that the laws did not recognise the existence of clans.[12] This seems to be in strange contradiction to the function and jurisdiction of the Lord Lyon and the Lyon Office of determining and recognising claims to be the chief of a clan. It also runs counter to the creation and activities of clan societies that were to become a feature of our period.

One fortuitous circumstance from which benefits had been derived may be mentioned. From the Act of Union of 1707 till the Reform Act of 1832, those chiefs who held land by royal charter became involved in great activity over parliamentary elections, and considerable clan feeling was developed. As Lewis Namier showed in his *Structure of Politics at the Accession of George III* (1929), eighteenth century political history was built not on the high political Whig principles of 1688 but on the exercise of local political influence and of patronage or, as we might term it, corruption. Nowhere was this more significant than in Scotland, where the union of the parliaments had reduced the number of constituencies from 159 to 45, and the franchise was strictly limited to the freeholder whose land, held of the crown, was valued either at forty shillings of old extent, the medieval assessment of taxable capacity, or at £400 Scots of current valuation. With a limited number of freeholders and therefore electors, a system of political management grew up. To secure and control votes, the family, kin and patrimony were of cardinal importance, and a legal manoeuvre of creating fictitious votes began after the Union. Large freeholds could be split into franchises which still met the qualifications. These 'parchment barons' would hold a sort of life-rent superiority and often only a nominal title to the land. The hands of the lairds and chiefs were also strengthened by heritable sheriffdoms (before their abolition in 1747) and the offices of commissioners of supply, justices of the peace and lords lieutenant. Nobles such as Argyll had an automatic advantage, and such was his influence that he controlled Scottish politics with his brother and successor, the Earl of Islay, until the latter's death in 1761. The apotheosis of the system was achieved by Henry Dundas, especially after his appointment as Lord Advocate in 1775. He made it his business to be acquainted with as large a part of the county electorate as possible, and by the free use of the spoils system he could influence most of the members of parliament and the electors. It could therefore be of enormous material advantage to be represented in parliament by a member sympathetic to one's interests and also in one's debt for his due election. Rivalries might sometimes reach the point of violence at election times, especially in the burghs, as the system of grouping for parliamentary seats made it difficult to control them. Burghs such as Inveraray clearly fell under the control of Argyll as the local patron, but others such as Dingwall were courted or coerced by local lairds such as the Monros and the Tullochs. In the excitement of elections, the old clan spirit could be revived and added to the heat of the contest. To quote one comparatively late example, the last rising of a clan is said to have been when the men of Clan Grant marched down to Elgin in force in March 1820 to defend their chief and his family who had become involved in a bitter electoral contest between rival candidates.[13]

It was especially important for the lesser gentry of the Highlands that the end of our preceding period, that is the years after the Act of Union of 1707, had seen the beginning of opportunities for a career overseas in North America and the West Indies and in India. At home there were also more openings in the professions. They had meanwhile been coming into contact with Lowland Scots and Englishmen and had begun to be affected by their higher standard of living in the same way as had the chiefs and their families earlier. At the same time, Highland landowners, themselves feeling the financial stringencies, were putting up the rents of their principal tenants or tacksmen. The introduction of large-scale sheep farming and the changes summed up by the term 'the Agricultural Revolution' both affected the position of the tacksmen and eventually led to their elimination as an important element of Highland society.[14] There was therefore a growing inducement for them to take advantage of the greater number of openings in the south and overseas. Emigration to America, for instance, was offering excellent opportunities to settlers with capital in the second half of the eighteenth century, at least until the outbreak of the American War in 1776. In some cases such settlers took their sub-tenants with them. The Society for the Propagation of Christian Knowledge estimated that between 1772 and 1791 sixteen vessels left the west of Inverness-shire and Ross taking across 6,400 people and at least £38,000 sterling in specie.[15] Such people were in a position to make satisfactory arrangements and they left in good heart. About the same time, with the extension of British colonial activity, and especially during the administration and ascendancy of Henry Dundas, Viscount Melville, great opportunities for a career were opening to young men in India and the East and West Indies. And the Continental wars also supplied the opportunity for a military career.

The tacksmen had been an element in the clan organisation. They and their kindred formed an important but fluctuating element in Highland society. They could be generous to their own tenants, supplying the money to buy in essential seed corn after a dearth or in marketing their cattle; but many hard things were said of them, especially by the agricultural reformers, under whose plans they were becoming obsolete. Nevertheless, in this period of transition they could be a valuable element in Highland society. Living closer to the land than the laird or chief, they maintained the old language and traditions. Many were retired officers returning to their native strath, living in simplicity and yet maintaining a high degree of breeding, nurturing families that were to bring honour to their race at the far ends of the earth. Boswell and Johnson left vivid pictures of the homes of some of the Skye tacksmen, with good country fare, fine napery, books of Latin and Greek, literature and history, Gaelic songs and a silver tea set such as they found at Coirechatachan. Thomas Pennant in his *Tour* described the same sort of life among the ex-officer farmers of Easter Ross, who 'assumed the farmer without flinging off the gentleman'. At Scottos in the 'Rough Bounds' of Knoydart, John MacDonell said that he lived in the company of 'a numerous society of gentlemen, well polished and educated'.[16] In spite of their manners, tastes, learning, breeding and abilities, the tacksmen often lived in what outsiders considered to be very mean dwellings, having only the most meagre of worldly goods. Elizabeth Grant of Rothiemurchus gives delightful pen pictures of neighbours of the tacksman class such as the last Shaws of Dalnavert who lived in a turf house. It must be emphasised that the tacksmen and local gentry were not a distinct class. Some farmed considerable estates; others merely rented a small holding. They had ties of blood with their chief and the head of their house; and, as every Highlander was a genealogist, everyone knew their own and their neighbours' pedigrees.

In most cases, loss of their land, and in general the rising standards of living had a cumulative effect. In *Minor Septs of Clan Chattan*, Fraser-Mackintosh gives details of the wholesale disappearance of nearly all the families of the lesser gentry in the straths of eastern Inverness-shire; in Strathdearn, for instance, out of nine small properties all but two changed hands during our period. Duncan Campbell in his *Reminiscences and Reflections* gives similar examples in Perthshire. Their going altered the social pattern of the Highlands and undoubtedly still further depressed the native Gaelic culture. This was probably recognised by contemporary poets; John MacCodrum, for example, laments the departure of the Uist tacksmen of the MacDonalds in 1770 and has sharp words to say of the incoming tenants. The elimination of the tacksmen was, however, inevitable in the changes that affected the whole appearance of Highland agriculture over the greater part of the mainland. It was the settled policy of good agricultural reformers to replace the methods of joint cultivation carried on by groups of eight or more sub-tenants, growing an unvaried succession of crops of grain on high, intermixed rigs, by working farmers on demarcated holdings and growing a rotation of crops.[17]

There was another important addition to Highland society. A number of Highlanders who had sought and some who had amassed their fortunes overseas returned with comfortable financial provision. They founded or restored the fortunes of families among the lesser gentry, to some extent stepping into the shoes of those who left the country, although the old ways of life and traditions could not be restored. Capt Alexander MacLeod of the Berneray family had made a fortune as owner of an East India merchantman, and bought Harris, Berneray and St Kilda for £15,000 in 1779 when MacLeod was obliged to sell it. Capt Alexander thus secured parts of the MacLeod estates which were then in danger of being lost to the clan. He was a model landlord and undertook many projects, especially in South Harris, for helping the people. James Matheson, a Sutherland man, was in business in London, Calcutta and latterly in China, where he had made a large fortune. He bought the Island of Lewis from the MacKenzies of Seaforth in 1844 and spent most of his fortune in trying to bring prosperity to it. He arrived just before the onset of the famine years and was faced with the task of trying to alleviate the wretched conditions which beset the islanders. In 1850 his efforts to bring relief were recognised by the award of a baronetcy.[18] The influx of this new element into society helped to bring about a change in manners and customs. Sir Aeneas Mackintosh of Mackintosh, whose reminiscences relate to the third quarter of the eighteenth century, described the dinner parties which he attended in Inverness:

> The gentlemen having a turn of going abroad, generally run to the Army, or turn Merchants, so that they mix the Ideas of one Country with the other, and make good Companions; after a long Absence people naturally converse on their different Adventures, the Bottle imperceptibly goes round, nor do they think of retiring till the wine gets the better.

With this convivial scene, so typical of the eighteenth century, one must compare Scott's description in *Waverley* of a chief's hospitality less than fifty years earlier and before the '45. He kept open house to his clansmen, who were seated strictly in accordance with their degree and who were entertained by the recitations of the family bard. According to strong tradition, the principal element in an evening's entertainment from the seventeenth century onwards had been the playing of *piobaireachd*, and as Sir Aeneas Mackintosh noted, families such as Fraser of Lovat, Farquharson of Invercauld and Grant of

Rothiemurchus still maintained family pipers, each of whom derived his skill in *piobaireachd* from the MacCrimmons in Skye.[19]

At the same time, with so much more contact with the outside world, the merchants in the burghs had better opportunites for trade. Hugh Miller described the activities of an eighteenth century Cromarty merchant:

> He supplied the proprietors with teas, and wines, and spiceries; with broad cloths, glass, delft ware, Flemish tiles, and pieces of japanned cabinet work; he furnished the blacksmith with iron from Sweden, the carpenter with tar and spars from Norway, and the farmer with flax-seed from Holland.[20]

The family of Forbes of Culloden, however, were quite exceptional not only in their success as merchants, but in the case of Duncan Forbes (1685-1747) for service to the nation; he was successively a member of parliament, Lord Advocate and Lord President of the Court of Session, as well as a farmer and man of business.

Contemporary descriptions of the lesser folk generally allude to their poverty. Burt in his *Letters*, in describing the Highlands and its people in the period before the '45, is the most explicit and gives fullest details. Other visitors, in commenting on the country people's poverty, noted other characteristics. Boswell has the delightful account of how the voices of the boatmen, singing as they rowed him to Raasay, blended with the song of the reapers on the shore. The natural dignity and beautiful manners of the people are also mentioned by most travellers. A French traveller who visited the Highlands in 1810 described it best when he wrote of their 'superiority to want'.[21] The accounts of such visitors are fully endorsed and amplified by the author and soldier General David Stewart of Garth (1772-1829). From long close contact with his fellow Gaels, he wrote sympathetically in his *Sketches*, published in 1822, of their character and temperament and his heartfelt concern about the loss to the nation consequent on their emigration. He also recalled how the country people used to enjoy the epics of the Fianna and traditional songs and poetry.

Something has been said of the essential need for a chief under the old clan system and of the devotion of clansmen to him. These ties died, but only gradually. After the '15 and '45, the tenants on several of the forfeited estates continued to give their rents to their old landlords; Seaforth, Lovat, Lochiel and Cromarty are prime examples. Iona had come into the possession of Argyll, but in one of the most moving passages in his *Journal*, Boswell describes the devotion of the MacLeans there to their old chief.

In this period of the Industrial Revolution in which new industries were being created and new resources exploited in the rest of Britain, the main economic resource in the Highlands continued to be its stark and weather-beaten land. How this could be turned to account was the main problem of our period. Before discussing the ways in which the proprietors tried to make some profit from the land, it is worthwhile considering what most parts of the Highlands looked like about the middle of the eighteenth century. For this we are dependent on the written descriptions of travellers, maps such as the military survey of Major General William Roy made between 1747 and 1752, and maps and plans in family muniments and official papers like those of the Annexed Forfeited Estates or the Breadalbane Estates. The accumulation of official records by burgeoning government departments created new sources of evidence and a new prejudiced view of the Highland economy. One of the first tasks of the Board of Agriculture, founded in 1793 through the efforts of Sir John Sinclair, was to commission a series of reports on the state of agriculture in different parts of the Highlands. The description in these reports of the method of agriculture practised all over the Highlands paints a fairly uniform picture which agrees with the contemporary parish accounts done by the ministers of the established church. These methods were then considered to be very primitive. Patches of the best land, known as 'infield,' were kept under constant cultivation with annual crops of grain, either of oats, including the primitive varieties of black oats, or bere, which was an inferior kind of barley. By constant ploughing, the infield arable land was worked into high narrow rigs or ridges, which at least provided a measure of simple drainage all too necessary on sour and impermeable soils. Portions of land once cultivated in this way and long abandoned can be recognised under the heather or rough grass like ripples on water. The toilful and unproductive system was worked by groups of tenants holding land jointly from the tacksman or the laird. To ensure equality in the communal work and a fair share of the fruits of the earth, the holding of each tenant consisted of a number of separate rigs, unfenced and periodically reallocated under the system known as 'runrig'. The infield ground was generally situated on the lower slopes of the hills, and the houses of the joint-tenants were built in a cluster beside them. The alluvial land along the rivers, now the most fertile land on a farm, was then boggy and water-logged, and patches of wet ground on the hill slopes were similarly uncultivable. All the available manure was deposited on the infield. No other means of improving the quality of the land were used except the wasteful process of skinning the surface of the less fertile and inaccessible ground, burning the cut turf and spreading the ashes on the infield. Scattered in the rough ground further from the dwellings were the areas of land designated as 'outfield', in varied stages of use or recovery. These were cropped without intermission until their fertility was exhausted and then allowed to lie waste until they had recovered some fertility.

The implements of the old methods of farming were few and simple. Hugh Miller described them in Ross at the end of our period as:

the one-stilted plough, the wooden toothed harrow, and the basket woven cart with its rollers of wood.[22]

The plough was made entirely of wood except for the small iron sock or share and coulter. On light soils it was drawn by four horses yoked abreast, and one man led the horses while another steered the plough. On heavier soils, teams of eight oxen or oxen and horses yoked in tandem might be used. Reaping was done with the sickle, usually a small toothed implement, and the workers organised themselves into bands. The joint-tenants were subsistence farmers, depending for their food on what they grew and the stock that they raised. Their cattle also supplied a little money for the few extra expenses that they had to meet. It was customary to send the cattle and other animals up to the grassy head waters of the rivers and burns in the summer months, to the areas known as 'sheilings'. A section of the community accompanied them and stayed at the sheilings through the summer to herd and milk the cattle and to make cheese for the winter. During the winter, the cattle had to subsist on the straw of the corn and what they could pick up of natural herbage and by foraging over the infield after the crops had been harvested. All accounts agree in condemning the inefficiency of the system and the poorness of the returns even in normal and good seasons. The account book kept by a forebear of one of the writers analysed in *Every Day Life on an Old Highland Farm* provides more actual figures. Under the old system their ordinary dietary was below even the standards estimated as necessary for industrialised working families of the time. Sir John Sinclair, writing of the fertile Black Isle, described the people's dietary and said that it enabled them only 'to subsist' but 'hardly in a manner adequate to give spirit of strength for labour'.[23] Unfortunately, and particularly in the high straths of the central and eastern Highlands, the severity of the climate reduced the already meagre rents and caused recurrent dearths. The worst shortages and famine were in 1763-4, 1782 (known in tradition as *Bliadhna na Peasarach Bana* or the 'Year of the White Peas'), 1802-4, 1817 (coupled with the post-war depression in cattle prices), 1826, and the disastrous famine years of the 1840s. Generally, there was a more or less serious shortage about every ten years, when the precious stocks of seed corn were used as food and much of the livestock was killed or died of starvation.

The Clearances have absorbed so much public attention that it may not be generally realised that at the same time and over wide areas of the Highlands, a different programme of agricultural reform was being carried out. Economic conditions at the end of the eighteenth century were propitious. The demand for meat increased, and during the war years up to 1815 the growing of cereals could be even more profitable. At the same time the spirit of enterprise and activity that engendered the Industrial Revolution had brought about sweeping changes and improvements in the south, and an agricultural revolution there was well under way. Its lessons had only to be applied. Several of the great Scots landowners became interested in these agricultural reforms. The group included three Highland proprietors with very large estates, the Dukes of Argyll and of Gordon and the Laird of Grant. Many owners of lesser estates shared their interest. The response of these three magnates is well documented, but lesser landowners such as MacDougall of MacDougall and Mackintosh of Mackintosh undertook improvements for which some details have also survived. Surviving tacks of the MacDougall farms on Kerrera show how they encouraged good stocking and cropping, the use of lime-rich shell-sand, seaware, lime itself imported from neighbouring Lismore, and the building of substantial byres, barns and dwellings; by the turn of the nineteenth century, they were letting their farms to the existing tenants with generous leases.[24] The pace was set for these changes by the House of Argyll which at the turn of the eighteenth century controlled hundreds of square miles of Argyllshire and Inverness-shire.

It was in the time of the 2nd Duke (1703-1743) that the tenurial system began to be reorganised on the Argyll estates. In Kintyre, about 1710, tacks or leases were offered to the highest bidder. Argyll represented himself as a landlord, albeit a benevolent one, rather than a Highland chieftain, and regarded his land as a productive capital asset. The reorganisation of the ducal land to the north, in Mull, Morvern and Tiree, was undertaken in 1737 by Duncan Forbes of Culloden as Argyll's commissioner. He was an avowed enemy of the tacksmen, whom it was his objective to remove. He divided the farms and then let them to the previous sub-tenants or to joint-tenants who then held his individual share of land directly of Argyll on a written lease for terms of years and at a significantly increased rent. This stroke against what Forbes held to be 'the tyranny of tacksmen' was the earliest manifestation of the coming social and economic changes; at the same time it met with doubtful success and disappointed its architects. In 1776, Campbell of Shawfield was letting his land on nineteen year leases and dividing it into reasonably sized holdings. Sir James Grant of Grant also carried out the policy of terminating leases of the large holdings and redeeming wadsets, of which there were a number in Strathspey, and of letting his land in farms of moderate size to individual farmers. He carried out the same policy in Glen Urquhart in 1808.[25]

The plans and the nature of the changes varied from district to district and even within a single estate owned by one proprietor. On the Argyll estates, for example, the process was quite different in Tiree and in mainland Knapdale. It could vary within one parish; for example, in the parish of Moy and Dalarossie, where the arable land lies on each side of the Findhorn. On one farm, Clune, the farmer was awarded a prize for his turnips in 1804 by the Badenoch Agricultural Society, whereas the farm of Woodside, nearly opposite on the other side of the river, still had four tenants in 1860, according to the account of the great-grandson of one of them. Long before that, however, before 1820, there are circumstantial traditions and actual records of at least nine farms being farmed by single tenants and more by two or more joint-tenants. Everywhere the reforms were only gradually accomplished, but the spread of drainage and the introduction of new crops, notably roots and hay, went some way to overcome the problems arising from the winter shortages of foodstuffs for man and beast. These changes greatly raised the standard of living of the country people, while the density of the population decreased.

The high prices of cereals during the Continental wars encouraged the spread of arable farming, and in the early years of the nineteenth century there must have been noticeably more land under cultivation than either before that date or at the present day. In the first stage, the introduction of field drainage by an old method of making a water channel in the bottom of a trench with stones picked off the land not only eliminated boggy patches and made the land more uniformly workable but also brought a great deal of what had been marsh along the valley bottoms under cultivation for the first time. The appearance of the land was thus radically changed, and these riverside fields are as much period pieces as are Regency houses with their elegant furniture. An entry in the account book of William Mackintosh of Balnespick records the making of field drains on the farm of Dunachton in 1775. He paid the man who made them 6d a day or gave him the equivalent value in meal. Sir John Sinclair described how they should be made in 1795, at least 3 ft deep, the bottom lined and the sides built up with stone, and a stone or flag laid on the top allowing at least 18 ins for ploughing depth. He recommended fussily that they should be cleaned out every second or third year, but, as country folk know, many of these drains, when well made, continue to function efficiently up to the present day.[26]

Another essential of improvement was the levelling of the old rigs and baulks, the uncultivated strips between the rigs which customarily grew a luxuriant crop of weeds, whins and thistles. This was undertaken by the estate when the joint holdings were divided, as the MacDougalls were doing on Kerrera in 1798 and as accounts in the Seafield Papers show of payments being made for the levelling of land.[27] Alternatively, the levelling of rigs was made a condition of leases, to be accomplished within a term of years during which a reduced rent was taken. The new shares of land were then demarcated, often by a professional surveyor, and the tenants accommodated in new houses, each with its attendant byre and barn on their own piece of land instead of in a farmtown cluster as of old. In some parts of the country, farms might go through a preliminary stage of joint tenancy by two or sometimes more farmers. Basic improvements such as the rebuilding of house and byre would be demanded in the lease, but the introduction of crop rotations and other improvements were often delayed.

Evidence exists both in historical sources and on the ground to show that by the extension of field drainage and the intake of rough grazing or waste, a great deal of additional land was coming under cultivation both in the Highlands and the Lowlands during the war years. In the high lying glens of the Highlands, the intakes were usually made on the sheilings. In the later eighteenth century, tacks were created on the hill where the hefting places of cattle had manured and enriched the ground. The seasonal grazings were then separated from their parent farms or 'wintertowns' and became permanent crofts.[28] When the prices of cereals and cattle fell after 1815, and especially during the agricultural depression of the 1820s, these crofts were generally abandoned. In many areas, there is a fringe to be seen of such abandoned intakes above the arable land of the upland valleys.

As these changes progressed, the appearance of the land had changed by the mid-nineteenth century. The Victorian period is well marked in the manners and customs, the houses, furniture and even plumbing, of the middle classes and of artisan working class families. A fairly uniform type of upland farm can be related to the same period. A fascinating pattern of small rectangular fields in the varied colourings of land under a five-year rotation of crops had gradually spread across the valleys and up the lower slopes of the hills. The size of the holdings had come to depend on horsepower, in other words how much land a pair or two pairs of horses could cultivate. This would, of course, vary greatly according to the lie of the land. The farmer's dwelling house would be strategically placed to give the fullest view of his domain and his crops of oats, barley, turnips, sown hay and fallow, his sheep grazing on the inbye land and perhaps some store cattle. As a period piece, the upland farming straths of the Highlands illustrate the frugal independence that came to be as characteristic of one aspect of the Regency and Victorian era as was the plushy opulence of another.

The introduction of a new, hardy breed of sheep in place of the fine, small, delicate breed kept in the Highlands produced the most regrettable

Leading sheaves from the harvest field on an early nineteenth century upland farm by Killiecrankie

phase in all the periods of Highland history, but before dealing with their direct effect, it is necessary to remember that the hardy blackface sheep that brought about such devastation in many unfortunate areas were a boon to farmers in districts where the agricultural reforms had taken place. In fact, the improved sheep of Tweeddale and the Border uplands, often referred to at the time as 'Linton' sheep after the Peeblesshire market where they changed hands, became the mainstay of the economy of upland farming, better able to support themselves on heathery moorland for most of the year than were the cattle, most of which had to be sent anything up to twenty miles to the sheilings, whereas the new breeds of sheep picked up their feed for a large part of the year on the nearby hill faces. The solvency of upland farms in northern Scotland came to depend on sheep. Setting aside the obvious social upheaval, the perspective of nineteenth century Highland history might be modified by a comparison of the actual acreage of arable lost by the Clearances with that which remained under cultivation in the sheep-raising upland farms.

The agricultural reforms in the Highlands were, of course, part of a movement that had affected the rest of Britain. It was a feature of the great stir in activity and enterprise in industry, commerce and the exploration of new resources that began to stir in the late seventeenth century and that we refer to as the Industrial Revolution. We referred to early prospectors for mineral deposits in the Highlands just as the great wealth of coal and iron ore was beginning to be exploited in England and the Lowlands. These were failures. Unfortunately for the future of the Highlands, two more methods of extracting a profit from land were introduced. It was discovered that an alkali for the production of iodine and soda could be made from kelp, the golden seaweed that grows so densely especially along the rocky shores of the West Coast. Alkali was an essential ingredient for bleaching linen which, in the eighteenth century, was one of the major manufactures of Britain and especially of Scotland, and also for soap and glass making. A beginning to kelp burning was made as early as 1722 on the shores of the Forth and in Orkney and soon spread to the Hebrides where the burning of kelp developed, especially by the end of the century.

An alternative source for alkali was barilla, which came from Spain, and supplies were first subjected to a duty and were then interrupted during the Napoleonic Wars when the price of kelp rose from £1 to £20 per ton. About 7,000 tons of kelp were produced in 1810, after which date production fell away. The value of land with this 'golden fringe' had jumped, and inducements had been offered to people who would come and help to make the kelp. This industry required little capital but plenty of labour. The work was hard and harsh — 'silly talk won't make kelp' said the proverb. Between 1755 and 1831 the population of the Long Island more than doubled, and the already small farms and 'lots' were further subdivided to accommodate the kelp burners. Unfortunately, when the duty on barilla was removed in 1825, the demand for kelp and

Kelp burning at Gribune Head, Mull, c.1823

its price fell, and eventually stocks of unsaleable kelp ash were not worth collecting and the industry almost died out.[29] Various attempts have since been made to revive kelping for iodine making and now plastics, but without dramatic success.

The collapse of this industry was disastrous for those who had been encouraged to settle on small subdivided holdings in order to make kelp. Not only did they lose the main source of their livelihood but they also suffered from acute shortage of land. This unhappy situation was aggravated in many areas by people who had been displaced by Clearances in the interior coming onto the coast to settle wherever they could, and, as the official censuses show, population continued to increase. In spite of the worst of the Clearances and in spite of two generations of sustained emigration, it was not until the 1841 census that the population of the Highland counties reached its high point of 472,487. In the 1820s and 1830s the subject of destitution and emigration was discussed in press and parliament. In bad years people were said to have been reduced to a diet of 'shellfish and a kind of broth made of seaweed, nettles and other wild plants'. Signs of changing attitudes can be seen after the harvest failures of 1835 and 1836, when it was felt that the balance of funds collected to relieve destitution should be spent on promoting systematic emigration, a policy that the government had opposed. With the steady increase in population and little immediate hope of more prosperous times, the government began to accept that emigration was the only solution to destitution. A national Colonial and Emigration Department was created in 1840 to provide free or assisted passage to would-be emigrants, and in the following year a Select Committee on Emigration was convened to report on conditions in the Highlands and Islands. But the problem of what came to be known as the 'congested districts' was to continue through all the changes and developments that occurred during the rest of our period and until the Crofting Act. Of course, the contemporary agricultural reforms had not been introduced in these districts. Runrig farming continued but was often reorganised into townships, with the arable still held in runrig and grazing in common. Another expedient to make land more profitable had yet more disastrous consequences and affected a larger area of the Highlands.

About the middle of the eighteenth century it was discovered that flocks of the hardy, coarse-woolled Border sheep could be kept on the higher hills of the Highlands on land that had hitherto been used for cattle during brief periods in the summer. Border sheep-masters began to rent great stretches of the Highlands as sheep-walks. The movement started in Argyll and west Perthshire about 1760 and steadily spread over the north and west. By 1782 flocks of Border sheep were being introduced into Glengarry, and in the next decade they had reached Cromarty and Sutherland. The market for mutton and wool was expanding with the growing population of the south, and Sir John Sinclair confidently asserted that the value of a farm stocked with Highland cattle would be quadrupled if they were replaced by sheep. As a matter of fact, a sheiling in Glengarry had been customarily let to local men for £15 per annum, and a sheep farmer offered a rent of £250 for it, which was about half the value of the whole estate, and he died a rich man. The rental of Glengarry between 1768 and 1802 increased from £700 sterling to over £5,000 sterling. For a time sheep farming boomed. To meet the growing demand for wool and the requirements of the English manufacturers, the Inverness Sheep and Wool fair was established in 1817; the prosperous sheep-farmers of upper Strathspey were known as 'the gentlemen of Badenoch' in these promising times.[30] It was disastrous that these flocks of sheep occupied the hill grazing and sheilings essential to the old Highland economy, and much of the

Runrig farming organised into a fixed pattern of arable strips allocated to each croft house in the township on St Kilda, 1860

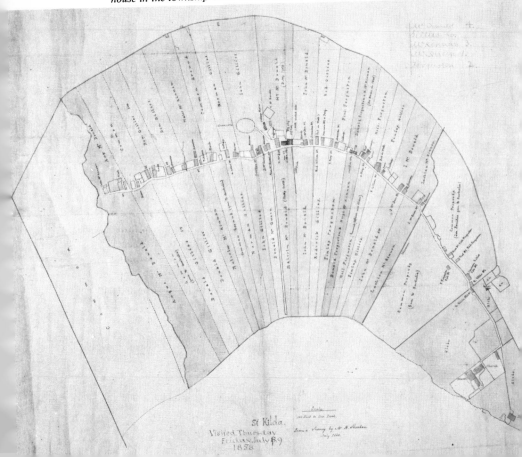

precious agricultural land was required for wintering the ewes and hoggs; wholesale evictions began to take place.

In many cases the proprietor was dependent on the land as his main source of income, and it was becoming inadequate because standards of living were rising and the returns on the land were low, especially as in many instances there were serious arrears of rent by the tenants. But all too often one senses indifference or, what is more sinister, hostility, and the whole problem of 'clearing' was the sign of a changed attitude to the country people. In his *General View of the Agriculture of the Central Highlands*, William Marshall wrote in 1794 that in the old days 'a good soldier, or a foolhardy desperado was of more value than a good husbandman' and that therefore the farms had been 'frittered down to the atoms in which they are now found' and the country 'burdened with a load of tenantry'; and Scott quoted the words of an old Argyllshire chief who said in 1788: 'I have lived in woeful times; when I was young the only question asked concerning a man of rank was, How many men lived on his estate?, then it was, How many black cattle it could keep?, but now it is, How many sheep will it carry?'. The Clearances have left a heritage not only of the desolate sites of ancient homesteads, but their memory has bred an enduring bitterness that has spread beyond the Highlands.

Many of the people who had been evicted or 'cleared' emigrated. It was estimated that 12,000 or more people left the Western Highlands between 1782 and 1803. The passing of the Passenger Shipping Act in that year resulted in the fares becoming much more expensive and put a halt to emigration for a while. Clearing then declined. But again by about 1820 it had reached its worst phases and continued for over twenty years all over the Highlands and the Islands, much to the dismay of the authorities. Occasionally the emigrations were voluntary and well organised, like that of three ship-loads of disbanded fencibles in 1802 from Glengarry; they sailed from Fort William, took their priest with them and settled on free government land in Ontario, Canada, in a compact colony.[31] Assisted emigration was recommended in 1805 by the Earl of Selkirk in his *Observations on the Present State of the Highlands of Scotland*, but this was not well received. He was unusual for his clear and sympathetic views of the unprecendented pressures on the small tenantry imposed by rising rents and prices and the rapid spread of sheep farming in his own day. As good as his word, the Earl sponsored settlements in Canada, most notably the Red River Settlement in Manitoba in 1814. Their conspicuous lack of success merely encourged his critics. In several other cases proprietors made careful provision for the emigrants' welfare. But only too often the poor and uninformed people were huddled in 'coffin ships' under wretched conditions. And when the people reached their destinations, they might find to their cost that all was not as inviting as the glowing picture painted by the lairds or emigration agents. This unhappy note comes through in John MacLean's poem *Am Bard an Canada*, which belongs to this period.

Some of the clearances were made by incoming proprietors, such as the South Uist evictions of 1851. But many were the descendants of the old lairds and chiefs such as Glengarry and Chisholm. The most notorious evictions and those which symbolise the evils of the system were those that took place in Sutherland from 1807 onwards. The *dramatis personae* of this episode were the Marquis of Stafford, later the first Duke of Sutherland, and his wife Elizabeth Gordon, Countess of Sutherland in her own right, William Young and Patrick Sellar, their ambitious commissioners, and James Loch, the factor, estate manager and architect of the improvement of the Sutherland tenantry, cottars and squatters. In 1803, Stafford had inherited his father's vast estates in Staffordshire and Shropshire and also the Bridgewater Canal fortune from his uncle. He and his wife wanted to apply some capital to the improvement of their Sutherland estates in the current mode, rather than to continue to pour money into famine relief or other non-productive schemes.[32] When Sellar directed the first clearance of Strathnaver in 1814, known in tradition as the 'Year of the Burnings', he was brought to trial, but a conviction was not secured. Doubts and reservations were expressed as to the humanity of the Loch and Sutherland policy when the clearances were reported in the press, but nothing prevented their continuing as they did in 1819 in Strathnaver and Kildonan. The most strident indictments were to come later from Donald MacLeod, the Strathnaver stonemason, in *Gloomy Memories in the Highlands of Scotland* (1857), his riposte to Harriet Beecher Stowe's *Sunny Memories*, Rev Donald Sage in his *Memorabilia Domestica* (1889) in which he describes the clearances of 1819, and Alexander MacKenzie in *The History of the Highland Clearances* (1883). In spite of their shortcomings as historical accounts, these books were taken up by the protagonists of the Crofters' cause in the 1880s and have since formed a rich source for social historians and those critical of Highland landlords. They and the events themselves have also prompted works of fiction where the well-known figures are thinly disguised and the old society presented as harmonious and traditional. Perhaps the best and most vivid are Neil Gunn's *Butchers' Broom* (1934), Fionn MacColla's *And the Cock Crew* (1945) and Iain Crichton Smith's *Consider the Lilies* (1968); all three are set in Sutherland and draw on sources such as *Memorabilia Domestica*.

But what of the victims of the process? The poetry of the period of emigration is disappointing in comparison with the surge of the eighteenth century. The few published outbursts of Gaelic poetry tend to be couched in general terms, as if pride, breeding and loyalty forbade the poet to sink to naming names and personal invective. It seems strangely appropriate condemnation of the unseen, intangible, unidentifiable 'economic forces' which bore so hardly on the Highlands in this period. There are few indictments of the calibre of the Glengarry bard, Allan MacDougall's *Oran nan Ciobairean Gallda*, which attacks the shepherds and sheep farmers from the Lowlands; Duncan Ban MacIntyre was also very aware of the ingredients of the disaster, as he described in *Oran nam Balgairean*, Song to the Foxes, in which he heaps praise on the fox as the enemy and destroyer of sheep. It is rare to find the degree of sorrow and bitterness which Alexander Carmichael recorded in the words of a South Uist cottar, Catherine MacPhee. In recalling times past, she described the evictions and deforcement in Iochdar in the north of the island as *obair ghraineil dhaoine*, 'the loathsome work of men'. One must assume that her feelings were typical of those left behind in cleared districts such as South Uist, and certainly the note of bitterness was echoed by many of those who testified to the Napier Commission in 1883.[33]

Not all the displaced people emigrated; many drifted south and became labourers and machine hands or entered the doomed handloom weaving industry under the urban conditions of the early phases of industrialisation. Yet others were placed by the proprietors in what were intended to be fishing settlements along the coasts. Being untrained as fishermen, having no capital with which to start, and faced with a period of decline in the industry, their conditions were little better. Their wretched conditions in the parish of Farr, for instance, were described by Rev David MacKenzie in restrained tones in 1834.[34] In their turn the great sheep farmer began to suffer a decline in prosperity as the price of the coarse wool produced by the blackface sheep fell. In many cases the proprietors turned land that had become unprofitable under sheep into grouse moors and deer forests. About 1820 or a little earlier grouse shooting had begun to be fashionable.

In this eventful period there were other industrial enterprises in the Highlands for good and ill: for instance, iron-smelting at Invergarry in 1727, Bonawe, Taynuilt in 1753 and in 1775 on Loch Fyne, in which the iron ore mined in England was brought to be smelted with charcoal made from the abundant supplies of scrub timber and the resulting pig iron was shipped to England. After the '15 a London company, the York Buildings Company, had bought up many of the Forfeited Estates in a fever of speculation and they felled the fine timber on the Struan Estate. They also bought the great fir forests of Strathspey and Abernethy and carried on extensive lumbering in the 1730s. A little shipbuilding industry temporarily sprang up at Garmouth, to which the timber was floated down, and the Company attempted to run an iron mine at Tomintoul, although this venture rapidly ran into debt and closed down. A lumbering scheme had also been started at Loch Broom. The same hopeful spirit hailed with enthusiasm the discovery that the Shetland Islands had a breed of exceptionally fine-woolled sheep. But these enterprises did not expand as the speculators hoped and generally made only a small and temporary impact on the local communities.[35]

During this period, as we have seen, the Highlands were governed with some degree of efficiency, and law and order was a phrase which came to be more clearly understood. The state also, during at least the earlier part of our period, began to assume some responsibility for the welfare of the people, although by the middle of the nineteenth century areas of economic disadvantage such as the Highlands were submitted to an unsympathetic lapse into Malthusian doctrines and the fullest application of the rigours of classical economics. During this earlier phase of assistance, the government had shown some interest in the three main Highland industries of this time, textiles, fishing and distilling. The fishing and distilling suffered from restrictive regulations, although some financial provisions were made for the fishing and textile industries, 'manufacturing' being seen as the road to economic, political and moral salvation. Under an act of 1753, Parliament voted a substantial sum in order to encourage the linen industry, but such advances as occurred were geographically limited to the southern Highlands. Help was renewed for fisheries and manufactures after the disastrous famine of 1782-83.

A yet more comprehensive plan was instituted in 1801 when the government, in order to reduce the acute distress in the Highlands due to a series of bad harvests, the effects of clearing and the disturbing symptoms of extensive emigration — 'the present rage for Emigration' — commissioned the great civil engineer, Thomas Telford, to draw up a programme of public works to alleviate the poverty and promote the economic development of the Highlands. His plans, submitted to the Parliamentary Committee on Highland Roads and Bridges, included the making of a canal through the Great Glen, improvement of communications by roads and bridges, and the building of harbours for the fisheries. His recommendations and their acceptance and endorsement by the Committee mark a significant step forward in the assumption of social responsibility for the social and economic problems of the Highlands. Work began immediately in 1803 on the Caledonian Canal, and this project was completed in 1822. A convenient and well planned system of roads, the 'parliamentary roads', with the necessary bridges was completed by 1823. The bridge over the Tay at Dunkeld, completed in 1809, is a particularly fine example of Telford's work.[36] The work which he initiated had a direct and widespread effect. His harbours, such as Aberdeen and Wick, with the attendant settlement which he planned and built at Pulteneytown, were especially valuable for the northern fisheries which, though fortunes varied, continued to prosper, and the roads and bridges changed the face of the country, and even more, the way of life of the people.

It is a matter of surprise that the Highlanders, suffering as they did from frequent food shortages, should have made so little and such inefficient use of the excellent supplies of fish round their shores. The Royal Burghs had claimed a monopoly of herring fishing and had complained when local people infringed it. On the east coast, the fringe of small inshore fishing communities had been slow to extend itself up the Highland coasts. On the West coast, where boats had played so important a part in the people's lives, in travel, raiding and the cattle trade, sea fishing did not figure in poetry or tradition. John Knox, an eighteenth century writer and philanthropist, campaigned for the improvement of the fishing industry and the organisation of fishing stations and villages round the coast. In 1786, he published the journal of his *Tour through the Highlands of Scotland and the Hebride Isles* in which he castigated the primitive and insubstantial fishing equipment of the Highlanders.

Meanwhile the Dutch had made use of superior equipment and had exploited the rich harvest of the herring shoals. The wars at the end of the eighteenth century had, however, destroyed these successful Dutch fisheries which had led the fishing industry of Europe for two centuries and had taken the cream of the herring shoals. Unfortunately, the mistaken policy of the government in encouraging only large decked fishing boats, the 'busses', by bounties and remissions of duty, and by imposing a heavy duty on salt, had so far given almost a monopoly of the herring fishery to the southern owners of these larger fishing boats. The plans to stimulate industry and employment in the Highlands led to the formation of the British Fisheries Society by private initiative and under distinguished patronage. The principal object of the Society was the creation of fishing villages and fishing 'stations' in the Highlands, and the monuments to its efforts are the villages it established at Tobermory and Ullapool. A third site at Lochbay in the Waternish district of Skye failed to develop according to the Society's expectations. Shortly afterwards, in 1806, Government policy changed; bounties were given on barrelled fish of a required standard no matter what the size of the boat in which they were caught, which benefitted the small scale enterprise of most Highlanders. In 1825 all duties on salt were repealed. This was of special benefit to fishermen in small boats and in less accessible places.[37]

For about a century some elements of the Highland fisheries flourished. They developed different methods in the different areas with their distinctive types of boats. Round the Moray Firth and up the coast of Sutherland and Caithness the fishing was done by full-time fishermen. In the North larger Highland communities grew up at Lybster, Portmahomack and Helmsdale, as well as the English-speaking town of Wick. Very large numbers of men from the West coast, from the poverty stricken 'congested districts', found part-time work at the herring fishing in the larger boats of the northern fisheries. On the West, besides fishing in small open boats for family needs, there were areas of special skill, such as the Islands of Lewis and Barra, or the specially created fishing villages like Tobermory and larger centres such as Stornoway. Loch Fyne became distinguished for its kippered herrings. The shape of the boats varied. Both in the North and West, in the very places where one might expect the tradition of the high, sharply raking stem to have survived from the days of the galleys, the oldest descriptions of their boats mention upright stems, whereas in the 'skaffies' of the Moray Firth, both the stems and sterns are sharply raked. This style of boat building was probably derived from Orkney, where the boats had continued to be built with a raked stem. The Orkney boats were particularly good and some were introduced into the Highlands.

The fishermen in the smaller boats suffered when the herring shoals, in a sudden change in their habits, took to swimming further out to sea, but an even more crippling blow to fishing as a rural industry was the introduction of the steam trawlers. These first came into use at Aberdeen about 1882. They were large and expensive vessels requiring more elaborate harbour facilities, and with them came a marked change in the Highland fisheries. On the Long Island and in the North and West, the fishermen took to working on the steam drifters and trawlers sailing out of the East coast ports, following the shoals of herring from north to south. Local fisheries declined into unimportance. But many traditions survive about them. The men had their own customs; the taboo on the use of certain words and the allusion at sea to particular people or things such as priests or rabbits are good examples. The courage of the fishermen of Lewis is still spoken of: great skill was required at the cirtical moment of beaching the open boats on an open shore in the troughs between the surging Atlantic rollers and depended on the daring and judgement of the skippers. The terrible losses suffered by these fishing communities are also remembered: for instance, Ness on the northern tip of Lewis lost seventy men in the space of about twenty five years.[38]

The other potential source of wealth was thought to be the extension to the Highlands of the linen industry, which had been the principal economic mainstay of the Lowlands in the penurious early eighteenth century. Both woollen and linen cloth had been made in the Highlands from remote times. Very fine woollen cloth, woven with combed yarn and dyed in brilliant colours, had been produced, especially in the Islands, as well as the coarser fabric for daily use. The industry was a domestic one with some local craftsmen weaving for the people's own use and this continued during the early part of our period.

Flax was grown, processed, spun and woven into linen on a small scale in the Highlands. In 1728, when the weaving of linen had become a significant and developing industry in the Lowlands, out of more than 2,000,000 yards of linen stamped as required by contemporary regulations, only 22,000 yards came from Argyll, Cromarty, Ross, Caithness and Orkney. The spinning of yarn also became established in some areas of Highland Perthshire, especially those adjacent to the heart of the Scottish linen industry and within reach of the busy marketing centres of Perth, Crieff and Dunkeld. It also developed in the burgh of Inverness, which had become the base for some merchant manufacturers. The eighteenth century saw the change in flax spinning from a domestic craft to an organised rural industry. One of the writers has been shown the site of an old 'retting pool', the pool in which flax was put to soak and to 'ret' so as to rot the soft outer skin of the stems and free the fibres. It was said that this was a smelly process — the retting pool was a good place in which to keep anything in which the excise officers were likely to take an interest. Implements for scutching and dressing the flax became more elaborate and, at a further stage of organisation, scutching mills were built, and eventually merchants supplied the spinners with the processed flax and collected the yarn. For instance, William Forsyth in Cromarty imported flax from Holland, prepared it in the town and then distributed it by boat to the spinners in the many small communities round the Beauly, Cromarty and Dornoch Firths.

It was to encourage home industry as well as fishing that the act of 1753 was passed by which Parliament voted £3,000 annually for nine years to the Board of Trustees for Fisheries and Manufactures. It was their plan to extend the industry to less accessible places in which they could have the co-operation of the Commissioners for the Annexed Forfeited Estates. Centres or 'stations' for introducing the latest methods of the linen industry were established at Loch Carron, Loch Broom and in Glenmoriston, districts to which it was hoped the industry would spread.

The production of linen in the Highlands did increase in the 1750s and 1760s, but the results were not spectacular or encouraging. In 1778 the value of the linen produced in the Highland counties together with

Orkney and Shetland but excluding the burgh of Inverness was only about £4,000.

As cotton began to replace linen in general use, the industry contracted, and at the same time the spread of improved methods of agriculture did away with the need for part-time work. But in Sutherland, in areas where the introduction of the improved agriculture was slower than the decline in demand for part-time workers, small scale attempts were made to introduce other such industries as straw plaiting.

The introduction of water power ended the spinning of linen in the Highlands as an organised rural industry, although we remember one element of that way of life. Previously in the Highlands, women had always spun their wool and flax with the spindle and distaff. The simpler form of spinning wheel, generally known in Scots as 'the muckle wheel', and then the more advanced and familiar form of spinning wheel, both long in use in the Lowlands, were both introduced into the Highlands at this time. One of the main objects of the linen stations and the spinning schools was to teach the women how to use them. For example, the spinning wheel was unknown in Glenmoriston before 1756, and the women used only the distaff and spindle. In that year, the Board of Trustees set up their linen and woollen factory at Invermoriston and began to distribute spinning wheels in the parish. Between April and December of 1764, their records show them to have distributed 30

Spinning wool with the distaff and spindle at Black Corries, Glencoe, in the 1890s

spinning wheels and 17 reels for winding and measuring yarn in Urquhart and neighbouring parishes. The spinning wheel continued to be used by the country women for spinning woollen yarn for their own domestic use, and in remoter areas the spindle was used for twisting plies until recent times. In some districts also the processes of carding and fulling continued to be done by hand. In the West the fulling of cloth, known as *luadhadh*, had been made into a festive communal occasion. In other areas, mainly in the Central and Eastern Highlands, water power was introduced for fulling. The mechanisation of the spinning and weaving of textiles gave the Highlands a small, semi-rural industry in the form of small woollen mills, some of which survive to the present day, although most of them were forced out of business by competition from the South.[39]

Quite distinct from the industries that were planned and encouraged during our period, the distilling of whisky developed into an important industry with no such assistance. It is unique in being, even more than tourism, the only industry in which the Highlands have supreme physical advantage because of the local peat and water, and it is the only one which has continued to flourish. In earlier times ale was regularly brewed, and the chiefs drank quantities of imported wine, as the

*The **luadhadh**, the process of fulling the woven cloth, taking place in the open air in the Outer Hebrides, c.1900*

strictures of the Privy Council in the seventeenth century show. In the eighteenth century a locally made spirit known as *uisge beatha* or 'water or life', anglicised as 'whisky', was being drunk. The growing of barley was also becoming more widespread, and a growing proportion of the crop was absorbed in distilling. Duties on distilled whisky were imposed from the early eighteenth century onwards, and they were frequently changed and increased. The industry flourished in Easter Ross, where the name of Ferintosh had become synonymous with good whisky. The laird had been granted the privilege of producing duty-free whisky in 1690 as compensation for losses suffered at the hands of the Jacobites. The stills provided an important local market for agricultural produce, and it was exported by boat and carried on horseback across the country to areas such as Gairloch where whisky was not being made. Whisky is alluded to by many contemporary writers, who often noted the large amounts which the Highlanders could drink, as one writer commented 'with much practice'. It was the only drink which Prince Charles Edward could obtain when he was a fugitive in Skye. A prohibition on the import of claret and foreign wines during the Continental wars of the period encouraged people to drink it.

A local burn supplied the water, the finest in the world, and specially suitable barley was also locally grown. The equipment used at that time, though perhaps not the most ancient, consisted of a pot-still of hammered metal with a 'worm' or coil of metal tubing. The wash of a fermented barley is heated in the still to evaporate the alcohol, which condenses in the worm leading off the top of the still; the spirit is collected in a cask set at one side. Martin Martin described how the wash was distilled once, twice, three times or even four times in the pot-still. The third distillation, *treas-tarraing*, was a strong brew, and the fourth could be dangerous.

This little industry was at its busiest after the Distilling Act of 1786, when duty was imposed on whisky from stills above a certain productive capacity. Duties and prices varied between districts and between Highlands and Lowlands. Small unlicensed stills flourished, and lairds and farmers found it in their interest to sell their surplus barley to them in spite of the sanctions. The onset of the Napoleonic Wars in the 1790s cut off wine imports, and whisky became a more popular drink with the lairds and gentry all over the country. Smuggling and illicit distillation had become a profitable local industry, and the government stepped up its attempts to stamp them out. Tales of the skill and daring of the smugglers in evading the excise officers or 'gaugers' still survive. The pot-still has passed into tradition as 'the ewie wi the crookit horn', and in the *port-a-beul* song comes the line 'all the sheep have milk but the ewe with the crooked horn has a gallon'. In 1823 a determined effort was made to end the irregularities into which the industry was drifting. A flat and reduced rate of duty was imposed on the whole of Britain, and stills of 40 gallons and over were licensed. Since this became the legal minimum size, the small illicit stills became outlawed and a serious effort was made to stamp them out. Since the 1823 Act the distilleries which are household names in Scotland began to spring up, and the industry went from strength to strength. The work in it seems to be congenial to the local people, but control is now in the hands of large companies, some of which are under foreign control, and it is the object of penally heavy taxation.

The development of one of these industries, textiles, was one of the most important incentives to the building of new settlements, the 'planned villages' of the second half of the eighteenth century, which have survived as a visible memorial to this period. Most of them originated in the estate improvement and capital projects of lairds interested in agricultural reforms, and the building was generally closely controlled by the laird. Such villages were numerous in the north east of Scotland, but Kenmore is a good example in the Perthshire Highlands, and Plockton, Kyleakin and Poolewe on the West coast. Some were founded in remote places such as Tomintoul. Some have disappeared and can be traced only with difficulty, such as Lewiston in Glen Urquhart. The original layout of others has been obliterated by later building. Grantown, founded in 1766 by Sir James Grant, 'the Good Sir James', is an early example and one of the best preserved.

The formal layout of such villages is still easily distinguishable. They consist of rows, or more often, a square and streets of small houses, each one with a plot of land for workshops and garden ground behind them. They were specifically built for the craftsmen, masons, carpenters and other tradesmen needed to supply the improved houses with the standards of comfort that increased contact with the south was making customary, and to encourage the two contemporary rural industries of linen weaving and fishing. The British Fisheries Society was also responsible for the laying out of villages, such as the fishing stations of Tobermory and Ullapool on their own land, and the Commissioners for the Annexed Forfeited Estates also managed some, such as the successful villages of Callander and Crieff.[40] The survival of many of the planned villages has been due to factors quite different from those which they were intended to serve, and this change marks a new and later stage in Highland development. These villages are striking examples of a great change in the housing of the Highlanders that began during this period. They had been very skilled in the beautiful craft of dry-stone dyking, but apart from castles and tower houses and many of the churches, there was little or no mortar work in the Highlands.

In much travelling through the Highlands, it is very difficult to recall any small or moderately sized houses with mason work obviously older than the eighteenth century. A very charming house at Laide in Wester Ross is exceptional. We know that a chief of the MacGregors in the sixteenth century had lived in 'a coupled house' (a house built in the traditional style of Central Scotland) and that even well into our period some of the gentry had continued to do so. For instance, about 1770, when Sir Aeneas was writing his *Notes*, Sheriff MacQueen of Corriebrough, a man both of means and position, was living in a turf house, and even later the house of the last of the Shaws of Dalnavert, one of the oldest families in Badenoch, was equally primitive. In the second half of the century when building an addition to Castle Grant, the Laird of Grant had to bring a mason and a joiner from outside to direct the work and instruct local assistants. It was thought so extraordinary that the Laird of Grant's 'Champion' (painted in 1714 by Waitt) should have built a 'lime and mortar' cottage for his mother that the tradition of it was handed down. It is significant that when Burt took the age-old track southwards from Inverness about the 1740s, and stopped the first night at a primitive change-house close to the ford over the Findhorn at Tomatin, his accommodation and that of his horses was extremely primitive. This was shortly before Wade built his road along the route. He established inns along his roads, and in 1732 what has now become the farmhouse of Dalmagarry was built. The four-square house of two floors and a garret is the prototype of any number of sturdy little houses all over the Highlands dating from the agricultural reforms and the improvement in means of communication.

There was joinery as well as masonry in these new little houses. The great development in the mining and working of iron in the South was making iron tools and utensils more available to the Highlanders. The importance of the introduction of the iron plough is often noted, but a range of tools and the skill to use them encouraged the building of more comfortable houses. Up till the eighteenth century and in many districts until even later, the only woodworking tool was the adze, which could be used to shape existing baulks of timber (as in the 'couples') or conveniently shaped branches to use in making furniture or could hack the centre of a tree trunk into a plank. There had been neither nails nor iron bolts to fasten pieces of wood together: instead, a hole was burnt with a red-hot iron and another piece of wood fitted into it. Tools and the craftsmen to use them now became available in the village for joinery and carpentry and could serve wide areas.

An even more widespread amenity was the arrival of the cast-iron cooking pot. Iron pots to hang upon chains over the fire had, of course, been made by the local blacksmith, but surviving examples are very rare.

One cannot believe that they were ever as plentiful as the cast-iron pots made available by the industrial development of the Lowlands because of the added skills and inventions in working iron. Such pots must have already come into general use in the Highlands before the fashion for paintings and prints of old fashioned Highland cottage interiors, for one can recognise their well-defined shapes. In the most inaccessible districts they can be found in great quantities. One wonders how, in earlier times, in spite of difficulties of transport and the poverty of the people these bulky things found their way from the 'workshops of the world' to the archaic setting of *Ultima Thule*.

Cast-iron cooking pot over a peat fire and hanging from a canopy chimney in a small Highland house, 1840

PART 2

During this period of chaotic change in the social and material life of the Highlanders and at the very moment when our racial culture was in acute danger of extinction, a new kind of patronage so necessary for the encouragement of the arts suddenly evolved. As we have tried to show during the preceding period, the patronage of the chiefs had largely been supplemented by that of the lesser gentry. From the early eighteenth century onwards, tacksmen, younger sons and impoverished feu-holders had tended to seek their fortunes overseas, and lesser folk had followed them. It was often said as a jest that if a few Highlanders met, they immediately proceeded to form a Highland Society.

During the earlier part of our period, in particular, amid the havoc and change in accepted ways of life, the influence of these societies was of vital importance not only in conserving some fragments of the heritage of the Gael but in adapting them to the ways of contemporary society. It was in this tradition that in 1778 twenty-five Highland gentlemen resident in London resolved to found a society that might prove to be beneficial to the northern part of the kingdom, and founded the first Highland Society with Simon Fraser of Lovat as president. In appreciation of the value of what they did, it must be remembered how greatly the repressive measures against Highland things after the '45 had broken the links of continuity and how much valuable material was in danger of being forgotten. The new Society aimed at preserving the dress, music and literature of the Highlands. It did much educational and charitable work; it helped to initiate the founding of Inverness Infirmary in 1800, a Gaelic Chapel in London, the Royal Caledonian Asylum as an orphanage in 1816, and it gave much individual relief. It has been interested in the Highland regiments and in 1859, it took a leading part in the formation of the London Scottish Volunteer Rifles. It established branches of the Society in Glasgow (1780), Madras (1814), Canada (1818), Bombay (1822) Nova Scotia (1838), Prince Edward Island (1838) and Melbourne (1864). But from our point of view its most interesting work was cultural. As we noted in the Macpherson controversy, it published the Gaelic translation of Ossian in 1807 and a later translation of the 'literal remains of Ossian'. A prize offered for the best history of the Highlands was won by William Forbes Skene, and his book is a useful text-book down to the present day. The Society also formed a collection of tartans, their 'Certified Tartans', showing the designs approved by the reigning chiefs of the day.

One of the most important of the Society's services was its work for the preservation of piping. It was the first society to revive the old art of *piobaireachd* or *ceòl mór* which had been slipping into limbo. In 1781, 1782 and 1783, it organised competitions at the great Falkirk Tryst. Their management was entrusted to a newly formed branch at Glasgow. In 1783 there was a procession to the churchyard, where the winners played 'MacCrimmon's Lament' round the tomb of the immortal heroes, Sir John Stuart, Sir John the Graham and Sir Robert Munro. Unfortunately, however, the competitors were dissatisfied with the awards and applied to the newly founded Edinburgh Highland Society for patronage, and thereafter that Society organised the competitions, although the London Society magnanimously continued to supply prizes.[1] By its interest at this critical time, the Highland Society of London inaugurated such competitions, which drew forth the talents of Highland music, neglected except in a few households, and set standards of playing which ensured that more and more skilful players have offered themselves in the competitions. Many societies in many parts of the world have carried on the work. When the Edinburgh competitions finally came to an end in 1844, the London Society continued its interest in piping; and it still presents gold medals, the highest awards for piping, one at the Northern Meeting at Inverness, and another at the Argyllshire Gathering at Oban.

In Edinburgh meanwhile, following the very bad harvest of 1782, and the succeeding season of dearth of 1783, a group of Highland gentlemen decided in 1784 to found a society to assist the Highlands. The membership rapidly grew to embrace all sorts and conditions, benevolent landlords, university men, scientifically-minded farmers and practical ministers. The Society was very typical of the Edinburgh of the age when moral philosophy, social progress and improvement, and literary achievements were so much in vogue. Its secretary was the ageing Henry MacKenzie, the 'Man of Feeling', and certainly while he presided, literary and cultural considerations were high on the syllabus. The Society's objects were wide and included an enquiry into the existing conditions of the Highlands, the development of its agriculture, industries, fisheries, and means of communications, and also the preservation of the language, poetry and music of the Highlands. It early ceased to be a purely Highland society and found its most important sphere of work in the promotion of every aspect of Scottish agriculture, by prizes or premiums and medals, essays and competitions in ploughing and crop and animal husbandry. In 1822 it began to organise fatstock shows held in turn in a number of towns all over Scotland.

It did its most valuable work for the culture of the Highlands in the early days. By its constitution it had a bard, a piper and a 'Professor of Gaelic'. It took a most important part in the Ossianic controversy. In 1797, after Macpherson's death, it instituted a thorough and impartial investigation into the existence of ancient Highland heroic poetry and how far Macpherson's translations were genuine, the findings of which enquiry were published in 1805. The Gaelic manuscripts collected during the enquiry were deposited in the Advocates' Library and form the main part of our collection of surviving Gaelic manuscripts. Among them was the *Book of the Dean of Lismore*, which had probably been acquired by Macpherson about 1760. The Society gave financial help towards the publication of a Gaelic vocabulary in 1794, a new edition of the translation of the Old Testament in 1803, and it published its Gaelic Dictionary in 1828. It also gave financial help to Alexander Campbell to travel in the Highlands in 1815 and collect songs for his *Albyn's Anthology*, and towards Capt Simon Fraser of Knockie's collection of airs and melodies of the Highlands.[2]

As one of its earliest activities, the Society also took over from the London Highland Society the supervision of the piping competitions at the Falkirk Tyrst. But it was found to be more convenient to transfer this to Edinburgh, as the judges and others concerned were too busy doing business during the Tryst to conduct the competition. The first Edinburgh competition was held in October 1784. These competitions were held with considerable circumstance. A salute was played by John MacArthur, the Society's piper, said to be one of the last survivors of the pipers trained at MacCrimmon's college. The piping competitions were interspersed with dancing and recitations of Gaelic poetry. From 1818 for a few years there were prizes for the pipers 'most correctly and neatly dressed in the ancient garb of this country', but this was later given up. After 1826, the piping competitions were held only once every three years and the last one was in 1844. The dancing competitions were, however, developed. In 1832 the 'ancient Gille-Caluim' was first performed and became a regular feature. The Edinburgh, Glasgow and Inverness Societies also concerned themselves with teaching children in their mother tongue. They established 77, 28 and 65 schools respectively, with a total of 9,900 pupils in the most remote and neglected districts.

A very different society, the Society of True Highlanders, was founded in 1815 at Inverlochy by that exhibitionist, Glengarry. Various members of the clan and other Highland gentlemen disported themselves at the yearly meetings in imitation of ancient festivities. On one occasion they staged a three-day deer drive after the old style with deer driven by a circle of beaters into the *eileirig*, the enclosed valley or chosen spot where the deer were dispatched by sportsmen. For the founding of the Society, Ewen MacLachlan composed a 'Metrical Effusion', an ode in extravagant style appropriate to the gathering and sentiments of the occasion. The Society of True Highlanders flourished as long as Glengarry lived. Two others among these Highland societies have laid students under a deep debt. The short-lived Iona Club was founded in 1834 and owed much to the scholarly activities of Skene and of Donald

Gregory; they published the *Collectanea de Rebus Albanicis* in 1839, a mine of valuable information for Highland history. A more lasting venture was created in 1871 with the founding of the Gaelic Society of Inverness, largely due to the enthusiasm and initiative of the young Dr William Mackay, the able author of *Urquhart and Glenmoriston*. Within a year the Society had 182 members and it soon became a focus of opinion, a sort of Gaelic lobby, to be reckoned with. In the 1870s and 1880s, its members took an active interest in the land reform movement, in Gaelic, in education and in the need for a Gaelic census to be incorporated in the decennial census. The Society began to publish volumes of *Transactions* which have continued to the present day as a valuable contribution to Highland and Gaelic scholarship and history.[3]

During the nineteenth century literally hundreds of Highland societies of various kinds were formed all over Britain and wherever in the wide world Highlanders were to be found, and the list of the names of such societies and their branches covers pages in Scottish Year Books. In the dark early days some were partly benefit societies, and most were concerned with the distress of the Highland people crowding into the towns. The first Dundee Society had a school to teach English to adult emigrants. But in spite of many useful activities, such as the provision of comforts for Highland troops in wartime, by and large their activities are mainly social. That they have maintained the pride and feeling of solidarity of the Gael through more than a century of depression and frustration and often when he was a stranger in a strange land is no small contribution to Gaeldom. The wearing of the Highland dress, if only on ceremonial occasions, the love of the pipes and the old songs, and to a much more limited extent, the speaking of the old language, have been fostered by them. Most of these societies have waxed and waned, have died and been reborn.

A rather similar influence is exercised by the Highland Games held in so many districts of the Highlands. Although the purist may not admire all the items in their programme, it must be remembered that they not only preserve something of the dress and music of the old Highlands and bring money to the country, but that they are also warmly supported by the country people themselves. The Highland character of the crowds that attend the local meetings is genuine, and to supply those people who do the country the greatest service that can be done to it — that of living and working there — with what they enjoy is a most worthy development. About 1826 the Strathfillan Games were started by a local landowner for his tenantry on the Drummond estates, but pride of place must be given to Braemar. In 1800 some local workmen began a charitable society. It was in the days of dear corn, and one of the chief activities was the buying of meal; this was continued until 1846, when the

Corn Laws were repealed. But in 1826, the name of the society had been changed to that of the Braemar Highland Society, and in 1832 the first Highland Games were held. These games proved to be very popular and were crowned with distinction when, in 1849, Queen Victoria was present. It has been claimed that those games are the revival of ancient games held by Malcolm Canmore. This may be regarded as a survival of the Highland habit of pedigree-making, but genuine traditions exist of trials of strength such as putting the *Clach Neart* or Stone of Strength; and the Wardlaw Manuscript has several descriptions of the athletic exercises in which a good chief encouraged the young men of his clan. The new fashion for Highland Games spread. In Inverness a Northern Meeting had been held since 1788 by some of the local gentry as a week of social activities. Members wore a uniform, but this did not consist of the kilt or of tartan. The entertainment consisted of balls, dinners and hunting, and after 1816 of pony racing. In 1840 the holding of Highland Games was added and became an important function. It will be remembered that it is to this gathering that the Highland Society of London gives a highly esteemed gold medal for piping. Another is given at the equally important gathering in the Western Highlands which was founded about the same time. The new movement spread all over the Highlands.

If many aspects of the Highland Games are artificial, the fostering of shinty revived a pastime which was genuinely old. Shinty or *camanachd* is a variant of the ancient Irish game of hurley, whose ancestry goes back to the sagas. It was played by Cù Chulainn, whose superhuman feats in the game were recounted. Shinty flourished through the vicissitudes and cataclysms of Highland life as an unorganised contest between the men and boys of neighbouring parishes or districts. The biggest gatherings traditionally took place at Yule and New Year. Even now, although *camanachd* has been formalised by leagues and rules, feelings run very high at local contests.

Great as were the services of the Societies in providing patronage for the arts of Gaeldom, poetry, one of the finest arts of all, still drew its inspiration from the more ancient way of Gaelic life and from the period of extreme stress and change that saw the final struggle for the throne by the House of Stuart and the destruction of Gaelic armed power that followed. It is highly significant that five of our greatest Gaelic poets should have lived and composed during this period and its aftermath.

It should be emphasised that Gaelic society produced no less than five major poets within a comparatively short space of time: Alexander MacDonald, *Alasdair MacMhaighstir Alasdair* (c.1695-1770), best known for his great sea poem, 'Clan Ranald's Galley' and his songs which breathed life into heroic and traditional values; Duncan Ban

MacIntyre (1724-1812), author of 'Song of the Misty Corry' and 'Praise of Ben Doran', songs still current in the repertoire of traditional singers; John MacCodrum (c.1693-1779), who composed songs on everyday affairs and eulogies to his patrons, the MacDonalds of Sleat; Robert Mackay (c.1714-1778), familiar as Rob Donn, the Sutherland poet, and Dugald Buchanan (1716-1768), whose religious poetry voiced a movement in Gaelic society that has continued down to the present day.

Our native literature shows both the changes and the surviving traditionalism so marked in our period. The defeat of the Jacobite forces in the '45 and the break-up of the traditional society of the Highlands in the eighteenth century were traumatic both in their causes and in their effects for the ordinary Gael. This was bound to be reflected in the people's poetry, and yet the changes and the weight of economic forces are not so readily evident in stark terms in the poetry of the eighteenth and nineteenth centuries. There was comparatively little spirited reaction, for instance, to the Clearances, although this must have been a stark experience for many Highlanders in the worst affected areas. The main reason for the lack of resistance may well have been religious. Sorley MacLean has characterised the poetry of that period as 'naturally depressing and even hopeless in tone'. Not surprisingly, some of the responses were more negative, such as awareness of and regret for the decline of traditional learning and for the disappearance of the chiefs and clanship. Such themes were, of course, the support and inspiration of the poets, and it was the poets who tended to carry over and perpetuate many of the traditional values. Thus it was the poets who publicly kept alive some of the spirit of Jacobitism after 1745 and who saw the feats of arms of 1793-1815 as the revival of clanship and of the traditional martial achievements of the Gael. Several songs have survived which denounced the proscription of Highland dress, some by poets whose people had been officially Hanoverian during the '45. None of these songs has the force and conviction of *Am Breacan Uallach*, 'The Proud Tartan', by Alexander MacDonald, *Alasdair MacMhaighstir Alasdair*. He finishes his song with a warning:

> And though you gained the upper hand
> Over us once by a kind of mishap,
> In devil the battle during his life
> Will the Butcher ever be successful again.[4]

In no other poetry of the period are the traditional values more evident than in Alexander MacDonald's, although this poet together with his contemporaries shows that he and his society were opening up to new influences. The new strains are particularly well seen in nature poetry of a new and highly descriptive sort. It seems that James Thomson, the

Lowland Scot, whose *Seasons* appeared between 1726 and 1730, influenced Gaelic poets as well as English. MacDonald's Sugar Brook, Song to Winter and Song to Summer are often quoted in comparison. He was, however, above all, the champion of Gaelic and the Gaelic people and he was one of the last poets of the old school who looked to an ideal of the resurgence of Gaelic nationhood.

The decline in the old values must have lightened the constraints on the village poets who appear for the first time in the eighteenth century, but yet whose work and style seem already mature. John MacCodrum gained an appointment as bard to Sir James MacDonald of Sleat in 1763, receiving a croft rent free for life together with appropriate remuneration in kind and specie in his native North Uist. The importance of his surviving verse lies not so much in the eulogies and elegies to his patron and Clan Donald, but in the local and reflective verse of serious, humorous or satiric nature. Rev Finlay MacRae wrote of his parish of North Uist in 1837: 'In the last generation, every farm and hamlet possessed its oral recorder of tale and song. The pastoral habits of the inhabitants led them to seek recreation in listening to, and in rehearsing the tales of other times; and the *seanchaidh* and the bard were held in high esteem'. MacRae noted the passing from fashion of the old songs and tastes, and in the ancient convention, MacCodrum compared himself to Ossian surviving to tell of the deeds of the Fiann to St. Patrick.[5]

Comparisons are often drawn between *MacMhaighstir Alasdair* and his young contemporary Duncan Ban MacIntyre, especially in their love poetry and songs to nature and the seasons. The similarities are more superficial then real. What really puts these two Gaelic poets into the modern era is that they both saw their works in print in their own lifetime, MacDonald in 1751 and MacIntyre in 1768. MacIntyre also composed to the Seasons, probably directly inspired by MacDonald. He is best remembered for his longest poem, *Moladh Beinn Dobhrainn*, Praising Ben Doran, composed in imitation of a piobaireachd with varying metres and with the most refined and penetrating descriptions of the deer on the hill. Other poets of the later eighteenth century who also composed on nature are William Ross, famous also for his love poems, and Ewen MacLachlan who was author of poems on each of the four seasons, although more generally referred to as translator of the *Iliad* into Gaelic.

Another local poet who has never attracted the attention which he undoubtedly deserves is Robb Donn, who belonged to the Reay country of north west Sutherland. He too was obviously sympathetic to the Jacobite cause, though his people had taken the opposite side in the '45. But like other Gaelic poets he looked to the situation which would restore the ideals of Gaelic society as the poets envisaged them. Much of his verse is local in reference, humorous in vein but never parochial or narrow in attitude. In his 'Lament for Ewan', composed in 1754, a sort of mock elegy, he considers how Death stalks mercilessly and impartially from cottage to court and in the same hour may take, as it had just done, prime minister Henry Pelham in London and poor Ewan in his hut by Loch Eriboll:

> I think that that must be true,
> That your vision takes in high and low,
> You took Pelham from the summit of greatness,
> And did you not take Ewan from Polla?

Robb Donn's editors have suggested that his verse, especially the satire, demonstrates the influence of the contemporary English poet, Alexander Pope, and the catalyst in this acquaintance was the pious and learned minister of Durness, Murdo MacDonald. He was the subject of one of Robb Donn's elegies; he translated Pope's *Messiah* into Gaelic and recited it to his parishioners.[6] Though we may think of a stereotype evangelical Highland minister as narrow, Murdo MacDonald was the antithesis. Widely read and catholic in his literary tastes, he was also a musician, composer of Gaelic airs and the father of the two gifted MacDonald brothers, Patrick and Joseph.

The contrast offered by the exuberance of eighteenth century poetry and the relative poverty of that of the nineteenth century is unfortunate, and here must be the effects of the social and economic upheavals of the period at their most depressing and negative. Much of the published verse of the nineteenth century was composed by *emigré* Gaels either in the southern cities or in North America or elsewhere. It takes as its theme the homeland, *An Gleann 'san robh mi og* — My native Glen — or praise of their language and land, and too often is overly sentimental. The rise of the many Highland societies in the cities and abroad encouraged the composition of sentimental, nostalgic, humorous and light-hearted verse which was always well received at the ceilidhs and concerts. Much of it made its mark and is still popular; and it would be wrong to be entirely deprecating of this class of poetry, if we consider such compositions as *Eilean an Fhraoich*, in praise of Lewis, and *An t-Eilean Muileach*, in praise of Mull. There is a mass of ephemeral verse, however, belonging to the nineteenth century which could be regarded as unsuited to polite taste and for which there must have been a reluctance to publish. Some of it found its way into the outstanding collection of Rev Alexander MacLean Sinclair in 1879, *An t-Oranaiche*, 'The Songster'. Some of it was prompted by the political issues of land reform.

Surprisingly late in this period the social and economic problems of the

Highlands and Islands and the burgeoning land reform movement gave rise to poetry of protest. Some of the most vigorous verse, like the political pressures, came from the Gaels in exile, and therefore tends to be coloured by sentiment or a romantic reconstruction of events contemporary and historical, and also the influence of English on language and metre. The most famous of the land agitation poets was Mary Macpherson, *Mairi Mhór nan Oran*, who became a legend in her own lifetime. But the most stringent comments came from men such as William Livingstone in Glasgow and John Smith of Uig in Lewis. William Livingstone (1808-1870) was born in Islay and was a self-taught man with a keen intellect. He was a Scottish nationalist when the cause was being born and he had an enthusiastic sense of history which he deployed cunningly in his writings. The most striking of his 'political' verse is his *Fios thun a'Bhàird*, in which he presents the contrast between his native island, happy, busy and populous, and the desolation caused by sheep and 'Lowland spite'. The same bitterness is to be found in John Smith's poetry. Though he died young in 1881, he lived through the first outbreaks of local resistance which was to lead to land reform in the 1880s. His most pointed statements are in his 'Song for Sportsmen', which mocks the deer forest owners who have absorbed the country of a land-hungry population, and 'The Spirit of Kindliness', which was prompted by the contemporary Lewis land troubles.[7]

The propaganda verse of the exiled Gaels tended to receive the attention which might have been lavished on the work of local poets with more reward. But the local poets echoed the messages of the public verse with more directness and less sentiment. Local folk, after all, would often have expected this of the village poets, and the Gaelic communities may have looked to their poets to sustain the bardic traditions, not necessarily of criticism but at least of comment and satire. One result was the voicing of beliefs in natural rights, doctrines which had surfaced frequently in seventeenth and eighteenth century Britain, and which were given a thorough airing in the Highlands in this period. The main element of this stated that the land belonged to the people, though there was nothing in law to bear this out. Often evangelical teachings added authority to this by maintaining that God gave the land to the people. A Tiree poet for example, John MacLean of Balemartin, gave expression to the compelling belief in natural rights in a song composed in 1886, which was a year of rioting in Tiree. In one verse he says:

> Before a Duke came or any of his people
> Or a kingly George from Hanover's realm,
> The low-lying isle, with its many shielings
> Belonged as a dwelling to the Childen of the Gael.

Non-political Gaelic poetry also continued to be extensively treasured and written. The Turner Collection, the manuscript collection made by Peter Turner, ex-soldier and packman in Argyll and Kintyre, gives an idea of the wide range of poetry enjoyed in these areas about the middle of the eighteenth century. The pieces included narrative poetry founded on the old epics, poetry in honour of the Duke of Argyll, nature and religious poetry and poetry on topical themes such as piping and whisky, sometimes descending to the scurrilous.

It is not easy to assess the extent to which the finer art of piping was lost after the '45. The tunes had been handed down by fingering or by *canntaireachd*, and knowledge of the latter was dying out. In 1784 three pipe tunes were recorded for the first time in ordinary musical notation in the *Collection of Highland Vocal Airs* of the Rev Patrick MacDonald of Kilmore. In the first few competitions held by the Highland Societies, it seems that few tunes were offered by the competitors. Favourites were *Failte a'Phrionnsa*, 'The Prince's Salute', *A'Ghlas Mheur*, 'The Fingerlock', and *Spaidsearachd Dhomhnuill Ghruamaich* or 'Grim Donald's March'. Fortunately a number of efforts were made to rescue the old tunes. Probably Sir Walter Scott, who did so much to interpret the Highlands to the world, was partly responsible. It was he who popularised such words as *piobaireachd* in the anglicised form 'pibroch'. Several collections of the old tunes were made. In 1822, Donald MacDonald, the well-known bagpipe maker in Edinburgh, who had been encouraged by the Highland Society to collect pipe tunes, published his first collection. His *Ancient Martial Music of Caledonia* included twenty-three tunes in staff notation, and its publication apparently almost ruined him. A second volume which he prepared remained in manuscript. This came to the attention of Major General C S Thomason, who prepared his own collection of 278 tunes which was published in 1900. Being unknown in the piping world and not himself a skilful player, his massive collection was never influential, but undoubtedly it did much to stimulate interest in *ceòl mór*. It has been superseded by the twelve (to date) published volumes of the Piobaireachd Society and Archibald Campbell's *The Kilberry Book of Ceòl Mór* (1948). Much more influential for the survival of the piper's art were the manuscript and printed collections of Angus Mackay of Raasay. In 1838 he published his *Collection of Ancient Piobaireachd*, which included notes on the history and traditions of the music and its masters. Angus Mackay was the most celebrated pupil of his father, John Mackay of Raasay, who had been taught by the MacCrimmons and whom we now consider as the most important link with the past, because so many of the best players of *ceòl mór* derive their music from him and his pupils. Another of his pupils who has been so influential was John Ban MacKenzie (1796-1864), who was said to be the finest player of his time.

A pupil both of John Ban and of Angus Mackay was Donald Cameron, who was piper to Seaforth. His reputation stood very high, and his playing was said to be like the playing of the MacCrimmons. Another link with the past has been the Macphersons; the father of *Calum Piobair* (1828-1898), piper to Cluny, was taught by Iain Dubh MacCrimmon and John Mackay of Raasay, and Calum's pupils such as Pipe Major John MacDonald, Inverness, are the masters to whom today's pipers owe their debt. This tenuous but unbroken link with the past is still recognised and cherished in the piping world today.

Until 1844, although the pipes were played for dancing competitions, the tunes played in the piping competitions were limited to *ceòl mór* or *piobaireachd*, which was considered to be the only form of pipe music worthy of serious playing by pipers of the highest class. After 1844 there was a great change, perhaps because the Highland Society's firm hand had been removed from the annual competitions; the pipers themselves competed in the playing of reels and strathspeys, and the latter tunes, probably orginally composed for playing on the fiddle, were elaborated for the pipes. Another change was the introduction of the elaborate competition marches in 2/4 time specially composed for the pipes. One of the earliest of these marches which is still played today is 'The Crags of Stirling', composed by Hugh Mackay about 1856, and when the Highland Society of London began to offer prizes for piping at the Inverness Northern Meeting, marches were included. Angus MacKay is thought by some to have been the first to compose a competition march, and tunes such as The Abercairney Highlanders and the Duke of Roxburgh's Farewell to the Blackmount Forest are usually credited to him. In the second half of the nineteenth century many of these 2/4 marches were composed, and among pipers, this is still the most popular form of music and the competiton tune *par excellence*. Competition strathspeys and reels also began to be played, some elaborations of older melodies and some new compositions; examples of the new slow strathspey are 'Blair Drummond', 'Maggie Cameron' and 'Shepherd's Crook', and of the reel, 'Duntroon', 'Mrs Macpherson of Inveran' and 'Sandy Cameron'.

Something has been said of the close connection that existed between Highland regiments and piping. The value of pipers was fully appreciated in the great wars of the eighteenth and nineteenth centuries. But the individual pipers were attached to each company and played separately, and they were paid for by the officers and received no official recognition by the War Office until 1854. After 1854 the pipers began to be formed into pipe bands, later drums were added to them, and they began to take the place of the fife and drum bands. Until then the piper had mainly played *ceòl mór*, but with the introduction of these bands,

the playing of what were then called quicksteps but are now called
regimental marches came into fashion. They were derived from well-
known melodies and songs such as 'Bundle and Go', 'Bannocks of Bere
Meal', *Caidil mo ghaol*, and not directly from *ceòl mór*, although this
music often influenced them and styles of playing.

The making of bagpipes also underwent a change. In the eighteenth
century and before, they were made by local craftsmen, often by wood
turners working in the burghs. Early surviving sets vary in size, design,
bore and finish, but they are generally made of local hardwoods such as
laburnum, boxwood, holly or fruitwood. With greater numbers of
troops being raised in Scotland and the Highlands after the Seven Years
War, the demand for pipes and pipers rose, and it is probably no
coincidence that one of the first references to a professional bagpipe
maker occurs in 1775, when Hugh Robertson of Castlehill was entered in
the Edinburgh Directory as such. And this falls within the period when
the proscriptive laws against things Highland were still on the statute
book. The use of the Highland pipes, the 'great pipe', in the forces has
tended to set the pattern for bagpipes, and since the beginning of the
nineteenth century, they have been made in a standard form, and the
other bagpipes which have been commonly played here have dropped out
of fashion accordingly. At the same time, imported hardwoods began to
be used in their manufacture, *lignum vitae*, cocus wood, ebony and later
African blackwood, and ivory mounts replaced bone, horn and 'sea-
ivory'.

Like piping, Highland dancing has been much encouraged by the
competitions organised by the early Societies and at the Highland
Games. The early history of Highland dancing is very obscure. The
ancient Gaelic epic stories contain no allusions to dancing, although
there are several descriptions of the amusements that people enjoyed at
feasts. These consisted of entertainment by jugglers and the performance
of weapon feats by the heroes; nor is dancing mentioned in the *Book of
the Dean of Lismore* nor in the early clan stories, and the Wardlaw
Manuscript only alludes to it twice, and then among 'manly exercises'. In
1574, when Lovat was training his young men in military exercises, 'At
intervals they used swimming, arching, football, throwing of the barr,
fencing, dancing, wrestling and such manly, sprightly exercises and
recreations, very fit for polishing and refining youth'. About 1667, when
on a hunting expedition, they danced to the fiddle and the trumpet. But
in several descriptions of weddings and other festivities, dancing is not
mentioned among the diversions.

Nevertheless, there is evidence that the people did dance in the
Highlands. The *port-a-beul*, mouth music for dancing, is generally
accepted as being very ancient. The unattractive custom of dancing by

the nearest relations at a wake, as described by Rev Lachlan Shaw, is surely primitive. One of the earlier allusions to dancing in the Highlands was in the report of a trial of Inveraray in October 1677. Donald Dubh MacGregor, accused of stealing a cow in order to get the tascal money for it, described how he found his way into several fairy mounds and saw there a number of men and women dancing and how he played for them on his trump. They told him of various stolen goods so that he might get the reward for informing. He was hanged.[8] As in this tale, the Jew's-harp or trump was used, but the fiddle was *par excellence* the musical instrument for dancing, and with the introduction of this instrument the fashion for country dancing spread over western Europe in the seventeenth and eighteenth centuries, and by the eighteenth century the habit of dancing is constantly mentioned in accounts of the Highlands. In those of the '45 there are many allusions to dancing by the Highlanders, and the Prince himself danced to cheer the hearts of his faithful companions on his long flight, skipping 'so nimbly, knacking his thumbs and clapping his hands' and even singing the tune of a 'Strathspey reel' for his own dancing. John Stoddart, a London journalist travelling in Scotland in 1799 and 1800, wrote that dancing was 'the favourite amusement of the North', and described young boys dancing the reel, the 'shean-trews', the hornpipe and the Highland fling with 'a Life and Spirit that few but the native Highlanders could attain.' Elizabeth Grant of Rothiemurchus said the Highland country people took regular dancing lessons and took great pride in their skill; and one of the writers has recollections of the regular visits of the dancing master in Strathdearn and Strathspey, carrying on the old tradition into the middle of last century. The Outer Isles have had their own particular style of dancing, for which the Royal Celtic Society has given prizes. Alexander Carmichael describes a number of old Highland dances which survived longer in the Hebrides than on the mainland. They included the ancient dance, *Cailleach an Dudain*, the Old Woman of the Mill Dust, danced by a man and a woman, for which the music was played 'by a piper or a fiddler, or sung as a port-a-bial, mouth-tune, by a looker-on, or by the performers themselves'.[9] Dancing is mentioned in a number of songs and poems in modern Gaelic and evidently of no great antiquity, but the word used is *dannsa* and never the old Irish word *rinnce*.

The word 'reel' appears first in the late sixteenth century, and one of the first references is in a witch trial in the Lothians in 1591. 'Ports', the likely progenitors of the slower Strathspey tunes, are recorded in the Skene (1615-30) and Straloch (1627-29) Manuscripts. The first composer of a Strathspey of whom a tradition has come down to us was James Macpherson, the cateran, who in 1700 played 'Macpherson's Rant' at the foot of the gallows on which he was hanged, and smashed his fiddle because no one would accept it. A number of other tunes were being or had been composed; for when about 1757 the first collection of reels was published by Robert Bremner, it contained a large number of our present favourite tunes such as Gille-Caluim, Tullochgorum and others. Although the playing of dance music was considered below the dignity of pipers, Joseph MacDonald commented that some pipe tunes for jigs were very ancient, and Patrick MacDonald included a few of them in his 1784 collection, calling them reels in 6/8 time. Although these tunes are still played by pipers as marching tunes or for their own amusement and practice, the dances themselves seem to have passed from memory.

Between 1750 and 1830 was the zenith of the composing and playing of reels and strathspeys. Most of the leading composers came from the Central and Eastern Highlands, although so great was southern appreciation that many of them such as the Gows moved to Edinburgh or London. Among the most outstanding were William Marshall of Fochabers, who wrote among others 'The Marquis of Huntly's Farewell'; Niel Gow (1727-1807), of Inver by Dunkeld, best known as a player; his son Nathaniel Gow, composer of 'The Fairy Dance'; and Red Rob Mackintosh, who published four collections of Scottish dance music.[10]

Highland songs are perhaps the most widely appreciated part of our heritage, and a good deal has been done to preserve them. Patrick MacDonald, who with his brother Joseph were the earliest collectors, described the singing of Highland songs in his day: 'Over all the Highlands, there are various songs, which are sung to airs suited to the nature of the subject. But on the western coast, benorth middle Lorn, and in all the Hebrides, *Luinigs* are most in request. These are in general very short, and of a plaintive cast, analogous to their poetry: and they are sung by the women, not only at their diversions but also during almost every kind of work where more than one person is employed, as milking the cows, and watching the folds, fulling of cloth, grinding of grain with the quern or hand-mill, hay-making and cutting down corn. The men too have *iorrams*, or songs for rowing, to which they keep time with their oars, as the women like-wise do in their operations, whenever their work admits of it. When the same airs are sung in their hours of relaxation, the time is marked by the motions of a napkin, which all the performers lay hold of. In singing, one person leads the band; but in a certain part of the tune he stops to take breath, while the rest strike in and complete the air, pronouncing it to a chorus of words and syllables generally of no significance.'[11] He and Joseph MacDonald recorded the airs without the words, but in the early nineteenth century more was attempted. In 1816 Captain Simon Fraser of Knockie published *The Airs and Melodies Peculiar to the Highlands of Scotland and the Isles*, and dedicated it to the Highland Society of Scotland. That Society also gave a grant to Alexander Campbell to travel in the Highlands to gather music and songs. He was a Highlander, born by Loch Lubnaig, the son of a joiner, whose family moved to Edinburgh, where the boy studied music. His *Albyn's Anthology* was published in two volumes in 1816 and 1818 and was a more comprehensive collection, including words as well as music; the editor must have had his eye on a wider public, because English versions of the songs are given, written to fit the music by distinguished authors such as Scott and James Hogg, the Ettrick Shepherd. It was, of course, a time when public taste had been educated by Burns and Hogg, and Lowland folk-songs were receiving much attention. In the many collections of Scots songs that were being made, Highland airs were included.

The setting and the singing of Highland songs has changed with the taste and fashion of the age, often to the detriment of old tradition. Songs fashionable in the 1870s and '80s differ from those sung today, which may not be surprising, but many have felt that Gaelic singing, style and tonality, were being swamped by Lowland and English taste and conventions. The chorus songs or *orain luadhaidh* were passing out of fashion, and the *oran mór* was no longer tolerated by modern audiences. In a later period, Miss Lucy Broadwood, editor of the *Journal of the Folk-Song Society* and collaborator with Miss Frances Tolmie, collected songs in Arisaig in 1906 and 1907; the old women who gave her some songs spoke scornfully of the debased and hackneyed setting of many published Highland songs. There was grave danger that the less hackneyed songs and the traditional ways of singing them would be lost. Besides being working songs, with a splendid rhythm, the words had been regarded as of great importance and were carefully enunciated and many verses were sung. Many old people used to speak of this difference. There had also been great variations in the interpretations of the songs according to the mood of the singer, and there was much improvisation in the waulking songs, for instance, and this was part of the fun. Pairing-off songs might be sung in which the names of young folk attending the waulking could be paired off by name. *Có bheir mi leam air an luing Éireannaich*? — whom shall I take with me on the Irish ship? — provided the formula for much light-hearted fun.[12]

It is to the abiding honour of the folk of the Highlands and Islands that all through the changes, crises and privations of the eighteenth century, they should have preserved that splendid heritage of stories, songs and traditions and, above all, the great epics of a golden age of Gaelic culture. But it was not until later, when links with the past had been further eroded, that attempts were made to save some relics of our heritage of story and song. In the third quarter of the nineteenth century, there was still a wealth of oral tradition in the Highlands. Local clan stories, the relics of the ancient epics, strange stories of wonders and adventure that survived and changed with the great migration of remote ancestors, floated about all over the Highlands. Night after night, through the long northern winter, the skilled story-tellers entranced their listeners and handed on the tales that had come down to them. In Campbell's collection of *Popular Tales* we read that at Poolewe 'it was the custom for the young to assemble together on the long winter nights to hear the old people recite the tales or *sgeulachd*, which they had learnt from their fathers before them'. The itinerant tailors were generally skilled narrators, and the people still spoke of and discussed the Ossianic heroes while the readers of the newspapers were discussing war news from Russia and India, as this was the time of the Crimean War and the Indian Mutiny. There are many instances of story-tellers who could keep a hamlet going for a month with different stories. The Ossianic themes were 'recited rapidly to a kind of chant'. Campbell of Islay has left a wonderful word-picture of such a teller of tales. His cottage, double-walled and thatched, with the interior crowded with kists and box beds, a dresser, and gear of all sorts, with the sunlight slanting down the chimney hole through the wreaths of peat smoke, and the tense listeners. The old man himself 'had the manner of a practised narrator, and it is quite evident that he is one; he chuckled at the interesting parts, and laid his withered finger on my knee as he gave out the terrible bits with due solemnity'.[13]

By the time these descriptions were written, the old culture was in almost its last stage of decline. Something has been said of the loss of cultural focus or centre of learning by the seventeenth century. Only too often it was discouraged on religious or educational grounds. To their honour, however, some of the best collectors were ministers and schoolmasters. Unfortunately the visitors who more and more were penetrating to out-of-the-way places brought with them an alien culture. Alexander Carmichael, who was collecting for his *Carmina Gadelica* from the 1850s onwards, noticed the progressive decline and finally found the 'traditions meagre in quantity, inferior in quality and greatly isolated'. It was from the old, the isolated and the poor that there was just time to gather something of their great Gaelic heritage.

In the nick of time the impulse of a new European movement began to affect the Highlands. Early in the nineteenth century an appreciation of 'folk-tales' had dawned on men's consciousness. The brothers Grimm had published their *Household Tales* in 1812-15, and these were translated into English in 1823. They were scrupulous in recording the stories verbatim. Hans Christian Andersen (1805-1875), Danish poet, dramatist and novelist, is chiefly known in Britain for his series of fairy tales. Unlike Jacob and Wilhelm Grimm, linguists and philologists rather than poets, Andersen fashioned such folk-tales into works of delicate art. The first English translation appeared in 1846. Jacob Grimm had urged G W Dasent to study Scandinavian language, history and mythology, and in the course of two decades Dasent published several works in English which were very influential. His *Popular Tales from the Norse*, published in 1859, suggested that similar work could be done in Scotland. These works were recognised for their value to the new science of ethnological studies then in its infancy in Europe. Campbell of Islay, *Iain Og Ile* (1822-1885) was learned in what he called 'this new science of "storyology",' and was personally acquainted with Dasent. Being a thorough-going Highlander as well as a man of vigorous intellect, he was well fitted to be a folklorist. He published his *Popular Tales of the West Highlands* in 1860-62. This work is in marked contrast to that of the earlier 'translators', in that he and the team of helpers which he had enlisted up and down the West Coast were most careful to take down and record the stories in the dialects and idiom of the people. 'It is generally the Gaelic of the people — pure from the source'. The success of Campbell's venture depended on his collaborators. The most outstanding of these was Hector MacLean of Ballygrant, Islay, who did much of the work of preparing Campbell's material for the press. His other helpers were John Dewar, woodman on the Argyll estates, seconded by the 8th Duke to collect stories, and Hector Urquhart, gamekeeper at Ardkinglass, both men untutored geniuses and enthusiasts. Dewar's work in five large bound volumes in immaculate script is preserved at Inveraray.[14]

Campbell inspired Lord Archibald Campbell to attempt something similar. The latter initiated the work on five volumes of *Waifs and Strays of Celtic Tradition* (1889-1895) which, like the *Popular Tales*, depended for their success on a group of collectors such as Rev James MacDougall and Rev John Gregorson Campbell of Tiree, who himself edited two of the volumes. Gregorson Campbell was a famous hypochondriac, whose long spells in bed in his manse on Tiree enabled him to copy out and properly edit all his material, and both he and MacDougall published other volumes of folklore and tales which are important source books. The work of collecting was carried on by Alexander Carmichael, one of this group. Carmichael (1832-1912), a native of Lismore and an Exciseman, was also one of the first to realise the wealth of material to be collected from the unlettered Gaelic population of the west and islands. He was particularly interested in sacred and religious poetry dating back to before the Reformation and in charms and incantations, many pre-Christian or pagan. His publications *Carmina Gadelica* (1900) in two volumes represented only a fraction of

Three men of Islay, John Francis Campbell, the pioneer Celtic Folklorist, and Hector MacLean of Ballygrant taking down a version of a long Gaelic folktale from the recitation of Lachlin MacNeill in 1870

his fieldwork and later scholars, including his grandson James Carmichael Watson, have published a further four volumes. Carmichael was sharply aware of the decline in the Gaelic tradition and was intent on exalting the Gael in the regard of the outside world. To this end, he recast some of his material, employing archaisms and deliberately drawing the sanctity of age about the material.

These late nineteenth century collections consist mainly of *ùr-sgeulan* or wonder-tales that the earlier collectors and the 1805 Report on Ossian had dismissed as late and unworthy of notice. It was Campbell of Islay who first proved their antiquity in published form and showed their value to the world. When he had finished his work on the *Popular Tales*, he moved on to the Ossianic controversy, to analyse the great corpus of Fenian ballads in his own collections and in the manuscripts in the Advocates' Library, now the National Library of Scotland. The results were published in his *Leabhar na Feinne* (1872). He demonstrated the falsity of Macpherson's and others' claims and he showed which of the earlier recordings were genuine and which had been more or less altered in accordance with contemporary southern taste, and he recorded the age-old versions of heroic poetry that the people were still repeating up and down the Highlands. Another important and scholarly study in folk culture was Sheriff Alexander Nicolson's *Collection of Gaelic Proverbs*, published in 1881, containing over 3,000 proverbs.

Alexander Carmichael, the scholar-collector of religious, devotional and traditional lore, literature, songs and poetry which he published in his **Carmina Gadelica**

The relative importance of the songs as a part of the people's heritage has also changed. They have increased in importance while that of the riddles, proverbs and of the poetry and stories has declined. The modern idea of a *ceilidh* is mainly a gathering for singing, but even in the mid-nineteenth century descriptions the emphasis in the informal evening gatherings in the people's houses was still on the tales. The songs themselves, however, were being altered. As part of the movement to collect the folk heritage of stories, Frances Tolmie (1840-1926) was the pioneer in a new effort to preserve the songs of the people. Born and bred in the Highlands and Islands, she had the understanding of the people as well as the musical talent necessary, and she devoted much of her life to collecting their songs. She lived at the time when the old ways of life were changing and she took down songs that were almost forgotten. Her descriptions of how she collected them give enchanting pictures of the people themselves and their settings. The verse and song which she collected had received very little attention from the collectors and scholars, and, as she said herself, the songs of Skye women which she had learnt in her youth 'were already nearly forgotten by the people in 1860, and amongst my contemporaries my pleasure in these old wives' songs was considered very odd, for they were not deemed "poetry" or worthy of notice by song-collectors of that period'. A woman of great generosity, she gave freely of her knowledge and of her collections; she gave forty-five songs to Dr Keith Norman MacDonald, the compiler of the *Gesto Collection of Highland Music* (1895). She also gave music and texts to Marjory Kennedy-Fraser, whose *Songs of the Hebrides* began to be issued in 1907 and owed twenty-one of its songs to Frances Tolmie. It is fortunate for posterity that her work was not plundered any more and that parties interested in musical tradition, such as Dr George Henderson and Lucy Broadwood, saved her manuscripts for their publication in the *Journal of the Folk-Song Society* in 1911, which included 105 songs and Miss Tolmie's own notes and memoirs.[15]

The way of life of many Highland people changed with time during the Victorian era. It became usual to sing songs with a piano accompaniment, and this was a normal form of entertainment in the home. A collection of well-known songs with easy piano accompaniment with lyrics in English but several with Gaelic choruses gained wide popularity and exercised considerable influence in conserving the pride of race and sense of individuality among Highlanders. This collection was called *Songs of the North*, and the principal compiler was Sir Harold Edwin Boulton (1859-1935). The first volume was published in 1885 and it ran through 99 editions.

The speaking of Gaelic was sinking into a folk-language of the remoter districts, and the critical, educated support necessary to encourage work of high literary quality was minimal. In this age of prose-writing, Gaelic work was almost absent. The use of the press was limited to religious works such as sermons and catechisms, which became numerous during periods of religious revival and around the time of the Disruption.

In the 1760s Gaelic ceased to be regarded in the official view as an obstacle to the spread of the reformed faith or as a threat to the Hanoverian dynasty. In fact, most of the most distinguished Gaelic scholars of the eighteenth century were ministers of the Established Church. Rev Donald MacNicol (1735-1802) was a Gaelic poet and minister of Lismore who made the redoubtable Dr Johnson smart for his denunciation of Ossian. He published his *Remarks on Dr Samuel Johnson's Journey to the Hebrides* in 1779 and took down about 6,000 lines of Duncan Ban MacIntyre's verse from his own recitation. Rev James MacLagan (1728-1805), minister of Blair Atholl, translated part of the Scriptures into Gaelic for the S.P.C.K. and formed a collection of Gaelic manuscript material, which is now in Glasgow University. Other notable scholars were Rev Donald MacQueen of Kilmuir, the friend of Thomas Pennant, Rev Alexander Pope of Reay (1706-1782), who made a collection of Ossianic material about 1739, and Rev James Stuart of Killin (1701-1789), who translated the New Testament into Gaelic. By 1767 the S.P.C.K. had amended its absurd educational methods and had rescinded the embargo on the use of Gaelic in its schools; it admitted that the children had been merely learning by rote. Nevertheless, cases of the beating of children in schools for speaking Gaelic still occurred. The beginnings of the change of heart were partly due to Dr Johnson. Hearing that there was opposition to a proposed translation of the New Testament, he wrote so formidably that the opposition was withdrawn. In 1767 Rev James Stuart's translation of the New Testament from Greek into Gaelic was published, followed by the Old Testament by 1801. Thus, nearly 250 years after the Reformation, the Highlanders although they had Psalters and Catechisms in Gaelic, were at last enabled to read the Scriptures in their own tongue. The British and Foreign Bible Society printed large editions of this translation. How deeply people appreciated the translations of the Scriptures was particularly evident to one of the writers when she was collecting for a folk museum. Most of the Bibles she came across had their pages worn thin from much handling and many of them had been carefully rebound by the people themselves with home-made materials.

As the number of people who could read as well as speak Gaelic was comparatively small, written Gaelic work was mostly confined to periodicals. They served a useful purpose in a period when there was still a large population of monoglot Gaelic speakers, an appreciable number of whom were literate in their mother-tongue in spite of the efforts of governments to obliterate the language. The moving spirit behind the periodicals of this period was Rev Norman MacLeod, known to all as *Caraid nan Gaidheal*, — the Friend of the Gael. With *An Teachdaire Gaelach*, the Gaelic Messenger, which first appeared in 1829, we have the beginning of original Gaelic prose. Twenty-one numbers appeared between 1829 and 1831. This was followed by *Cuairtear nan Gleann*, of which forty numbers appeared between 1840 and 1843. These were enormously popular and had a heavy religious and moralistic bias. They were, however, topical and informative. MacLeod inspired successors later in the century and set the standards for writing in Gaelic for many years.

The wearing of Highland dress and of tartan has great significance to Highland people; with music and literature it is part of their racial heritage, but it has gone through various vicissitudes. In more affluent circles in the later half of the eighteenth century, it largely went out of fashion. The uniform worn by members of the Northern Meeting

Association at Inverness at the end of the century had nothing Highland about it, and Sir John Graham Dalyell, writing in 1849, said: 'Thirty or forty years ago no reputable gentleman would have appeared in a kilt in the streets of Edinburgh; and I recollect some expressions denoting surprise, not unmixed with disapprobation from ladies, that a young Highlander, though a person of family distinction, should appear in one at an evening party where I was present'. We owe it mainly to Sir Walter Scott that it became highly fashionable and that in 1822 George IV was received in the northern capital in a welter of tartan. But among the country people, the wearing of Highland dress followed an opposite course. They seemed to have resumed wearing it even in those districts where its proscription after the '45 had been most severely enforced, and several visitors at the end of the century allude to this. For instance, Stoddart in his *Remarks on local scenery and manners* said that when he reached Luss he began to hear Gaelic spoken, and 'here also begins the use of the plaid with all its accompaniments'. Dr Thomas Garnett describes the dress worn in Strathtay at the turn of the century: 'The Highland dress is more common here than in any other part of the country through which we passed ... It consists of a short jacket of tartan or woollen cloth, woven in squares of the most vivid colours, in which green and red are however predominant; the Philabeg or Kilt ... of the same stuff', diced hose in red and white, sporran of badger or fox, tartan plaid and a blue bonnet with a red and white band or border. But he also remarked that Highland dress was 'fast wearing out in the Highlands; many dress in the English manner ...' The change from home-produced to bought clothes was very much a part of this. The Statistical Accounts of many parishes record how the introduction of town-made clothing drove out traditional home-made styles. Elizabeth Isabella Spence, a novelist and traveller who wrote *Letters from the north Highlands* in 1816, said that the wearing of Highland dress had almost gone out in Inverness, but that at a funeral in Glen Urquhart the men and women were dressed 'in bright showy tartan'. Lord Cockburn, who was constantly on circuit during the 1840s, in his shrewd descriptions only comments on the absence of the kilt. In Skye about 1840 the people still wore homespun clothes, but the kilt had so entirely gone out that it was thought that it had never been worn there.

We owe it largely to the renown of the Highland regiments and to the sentiment fostered by the Highland Societies that the wearing of the Highland dress has survived. But inevitably, like other clothing, the fabric is mainly factory woven and made up by tailors. The wearing of feathers in the bonnet had certainly been in fashion in the seventeenth century. In the early nineteenth, some bonnets look like millinery confections. It was rather later that the Glengarry bonnet came into fashion. The shoulder plaid became a purely ornamental rather than a functional garment, and accoutrements were made by town craftsmen and mainly for display, such as dirks with cairngorms and brooches bejewelled or decorated with the chief's crest succeeded the zigzags or hatchings to which the fine Gaelic designs had declined by the end of the eighteenth century. The large skin sporrans with brush-like tassels had come in about 1770 and were referred to as handsome novelties introduced by the military. The long white goatskin sporrans became fashionable about 1800. Pistols of an inferior make, many from Birmingham, were worn for a time but have gone out; but reproductions of the powder horn, which had actually become obsolete before the flint-lock gun did so, are still occasionally worn. The *sgian-dubh* was added to the outfit in the early nineteenth century and by the end of it had become almost *de rigueur*. By the middle of that century the old combed, hard fabrics were going out and the thin, soft, Saxony type of cloth had come in and with it the use of vivid aniline dyes. In recording these changes, it is not for a moment suggested that the kilt and other parts of the Highland dress should not have been modified. All living things change with a changing society, and the dress of the Highlanders is very far from dead.

Among well-to-do women, the plaid has shrunk to a silk tartan scarf or sash worn on gala occasions, such as Highland balls, and about the middle of the nineteenth century there was a fashion for fine Saxony cloth tartan shawls. By the end of the eighteenth century the kertch or coif had given place to the mutch. But in the people's songs the word *breid* lingered on, significant as it was as the badge of matronhood, as distinct from the *stiom* or snood of maidenhood. Alexander Carmichael was told of the ceremonies associated with the kertch by a woman in Ness: 'On the morning after the marriage the mother of the bride .. placed the *breid tri chearnach* or three cornered kerch on the head of the bride before she rose from her bed. And the mother did this in the name of the Sacred Three ......' When she was dressed, she joined the wedding company and the festivities continued throughout the day. Carmichael also collected a beautiful address to a bride on first donning the *breid*. Henry Cockburn described the women attending the church service at Broadford in Skye in the 1840s wearing 'red tartan cloaks or shawls and clean mutches'. It was within living memory that the petticoats and skirts of striped homespun stuff, called 'drugget', went out of use.

The origin of tartans, a most controversial subject, has been alluded to, and also the debatable point of what tartan the Independent Companies might have worn. But it is certain that so early as 1740 the Black Watch were known by their dark tartan. The 93rd or Argyll and Sutherland Highlanders took over this tartan with modifications in the sett. The 92nd or Gordon Highlanders wear a dark tartan with a yellow over-check. The 78th or Seaforth Highlanders, though for a time only one battalion, wore a red tartan, then wore the old dark green government pattern with red and white over-checks, which had already been worn by the Ross-shire Fencibles and three Regiments of the Line raised in Ross-shire during the Continental wars. These three tartans are now regarded as the clan tartans of the Campbells, Gordons and MacKenzies. It is a moot point whether their origin is earlier than their introduction as regimental tartans. There is no evidence of the existence of an earlier MacKenzie tartan, and there is some indication that red tartan was once worn by the Campbells. Lord Duffus, painted by Richard Waitt in about 1710, shows him wearing a fairly bright tartan, and a portrait of Rachel Gordon of Abergeldie shows her wearing a red and green tartan with a black over-check. The regimental tartan worn by the Camerons is exceptional; it was devised by the mother of Cameron of Erracht who raised the Regiment in 1793. It is supposed to be a form of tartan worn by the MacDonalds of Keppoch with a yellow stripe associated with the Camerons, and was adopted by the family as well as by the Regiment. This is one of the strongest pieces of evidence for the age of an existing clan tartan. As James Scarlett convincingly points out, a far more ancient origin for a number of other tartans, as for instance that of the Grants, Mackintoshes and MacGillivrays, is the fact that the clans in adjacent districts had adopted distinctive variations of a mainly red and green 'district pattern' that for convenience the local weavers had adopted in setting their warps.

The order books of weavers of the late eighteenth century show that at first the demand was for checked designs, not definitely the setts of clan tartans. In the early nineteenth century, however, clan tartans became popular and the fashion received great stimulus from the visit of George IV to Edinburgh in 1822, with the 'Wizard of the North' in attendance as Master of Ceremonies; and the list of tartans grew and grew. The earliest list, published by James Logan in 1831, in his *Scottish Gael*, numbered fifty-three. There must now be hundreds of different variations of tartan.

In many cases the tartans now sold were reproduced from old family portraits or even from surviving pieces of fabric. D W Stewart in his *Old and Rare Scottish Tartans* mentions nearly a dozen of such cases. They include the dress tartan of MacDonald of the Isles from Jeremiah Davison's portrait of 1750, and the hunting tartan from one of 1765 of the first Lord MacDonald. Early portraits of this family show a number of other patterns. The Fraser tartan was taken from a 1790 collection of specimens, but several eighteenth century Fraser portraits show variations of the same tartan; Grant from a portrait of Robert Grant of

Lurg, who served in the Independent Companies; MacDonald from the remains of a waistcoat given by MacDonald of Kingsburgh to Prince Charles Edward; MacDonald of Keppoch from a plaid given to Prince Charles Edward; MacIan from a portrait of Alasdair Ruadh of Glengarry of the '45. The tartan worn by MacLaine of Lochbuie is known to be very old; MacRae is from a piece of old hard tartan from a kilt worn at Sheriffmuir; Murray of Tullibardine is also copied from an old portrait. Unfortunately an element of doubt was introduced when the Sobieski Stuart brothers published their *Vestiarium Scoticum*. The sumptuously produced book was claimed by the brothers to be the reproduction of the sixteenth century manuscript, but the existence of this manuscript has never been incontrovertibly proved. The patterns in the *Vestiarium* differed in some cases from those which had then come into general use.

If it is not possible to make good the claim that the present clan tartans have survived *en bloc* from remote antiquity, it can at least be said that in their complex and stylised beauty, they have the characteristics of the old Gaelic arts and that with their possession, the old pride of race of the Highlanders had found a contemporary form of expression. It is of even greater importance that for most Highlanders clan tartans have acquired a real significance and that for them they represent the tangible survival of a pride in descent and of a loyalty to a community. These are more fundamental characteristics of the Gael than the periodic variations in their culture that this book has tried to trace. Although the formation of the Highland corps contributed to the survival of Highland piping and dress, the movement probably tended to discourage the old *calanas* or women's home woollen and linen industry. The Independent Companies of 1729 and the later corps were supplied with their outfits by their commanding officers who were repaid by the government. Tartan was obtained through a military agent, and important manufacturers sprang up outside the Highlands, at Bannockburn and Stirling, as well as just within it, at Aberfeldy. Home spinning and weaving by the local people for their own use eventually passed away in district after district.

The making of dirks, brooches and other ornaments enriched by the traditional patterns, which had been mainly carried on by the 'cairds' or tinkers, ceased when the country people gave up wearing Highland dress. Boswell in his *Journal* mentioned the 'plaited carving' commonly found on the Highland dirks or forks and knives. Many old tinkers still remember that their ancestors were fine craftsmen. Like music, poetry and the lesser arts, the carrying on of home crafts such as these had been a form of self-expression.

It may be pointed out how much originality went into the form of even the simplest artefacts, how much ingenuity can be found in the use of local materials such as straw and heather or an unusual knot or bend in a branch of a tree, and how much social history lies in the shapes of home-made chairs, sometimes made in the crudest way and yet reflecting the influence of the great styles of the past — Queen Anne, Chippendale or Sheraton — which must have been seen and copied all down the scale of gradations of the old, closely-knit fabric of Highland society. When these survive, they are tangible links with a distant past and a pride of race of which the old Gaelic arts, which we have described, are one form of self-expression. These may be more fundamental characteristics of the Gael than the periodic variations in their culture that this book has attempted to trace.

Period VII

Later nineteenth and twentieth centuries.
Survival within integration

Our final period deals with events from the 1880s down to the years following the Second World War. It covers one of the most momentous times in the history of Britain. The results of the desperate struggle for national survival have not fully worked themselves out. Our period falls into two sections. The first one covers the time up to the First World War (1914-1918), which, in the writers' opinion, most definitely marks a watershed in British history. This was followed by an interim period of about twenty years and then by the Second World War (1939-1945), which intensified and widened the effects of the earlier conflict. The pre-War period, with the outstanding exception of the crofting legislation, was, for the main part, a continuance of the conditions that had been evolved during the second half of the nineteenth century. Farming, sport and tourism were run upon the same lines. There was more intervention by the state in private lives and enterprises. The openings overseas that since the beginning of the eighteenth century had been of such value to the Highlanders were still available. At the very beginning of our period, one innovation of cardinal importance was introduced; it opened a new chapter in Highland history. This was the series of acts and organisations for the improvement of the conditions of the crofters. The conditions limiting the absolute ownership of land and the obligations assumed by the state and imposed upon the landowners were revolutionary changes in current legal and economic thinking. This new concept of the responsibilities of the state has persisted down to the present day, and there has been a succession of further acts and provisions by the state for the benefit of the crofters. It is a most striking illustration of a complete change in the climate of public opinion.

During the eighteenth and nineteenth centuries, the condition of the people in many of the coastal districts and islands of the North and West Highlands had become progressively worse. Apart from the introduction of the potato, which itself had led to a disastrous famine, there had been little improvement in the people's distinctly unsophisticated means of gaining a livelihood, and serious overcrowding had developed on land that was already inadequate to furnish proper support. Public opinion, especially among expatriate Highlanders, had become increasingly concerned over the people's plight and shocked by the worst of the

270

Clearances. Accounts began to appear in English newspapers, and the Gaelic movement itself produced papers such as John Murdoch's radical *Highlander*, founded in 1873, and *The Oban Times*, which took up the cause of the local people under the editorship of Duncan Cameron. The attitude of the local people changed but slowly from passive resignation to bitter outrage and the first manifestations of active resistance. In the 1880s this gave voice to a poetic resurgence, especially in Skye and Lewis. What seemed a relatively small incident attracted a good deal of attention and turned out to be the first blow of the so-called Crofters' War. The indiscriminate reallocation of grazings and summary eviction notices served on families on Bernera, Lewis, in 1874 turned into a *cause célèbre* when Sir James Matheson's Lewis chamberlain was forced out of office. Various other incidents hit the headlines, but none was to raise the same outcry as the Battle of the Braes in Skye in 1882 and the case of the 'Glendale Martyrs' in the following year, when a gunboat was sent to help with the arrest of five Skyemen. Refusals to give up grazings and also to pay rents became commonplace, and eventually, in response to overtures from many parties, the Government appointed a commission of inquiry into conditions in the Highlands and Islands under the chairmanship of Lord Napier in 1883.

Contemporary observers were struck by the comparative lack of violence in the period of land reform agitation, especially when the conspicuous example of Ireland offered so great a contrast. But there were sympathisers in the cities who wanted to put more political muscle in to the crofters' cause. Regarding the Napier Commission as an inadequate expediency, they formed the Highland Land Law Reform Association and, taking advantage of the extension of franchise in the 1884 Reform Act, they ran candidates in the Highland constituencies in the 1885 general election and captured four seats for members supporting their cause. The obvious mass support which they enjoyed in the North and West helped to push the legislation of the Crofters Holdings (Scotland) Act of 1886 through Parliament. This made a complete break with the classical nineteenth century ideas of *laissez-faire* and the sanctity of property. The government had now assumed oversight of the crofters. The legislation applied to parishes within the counties of Argyll, Inverness, Ross and Cromarty, Sutherland, Caithness and the Northern Isles, where crofting townships of arable holdings with common grazing rights existed. The Act gave crofters security of tenure, the right to compensation for improvements and the right of the heir to succeed, and it set up a court, the Crofters' Commission, to administer the terms of the Act and to fix fair rents. The work of the Crofters' Commission was superseded by the Land Court and the Board of Agriculture in 1911. The Board was very active in introducing new settlement schemes. By the 1920s most of the arable land in the crofting areas had been resettled. The Congested Districts Board was established in 1897 to give practical help and was merged with the Board of Agriculture in 1911.

The term 'croft' and 'crofter' have been long used in a loose and general sense; both were defined in the 1886 Act. The crofter is tenant of an agricultural holding known as a croft, registered as such and paying a certain annual rent. The area of inbye land was not to exceed 30 acres, later changed to 50 acres, and is generally much smaller, and the tenancy includes pasture rights in common. The crofter therefore rents his land but supplies dwelling house, farm buildings, fencing and draining; elsewhere in the country it should be remembered that the farmer leases both land and buildings. In recent years there have been about 18,500 crofts on the Crofters' Commission register, of which about 60 per cent are in the Hebrides, and Lewis alone has over 3,500. When the 1886 Act was passed, the crofters, many occupying very small crofts, were mainly subsistence farmers using simple methods of husbandry, cultivating the ground in the form of lazy-beds with the *cas-chrom* and spade. Their additional sources of income in coastal districts had been mainly fishing in open boats, seasonal work in the Lowlands and the sale of a few cattle. Housing, fuel, most of the implements, utensils and clothing were home-made. Returns were always small and uncertain for the toil required, and at times the people suffered material privation. On the other hand, their intellectual and social life was enriched by the splendours of a great inheritance. But the way of life of the crofters was changing. The croft has become less and less the sole support of the family, and alternative work was found, especially in the fisheries of the North and East coasts, the Services and the Merchant Navy. Emigration continued, and although it offered new opportunities for many, it has broken family ties and lost to the country some of the finest youth. Those who witnessed the departure of the emigrant ships *Metagama*, *Marloch* and *Canada* in 1923 and 1924 from Stornoway will describe the harsh side of emigration and what it means in human terms. It has been said that the main export from the Long Island was men, borne out by the fact that these three ships took about 860 mostly young people in two years. By an Act of 1911 permanent residence was no longer required of a crofter. Mainly with the money thus earned, the people imported more and more of their needs and assimilated their social ideas more and more to those of the outside world. But observers have said that the change has been specially marked since the two World Wars. Legislation has continued to be framed to deal with the position as it had developed and with conditions as they actually were.

In the severe pressure of over-crowding the old Highland system of running farming had been continued. Each individual's small share of the arable land was cultivated under an 'open-field' system, and in some cases the individual lots were re-allocated every year. The grazing was pastured in common to a limited extent, and this system lingered on. But from the early days of the crofters' legislation, a definite type of lay-out for crofting townships was evolved so far as the actual lie of the land allowed it. The crofters' houses are usually spaced along a road, each of them at the end of the individual crofter's strip of arable land. According to a rotation of crops, each crofter divides his land into strips yet narrower for growing cereals, turnips, etc. Where separate crofts are still fully cultivated, this lay-out is a very distinctive pattern on the landscape.

It may be pointed out that this agricultural lay-out, although imposed as a new development, had certain links with the past but that socially it created a new kind of community of small agriculturalists quite unlike the old Highland society of many gradations of land-holding.

The Crofters' Act did nothing for the landless cottars, and their frustration led them to occupy ground, often to build houses on it and always to cultivate it as a sign of their determination. These 'land raids' intensified. One of the best remembered was the great 'Deer Raid' of Park. Falling agricultural prices and a depression in the herring industry had reduced the already small incomes of crofter and cottars. They had also reduced the profits of sheep farming, and when no tenant could be

Spring ploughing on a croft at Blathaich, Ardgour

found for the Lewis sheep farm of Park, it was then let by the Mathesons as a deer forest. It was occupied in 1886 by the landless population of the surrounding townships, who killed a number of deer to reduce the attractions of the property as a sporting let. In Lewis, where the increase of population and pressure on land has been greatest and hence also the effects of falling prices, there were other attempts to break up sheep farms. The establishment of the Congested Districts Board in 1897 represented a radical attempt to make more land available and to sponsor schemes of employment in weaving and fishing, borrowing the name and the policy from the experience of Ireland. The functions of the Board were taken over by its successor, the Board of Agriculture, in 1911. But the problem of a landless population and the trouble that it aroused was solved only gradually. The Board of Agriculture introduced land settlement schemes, sometimes buying the land in order to implement them. Between about 1896 and 1924 almost all the land of the big farms was restored to crofting tenure. The last of these farms to be broken up into crofts was at Eoligarry, Barra, in 1939. By the 1920s most of the useful arable land had been resettled.

It seemed to be fitting to date this period in Highland history with the passing of legislation fundamentally new in concept and that deeply afftected a considerable area of the Highlands. The changes were, however, local in their effect. The pattern of life over the rest of the Highlands continued with little change up to 1914 and the outbreak of

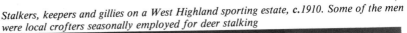

Stalkers, keepers and gillies on a West Highland sporting estate, c.1910. Some of the men were local crofters seasonally employed for deer stalking

the First World War. The main source of revenue and work continued to be the rental and rates of sporting estates and, to a lesser extent, 'summer visitors' of the old type. It is difficult to summarise a general social attitude of mind that largely persisted until the Second World War; the writers are obliged to pick out illustrations.

The survival of the old affection for the clan chiefs can be traced in unexpected places. Of course, clan societies abounded both at home and overseas. Almost invariably, their most important function has become that of forming friendly associations and welcoming links with fellow clansmen overseas. The chiefs were still figureheads and focal points for these activites. Many have taken their position, duty and social obligations very seriously and, because of this, have rendered valuable service to the local government of the period. The boundaries of the counties followed the lie of the land in the same way as had past social organisations. Sheriffdoms were formally established by the Local Government (Scotland) Act of 1889, by which the administrative powers and duties of the Commissioners of Supply were transferred to County Councils constituted under the Act. The estates that the chiefs of the clans had built up lay in the main within the confines of a county. As the Highlands are a rural area, there tended to be a strong territorial element among the members of each Council. Although clan societies could give loyal suport to chiefs who had lost their land, the links of clanship were greatly strengthened when a chief could offer the traditional hospitality to his clan from his ancestral home. The MacLeans of Duart had good reason to feel this when Sir Fitzroy MacLean of Duart bought and restored Duart castle just before the First World War. When the chief of an important clan was chosen as chairman of the Council of his county, as were Mackintosh, Lovat, Lochiel and Lord Macdonald successively of Inverness County Council, besides general appreciation of their own qualities as chairmen, there was the sense of a warming link with the past. Recently County Councils have, of course, been abolished and local government entirely reorganised.

The prestige element attaching to the rank of a clan chief in the plushy Victorian and post-Victorian period is illustrated by several contemporary lawsuits. They aroused great interest at the time. An outstanding one arose because there were words between the Duke of Argyll and Angus Campbell of Dunstaffnage after the latter had claimed that he no longer held the ruined castle of Dunstaffnage as a vassal of the Duke, since the obligation to defend it (which was the condition upon which his ancestor had been granted the title to hold it) had ceased to exist with the abolition of the feudal due of military service in the Act passed after the '45. In 1912 there was a case before the Court of Session which Dunstaffnage lost.[1]

In 1921 a case was brought in the Court of Session by Colonel James A. F. Humbertson Stewart MacKenzie of Seaforth, afterwards Lord Seaforth of Brahan, to prove that Mrs Beatrice Anna Fraser-Mackenzie of Allangrange was not entitled to have upon her gateway a coat of arms which he claimed was that of the chief of Clan MacKenzie. She won the case and also an appeal by Colonel Stewart MacKenzie to the House of Lords. To her friends she freely stated that, if she had lost, the many legal costs would have crippled her financially very seriously.

In 1940 there was a rather similar case, in which the heiress to MacLean of Ardgour, having applied to the Lord Lyon for recognition of her position as chief with the appropriate arms, had her claim opposed by the nearest male heir to the chieftanship upon the grounds that a woman could not be a chief. The Lord Lyon found that the heiress was entitled to the arms of the chief of the clan, but the male heir appealed from the Lyon Court to the Court of Session and again lost his case.[2] These cases, especially the last one, aroused much interest in the Highlands, and many theories regarding an imaginary code of clan law were advanced. Such cases would be most unlikely to be taken to court in the post-War years.

Unfortunately, during these years before the First War, the agricultural depression continued. Highland agriculture, with its dependence upon the price of the coarse wool of the blackface sheep, was especially hard hit; the crofting communities were badly affected too. There were signs of the beginning of other changes in agriculture. No one seems to have recorded the progress of the replacement of the sickle by the scythe, involving a change in methods of harvesting. This had long ago taken place in most areas and even upon the small upland farms the horse-drawn reaper and then the reaper and binder, which bound the sheaves ready for stooking as well as cutting the corn, were coming into use. It marked the end of one of the most important occasions for seasonal part-time labour and had economic as well as social effects. The old profitable forms of tourist industry continued. Changes in transport did not much affect it. The bicycle, which came into general use at the beginning of the twentieth century, gave local people a welcome mobility. The motor-car, even just before the War, was still a complicated machine, driven only by chauffeurs or the mechanically minded. It had not seriously challenged horse-power on the roads and even less on the farms.

A vitally important development was the beginning of a new form of support for Gaelic culture. In a society that had been Gaelic-speaking and had gradually become bi-lingual, the patronage of Gaelic literature had rested with the chiefs and its encouragement with the lesser gentry. But by the nineteenth century the aristocracy was with few exceptions ignorant of Gaelic and its Gaelic roots. By the twentieth century, a growing section of the community had little or no Gaelic. It had had no status in official education and its fortunes had been in the hands of too many different agencies from parish schools to church schools. The 1872 Education Act applied a universal principle of education through the medium of English, and Gaelic was not even mentioned. A few individuals and groups such as the newly-formed Gaelic Society of Inverness campaigned for some recognition of the importance of the language as the mother-tongue of Highlanders, but the official attitude remained antagonistic. The 1918 Education Act included a 'Gaelic Clause' recommending adequate provision for teaching Gaelic in Gaelic-speaking areas, but an attitude of official indifference continued until after the Second World War. The 1956 Schools Code took account of the Gaelic-speaking areas in making a broader provision for instruction in Gaelic language and literature and the use of Gaelic where appropriate for instructing in other subjects. Since then there has been an increasing emphasis on the sympathetic use of Gaelic in teaching Gaelic-speaking children to read, write and count in the language.

It will be remembered that the teaching of Gaelic had been first included in the curriculum of state education in 1878, when formal permission was first given to school boards to pay the salary of a teacher of 'Gaelic, drill, cooking or any other special subject'. This opening was turned to good account in developing the teaching of Gaelic in many schools. An outstanding example is the Nicholson Institute. It began as an institution to educate local boys, founded in 1864 with money left by a Stornoway man named John Nicholson, an engineer who died as the result of an accident. Enlarged by amalgamations with other schools and helped by Sir John Matheson, the present Nicholson Institute was opened in 1901. Its pupils have achieved high academic honours and are regular winners in competitions at the *Mòd*.[3]

At this point the efforts of enthusiasts, most notably Professor John Stuart Blackie, enlisted a new and powerful agent for its preservation. Gaelic became a subject for academic study. A Chair of Celtic Studies had been founded in Edinburgh in 1882 and a succession of Gaelic scholars have held it. A great deal of valuable work was done in preserving original Gaelic writings, for instance, by the Scottish Gaelic Text Society whose first work was produced in 1937, and also by scholars who made prose and poetry available, such as Professor William J. Watson with his collection of Gaelic poetry, *Bardachd Ghaidhlig* (1918), and his collection of Gaelic prose, *Rosg Gaidhlig* (1915). Gaelic prose was also made available to a much wider circle of readers by the Gaelic Supplement of the Church of Scotland's magazine *Life and Work*, founded in 1879. The Rev Donald Lamont, minister of Blair Atholl, rendered valuable service as its editor for forty years. Even the general public became aware that the eminent German philologist, Prof. Kuno Meyer, was studying the Gaelic language. He was, as a matter of fact, a member of a group of four scholars of distinction and they were followed by an equally distinguished group of Scandinavian scholars. About the same time people's appreciation of the old Highland handcrafts was stimulated by an exhibition held in Glasgow in 1888 and 1890 and also by the admirable catalogue prepared for it by James Paton. One of the writers well remembers what a fascinating eye-opener it was.

In the field, valuable work that did not reach the general public until the inter-war period was being done by Alexander Carmichael, the author of *Carmina Gadelica*, by Miss Frances Tolmie, the collector of songs, and Kenneth MacLeod, the translator, who both generously contributed to many contemporary publications, and by Mrs Kennedy-Fraser who was influenced by such composers as Brahms and Bartok who embodied local folk melodies in their own compositions. Her *Songs of the Hebrides* came out about the time of the First World War.

It is a matter of great satisfaction that the most distinctive art of the Gaels, piping, survives with renewed vigour. The popularity of the nineteenth century led to the neglect of *piobaireachd*. The composition of it declined as the hereditary piping families disappeared, and for about a century the generative spirit of *piobaireachd* seemed to be dead. Since the 1930's, however, and especially in the last twenty years, some very fine tunes have been composed in this traditional genre, beginning with the late Angus Macpherson's *Salute to the Cairn at Boreraig*. Further stimulus had been given to the art by the founding of the Piobaireachd Society in 1902 and its work in teaching piping with the untiring aid of the late Pipe Major Willie Ross and their publication of *ceòl mór*.

But of far greater importance in keeping the traditional music of Gaeldom in people's ears and mouths was the formation in 1893 of *An Comunn Gaidhealach*, inspired by the Welsh Eisteddfod and holding its first *Mòd* or Gathering in Oban for competitions in literature and music. The attendance at the yearly Mods has become so large that they can now only be held in the big halls of the larger towns, and expatriate Gaels take an active part in them. The local Mods held in the Gaidhealtachd however, give great stimulus to the country people, and the movement has encouraged the singing of Gaelic songs and the writing of verse and prose. Perhaps of all the attempts at reviving the old Highland arts, this has become most thoroughly acclimatised.

The narrative of events from the passing of the first crofters legislation till 1914 and the outbreak of the First World War has not been a local Highland affair. The danger, the effort, the losses, the destruction of materials and the expenditure affected the whole of Great Britain, and so did the drastic re-orientation of social life. The First World War marks a landmark in the life of the nation. A period of about twenty years followed. We, who lived through it, vainly hoped that the 'War to end all Wars' had been fought, and most people assumed that society would gradually revert to its pre-War condition. Instead, it was an interim period till the Second World War broke out in 1939. In this tremendous cataclysm, in which the whole nation was involved, the Highlands like the rest of Britain endured the terrible losses of our young manhood and the material destruction, the burden of national debt and the heavy burden of taxation, especially upon inherited and unearned wealth. As the Highlands so much depended upon the fashion element in sport and a relatively luxurious form of tourism, this post-War development especially affected it. As one remembers the general attitude, people in general were anxious to resume the pre-War way of life. This was the case in what was still the most valuable source of revenue to the Highlands, the use of land for sporting purposes. Financially, the people who rented or bought sporting estates were specially hard hit. Social changes, especially the shortage of domestic staff to run the shooting lodges, diminished their attractiveness, but to a certain extent the shooting season continued to be a matter of importance financially and socially until the outbreak of the Second World War.

Agriculture upon the upland Highland farms had shared in the wartime prosperity, and some land that had gone out of cultivation was temporarily brought back under the plough. Then wartime agricultural prosperity ceased, and upland farming again became a depressed industry. There was a fashion for raising beef cattle, but on the lesser hill farms at least no major changes in farming practice developed. The tourist industry also did not suffer a fundamental change, although towards the end of the period there were stirrings of innovation. The period saw the coming of the motor-car but it was little more than an added amenity and did not greatly displace the use of horses.

During this period, when old ways often tended to be deliberately resumed, the great innovation was the increased activity of the state and of public reliance upon it, although the term 'Welfare State' was not actually formulated until the middle of the Second World War. Two of these new state enterprises especially affected the Highlands. One of those was forestry. Landowners had done a great deal of planting before 1914, and forestry in some districts was a valuable asset; but during the War there had been wholesale felling of timber, and it was largely to make good this loss that the state took action. The Forestry Commission appointed in 1919 has been extremely active in Scotland. According to recent reports, approximately three quarters of their planting has been there, and by 1954 they had acquired over a million acres of ground, although something less than half of this was plantable, some of it being wet and sour and some lying at a considerable altitude. With developments in transport and technology, remoter areas have become viable for afforestation. In a few places, the Forestry Commission has set down settlements of attractive houses for the families of workers who are servicing the forests. The national policy aimed at rebuilding home stocks in case of further crises, and considerable state aid has been produced for private forestry as well as the Commission's work. A forest fleece of trees has spread over many thousands of acres of hill. It was very unfortunate that the species most favoured in post-War afforestation was the recently introduced non-native Sitka spruce, and Scots pine and the slow-growing broadleafed trees, such as oak, beech and ash, were entirely neglected. But in the last decade, new planting has tended to be broken up so as to include a variety of tree species, especially native ones. Another new organisation, the Nature Conservancy, pointed the way to more interesting and enlightened planting policies.

Of great local importance and in the quest for sources of power, another statutory body was formed to utilise the waters of the Highlands. The harnessing of water power in Britain had been pioneered by the British Aluminium Company, which was processing imported aluminum and installed a hydro-electric plant at the Falls of Foyers on Loch Ness in 1896, making use of one of the few natural resources of the Highlands. This was followed by other schemes. The most ambitious involved a new township of 300 houses at Inverlochy and a tunnel through the Ben Nevis range to bring the water 15 miles from the catchment areas. Between the Wars, three projects for the supply of electricity were proposed in Inverness-shire and Perthshire. Further development in the Highlands was thwarted by powerful opposition and rejected by Parliament. The future of Highland hydro-electricity was ensured by the vision of Tom Johnston, who was Secretary of State for Scotland in Churchill's War Cabinet. He piloted a Bill through Parliament which set up the North of Scotland Hydro-Electric Board in 1943. A clause in the Act makes the 'Hydro-Board', as it is known, unique among such bodies. As far as it is within the Board's competence it should co-operate in measures for the economic development and social improvement of its area. The Board's priorities were to develop water power in the Highlands in order to bring light and power to those areas beyond existing electricity supplies. In the sparsely populated areas, this enterprise has always made a loss, and therefore the Board stores electricity and sells it to the South of Scotland Electricity Board, and huge pylons carrying transmission lines march across the landscape from the hills to the centres of population and industry in Central Scotland.

The Western Isles, Orkney and Shetland lie within the Hydro-Board's area of operation and they are powered by diesel generators as well as small hydro-generators. All but a few remote houses have come within the Hydro-Board's orbit, and so now the people of the Highlands have the benefit of power and light through the long hard winters. The Board's social clause has operated on a small scale to the advantage of individual crofters and also on a large scale, the potential of power supplies offering possibilities for industry and new jobs in its train. This was the determining factor in the decision of the British Aluminium Company to establish a smelter at Invergordon in 1967, an enterprise that requires a large amount of power throughout the year.

One important private enterprise was attempted. It is significant that it foundered on the situation created by the crofting legislation. The provisions of the Crofters' Act had been extended by the Small Landholders (Scotland) Act, passed shortly before the 1914-18 War, which empowered the Secretary of State to divide into smallholdings farms of 150 acres, and in 1911, under the terms of the Act, the Board of Agriculture made arrangements for the sub-division of four farms in Lewis. Seven years later the Island of Lewis was bought by Lord Leverhulme, who drew up a comprehensive scheme for developing the fisheries of the Island with auxiliary enterprises and proceeded to carry it out at his own expense. Unfortunately, as part of Lord Leverhulme's scheme the four farms that had been allotted for sub-division by the Board of Agriculture were to be preserved in order to supply the growing town of Stornoway with milk. A group of men who had applied for crofts upon the farms demanded that they be sub-divided and proceeded to raid them. Lord Leverhulme insisted that the farms should be retained and threatened to stop carrying out his great projects, and for a time he actually stopped the work. The authorities, who were committed to the division of the farms and yet did not wish to lose the great advantage of Lord Leverhulme's scheme, acted ineffectively. Negotiations continued. Lord Leverhulme offered other land for sub-division, but the raiding continued and was not dealt with by the authorities or by local opinion. In 1923 Lord Leverhulme finally abandoned his plans for the Island, stopped all work and offered the whole estate in Trust to the local District Councils. Some accepted, others refused and the land was sold.[4]

After the First War there was great activity in land settlement in accordance with the general demand for the provision of 'Homes fit for

Heroes'. The Board (later Department) of Agriculture was generous in grants for re-housing the crofters. The local styles of housing had varied to suit conditions such as shortage or abundance of timber and were built by the people themselves. The most perfect example was the Lewis-type of home, constructed with the minimum of timber, low and streamlined in shape to offer the least resistance to the high winds and, for extra protection, with double walls. During the 1930s, the steamers to the Isles were piled high with prefabricated doors, roofs and window frames. The new houses were built to a standard design and known among the people as *Tigh a'Bhuird*, literally 'the Board's house'.

There was a dramatic increase in the use of motor-cars during the inter-war period. They had become much easier to drive and they did not require the same attendance as horses. Their use began to affect the construction of roads, the mechanisation of heavier traffic and the tourist industry.

It was during this time that Mrs Kennedy-Fraser, in magnificent and archaic costume, sang her songs to crowded audiences in the larger cities and there was a certain vogue for her songs and also for the playing of the *clarsach*, the old Gaelic harp, in more sophisticated circles. Probably largely because of the elaborate accompaniment, her songs did not penetrate widely among country audiences.

Some of Carmichael's collections of the folklore of the Western Isles were printed in a more accessible edition with translations and were a revelation to many Highlanders. Professor W.J. Watson's translations of the texts of medieval poetry, made shortly before the War, now came to be widely appreciated.

The period between the Wars was the time of 'the Dancing Years' all over Britain, in the Highlands, as elsewhere. A society that became naturalised in the Highlands is the Scottish Country Dance Society, founded in 1923 by the late Miss Jean Milligan. Besides reviving old Highland dances, it has done valuable work in maintaining the old high standard of dancing which is in some danger of slipping in a renewed popularity of country dancing and other fashions for modern dance. The Society quickly inspired the founding of branches throughout the country and published books of dances. They had the advantage of inheriting a still living tradition. The Highland Dance and Reel Society have also encouraged the best standard of dancing. Only in a few areas have religious attitudes discouraged dancing. As an accompaniment to dancing, the 'trump' or Jew's-harp has long gone out of use, but, failing the accompaniment of the fiddle or the pipes, the 'box', the melodeon or accordion, will always fill the gap.

To deal with events since the last World War is to give an account of current affairs rather than to write history. Without the hindsight that the past confers it would be both presumptuous and invidious to attempt to record anything beyond a generalised summary. One of the writers has lively memories going back to an earlier period, and she would tentatively suggest that this post-War period is most markedly different from its predecessors in its egalitarianism, its disassociation with the past, and, beyond all else, by its belief in the efficacy of technological progress. A prime example of this is the state of euphoria produced by the discovery that oil and gas could be extracted from under the North Sea. There was a strong belief that special benefits would be derived from it by the Highlands. As we now know, the exploitation of this new source of wealth has been of special benefit to certain districts and to Scotland in general to a limited extent. To the Highlands and Western Isles it has brought some temporary large scale engineering projects as transient in their benefit to local people as was the building of the railways or the hydro-electric installations. Another general feature of the period is the disappearance of the 'fashion' element that had been so profitable to the Highlands.

The Highlands are becoming more and more integrated into the general life of Britain. With the rest of the country it suffered the devastating losses in war of men and material wealth. The loss of the Empire closed off what had been a wonderful area of expansion for Highland people. During the War, Churchill and Beveridge had promulgated the establishment of a Welfare State, completing a conception of public responsibility that Lloyd George had initiated before the First World War in his campaign for Old Age Pensions. Its benefits affect Highland people as much as anyone else. Since the War there has been an increase in the activities of both central and local government and a most important change has been made in local and community organisation by the passage of the Local Government (Scotland) Act of 1973. This Act superseded the County Councils, the organisation of which had contributed much to the old social life and territorial allegiance of the country. The most regrettable example is the new arrangement in the vast region of Strathclyde that stretches from the Point of Ardnamurchan to the Lowland Uplands with the great City of Glasgow in its midst.

To the Forestry Commission and the Hydro-Electric Board, the state now added another organisation intended to be of especial benefit to the Highlands, the Highlands and Islands Development Board. This was set up by an Act of Parliament in 1965 specifically to encourage new industrial enterprise in the seven crofting counties, a region where it was recognised that social and economic well-being was lacking. The Board's initial strategy was directed towards what it termed 'growth centre policy', that is, concentrating manufacturing industry at one or two points to minimise the high costs involved in establishing it in a remote area, to achieve economies of scale and to limit the effects of industrialisation. The area around the Moray Firth was chosen. The biggest single project was the aluminium smelter at Invergordon, representing a huge investment of capital but without the hoped-for mass employment. Unfortunately, though this is a spot conveniently situated for deep-water access, it also contains some of the best of the meagre proportion of good agricultural land in the Highlands. Many are now justified in feeling that such large-scale industrialisation is not the answer. The Board has also given financial help through its grants and loans scheme to many lesser ventures, and it has spent a good deal of money in the Highlands.

In the efforts at rehabilitation after the Second World War, the position of the crofters was felt to be unsatisfactory, and the 1951 Taylor Commission of Inquiry took comprehensive stock of the position of crofting. It pointed out that the crofting legislation had imposed a rigidity on the crofting structure in the size of the crofts, many of which, dating back to the days of land-hunger and dire need, were too small, and in restrictions on the use of the common grazings for different purposes. It emphasised the insuperable difficulties of remoteness from markets and high cost of freight. The Crofters (Scotland) Act of 1955 enabled a re-appointed Crofters Commission to amalgamate crofts into viable holdings, and to organise grazings committees with specific powers and duties. The main anomalies persisted, however; for instance, the crofter, although he was a protected tenant, still had to provide his own house and buildings, though generous grants and loans from the Department of Agriculture helped him. In 1968 the Crofters Commission recommended the reform of crofting tenure to the Secretary of State for Scotland, proposing that crofters should acquire full rights of ownership. After party political battles, the Crofting Reform (Scotland) Act was entered on the statute book in 1976. It gives the crofter the opportunity of acquiring the ownership of his croft at a price based on the rental value rather than, for instance, the market price of agricultural land, giving him the full property rights in his house and inbye land. This legislation came at an appropriate time when some crofters by inheritance and purchase were enlarging crofts to make them into small farms.

In spite of the expenditure of large sums of public money and the extension of services, the authorities have only partially solved the problem.Anyone old enough to have visited the Islands from time to time during the past half-century or more must realise the changes; gone are the signs of extreme poverty and much that was characteristic of Island life, including the local styles of the houses. Better stock and cultivation are to be seen, but also more and more derelict or under-cultivated land, and absenteeism has become a problem. From the 1930s onwards transport by air, sea and road has been greatly improved, but this advance has not solved the problem of the spiralling costs of fares and freight charges. Freight charges to the Islands are now so high that these areas are becoming, in modern parlance, severely disadvantaged because they are remote from urban centres. Transport has, however, given much more scope to tourism, and remote islands and communitites now have vehicle ferries which are not so much a benefit to the residents as an encouragement to the tourist industry in the remoter areas.

The adverse conditions that affected the crofters also affected the upland farmers of the main parts of the Highlands. Owing to many factors such as changes in markets and prices, labour shortages and mechanisation, the size of a viable hill farm increased, leading to amalgamations and some marginal land being forced out of cultivation. The use of tractors for general farm work had become an established practice by the end of the Second World War. The whistle of the ploughman as he turned his meticulously exact furrows had given place to the rattle and mechanical power of the tractor. It was one of the last of the rural crafts and yet in the remoter Highlands it was not two hundred years old. The introduction of binders and hay balers has obviated the need for groups of communal workers at harvest and hay-making, and the introduction of clipping machines has done away with the larger gathering of farmers and shepherds of wider districts for the annual clipping of the sheep at every farm within convenient reach. The kind of livestock seen grazing in the fields demonstrates the changes that have taken place. Work-horses have disappeared and so have milking cows, for all the milk in rural areas and even some Islands is imported from specialised dairies in the low country. Imported breeds of stock from abroad have made their appearance. On a mechanised farm, the farmyard is no longer the safe and happy place where children played that must linger in the memories of older readers. Ponies, generally pastured on the rougher ground, themselves illustrate the changes wrought by a new period. Ponies were used for carrying game shot on the hill which is now often conveyed in highly specialised motor vehicles, and also for carrying peat from the moss, work now done by tractors. Ponies are now kept in considerable numbers for the new tourist attraction of pony trekking.

The management of the shootings, financially so important to the Highlands, has also changed. During the interlude between the Wars, it had become increasingly diffcult to obtain domestic help. Since the last War, the shooting tenants have no longer occupied the lodges for about nine or ten weeks during the season bringing up a large domestic staff and entertaining. Instead they come for a limited number of drives, or the lease of a moor may be syndicated or let for individual grouse drives. A great deal of cheerful bustle and a certain amount of money has been lost. Country clothes, tweeds and hand-knitted stockings, are not so much worn, and the highly skilled tailors and shoemakers for such clothes have disappeared. The kilt has become more and more a garment for ceremonious occasions and may be specially hired. The fashion among women for wearing tartan skirts that came in when, after the War, tartan cloth was again available, has been replaced by the wearing of trousers.

Tourism, closely linked with transport, has become of increasing importance to Highlanders. In scale, it varies from big business, as in the sports complex at Aviemore, to the 'Bed and Breakfast' signs that have proliferated as transport has developed. The growing road traffic, lorries as well as cars, has led to the drastic re-making of the roads, and improvements have been made in taking cars to the Islands. It will soon be forgotten how recent is the introduction of Youth Hostels and of 'hitch-hiking'. Caravans began to clutter up the old roads after the War — well-stocked with provisions, the caravanners, like the occupants of 'weekend cottages', are not good spenders in the Highlands. Buses bring people to the Highlands, but bus tours are incompatible with long-staying visitors. As tourism develops into bigger business, a smaller proportion of the supplies and the staff is local. It is, of course, a great advantage that people from the areas of greater earning power should spend some of their money in the Highlands, so far as they do not interefere with the amenities of the people who live, work and pay the rates there, but it would be of interest to know how the actual financial benefit to the Highlanders of the pre- and post-War tourist industries compare.

The development of transport by road to a large degree as well as by sea and air has been very marked. Unfortunately, since the Wars, the use of the railways has declined. The report by Dr Beeching to the British Railways Board in 1963 made sweeping proposals, and several lines in the Highlands, such as the one between Boat-of-Garten and Forres, have been closed. The Highlands are now linked with the south by air. Another development of service by air was the delivery of feed to inaccessible farms during severe winters which began with the bad winter of 1954-55. Such a service is now undertaken by helicopters and has extended to air-sea rescue missions off the coasts and in the hills, and to the transport to hospital care of emergency cases, especially from the Islands. At a time when more and more visitors come to the Highlands, the resident population is declining and less Gaelic is spoken.

Celtic studies, of course, proceeded at the Scottish universities, but a great deal of research has also been undertaken by foreigners, especially Scandinavian scholars. Not only has a certain number of books been written in Gaelic, but it is even more significant of a growing literacy in Gaelic that the periodical *Gairm*, first published in 1952, as well as the Gaelic section of *Life and Work*, the Church of Scotland's monthly magazine, should be widely read. Looking back through our period, one is struck by the growing importance that is attached to the actual speaking or singing voice. This has, no doubt, been much encouraged by advances and improvements in the recording apparatus which has come to be widely used since the last War.

One of the most valuable activities of the School of Scottish Studies, founded in 1951 as a Department of the University of Edinburgh and specially active in work upon Highland subjects, has been the recording and also the storing of verbal records of tradition, songs and local dialects so that they may be available in the future. In 1976 the British Broadcasting Corporation inaugurated B.B.C. Highland as a channel for local self-expression. Another post-War development is the increased interest in the actual setting of the country people's lives, their houses, implements and furnishings. A small number of folk museums (to use a generic term not very applicable to the Highlands) was set up by individuals at their own expense, but support is now given by trusts and local authorities.

In this book, we have tried to trace the stages in the development of the Highlands as a distinct, self-contained entity and that of the clans into closely integrated groups consisting of people of varying status but warmed by the ties of kinship and friendship. We have tried to enumerate the differing attempts which her people have made to wring a living from their beloved, beautiful, sterile and storm-ridden land. We have endeavoured to indicate the processes that are merging the old distinctive way of life of the Highlands into the wider one of contemporary society. In doing so, what has illuminated our work has been to recognise how, down the centuries, the Highland people consistently upheld the high standards (though individuals may often have failed to live up to them) of courage, selfless devotion, superiority to material discomfort, good breeding and a creative and active love of music and poetry. This is no mean heritage.

ABBREVIATED TITLES

A.P.S.	T. Thomson and C. Innes (edd.) *The Acts of the Parliaments of Scotland*, Edinburgh, 1814-1875.
N.S.A.	*New Statistical Account*, 15 Vols, Edinburgh, 1845.
O.S.A.	*Old Statistical Account*, 21 Vols, Edinburgh, 1791-1799.
P.S.A.S.	*Proceedings of the Society of Antiquaries of Scotland*, 1851-
R.M.S.	J. M. Thomson *et al* (edd.) *Registrum Magni Sigilli Regum Scotorum*, Edinburgh, 1882-1914.
R.P.C.	J. H. Burton *et al* (edd.), *The Register of the Privy Council of Scotland*, Edinburgh, 1877-
S.H.R.	*Scottish Historical Review*, 1903-1928, 1947-
T.G.S.I.	*Transactions of the Gaelic Society of Inverness*, 1871-

References

Period I

1. J. A. Balfour ed., *The Book of Arran* Vol. I, Arran Society of Glasgow, 1910, 205; Arthur Mitchell, *The Past in the Present*, Edinburgh, 1880, 249-254.
2. Martin Martin, *A Description of the Western Islands of Scotland*, 1703 (ed. Donald J. MacLeod, Stirling, 1934), 107.
3. William Mackay ed., *Records of the Presbyteries of Inverness and Dingwall 1643-1688*, Scottish History Society, Edinburgh, 1896, 279-283.
4. Joseph Anderson, *Scotland in Early Christian Times*, Edinburgh, 1881, 191-193.
5. Frank Forbes Mackay, *MacNeill of Carskey*, Edinburgh, 1955, 105; Arthur Mitchell, 'Superstitions in the North-West Highlands and Islands of Scotland, especially in relation to Lunacy', *P.S.A.S.* 4 (1860-62), 274.
6. George Henderson, *Survivals in Belief among the Celts*, Glasgow, 1911, 262-263; Lachlan Shaw, *The History of the Province of Moray*, Edinburgh, 1775, 240-241.
7. Calum I. MacLean, 'The Last Sheaf', *Scottish Studies* 8 (1964), 193-207; see also his 'Traditional Beliefs in Scotland', *Scottish Studies* 3 (1959), 189-200; John Gregorson Campbell, *Superstitions of the Highlands and Islands of Scotland*, Glasgow, 1900, 20.
8. *N.S.A.* 14 (1845), 82.
9. John Gregorson Campbell, *op. cit.*, Chapter 3.
10. *Ib.*, 46.
11. R. Angus Smith, 'Descriptive List of Antiquities near Loch Etive', *P.S.A.S.* 9 (1870-72), 409-414.
12. Martin Martin, *op. cit.*, 288.
13. G. F. Black, 'Scottish Charms and Amulets', *P.S.A.S.* 27 (1892-93), 442.
14. Eoin MacNeill, *Celtic Ireland*, Dublin, 1921, and *Phases of Irish History*, Dublin, 1919, 79.
15. Douglas Hyde, *A Literary History of Ireland*, New Edition, 1967, 164.
16. William Forbes Skene ed., *John of Fordun's Chronicle* Vol. I. Edinburgh, 1871, 42.
17. William J. Watson, *Place-Names of Ross and Cromarty*, Inverness, 1904, lvii; George Henderson, *The Norse Influence on Celtic Scotland*, Glasgow, 1910, 342; Alf Sommerfelt, 'The Norse Influence on Irish and Scottish Gaelic' in Brian O'Cuiv ed., *The Impact of the Scandinavian Invasions on the Celtic-speaking Peoples c.800-1100 AD*, Dublin, 1975, 76.
18. Lachlan Shaw, *op.cit*, 164; Rev. J. M. Joass, 'Notes on the Curachs and Ammirs in Ross-shire', *P.S.A.S.* 15 (1880-81), 179-80.
19. Alan Orr Anderson, *Early Sources of Scottish History* Vol. I, Edinburgh, 1922, cxv-cxix; Kenneth H. Jackson, *The Gaelic Notes in the Book of Deer*, Cambridge, 1972, 102-110.
20. John Stuart ed., *The Book of Deer*, Spalding Club, Aberdeen, 1869; Kenneth H. Jackson, *op.cit.*, 33; William J. Watson, *The Celtic Place-Names of Scotland*, Edinburgh, 1926, 407-414.
21. Alan Orr Anderson, *op.cit.*, 83.
22. John Bannerman, *Studies in the History of Dalriada*, Edinburgh, 1974, 27-68, 115; William J. Watson, *The Celtic Place-Names*, *op.cit.*, 122.
23. James Robertson, *General View of the Agriculture of the County of Perth*, Perth, 1799, 95-6; Angus MacLeod ed., *The Songs of Duncan Ban MacIntyre*, Scottish Gaelic Texts Society, Edinburgh, 1952, 122.
24. Douglas Hyde, *op.cit.*, 122-3.
25. H. F. McClintock, *Old Irish and Highland Dress*, Dundalk, 1943; G. M. Crowfoot, 'Two Textiles from the National Museum', *P.S.A.S.* 82 (1947-48), 227; A. S. Henshall, 'Early Textiles found in Scotland', *P.S.A.S.* 86 (1951-52), 6.

26. Joseph Anderson, *op.cit.*, Second Series, 1-34; Robert B. K. Stevenson, 'The Hunterston Brooch and Its Significance', *Medieval Archaeology* 18 (1974), 16-42.

27. Maj. Gen. David Stewart of Garth, *Sketches of the Present State of the Highlanders of Scotland* Vol. I, Edinburgh, 1822, 73-4; Henry Cockburn, *Circuit Journeys*, Edinburgh, 1889, 127.

28. Standish H. O'Grady, *Silva Gadelica*, Dublin, 1892, 120-21.

29. F. W. L. Thomas, 'Dunadd, the Place of Inauguration of the Dalriadic Kings', *P.S.A.S.* 13 (1878-79), 33-34; J. Hewat Craw, 'Excavations at Dunadd', *P.S.A.S.* 64 (1929-30), 111-126.

30. J. R. C. Hamilton, *Excavations at Jarlshof, Shetland*, Her Majesty's Stationery Office, 1956, Chapter 6.

31. David MacGibbon and Thomas Ross, *The Ecclesiastical Architecture of Scotland* Vol. I, Edinburgh, 1896, 86-90.

32. Francis C. Eeles, 'The Monymusk Reliquary', *P.S.A.S.* 68 (1933-34), 433.

33. Donald MacKinnon, *A Descriptive Catalogue of Gaelic Manuscripts*, Edinburgh, 1912, 323-24; Joseph Anderson, *op.cit.*, 146.

34. Donald MacKinnon, 'The Glenmasan Manuscript', *Celtic Review* 1 (1904-05), 3-17, 104-31, 208-29, 296-315; Alexander Carmichael, *Deirdire and the Lay of the Children of Uisne*, Edinburgh, 1905; Alexander Carmichael, *Carmina Gadelica* Vol. I, Edinburgh, 1972, 6-11.

35. R. L. Thompson ed., *Foirm na n-Uirrnuidheadh, The Book of Common Order*, Scottish Gaelic Texts Society, Edinburgh, 1970, 11.

36. Kenneth H. Jackson, 'The Duan Albannach', *S.H.R.* 36 (1957), 125-37.

37. Martin Martin, *op.cit.*, 99.

Period II

1. William Forbes Leith, *Life of St Margaret Queen of Scotland by Turgot, Bishop of St Andrews*, Edinburgh, 1884, 40.

2. R. L. Graeme Ritchie, *The Normans in Scotland*, Edinburgh, 1954, xi.

3. William Mackay, *Urquhart and Glenmoriston*, Inverness, 1893, 15-17; W. Douglas Simpson, *The Province of Mar*, Aberdeen, 1943, 115, and 'Rait Castle and Barevan Church, Nairnshire', *P.S.A.S.* 71 (1936-37), 98-115.

4. G. W. S. Barrow, 'The Earliest Stewarts and their Lands' in *The Kingdom of the Scots*, London, 1973, 337-61.

5. G. W. S. Barrow, *Regesta Regum Scottorum* Vol. II, 'The Acts of William I', Edinburgh, 1971, 198-99.

6. Peter McNeill and Ranald Nicholson edd., *An Historical Atlas of Scotland c.400-c.1600*, St Andrews, 1975, 27-28, 126-27.

7. A. M. Mackintosh, *The Mackintoshes and Clan Chattan*, Edinburgh, 1903, 10-14.

8. William Croft Dickinson, *The Sheriff Court Book of Fife, 1515-1522*, Scottish History Society, Edinburgh, 1928, 347-68.

9. *Registrum Episcopatus Moraviensis*, Bannatyne Club, Edinburgh, 1837, 183-87; William Croft Dickinson, *op.cit.*, xviii (note).

10. G. W. S. Barrow, 'The Judex' in *The Kingdom of the Scots*, London, 1973, 69-82.

11. William Forbes Skene ed., *op.cit.*, 294-95.

12. *A.P.S.* Vol. I (1124-1423), 325.

13. *Ib.*, 122, 663-65.

14. Lachlan Shaw, *op.cit.*, 105-7, 113-17; W. Douglas Simpson, 'The Early Castles of Mar', *P.S.A.S.* 63 (1928-29), 102-38; J. R. N. MacPhail ed., *Highland Papers* Vol. II (1240-1716), Scottish History Society, Edinburgh, 1916, 114-245.

15. *Registrum Monasterii De Passelet, 1163-1529*, Maitland Club, Edinburgh, 1832, 125-26, 129.

16. Archibald C. Lawrie, *Early Scottish Charters*, Glasgow, 1905, 171; G. W. S. Barrow, *Regesta Regum Scottorum* Vol. II, *op.cit.*, 184.

17. W. Douglas Simpson, 'The Doune of Invernochty', *P.S.A.S.* 53 (1918-19), 34-35; David MacGibbon and Thomas Ross, *The Castellated and Domestic Architecture of Scotland* Vol. I, Edinburgh, 1887, 278-80; Peter McNeill and Ranald Nicholson, *op.cit.*, 28-29, 128.

18. Alan Orr Anderson, *Scottish Annals from English Chroniclers A.D. 500-1286*, London, 1908, 197-202.

19. Joseph Stephenson ed., *Scalacronika : By Sir Thomas Gray of Heton, Knight*, Maitland Club, Edinburgh, 1836.

20. *A.P.S.* Vol. I (1124-1423), 465-66.

21. Francis C. Eeles, 'The Guthrie Bell and its Shrine', *P.S.A.S.* 60 (1925-26), 409-20; Joseph Anderson, *op.cit.*, 226; Joseph Robertson ed., *Collections for a History of the Shires of Aberdeen and Banff*, Spalding Club, Aberdeen, 1843, 505.

22. G. W. S. Barrow, *Regesta Regum Scottorum* Vol. II, *op.cit.*, 354, 453-54; Joseph Anderson, *op.cit.*, 210-11, 216-17, 241-43; David MacRoberts *Catalogue of Scottish Medieval Liturgical Books and Fragments*, Glasgow, 1953.

23. J. Graham Callander, 'Notes on a Casket of Cetacean Bone', *P.S.A.S.* 60 (1925-26), 105-17; Joseph Anderson, 'Notice of a Casket of Cetacean Bone', *P.S.A.S.* 20 (1885-86), 390-96.

24. Joseph Anderson, *op.cit.*, 145-46.

25. Kenneth H. Jackson, *The Gaelic Notes, op.cit.*, 31; Alan Orr Anderson, *Early Sources* Vol. II, *op.cit.*, 253-54; John Stuart ed., *The Book of Deer, op.cit.*, 90.

26. David MacGibbon and Thomas Ross, *The Ecclesiastical Architecture, op.cit.*, 220-23, 421-26.

27. Gordon Donaldson, 'Scottish Bishops' Sees before the reign of David I', *P.S.A.S.* 87 (1952-53), 106-17; Archibald C. Lawrie, *op.cit.*, 63; *Origines Parochiales Scotiae*, Bannatyne Club, Edinburgh, 1851-55.

28. G. W. S. Barrow, 'Pre-feudal Scotland : shires and thanes' in *The Kingdom of the Scots, op.cit.*, 53-64.

29. E. R. Lindsay and A. I. Cameron, *Calendar of Scottish Supplications to Rome, 1418-1422*, Scottish History Society, Edinburgh, 1934, 129.

30. Donald MacKinnon, *op.cit.*, 93-94.

31. Ian B. Cowan and David E. Easson, *Medieval Religious Houses, Scotland*, 2nd Edition, London, 1976, 114-21.

32. G. W. S. Barrow, *Regesta Regum Scottorum* Vol II, *op.cit.*, 146-49; W. A. Lindsay *et al.*, *Charters, Bulls and other Documents relating to the Abbey of Inchaffray*, Scottish History Society, Edinburgh, 1908, xli-xliv, xlix.

33. E. R. Lindsay and A. I. Cameron, *Calendar of Scottish Supplications, op.cit.*, 137.

34. I. F. Grant, *Highland Folk Ways*, London, 1961, 254; A. and A. MacDonald, *The Poems of Alexander MacDonald*, Inverness, 1924, 370-401; B. R. S. Megaw, 'An Eighteenth Century Representation of a Highland Boat', *Scottish Studies* 5 (1961), 96-99.

35. Donald Gregory, *The History of the Western Highlands and Isles of Scotland*, 2nd Edition, London, 1881, 170; J. G. Mackay, 'Social Life in Skye from Legend and Story — Part III', *T.G.S.I.* 30 (1919-1922), 16-17; W. C. MacKenzie, *The Highlands and Islands of Scotland*, Edinburgh, 1949, 110, 168; John P. MacLean, *A History of the Clan MacLean*, Cincinnati, 1889, 337.

36. W. D. H. Sellar, 'The origins and ancestry of Somerled', *S.H.R.* 45 (1966), 123-42; Derick S. Thomson, 'The Harlaw Brosnachadh' in J. Carney and D. Greene edd., *Celtic Studies. Essays in Memory of Angus Matheson*, New York, 1968, 160-61.

37. William Forbes Skene, *Celtic Scotland* Vol. III, Edinburgh, 1880, 303-306; J. R. N. MacPhail ed., *Highland Papers* Vol. I (1337-1680), Scottish History Society, Edinburgh, 1914, 5-72; Alexander Cameron, *Reliquiae Celticae* Vol. II, Inverness, 1894, 148-309; A. O. Anderson, *Early Sources* Vol. II, *op.cit.*, 253-58; A. A. M. Duncan and A. L. Brown, 'Argyll and the Isles in the Earlier Middle Ages', *P.S.A.S.* 90 (1956-57), 192-220.

38. A. M. Mackintosh, *The Mackintoshes, op.cit.*, 1-6.

Period III

1. Michael Starforth, *An Official Short History of the Clan MacDougall*, Glasgow, n.d., 11-21.

2. W. M. MacKenzie ed., *The Bruce*, London, 1909, 201.

3. Charles Fraser-Mackintosh, *Minor Septs of Clan Chattan*, Glasgow, 1898.

4. E. W. M. Balfour-Melville, *James I, King of Scots*, London, 1936, 164-65, 284.

5. Robert L. Mackay, *The House and Clan of Mackay*, Edinburgh, 1829, 5.

6. William Mackay ed., *The Wardlaw Manuscript*, Scottish History Society, Edinburgh, 1905, 174-75.

7. William Fraser, *The Chiefs of Clan Grant* Vol. I, 'Memoirs', Edinburgh, 1883, 22-24.

8. William Matheson, 'Traditions of the MacKenzies', *T.G.S.I.* 39-40 (1942-1950), 212.

9. I. F. Grant, *The Clan Donald*, Edinburgh, 1952, 18-21.

10. W. C. MacKenzie, *The History of the Outer Hebrides*, Paisley, 1903, 85-91; I. F. Grant, *The Lordship of the Isles*, Edinburgh, 1935, 180-85; William Mackay, *Sidelights on Highland History*, Inverness, 1925, 281-302.

11. The Earl of Cromartie, *A Highland History*, Berkhamsted, Herts, 1979, 106.

12. E. M. Barron, *Inverness and the MacDonalds*, Inverness, 1930, 21-57.

13. Andrew Lang ed., *The Highlands of Scotland in 1750*, Edinburgh, 1898, 52.

14. *R.M.S. 1424-1513*, 462, 484-85.

15. William J. Watson, *Rosg Gaidhlig*, 2nd Edition, Glasgow, 1929, 182-83; *N.S.A.* 7 (1845), 384.

16. J. R. N. MacPhail ed., *Highland Papers* I, *op.cit.*, 24-25.

17. *Ib.*, 23-24.

18. *Ib.*, 45-46.

19. Derick S. Thomson, 'The MacMhuirich Bardic Family', *T.G.S.I.* 43 (1960-63), 276-304; Henry MacKenzie ed., *Report of the Committee of the Highland Society on Ossian*, Edinburgh, 1805, 278.

20. Sir Robert Gordon, *A Genealogical History of the Earldom of Sutherland*, Edinburgh, 1813, 268.

21. I. F. Grant, *The Lordship*, *op.cit.*, 409; Martin Martin, *op.cit.*, 167, 290; J. R. N. MacPhail ed., *Highland Papers* Vol. III (1662-1667), Scottish History Society, Edinburgh, 1920, 78; Andrew McKerral, *Kintyre in the Seventeenth Century*, Edinburgh, 1948, 11; J. R. N. MacPhail ed., *Highland Papers* I, *op.cit.*, 312, 314; Charles Fraser-Mackintosh, *Antiquarian Notes (Second Series)*, Inverness, 1897, 164-66; J. T. Clark ed., *Macfarlane's Genealogical Collections* Vol. I, Scottish History Society, Edinburgh, 1900, 212.

22. J. R. N. MacPhail ed., *Highland Papers* II, *op.cit.*, 9-10.

23. K. A. Steer and J. W. M. Bannerman, *Late Medieval Monumental Sculpture in the West Highlands*, Her Majesty's Stationery Office, Edinburgh, 1977, 167-87; J. S. Richardson, 'The Campbell of Lerags Cross at Kilbride near Oban, with a Note on Cross-heads of late Medieval Date in the West Highlands', *P.S.A.S.* 61 (1926-27), 143-162.

24. *A.P.S.* Vol. II (1424-1567), 168.

25. J. L. Campbell and Derick Thomson, *Edward Lhuyd in the Scottish Highlands 1699-1700*, Oxford University Press, 1963, Plate VIII.

26. Angus Graham, 'Some Carved Stones from Argyll', *P.S.A.S.* 60 (1925-26), 123-32; R. A. S. MacAlister, *Ecclesiastical Vestments : Their Development and History*, 1896.

27. J. R. N. MacPhail ed., *Highland Papers* II, *op.cit.*, 92.

28. *Ib.*, 22-23, and *Highland Papers* I, *op.cit.*, 210-11; John Major, *A History of Greater Britain*, Scottish History Society, Edinburgh, 1892, 361-62.

29. William Forbes Skene, *Celtic Scotland* Vol. III, *op.cit.*, 437-38.

30. William J. Watson ed., *Scottish Verse from the Book of the Dean of Lismore*, Scottish Gaelic Texts Society, Edinburgh, 1937, 2-3; Neil Ross ed., *Heroic Poetry*

from the Book of the Dean of Lismore, Scottish Gaelic Texts Society, Edinburgh, 1939.

31. William J. Watson, *Bardachd Ghaidhlig*, An Comunn Gaidhealach, Inverness, 1976, xxxvi-liv; Douglas Hyde, *op.cit.*, 273-74.
32. J. R. N. MacPhail ed., *Highland Papers* II, *op.cit.*, 73.
33. J. R. N. MacPhail ed., *Highland Papers* I, *op.cit.*, 41-43; William J. Watson, *Rosg Gaidhlig op.cit.*, 99-102.
34. Alexander Carmichael, *Carmina Gadelica* Vol. II, Edinburgh, 1972, 292; Alexander MacLeod ed., *Sar Orain*, Glasgow, 1933, 126-27.
35. H. F. Hore, 'Irish Bardism in 1561', *The Ulster Journal of Archaeology* 6 (1858), 167.
36. Donald MacKinnon, *Gaelic Manuscripts*, *op.cit.*, 5-71, 72-105, 298-301.
37. Rev. James MacDougall, *Waifs and Strays of Celtic Tradition* Vol. 3, London, 1891, 30-32, 44-46.
38. *Registrum Episcopatus Moraviensis*, *op.cit.*, 382-83.

Period IV

1. G. Gregory Smith ed., *The Book of Islay*, Edinburgh, 1895, 103, 112-113, 191-92, 199-230.
2. J. R. N. MacPhail ed., *Highland Papers* III, *op.cit.*, 159-61.
3. G. Gregory Smith, *op.cit.*, 62-65; A. M. Mackintosh, *The Mackintoshes*, *op.cit.*, 182-83; I. F. Grant, *The MacLeods. The History of a Clan, 1200-1956*, London, 1959, 192.
4. Donald Gregory, *op.cit.*, 270-72, 278-80, 290-99; I. F. Grant, *The MacLeods*, *op.cit.*, 192-97, 202-207.
5. *Collectanea de Rebus Albanicis*, Iona Club, Edinburgh, 1847, 115.
6. *R.P.C.* Vol. IX (1610-1613), 26-30; *Collectanea*, *op.cit.*, 120; *A.P.S.* Vol. IV (1593-1625), 548; Andrew McKerral, *Kintyre*, *op.cit.*, 138.
7. J. R. N. MacPhail ed., *Highland Papers* III, *op.cit.*, 295; *Collectanea*, *op.cit.*, 48-49.
8. G. Gregory Smith, *op.cit.*, 335, 424-29; Herbert Campbell ed., 'The Manuscript History of Craignish' in *Miscellany of the Scottish History Society* Vol. IV, Scottish History Society, Edinburgh, 1926, 248-49; Donald Gregory, *op.cit.*, 405-12.
9. J. R. N. MacPhail ed., *Highland Papers* III, *op.cit.*, 132; *Collectanea op.cit.*, 128-29.
10. G. Gregory Smith, *op.cit.*, 39, 41-43, 121-22.
11. J. R. N. MacPhail ed., *Highland Papers* III, *op.cit.*, 68-84, 302.
12. J. T. Clark ed., *Macfarlane's Genealogical Collections*, *op.cit.*, 235-37.
13. Donald Gregory, *op.cit.*, 107-108, 130; I. F. Grant, *The MacLeods*, *op.cit.*, 135-37.
14. John Stuart ed., *Spalding Club Miscellany* II, Spalding Club, Aberdeen, 1842, 83-84.
15. William Mackay, *Urquhart and Glenmoriston*, *op.cit.*, 85-87, 96-99, 105-12.
16. Sir Robert Gordon, *op.cit.*, 253-55.
17. *Collectanea*, *op.cit.*, 197-98; Cosmo Innes ed., *The Black Book of Taymouth*, Bannatyne Club, Edinburgh, 1855, 177-262.
18. Andrew Lang, *op.cit.*, 116.
19. *R.P.C.* Vol. IV (1599-1604), 425.
20. William Fraser, *The Chiefs of Grant*, *op.cit*, 99.
21. Donald Gregory, *op.cit.*, 157-63.
22. I. F. Grant, *The MacLeods*, *op.cit.*, 117-25.
23. William Forbes Skene, *Celtic Scotland* Vol. III, *op.cit.*, 429.
24. A. M. Mackintosh, *op.cit.*, 217-20, 267; I. F. Grant, *The MacLeods*, *op.cit.*, 192-96, 201-207.
25. *A.P.S.* Vol. III (1567-1592), 461-67.
26. Andrew McKerral, 'West Highland Mercenaries in Ireland', *S.H.R.* 30 (1951) 1-14; *Collectanea*, *op.cit.*, 28.

27. *R.M.S.* Vol. II (1424-1513), 204-205; Cosmo Innes ed., *The Black Book, op.cit.*, 420.
28. Joseph Bain ed., *Calendar of State Papers Relating to Scotland and Mary Queen of Scots* Vol. II (1563-1569), Edinburgh, 1900, 13; *Collectanea, op.cit.*, Appendix, 39.
29. H. F. McClintock, *Old Irish and Highland Dress, op.cit.*, 123.
30. Francis Collinson, *The Bagpipe*, London, 1975, 90, 140-41; George Penny, *Traditions of Perth*, Perth, 1836, 39.
31. Angus Macpherson, *A Highlander looks back*, Oban, n.d., 66.
32. J. P. Grant, 'Canntaireachd' in B. Seton and J. Grant, *The Pipes of War*, Glasgow, 1920, 179-90.
33. William J. Watson, *Bardachd, op.cit.*, xxxv, 242, 244-49, 259-62.

Period V Part 1

1. William Mackay ed., *The Wardlaw Manuscript, op.cit*, 289.
2. James Allardyce ed., *Historical Papers Relating to the Jacobite Period, 1699-1750* Vol. I, New Spalding Club, Aberdeen, 1895, 55-58, 132.
3. *Memoirs of Sir Ewen Cameron of Locheill*, Abbotsford Club, Edinburgh, 1842, 101, 188-89; *Collectanea, op.cit.*, Appendix, 42.
4. J. R. N. MacPhail ed., *Highland Papers* I, *op.cit.*, 245-311, 323-33.
5. William Mackay ed., *The Wardlaw Manuscript, op.cit.*, 454; A. M. Mackintosh, *op.cit.*, 244-67.
6. *R.P.C.* 2nd Series Vol. V (1633-1635), 503; Charles Fraser-Mackintosh, *Antiquarian Notes*, 2nd Edition, Stirling, 1913, 194-96.
7. I. H. Mackay Scobie, 'The Highland Independent Companies of 1745-1747', *Journal of the Society for Army Historical Research* 20 (1941), 4-12; I. F. Grant, *Highland Folk Ways, op. cit.*, 334.
8. J. T. Clark ed., *Macfarlane's Genealogical Collections, op.cit.*, 68; J. R. N. MacPhail ed., *Highland Papers* I, *op.cit.*, 198-239, and *Highland Papers* II, *op.cit.*, 312-23.
9. Duncan Warrand ed., *More Culloden Papers* Vol. IV (1744-1746), Inverness, 1929, 97; Frederick A. Pottle and Charles H. Bennett, *Boswell's Journal of a Tour to the Hebrides*, London, 1936, 331.
10. A. M. Mackintosh, *op.cit.*, 426, 498.
11. James Allardyce, *op.cit.*, 132-33, 174.
12. Edward Burt, *Letters from a Gentleman in the North of Scotland* Vol. II, Edinburgh 1876, 105-108; Niall D. Campbell, 'An Old Tiree Rental of the Year 1662', *S.H.R.* 9 (1911-1912), 343-44.
13. William Mackay ed., *The Wardlaw Manuscript, op.cit.*, 252, 296, 309; Charles Fraser-Mackintosh, *Antiquarian Notes, op.cit.*, 23-25.
14. William Fraser, *The Earls of Cromartie* Vol I, Edinburgh, 1876, xxv-xxxvii; *Collectanea, op.cit.*, 20-21; Herbert Campbell ed., 'The Manuscript History of Craignish', *op.cit.*, 224-26.
15. William Mackay ed., *The Wardlaw Manuscript, op.cit.*, 253, and *Urquhart and Glenmoriston, op.cit.*, 563-69.
16. G. Gregory Smith, *op.cit.*, 270; William Forbes Skene, *Celtic Scotland, op.cit.*, 318; J. R. N. MacPhail ed., *Highland Papers* I, *op.cit.*, 198-239.
17. William Mackay ed., *The Wardlaw Manuscript, op.cit.*, 250.
18. J. R. N. MacPhail ed., *Highland Papers* I, *op.cit.*, 219.
19. William Matheson ed., *The Blind Harper. The Songs of Roderick Morrison and his Music*, Scottish Gaelic Texts Society, Edinburgh, 1970, 58-73.
20. William Mackintosh, *An Essay on Ways and Means of Inclosing, Fallowing, Planting Etc. in Scotland*, Edinburgh, 1729, 229-31.
21. I. F. Grant, *Along a Highland Road*, London 1980, Chap 4.
22. I. F. Grant, *The Social and Economic Development of Scotland Before 1603*, Edinburgh, 1930, 309-11.

23. *Miscellany of the Scottish Burgh Records Society*, Edinburgh, 1881, 26; *Collectanea, op.cit.*, 151-52.
24. William Mackay, *Life in Inverness in the Sixteenth Century*, Aberdeen, 1911, 9, 12.
25. *R.P.C.* Vol. V (1592-1599), 10; Donald W. Stewart, *Old and Rare Scottish Tartans*, Edinburgh, 1893, 29.
26. I. F. Grant, *The Social and Economic Development, op.cit.*, 545-47; J. R. N. MacPhail ed., *Highland Papers* II, *op.cit.*, 30; Charles Fraser-Mackintosh, *Antiquarian Notes, op.cit.*, 30-31.
27. *Collectanea, op.cit.*, 153-54.
28. A. R. B. Haldane, *The Drove Roads of Scotland*, Edinburgh, 1952, Chaps 1, 2 and 8; *O.S.A.* 3 (1793), 335.
29. William Mackay ed., *the Wardlaw Manuscript, op.cit.*, 324, 487-89; George Bain, *The Lordship of Petty*, Nairn, 1925, 62-71; Sorley MacLean, 'Domhnall Donn of Bohuntin', *T.G.S.I.* 42 (1953-59), 91-110.
30. William Fraser, *The Chiefs of Grant* Vol. II, *op.cit.*, 76; William Alexander, *Northern Rural Life in the Eighteenth Century*, Edinburgh, 1877, 63-66; *R.P.C.* Vol. VI (1599-1604), 500-501.
31. *O.S.A.* 8 (1793), 500; *O.S.A.* 2 (1792), 457; Robert Chambers, *Domestic Annals of Scotland* Vol. III, Edinburgh, 1861, 616-18; J. T. Clark ed., *Macfarlane's Genealogical Collections, op.cit.*, 307; James Allardyce, *op.cit.*, 135-36.
32. G. Gregory Smith, *op.cit.*, 365-67, 456-67; Alasdair Cameron, 'A Page from the Past : The Lead Mines at Strontian', *T.G.S.I.* 38 (1937-41), 444-52.
33. Andrew McKerral, *op.cit.*, 132-33, 147; William Mackay ed., *The Letter Book of Bailie John Steuart of Inverness 1715-1752*, Scottish History Society Edinburgh, 1915.
34. Donald Gregory, *op.cit.*, 395; *R.P.C.* Vol. X (1613-1616), 777.
35. Andrew McKerral, *op.cit.*, 145; Martin Martin, *op.cit.*, 85, 86-87, 143; *Collectanea, op.cit.*, Appendix, 43; R. Scott-Moncrieff, 'Notes on the Early Use of Aqua Vitae in Scotland', *P.S.A.S.* 50 (1915-16), 266.
36. Robert Pitcairn, *Criminal Trials in Scotland 1488-1624* Vol. III, Bannatyne Club Edinburgh, 1833, 5, 9.
37. William Mackay, 'Education in the Highlands in Olden Times', *T.G.S.I.* 27 (1908-11), 252; William Mackay ed., *The Wardlaw Manuscript, op.cit.*, 192-93; A. M. Mackintosh, *op.cit.*, 283-84.
38. *R.P.C.* Vol. X (1613-1616), 671, 777; *R.P.C.* Vol. IX (1610-1613), 28-29.
39. Cosmo Innes, *Sketches of Early Scottish History,* Edinburgh, 1861, 371.
40. *A.P.S.* Vol. VII (1661-1669), 290.
41. Duncan C. MacTavish ed., *Minutes of the Synod of Argyll 1639-1653*, Scottish History Society, Edinburgh, 1943, xvi-xvii, 193.
42. *An Account of the Society in Scotland for Propagating Christian Knowledge from its commencement in 1709*, Edinburgh, 1774, 54; William Mackay, 'Education in the Highlands', *op.cit.*, 267.
43. Rev. Donald MacLean, 'The Life and Literary Labours of the Rev. Robert Kirk of Aberfoyle', *T.G.S.I.* 31 (1927), 328-66; *A.P.S.* Vol. VI Pt 1 (1643-1647), 195; *A.P.S.* Vol. VI Pt 2 (1648-1660), 766, 875.
44. Arthur Mitchell ed., *Macfarlane's Geographical Collections* Vol. II, Scottish History Society, Edinburgh, 1907, 217; *O.S.A.* 14 (1795), 205.
45. Dom Odo Blundell, *The Catholic Highlands of Scotland*, London, 1909; J. L. Campbell, 'Some Notes and Comments on "The Irish Franciscan Mission to Scotland" ', *Innes Review* 4 (1953), 42-48; J. R. N. MacPhail ed., *Highland Papers* III, *op.cit.*, 58.
46. I. F. Grant, *The Lordship, op.cit.*, 414; I. F. Grant, *The MacLeods, op.cit.*, 162-63; Martin Martin, *op.cit.*, 155, 238-39; Alexander Carmichael, *Carmina Gadelica*, Vol. II *op.cit.*, 78-80; Thomas Garnett, *Observations on a Tour through the Highlands and part of the Western Isles of Scotland* Vol. I, London, 1800, 148, 203.

Period V Part 2

1. William J. Watson, 'Classic Gaelic Poetry', *T.G.S.I.* 29 (1914-19), 207; Alexander Cameron, *Reliquiae Celticae* Vol. II, *op.cit.*, 264-75; J. Carmichael Watson ed., *Gaelic Songs of Mary MacLeod* Scottish Gaelic Texts Society, Edinburgh, 1965, 88-95.
2. Alexander Cameron, *Reliquiae Celticae* Vol. II, *op.cit.*, 238-40.
3. Alan Bruford, 'A Lost MacMhuirich Manuscript', *Scottish Gaelic Studies* 10 (1965), 158-61.
4. Alexander Cameron, *Reliquiae Celticae* Vol. I, *op.cit.*, 121-22.
5. J. L. Campbell and Derick Thomson, *Edward Lhuyd*, *op.cit.*, 33; John MacKenzie, *The Beauties of Gaelic Poetry*, 4th Edition, Edinburgh, 1877, 77.
6. Donald MacKinnon, 'The Fernaig Manuscript', *T.G.S.I.* 11 (1884-85), 323-24, 336.
7. Annie M. MacKenzie ed., *Orain Iain Luim. The Songs of John MacDonald, Bard of Keppoch*, Scottish Gaelic Texts Society, Edinburgh, 1964, 24-25.
8. I. F. Grant, *The MacLeods*, *op.cit.*, 188-90, 218.
9. Donald MacKinnon, *Gaelic Manuscripts*, *op.cit.*, 142-46; J. F. Campbell, *Popular Tales* Vol. III, *op.cit.*, Edinburgh, 1862, 185-281.
10. Alexander MacLean Sinclair, *Gaelic Bards*, Charlottetown, 1890, 161; Rev. W. Forsyth, *In the Shadow of Cairngorm*, Inverness, 1900, 275-76; J. R. N. MacPhail ed., *Highland Papers* I, *op.cit.*, 280; William J. Watson, *Bardachd*, *op.cit.*, 131-33.
11. Francis Collinson, *op.cit.*, 168-69, 170-71; B. Seton and J. Grant, *op.cit.*, 14; W. L. Manson, *The Highland Bagpipe*, Paisley, 1901, 113-14; William Mackay ed., *The Wardlaw Manuscript*, *op.cit.*, 379-80.
12. J. L. Campbell ed., *A Collection of Highland Rites and Customs*, The Folklore Society, Cambridge, 1975, 49; I. F. Grant, *The MacLeods*, *op.cit.*, 165-66, 377, 490; Francis Collinson, *op.cit.*, 98.
13. James Philip, *The Grameid*, Scottish History Society, Edinburgh, 1888, 136, 140, 143.
14. James Allardyce, *op.cit.*, 339; James Roy of Whitehaven, *A Compleat History of the Rebellion*, York, 1749, 391-62.
15. Donald C. Stewart, *The Setts of the Scottish Tartans*, 2nd Edition, London, 1974, 4-5; Donald C. Stewart and J. Charles Thompson, *Scotland's Forged Tartans*, Edinburgh, 1980.
16. Donald W. Stewart, *op.cit.*, 27.
17. *Ib.*, 29.
18. James Allardyce, *op.cit.*, 288.
19. *O.S.A.* 2 (1792), 390-91.
20. *Collectanea*, *op.cit.*, Appendix, 51.
21. J. R. N. MacPhail ed., *Highland Papers* III, *op.cit.*, 9.
22. J. R. N. MacPhail ed., *Highland Papers* I, *op.cit.*, 317; Herbert Campbell, 'The Manuscript History of Craignish', *op.cit.*, 243.
23. James Allardyce, *op.cit.*, 160.
24. J. R. N. MacPhail ed., *Highland Papers* II, *op.cit.*, 43.
25. Angus MacLeod ed., *The Songs of Duncan Ban MacIntyre*, *op. cit.*, 226-29.
26. J. R. N. MacPhail ed., *Highland Papers* IV (1296-1752), Scottish History Society, Edinburgh, 1934, 123.

Period VI Part 1

1. A.H. Millar, 'Note on the Proclamation for Disarming of the Highlands in 1746', *P.S.A.S.* 30 (1895-96), 210; Dugald Mitchell, *History of the Highlands and Gaelic Scotland*,Paisley, 1900, 663.
2. James Allardyce, *op.cit.*, 501; Colonel John MacDonell of Scottos, *Spanish John*, Edinburgh, 1931, 54.

3. Sir Aeneas Mackintosh, *Notes Descriptive and Historical*, Inverness, 1892, 30.
4. I.H. Mackay Scobie, *An Old Highland Fencible Corps*, Edinburgh, 1914, 2, 6-7.
5. A.J. Youngson, *After the Forty-Five*, Edinburgh, 1973, 43-44.
6. John MacInnes, *The Brave Sons of Skye*, Edinburgh, 1899.
7. Kenneth H. Jackson ed., *Celtica*, National Library of Scotland, Edinburgh, 1967, 14-23; Hugh and John MacCallum, *An Original Collection of the Poems of Ossian*, Montrose, 1816, xxxviii.
8. Derick S. Thomson, *The Gaelic Sources of Macpherson's 'Ossian'*, Aberdeen University Studies No 130, 1952.
9. Derick S. Thomson, 'Bogus Gaelic Literature c.1750-c.1820', *Transactions of the Gaelic Society of Glasgow* 5 (1956-57), 180-81.
10. James Holloway and Lindsay Errington, *The Discovery of Scotland*, Her Majesty's Stationery Office, 1978, 103-18.
11. *Parliamentary Papers* XXXVII, (1846) 497-507.
12. Charles Fraser-Mackintosh, *Minor Septs*, *op.cit.*, 26.
13. Rev. W. Forsyth, *op.cit.*, 258-62; W. Ferguson, 'Dingwall Burgh Politics and the Parliamentary Franchise in the Eighteenth Century', *S.H.R.* 38 (1959), 89-108; James Fergusson,' "Making Interest" in Scottish County Elections', *S.H.R.* 26 (1947), 119-33.
14. E. R. Cregeen, 'The Tacksmen and their Successors. A Study of Tenurial Reorganisation in Mull, Morvern and Tiree in the Early Eighteenth Century', *Scottish Studies* 13 (1969), 93-144; E.R. Cregeen, 'The Changing Role of the House of Argyll in the Scottish Highlands' in N. T. Phillipson and R. Mitchison edd., *Scotland in the Age of Improvement*, Edinburgh, 1970, 5-23.
15. Margaret I. Adam, 'The Highland Emigration of 1770', *S.H.R.* 16 (1919), 280-93.
16. Hugh Barron, 'Books belonging to a Highland Tacksman', *Scottish Gaelic Studies* 12 (1971), 56-58; Thomas Pennant, *A Tour in Scotland in 1769*, 5th Edition, London, 1790, 186; Colonel John MacDonell of Scottos, *op.cit.*, 51.
17. William Marshall, *General View of the Agriculture of the Central Highlands*, London, 1794, 30.
18. I. F. Grant, *The MacLeods*, *op.cit.*, 507, 573-75; Donald Macdonald, *Lewis. A History of the Island*, Edinburgh, 1978, 39-43.
19. Sir Aeneas Mackintosh, *op.cit.*, 36, 44.
20. Hugh Miller, *Memoir of William Forsyth Esq., A Scotch Merchant of the Eighteenth Century*, London, 1839, 15.
21. Louis Simond, *Journal of a Tour and Residence in Great Britain During the Years 1810 and 1811* Vol I, Edinburgh, 1817, 435.
22. Hugh Miller, *Tales and Sketches*, Edinburgh, 1863, 137.
23. Sir John Sinclair, *General View of the Agriculture of the Northern Islands of Scotland*, London, 1795, 43; *N.S.A.* 14 (1845), 110.
24. H. MacDougall of MacDougall, *Island of Kerrera. Mirror of History*, Oban, 1979, 29-33.
25. E. R. Cregeen, 'The Tacksmen and their Successors' *op.cit.*, 94-135; William Mackay, *Urquhart and Glenmoriston*, *op.cit.*, 443.
26. I. F. Grant, *Everyday Life on an Old Highland Farm, 1769-1782*, London 1924, 44, 216; Sir John Sinclair, *General View*, *op.cit.*, 39.
27. I. F. Grant, *Along A Highland Road*, *op.cit.*, 85-88; H. MacDougall of MacDougall, *op.cit.*, 30.
28. M. L. Parry, 'Changes in the Extent of Improved Farmland' in M. L. Parry and T.R. Slater, *The Making of the Scottish Countryside*, London, 1980, 183; Victor Gaffney, 'Summer Shealings', *S.H.R.* 38 (1959), 20-35.
29. James Barron, *The Northern Highlands in the Nineteenth Century* Vol. II (1825-1841), Inverness, 1907, 98-99, 273-74; Malcolm Gray, *The Highland Economy*, Edinburgh, 1957, 124-38.
30. Malcolm Gray, *op.cit.*, 86-104; Charles Fraser-Mackintosh, *Antiquarian Notes (Second Series)*, *op.cit.*, 131, 364-65; James Barron, *The Northern Highlands*, *op.cit.*, Inverness, 1903, 122.

31. Margaret I. Adam, 'The Causes of the Highland Emigrations of 1783-1803', *S.H.R.* 17 (1920), 74; Charles Fraser-Mackintosh, *Antiquarian Notes (Second Series)*, *op.cit.*, 130-31.
32. Eric Richards, *The Leviathan of Wealth*, London, 1973.
33. Angus MacLeod, *op.cit.*, 346-49; Sorley MacLean, 'The Poetry of the Clearances', *T.G.S.I.* 38 (1937-41), 293-324.
34. *N.S.A.* 15 (1845), 74-81.
35. David Murray, *The York Buildings Company*, Glasgow, 1883, 55-63; Henry Hamilton, *An Economic History of Scotland in the Eighteenth Century*, Oxford, 1963, 189-92.
36. A. R. B. Haldane, *New Ways Through the Glens*, Edinburgh, 1962, 31-35, 119.
37. A. J. Youngson, *op.cit.*, 109-13; Jean Dunlop, *The British Fisheries Society*, Edinburgh, 1981.
38. I. F. Grant, *Highland Folk Ways*, *op.cit.*, 270-76; Donald Macdonald, *Lewis*, *op.cit.*, 94-95, 99.
39. I. F. Grant, *Highland Folk Ways*, *op.cit.*, 222-26; William Mackay, *Urquhart and Glenmoriston*, *op.cit.*, 451-52, 554-55.
40. T. C. Smout, 'The Landowner and the Planned Village in Scotland 1730-1830' in N. T. Phillipson and R. Mitchison edd., *op.cit.*, 73-106; Victor Gaffney, *The Lordship of Strathavon : Tomintoul under the Gordons*, Spalding Club, Aberdeen, 1960, 34-61; Douglas G. Lockhart, 'Scottish Village Plans. A Preliminary Analysis', *Scottish Geographical Magazine* 96 (1980), 141-57.

Period VI Part 2

1. John Graham Dalyell, *Musical Memoirs of Scotland, With Historical Annotations*, Edinburgh, 1849, 94-95.
2. Alexander Ramsay, *History of the Highland and Agricultural Society of Scotland*, Edinburgh, 1879, 48-50, 132-38, 160-73, 481-90.
3. Mairi A. MacDonald, 'History of the Gaelic Society of Inverness from 1871-1971', *T.G.S.I.* 46 (1969-70), 1-21.
4. J. L. Campbell, *Highland Songs of the Forty-Five*, Edinburgh, 1933, xxiv-xxv; William J. Watson, *Bardachd*, *op.cit.*, 25-29, 115.
5. William Matheson, *The Songs of John MacCodrum*, Scottish Gaelic Texts Society, Edinburgh, 1938, xxiii-xxv; *N.S.A.* 14 (1845), 168.
6. Donald John MacLeod, 'The Poetry of Robb Donn Mackay', *Scottish Gaelic Studies* 12 (1971), 3-21; *Songs and Poems in the Gaelic Language by Robert Mackay*, Inverness, 1829, 332; Hew Morrison, 'Ministers of the Presbytery of Tongue 1726-63', *T.G.S.I.* 11 (1884-85), 293-310.
7. Derick Thomson, *An Introduction to Gaelic Poetry*, London, 1974, 236-37, 239-45.
8. J. R. N. MacPhail ed., *Highland Papers* III, *op.cit.*, 36-38.
9. John Stoddart, *Remarks on local scenery and manners in Scotland during the years 1799 and 1800* Vol I, London, 1801, 133; I. F. Grant, *Highland Folk Ways*, *op.cit.*, 352; Alexander Carmichael, *Carmina Gadelica* Vol. I, *op.cit.*, 206-207.
10. Henry George Farmer, *A History of Music in Scotland*, London, 1947, 233, 341-44.
11. *Journal of the Folk Song Society* 16 (1911) vi.
12. Margaret F. Shaw, *Folksongs and Folklore of South Uist*, 2nd Edition, Oxford, 1977, 268.
13. J.F. Campbell, *Popular Tales* Vol. I, *op.cit.* xii-xv, xxxiii, xxix-xxx.
14. John MacKechnie ed., *The Dewar Manuscripts* Vol. I. Glasgow, 1963, 46-50.
15. *Journal of the Folk Song Society*, *op.cit.*, 146; Ethel Bassin, *The Old Songs of Skye. Frances Tolmie and her Circle*, London, 1977, 80-83.

Period VII

1. *Duke of Argyll v. Campbell*, 1912, Session Cases, 458.
2. *Maclean of Ardgour v. Maclean* 1941, Session Cases, 613; *Stewart Mackenzie v. Fraser-Mackenzie*, 1922, Session Cases (House of Lords), 39.
3. Donald Macdonald, *Lewis, op.cit.*, 156.
4. *Ib*, 178-88.

Index

Caithness, 15, 37, 43-44, 55, 114, 115,
118, 236, 237, 271
Caledonian Canal, 234
Calp, feudal casualty, 111, 118, 123, 146,
160
Camanachd, shinty, 248
Camerons, 120, 123, 124, 137, 142,
145-146, 159, 183, 184, 208, 267
Campbell, John Francis, of Islay
(1822-1885), 4, 28, 176, 180, 213,
259-261
Campbell of Breadalbane, 7, 111, 118,
190, 204, 222
Campbell of Cawdor, 108, 111, 122, 145,
171
Campbell of Lochawe, 69, 91, 124, 267
Campbells, 57, 59, 61, 64, 69, 76, 91, 97,
101, 105, 118, 123, 124, 126, 145, 149,
178, 184, 267
Canntaireachd, pipe music notation,
133-134, 179, 253
Carmichael, Alexander (1832-1912), 27,
32, 188, 191, 212, 233, 256, 259-262,
266, 278, 282
Carmina Gadelica, 259, 262, 278
Carswell, Bishop John of the Isles
(c.1525-1572), 28, 58, 170, 171, 177
Caskets, 23, 24, 52, 87
Castles, 43, 45-47, 83, 102, 127, 143, 162
Caterans, cattle reivers, 147, 156-161
Cattle, 6, 19, 26, 59, 149, 151, 152-153,
155-160, 214, 223, 226, 230-231, 235,
272, 279
Celtic Studies, 90, 212-214, 277, 287
Chain-mail, 48-49, 91, 128, 151
Charm stones, 3, 5-8
Chisholms, 67-68, 154, 232
Chorus songs, 136, 179, 257-258
Christianity, 9, 11, 12, 22-23, 25, 29, 30,
31-32, 35
Clan Chattan, 6, 62, 65, 66, 68, 102, 115,
120, 142, 145, 152, 154, 167, 184, 217,
219
Clan Donald, 5, 60-61, 63, 70, 72, 81, 85,
105, 111, 113, 117, 122, 124, 129, 139,
140, 145, 152, 165, 174, 178, 184, 199,
219, 250
Clan Ranald, 58, 61, 70, 71, 74, 81, 106,
110, 116, 118, 121, 129, 146, 162, 163,
171, 174, 184, 215
Clans, 2, 15, 18-19, 35, 40, 59-62, 63, 65,
67-69, 92, 100, 116, 119, 121, 125, 137,
144-154, 190, 204, 209, 217, 218-219,
221, 249, 275, 287
Clarsach, 98, 282
Claymore, *Claidheamh-mór*, 87, 196
Claidheamh geal soluis, sword of light, 5

Clearances, 223, 227, 229, 231-233, 271
Comyns, Lords of Badenoch, 38, 39, 47,
49, 63, 65, 70
Congested Districts Board, 229, 236, 272,
274
Conn of the Hundred Battles, 60, 70, 74,
175
Cowal, 18, 43
Craftsmen, 11-12, 20, 23, 25, 29, 49, 93,
162, 195, 237, 241, 242, 255, 268
Crieff, 158, 237, 241
Crofters' Acts, 229, 270, 271-273, 278,
281, 284
Crofters' War, 232, 252, 271
Crofting, 226, 270, 272-274, 284
Crosses, West Highland, sculptured, 5, 25,
58, 85, 90, 102
Cu Chullainn, 27, 43, 94, 136, 248
Cuddichs, obligation of hospitality or
cuid oidhche, 45, 123, 147
Culdees, *Celi Dé*, 32, 35, 53, 54, 56
Currachs, 13-14
Culloden, Battle of, 140, 179, 181, 203
Cumberland, Duke of, 140, 181, 203

Dalarossie, Moy, 1, 160, 225
Dalriada, 12, 14, 18, 22, 124, 184
Dancing, 246, 255-256, 282
Davidsons, 121, 184
Davoch, 17, 44
Deer, Book of, Gaelic *notitiae*, 15, 17, 24,
32, 40, 42, 53, 54, 67
Deirdre, 26, 27, 94, 135
Dewar, 50-51
Diet, 154, 229
Dingwall, 2, 45, 73, 115, 218
Diocesan church, 55-57
Disarming Act, 197
Disruption, 263
Distilling, 110, 163, 234, 239-241
Donald Balloch of Islay, 75, 78
Donald Bane, King of Scots (c.1031-1100),
36, 37, 49
Donald, 2nd Lord of the Isles (d.c.1422),
67, 71, 72, 73-75, 78
Drainage, 225, 226, 272
Dress, 20, 21, 47, 87, 90, 91, 104, 125-127,
154, 185-195, 204-207, 210, 246, 247,
249, 264-268, 286
264-268, 286
Droving, 152-153, 155, 158, 192
Dunadd, Kilmartin, Argyll, 14, 22, 42, 80,
83
Dundee, John Graham of Claverhouse,
Viscount (1648-1689), 137, 139, 183, 189
Dunkeld, 12, 14, 37, 53, 56, 234, 237
Dunvegan, 47, 127, 153, 173, 176, 216